PRAISE FOR *Find the Perfect College*

"Rosalind Marie and Claire Law  volume that can serve readers who want ools
for understanding and choosing a co

...D., author of
Looking at Type: The Funda......us and Looking at Type and Careers

"This book is long overdue! At last two premier experts have combined qualitative research and their decades of experience with matching students with the right colleges to produce an insightful guide for students, parents and guidance counselors.

"In today's economy, mistakes can be costly, and parents are looking for a sure strategy to match their student to a college that fits them.

"Hats off to these two—They hit the bull's-eye!"
—*George de Lodzia, Ph.D., Emeritus Professor*
of Business Administration, University of Rhode Island

"The idea that applying to college should be about a 'great match' rather than a prize to be won has thankfully, entered into common thought. Yet how to divine a great match has been unclear—until now. Through this book, Marie and Law have brought scientific research and understanding of personality, motivation and learning into the mix in a way that offers new insights to students and parents as well as counseling and admission professionals."
—*Mark H. Sklarow, Chief Executive Officer,*
Independent Educational Consultants Association

"Students, their parents and their advisors will gain from the insights provided here. This is new and valuable college planning territory. Take a look. These pages take college planning to a new level."
—*Steven R. Antonoff, Ph.D., Certified Educational Planner,*
Antonoff Associates, Inc.

"This book presents a proven, effective tool for the job of finding a college! Each one of our high school seniors has been able to pick their major and find a college by working through this process. What a relief!"
—*Lori Pohly, parent, Huntsville, AL*

FIND *the* PERFECT COLLEGE *for* YOU

82 Exceptional Schools That Fit Your Personality and Learning Style

FOURTH EDITION

ROSALIND P. MARIE
& C. CLAIRE LAW

Find the Perfect College for You: 82 Exceptional Schools That Fit Your Personality and Learning Style
Fourth Edition By Rosalind P. Marie and C. Claire Law

Published by SuperCollege, LLC
2713 Newlands, Belmont, CA 94002
www.supercollege.com

Credits: Cover: TLC Graphics, www.tlcgraphics.com. Design: Monica Thomas
Layout: The Roberts Group, www.editorialservice.com

Trademarks: All brand names, product names and services used in this book are trademarks, registered trademarks or tradenames of their respective holders. SuperCollege is not associated with any college, university, product or vendor.

Disclaimers: The authors and publisher have used their best efforts in preparing this book. It is sold with the understanding that the authors and publisher are not rendering legal or other professional advice. The authors and publisher cannot be held responsible for any loss incurred as a result of specific decisions made by the reader. The authors and publisher make no representations or warranties with respect to the accuracy or completeness of the contents of the book and specifically disclaim any implied warranties or merchantability or fitness for a particular purpose. The accuracy and completeness of the information provided herein and the opinions stated herein are not guaranteed or warranted to produce any particular results. The authors and publisher specifically disclaim any responsibility for any liability, loss, or risk, personal or otherwise, which is incurred as a consequence, directly or indirectly, from the use and application of any of the contents of this book.

ISBN13: 978-1-61760-119-4

Manufactured in the United States of America
10 9 8 7 6 5 4 3 2 1

Library of Congress Cataloging-in-Publication Data

Names: Marie, Rosalind P., author. | Law, C. Claire, author.
Title: Find the perfect college for you : 82 exceptional schools that fit your
  personality and learning style / Rosalind P. Marie and C. Claire Law.
Description: Belmont, CA : SuperCollege, 2016.
Identifiers: LCCN 2016015719 (print) | LCCN 2016017173 (ebook) | ISBN
  9781617601194 (paperback) | ISBN 9781617601200 | ISBN 9781617601217
Subjects: LCSH: College choice--Psychological aspects--United States. |
  Personality. | BISAC: STUDY AIDS / College Guides.
Classification: LCC LB2350.5 .M344 2016 (print) | LCC LB2350.5 (ebook) | DDC
  378.1/61--dc23
LC record available at https://lccn.loc.gov/2016015719

FOR

PARENTS
AND STUDENTS
OF THE 2017 AND 2018
HIGH SCHOOL GRADUATION CLASSES

ACKNOWLEDGEMENTS

We would like to thank all the parents and students who selected our approach to college planning over the years and our readers. We are thankful for our publisher, SuperCollege, who supported our vision and continues to help us bring it into the collegiate public square. Our admiration and gratitude goes out to the twentieth century psychologists, Carl Jung, Katharine Briggs and Isabel Briggs Myers, whose research influenced us lastingly and remains our constant inspiration while advising high school students.

NOTE FROM THE AUTHORS

This book was born out of the authors' personal experience while advising college-bound students. Our philosophical perspective strongly points to starting the process by helping students better understand themselves through assessments, interest inventories and personal interviews. With those emerging student profiles we call upon our knowledge of individual campuses and their unique academic and social environments. Throughout each advising session, telephone discussion and meeting with student and family we seek to match and interface the student personality preferences and learning style with college and universities that support and appeal to those student profiles. We set out to capture that advising process in this book and elected to enter our individual, subjective views of college campuses into a qualitative research design.

Over the period of ten years, we consulted with professional educators and psychologists to develop and move forward with the methodical framework that resulted in this book. Our observations and advising are heavily based upon and follow much within the theories of student development and environmental theories which encompass the physical and social environment. The research and theories of Alexander Astin, 1962, 1968; and Astin and Holland, 1961; Holland (1973) and Myers (1980), Michelson, 1970; Moos, 1979, Pascarella, 1985; Stern, 1986; Strange, 1991 and Kurt Lewin, (1937) have influenced our work in this book. The *Myers Briggs Type Indicator*®, emanating from Jungian Psychological theory, is the foundation of our college advising process and lays the fundamental groundwork for this book.

CONTENTS

Acknowledgements   vii

Note from the Authors   viii

The Colleges   x

Foreword   xiii

CHAPTER 1
What's in This Book?   1

CHAPTER 2
Three Powerful Tools Viewed in Action on College Campuses   5

CHAPTER 3
Uncover Your Personality Preferences and Type   13

CHAPTER 4
The Exploratory Table of Majors and Minors for Personality
Types   19

CHAPTER 5
Description of Personality Types in High School   29

CHAPTER 6
The College Descriptions   47

CHAPTER 7
The Tables of Colleges for Personality Types   387

Endnotes   396

THE COLLEGES

Agnes Scott College 49
American University 53
Amherst College 57
Bates College 61
Beloit College 65
Boston College 69
Boston University 73
Bowdoin College 77
Brandeis University 81
Brown University 85
Butler University 89
California Institute of Technology 93
Carleton College 97
Case Western Reserve University 100
Claremont Colleges – Claremont McKenna 104
Claremont Colleges – Harvey Mudd 104
Claremont Colleges – Pitzer 104
Claremont Colleges – Pomona 104
Claremont Colleges – Scripps 104
Colby College 111
Colgate University 114
College of Charleston 118
College of Wooster 122
Columbia University 126
Connecticut College 131
Dartmouth College 134
Davidson College 138
Denison University 142
Duke University 146
Elon University 150
Emory University 154
Florida Southern College 158

Furman University 162
George Washington University 166
Georgetown University 170
Georgia Institute of Technology 175
Guilford College 179
Hamilton College 183
Hampshire College 187
Harvard University 191
Haverford College 197
Hendrix College 201
Johns Hopkins University 204
Kalamazoo College 208
Kenyon College 212
Lawrence University 216
Lynchburg College 220
Marquette University 224
Massachusetts Institute of Technology 228
Middlebury College 233
Muhlenberg College 237
New York University 240
Northeastern University 245
Northwestern University 249
Notre Dame University 252
Oberlin College 256
Occidental College 259
Pepperdine University 263
Princeton University 267
Roanoke College 273
Rollins College 277
Saint Louis University 281
Salve Regina University 285
Sarah Lawrence College 289
Stanford University 293
Swarthmore College 298
Syracuse University 302
Tufts University 306
Tulane University 310
Union College 314
University of Chicago 318
University of Miami 322

University of Pennsylvania 326
University of Redlands 331
University of Richmond 335
University of Southern California 339
University of Tampa 344
Valparaiso University 347
Vanderbilt University 351
Wabash College 355
Wake Forest University 359
Washington and Lee University 363
Washington University in St Louis 367
Wesleyan University 371
Williams College 375
Yale University 379

FOREWORD FOR STUDENTS

Hello Young Millennials. In the junior and senior years of high school, you will explore and make decisions like never before. It will be different for you and your family even if an older sibling headed off to college a few years ago. Now colleges are careful about how they communicate with you. Sometimes it is harder to tell them apart.

This is different than earlier years, and there have been some exciting changes. You might not know about the new degrees that college faculty have put together in the past five years. You are probably unaware of new career directions in psychology, health, engineering, research in physics and algorithms in computer science. You might be surprised that college administrators spend months every year redefining their curriculum, faculty and campus -- all for you.

The best helper you can find for this process is ... yourself. There is not a single admission officer, guidance counselor, friend, sibling or even parent who knows you better. Go online or ask a guidance counselor to give you a personality survey called the Myers Briggs Type Indicator® or MBTI© for short. If you can't do that, look at Chapter Two and Chapter Four and take a guess at your personality type. Then read over all the majors for your type in this book, highlighting them as you go. It will be your best birthday present ever. Call your parents on their cell phone and tell them about this.

FOREWORD FOR PARENTS

Hello parents. Does this sound familiar? There is a decision to make and you ask young Millennial a question as they head out the door. Which college to tour next week? What application still needs an essay? Did they get the scholarship form from the high school? They reply... Call me on my cell phone.

This is common for today's youngest members of the Millennial Generation born in the late 1990s. How else can you help? Try approaching the conversation through the idea of student personality and social environment. Does young Millennial want a campus with students who advocate for causes and possibly protest? Does reserved ISFP want a campus where all students join about five clubs? Does ISTJ like the idea of being an accountant? This innovative book presents a new way to talk about college and college degrees. With a small investment of money and time, you will get insight that clears away unimportant clutter in the college selection process and refocuses family conversation on the purpose of going to college.

CHAPTER 1

WHAT'S IN THIS BOOK?

The College Search

Starting the search for the right college can be both exciting and unsettling for families. Students are about to start an unfamiliar journey. Parents may or may not have much experience with the new college application process. Over the years, family, friends and neighbors have been good sources for help. Visits to the bookstores were a good bet for help too. Now parents and students find themselves back in the aisles or on the internet, but this time searching for college guides. There are many books to choose from with observations and statistics about selecting a college.

So why would you choose this book? Because it is the *only* college book that matches the student Personality Type using the Myers-Briggs Type Indicator® with the teaching philosophies at colleges and universities.* You will be able to use a proven method that highlights the specific learning style of each of the different Personality Type. Our book offers this original perspective for students, parents and high school guidance counselors because the focus is on the student learning style first and the college descriptions second.

Within these pages you will find 82 of our favorite colleges that run the gamut from the most selective to more or less open admission. By following our planning suggestions throughout the search, parent and student will begin to recognize differing learning environments. Families can then match Student Personality Type and learning style with the colleges they visit. As you do this, you can add a few colleges to your list that we suggest for your Type. The value in doing this is to confidently add new colleges for serious consideration. At the same time, the process can lead you to drop others. As you understand more about learning style and how it plays out in the lecture

1

halls and classes, you might also recognize college teaching environments that are not listed in this book.

Personality Type

So exactly where does this Personality Type research come from and how reliable is it? The concept grew out of the work of early 20th century psychologists Carl Jung and Katherine Briggs with her daughter, Isabel Myers, who developed a complex theory of human personality and the idea of personality preferences. Their understanding of human personality was put to practical use during World War II when GIs were successfully assigned to work tasks based on their answers to questions developed by Myers. Those questions, updated to reflect modern society, are in constant use today, in business, government and education. Our book highlights the career fields selected by each of the sixteen personality types as identified through decades of research. We then recommend the educational majors and minors that prepare undergraduates for those fields. We have found that high school students like to talk about majors on the list researched for their type and are less interested in talking about others.

In Chapters Two and Three you will explore and then uncover the likely student Personality Type**. With this selection, you can get started using our book to expand or slim down your college list. In the process you will learn about three powerful tools in college planning. They are the student learning style, educational majors preferred by each Personality Type and the college environments. We highlight each of these three tools for each of the college campuses. They are the heart and soul of our book.

Learning Style

Learning style is so important because it frees the student to be more creative and open to exploration if they are in a learning environment that works for them. The learner is quickly motivated when there is a good match between the college educational approach and their individual learning style. Undergraduate college students use a lot of emotional and intellectual energy in the classroom to understand information presented by the professor. The student who is taking in knowledge with their preferred learning style can focus wholly on the subject at hand. The student who is not so well matched to the learning style is doing two things: learning the information and then rearranging it into ways that can be remembered and utilized. Therefore, the student who learns best by working with others in pairs or small teams learns quickly and soundly if the professor requires student teams. The undergraduate who learns best by mulling over ideas in their mind without interruption learns well if the professor relies heavily on reference documents at the library or online. These two study methods utilize two of the eight potential learning preferences that make up a student's learning style. The primary use of our book is matching the student learning preference with the colleges that support them through collegiate educational practices in and out of the classroom.

Exploring Educational Majors

How many times have we heard about college undergrads who don't know what to declare for their major during the last two years of college? How many times have we heard from graduates who are questioning their degree after graduation because it has little relation to the job they want? A proven way to avoid this is to take advantage of the research that identifies occupations preferred by each of the Personality Types. In our book, we recommend majors and minors that pair up with the preferred occupations of each Personality Type as archived in MBTI® career research. Our second powerful planning tool therefore is the 1,300 short descriptions of majors and minors presently being offered on campuses across the nation. Once again, this is the *only* book that connects the dots between personality preference and educational majors. It is a great tool for most high school students who are undecided. For those who have a major in mind, we suggest considering a minor or double major that also appeals to student Personality Type.

College Physical and Social Environments

Our concept of identifying Personality Type and learning style at the colleges is unique. Yet, there is also the familiar and obvious campus social culture to consider when choosing a college. We explore it through the Social and Physical Environment sections found in each of the 82 college descriptions. Together they comprise the third powerful tool in our book.

Both the social and physical environments have strong influence in shaping the shared values, beliefs and behaviors of the student body. Social psychologists such as John Holland describe how certain people shape a social environment and are attracted to like-minded individuals. Lawrence Kohlberg, also a social psychologist, offers a foundation for understanding the development of college student morality. Research by pioneers such as these two theorists has influenced key practices in collegiate environments like the Honor Code. Environmental psychologists, such as Kurt Lewin, describe how the physical attributes can also shape specific behaviors.

You would witness the Person Environment Theories in action when students march for or against climate controls. Individuals on any particular campus tend to be like-minded, and would likely hold similar views or at least be sympathetic with each other on the growing divisions within our polyglot American culture. These important theories helped frame our observations of the illusive nature of campus social life that is so important during college selection.

82 Colleges

So why did we select these 82 colleges as a primer for matching learning style and Personality Type with college environment? *The simple answer is because these 82 colleges have very cohesive and well-crafted educational environments.* These colleges are consistently on target with their educational beliefs. They put their understanding into action every day, each semester. They have administration and faculty perspectives that fit a clear cluster of types among the 16 learning styles. These 82 colleges translate their beliefs into the academic courses and residential life. Their core courses required for graduation often harken back to the philosophy of their founders. The course curriculum is notable for what it offers and what it does not offer. The undergraduate time spent on and off campus, in internships or study abroad trips, reflects how the administration and faculty view acquiring knowledge. The option to double major or combine a single major with other minors reflects the administration's view of societal needs in the workforce. The advising for post-graduation options points to how the college expects its graduates to contribute to society. All of these reflect and support specific learning styles and define educational culture on the campus. This is why we selected these 82 excellent colleges.

Three Powerful Tools

The solid match between undergraduate student and college can launch the young adult into their first professional position with personal satisfaction and success. Learning style, best fit majors and social/physical environment are three powerful tools used to find the right college. They are not quickly absorbed, but the advising method presented in this book capitalizes on them. It lays out the basic concepts and hundreds of specific examples that you can access by tables or by reading the individual college reviews. We hope you will agree.

*Myers-Briggs Type Indicator®, MBTI®, and Myers-Briggs® are trademarks or registered trademarks of the MBTI® trust, Inc., in the United States and other countries.

**www.mbticomplete.com is recommended by the Association of Psychological Type as the official website for completing the MBTI® survey online.

CHAPTER 2

THREE POWERFUL TOOLS VIEWED IN ACTION ON COLLEGE CAMPUSES

In this chapter, we present a description of Personality Type with learning style, the benefits of exploring educational majors through personality preferences and key features of the physical and social environments.

Why is this important information to have? As a high school student, you can recognize your personality preferences and honor them. Your personality preferences typically lead to behavior and actions that are repeated almost daily. In this way through elementary, middle and high school you developed strengths and predictable style. We suggest that you use this valuable self knowledge to move ahead into college with confidence. Even though your choice may be very different than those of your friends, you can feel secure about your decision to enter a particular university or community college. Do this by taking time to discover and honor your personality preferences.

So what are those behaviors and actions that you repeat almost daily? Think about how often you changed up the hallways you used to get to the next class. Did you take a different route to catch more friends you've missed during the week? What was your reaction to a teacher who said the test would be an essay? Did you wish it would be fill in the blank? If an uncle tells a personal story about playing on a baseball team decades ago, does it help you with your teammates, or bore you a bit? Are you disappointed when your favorite frozen breakfast perigees and tamale breakfast bars are missing from the freezer Saturday morning? These examples point backward to the personality preferences that are in play every day in the high school classroom and will show again in college lecture halls.

We are going to take the forward approach in this book. We will alert you to the environmentally-focused college campus in the mountains that makes hiking mandatory, or, to a college located near others that often results in students being able to cross-register. We remind the reader that colleges with independent founders often explore morals and beliefs through their courses and in the classroom. Contrast this with the solitude of the public university that sticks to the subject content in their lecture halls. We know that you probably learn the sciences by detail/facts or by ideas/concepts. We will remind you to honor your preference for learning and understand how it will impact your college years. We know that all students lean toward four of eight learning preferences. This knowledge adds your personality to the college search and helps answer that nagging question—Why you are choosing to go to this college?

Personality Type and Learning Style in College

Each Personality Type has its very own learning style. The learning style can be thought of as how each individual takes in information and retains it for use. There are eight distinct preferences in combination that determine Type and learning style. Most college campuses honor and support certain of these eight preferences. Colleges develop teaching strategies over decades that favor some of the eight preferences over others. In this way, they honor some Learning Styles over others. Very few campuses successfully honor and support all eight of the learning styles associated with Personality Type. In our observations, we typically found that colleges serve a range of two to four distinct preferences quite well through their educational practices, curriculum and academic philosophies. With this information and other factors, we identified compatible Personality Types for each of the 82 colleges in this book. For those familiar with different research methods, we followed the tenets of qualitative research.

The eight preferences called out above are organized into four pairs. An individual student can be one or the other within each pair -- but not both. Therefore, each student will have four and only four preferences that make up their Personality Type. The student may borrow the opposite preference for an assignment or a particular course, but it will never become their preferred preference or change their learning style.

Extravert and Introvert Learning Styles

College students with the Extravert preference would like professors who require frequent participation or teaming with other students on projects anywhere on campus. The opposite choice is the student with the Introvert preference. They would like coursework that requires iPad research in their room or a quiet nook and reading a list of selected journals on reserve at the library. These are examples of educational practices that honor two preference opposites: Extraverts (E) and Introverts (I). Each of us has a preference for one of these, but not both. Most colleges have educational features that serve both of these preferences. However, some colleges lean toward one or the other.

Sensing and Intuitive Learning Styles

The Sensing (S) student prefers to learn by collecting all the facts and then arriving at a conclusion. The needs of this Sensing student would be met in a college freshman course like "Introduction to Experimental Biology." This would likely be taught in a step-by-step, building block approach through lab techniques. On the other hand, a freshman course like "Foundations in Biology" that probably starts first with the theories central to understanding life on earth meets the needs of the Intuitive learner. This Intuitive (N) learner likes to get the big picture first and then discover the facts. A student will have either the preference for Sensing courses or Intuitive courses, but not both.

Colleges may offer both types, sensing and intuitive courses. Sensing and Intuitive preferences are the predominant preference pair that underlies collegiate academic philosophies. Colleges tend to lean heavily toward one or the other. Educational practices influenced by these two preferences interface with all majors and minors as well as some extracurricular activities.

Thinking and Feeling Learning Styles

Objective analysis and logic rule within the preference for Thinking (T). A college emphasizing this preference would lean more toward analytical and precise subject matter. Advisors would encourage undergraduates to explore career fields. On the other hand, a college that mentors and advises with an orientation for the Feeling (F) preference would emphasize career exploration by defining personal beliefs and values followed by exploring the majors. Educational advising influenced by the Feeling preference would call attention to values and beliefs during an open-ended discussion between professor and student.

Many college courses are quite grounded in objective analyses as a preferred way to acquire knowledge which reflects the Thinking preference. A lesser number of colleges heavily emphasize exploratory, values-driven curriculum. The reader should know that each of these opposite learning preferences can lead to an exceptionally fine education. Colleges have historically leaned toward the Thinking preference. As society is changing with emphasis on relativist values, we have observed that colleges are offering more content and curricula through the lens of the Feeling preference. Students will be one or the other of these two opposite preferences.

Judging and Perception Learning Styles

The student who likes a course syllabus that is well organized with a list of to-do's and clear cut-offs for grades favors the learning style of the Judging (J) preference. The undergraduate who likes just a paragraph on the course objective at the start of the class leans toward the Perceiving (P) learning style. College professors often utilize a little of both of these orientations in how they organize the course objectives. However, the college administration policies outlined in the catalogs often lean toward one preference or the other. It will be reflected in the requirements for graduation, the regulations for residential housing, registration, research participation and more. These two tend to influence both the social and academic life on the campus.

College Educational Majors and Minors and the Best Personality Fit

As covered in Chapter One, there are preferred occupations for each of the sixteen Personality Types. Many decades of research with the MBTI® instrument support the connection between personality and occupation.* It is our belief that the student who is familiar with their Type's preferred careers/occupations will have a clearer, chartered path through their four collegiate years. The value of this book is to identify educational majors and minors that lead to those preferred careers and occupations.

Within these pages, the reader will find their Personality Type matched to specific majors at over half of the colleges that we reviewed. The purpose of each short description is to spark the interest of the high school student and encourage the exploration of that educational major or minor. We strongly recommend that over time, students read through each of the educational majors listed for their Personality Type. There are about fifty different majors recommended for each Type in Chapter Four. That exercise alone will likely trigger new ideas about how to evaluate other colleges.

The short major descriptions are not directing students to declare that major at that college. Instead, they should help high school students think about the purpose of their college degree. In this way, a student could read about a major recommended at College A. Yet that very major could be at College B, taught in the same way at a similar campus, but closer to home. Or perhaps a student might like the looks of a major at College C listed for a Type with two of the same preference letters in their Type. We hope you will be open and flexible in how you use the 1,500 major recommendations on these pages.

College Physical Environment

The environment is what you experience when you first visit a college campus. You scan the campus landscape and the views, flower beds, trees and buildings. Some buildings are easily recognizable icons. You notice how the undergraduates dress. You hear the sounds of city noise traveling across the campus. You hear what students are talking about. You feel the energy level across the campus on the day of your visit. Everyone notices the environment in some way. We believe that two features of the environment are particularly important for making the right college selection. They are the physical and the social environments.

Because colleges are aware that building layouts and floor plans actually influence students, new buildings are configured with specific goals for student behavior. Residence halls built after 2005 often form a village community where students can easily socialize. They include mini conference spaces to study with laptops connected to the college servers. Most new residence halls are likely to be suite-style apartments with a common living room. Semi-circular classrooms with smart boards are spaces that encourage discussion among students and professor. New student centers with lots of couches, multiple study nooks and snack locations encourage students to sit and read while friends finish the indoor climbing wall. Over a cup of coffee some will seize the opportunity to discuss the upcoming exam. Many colleges have also elected to build professional level theaters and music practice rooms with high quality acoustic stage and sound equipment. Students who might otherwise drop their musical instrument after the close of the football season may take up their flute again with new awareness of music's connection to math theory.

As colleges use physical space across the campus in new ways, professors are moving their offices into the residence halls. Upperclass students are given their own offices within the department. This is especially attractive to students who want to continue a discussion that started in class. It increases student options during free time when not sitting in lecture halls. These changes are supported by the theories of twentieth century psychologists, from Kurt Lewin (1936) to Alexander Astin (1984) and George D. Kuh (2004). Their research examined the effects of campus environments identifying variables that keep students more engaged on campus.

Taken as a whole, the Environmental Press influences how students spend their free time. The House System originating at Oxford and Cambridge Universities in England forms similar intellectual communities within the university, serving just about every need of students, from elegant dining to academic and social mentoring. If a student is at a university with the House System, they will identify more with their residence hall than the university itself. Yet other campuses may require off campus semester study, encouraging interaction and identity outside of the collegiate bubble. The "city drain" can also take students away from campus. Most large American cities are multi-cultural and students will quickly experience competing values and beliefs in action on our sidewalks. However, colleges located adjacent to American suburbs don't "drain." Suburban neighborhoods are quiet and empty during the working week, encouraging social interaction to remain on campus. Along with academic work, these variables associated with college location will very much impact student learning and experience.

College Social Environment

The social environment describes many experiences other than academic study at a particular college. When we visit colleges we note individual activity and groups that seem to color the social scene. By describing the social environment we offer the reader another lens to understand the differences between campuses that otherwise seem similar. At some colleges the grading policies generate competition while at others it's "all for one and one for all." While each student is unique, they are still members of the whole student body, and they influence one another. Along with the administration policies, structure, restrictions and rules, they define the college social environment.

While assessing college social environments we relied on the work of another prominent social psychologist John Holland, who proposed career clusters based on the simple concept that birds of a feather flock together. The Holland Typography®, used in high schools across the country was adapted to ACT's® World of Work Map. Holland's work predicts that artistic individuals are attracted to those who, like themselves, want to see creative, original results from their efforts. These artistic students together influence and agitate for an open, exploratory curriculum. So they may seek out a college where little or no connection is drawn to today's economic scene. In capturing the nature of the social environment for our readers, we often looked at the list of student clubs and closely read the student newspapers and the bulletin boards in libraries and dining halls. They pointed to what the whole student body experienced and requested during the semester.

Each of these defining physical and social features is important in that they melt together like a cake, once it is baked, to comprise the campus culture and environment. They are critical because students need to know before they apply to college whether they like chocolate, caramel or vanilla cake. With a little help from the concepts in this book, families will learn to recognize the physical and social press of the environment. Parents and students can now evaluate these environments as they follow along on the campus tour.

In the next chapter, we offer an exercise that allows parents or students to choose their four preferences that form a Personality Type.

* The MBTI® instrument has been the subject of hundreds of research projects studying the links between personality type and different aspects of life. The Center for Applications of Psychological Type™ (CAPT®) maintains the largest single collection of research about the MBTI® instrument in the world. (In the 1940s and 1950s, Isabel Briggs Myers first recorded her research notes on thousands of index cards, which are now part of the archives at the University of Florida in Gainesville, Florida.) www.capt.org

CHAPTER 3

UNCOVER YOUR PERSONALITY PREFERENCES AND TYPE

With a basic understanding of the eight preferences from Chapter Two you can move forward by making a choice on four scales. When you make your selection within each of these four pairs you will identify your likely Personality Type. At the same time, we recommend students formally complete the MBTI® assessment. It will likely improve your ability to use this book confidently and definitely will give you a heads up on self knowledge. Most counselors, psychologists, high school guidance counselors and educational consultants can administer the survey. Ask around because you may have access even without extra fees. However, you can also take the MBTI® online at www.mbticomplete.com

As you start utilizing Personality Type in the college selection process it is important to remember that any student can find success at any college. Adaptability, capability, strength of high school academics, motivation and other factors come into play. Yet students who know their Personality Type are more likely to visit and hone in on campuses that really fit them.

Extraversion and Introversion

The first scale is between Extraversion and Introversion. Please read and react to the information below. Which one sounds more like you? Which has more of your behaviors? Which describes you better?

Extraversion, referred to as **(E)**, appeals to those high school students who want to socialize with a large group of friends, from casual acquaintances to middle and best friends. The social butterfly gets energized by meeting many people and being involved in clubs and extracurricular activities. Extraverts are the first to say hello in the hallway and one of the first to raise their hand in class, volunteering to give answers. They could be attracted to the dance team, the mock trial or student council. Extraverts are often visible in activities, sports and projects and they are familiar to teachers and staff in the high school. They like to be expressive conversationalists, often using their hands for gestures. Extraverts are usually chatting on their smart phone and sometimes getting in trouble for chatting in class too. Their Facebook pages have a lot of info. Easy to know, extraverts often think out loud and quickly throw their personal thoughts into the classroom discussions.

Introversion, referred to as **(I)**, appeals to those high school students who want to have a few, select friendships. Introverts could possibly lose interest and enthusiasm in some of the rah-rah high school activities like pep club. The math team or cross country team could meet the Introvert's needs because they involve others, but nevertheless are mostly an individual effort. They rely on their own gathering of information and reflect with care and time as they reach conclusions or act on information. Texting is an ideal way to connect with friends. They have a short Facebook page or maybe not one at all. They enter the hallway without taking up a lot of room or gesturing, possibly absorbed in conversation with a classmate or a teacher. Introverts prefer to do homework alone. Outside of their closer friends, they typically communicate with a few other students once in a while. Art class may appeal to them because they can express themselves without excessive conversation. Introverts ponder and pause before voicing their opinions, in class often seeking a deeper explanation than the teacher provides.

Which of these two sounds like you?	
❏ **Extraversion**	❏ **Introversion**

Sensing and Intuition

Sensing, referred to as **(S)**, students love to study subjects that have a practical connection to the world. They use structure to assure that their facts are categorized and correct. They like step-by-step directions and feedback that is definite and measurable. Sensors in high school prefer not to have many open-ended questions from the teacher that require guesswork or interpretation. This preference learner tends to like subjects such as earth or life sciences and physics. Their memory is an asset that helps them get good grades on fill-in-the-blank and matching quizzes in high school. They follow instructions accurately. They are first class observers of what they can see, hear and smell. Generally speaking, they are not looking for hidden meanings, so when they text message it will be descriptive with facts and times. If a teacher does not move rapidly through the material or jump around, these students will get a solid understanding of the subject. Sometimes it is a struggle to get the whole concept from a lesson. Sensors might challenge a teacher if the facts in a lesson plan don't jive with their knowledge of reality. They can be good at athletics because they focus on today's game, tuning all their senses to the sport during the play. They are present and attending, happy with the organized teacher who covers what they need to know.

Intuition, referred to as (**N**), students prefer to explore theoretical information and abstract knowledge. They are driven by possibilities. They love to develop big ideas and random thoughts researching on their iPad. They are imaginative, global learners who appreciate the big picture and are disinterested in the nitty-gritty details. Intuitive students are able to see beyond the information presented by the teacher during the class period. They anticipate the subject matter and look forward to the next chapter. They can miss important details. They may not be looking or listening in class at any moment. They like to read books that have heroes or fantasy orientations or anything else that stretches the imagination. They rely on their hunches and can build connections between seemingly unrelated topics. These students like to add to the information presented in class. They are future-oriented and would like the model United Nations if their high school should offer it. They like a teacher who moves along quickly and offers choice in doing homework assignments. Intuitive students are ready to move on to new material and will automatically connect it to earlier knowledge. They prefer variety and new materials in the classroom; it brings excitement and interest to sequentially-based knowledge.

Which of these two sounds like you?	
❑ **Sensing**	❑ **Intuition**

Thinking and Feeling

Thinking, referred to as (**T**), students are analytical, logical and place greatest importance on the knowledge offered in the classroom. They often enjoy analyzing ideas and information with an objective point of view. They try to bring a "cause and effect" clarity to a free-roaming, off-task class discussion. They need logical principles and order. Thinkers would respond well to a teacher who presents complex issues without emotion and focuses on the underlying foundation. These students would not respond well to a teacher who tells stories about their own life experience as a way to bring understanding to the subject. Thinkers can simmer down a complicated problem because of their ability to logically organize complex situations. They can examine an event from the outside. Their precise conversation can even seem like a critique, yet it originates from the need to objectively square up what they know. Occasionally, their logic can rule over more gentle viewpoints that rely on instinct or intangible information. Students with the Thinking preference really expect and focus on fairness through order in the high school administration. They are motivated by assignments and accomplishments that lead to an objective report or grade. They like the high school website if it is up to date.

Feeling, referred to as **(F)**, high school students often place the greatest importance on the personal connections with the teacher and other students in the classroom. They gain energy through their friendships. They are aware of others' feelings. Those with this preference can seem diplomatic, capable of sizing up situations and able to avoid stepping on toes if needed in the situation. They find something to appreciate in most of their friends and not-so-friends. They need harmony at home and in the high school social groups in order to function well. The Feeler brings human stories to the subject and likes teachers who bring their life stories into the classroom. They shine with appreciation when the teacher compliments their contribution. Small group work in the class is a hit with them. They are supportive of their friends and would like each and every friend to support them in return. They would like pages on the high school website to highlight individual students rather than activities and schedules. They can be very persuasive in both academic and extracurricular activities if they choose because they understand the emotional needs of others. They will notice if the high school principal pays attention to the energy and needs of the student body as well as the lunchroom dust ups and grades.

Which of these two sounds like you?	
❑ **Thinking**	❑ **Feeling**

Judgment and Perception

Judgment, referred to as **(J)**, students like to plan their week, their school day and other activities in advance. Their day follows a routine if possible. As high school students, they usually like to finish their homework, closing the book, figuratively and literally. Those of this preference see homework and class assignments as immediate business that should be completed. They expect teachers to be consistent and clear in grading class work. After they have made a decision about class schedules, electives or extracurricular clubs to join, they are confident and are not likely to second guess that decision. Arriving at a decision may be an uncomfortable process. They like well-organized, purposeful teachers in the classroom. They often arrive at class on time. They quickly end rambling conversations on their smart phones. Their iPad screen and files will be well organized. They don't run out of gas on the way to school or show up late at after-school jobs. They like high school administrators who are consistent and ensure a predictable calendar of activities from year to year. If the parking lot empties quickly with two exits during sophomore and junior year, it doesn't need a third exit, rearranging the lanes, in senior year to see if it can be done faster.

Perceiving, referred to as **(P)**, students like to gather information and explore at length and without deadlines or time limits. Perceiving students value the unknown. They are comfortable while considering the alternatives in a decision, needing to examine them for a good while. After the decision is made, they may still ponder the other options they did not choose. They appreciate a high school teacher who responds positively to alternative viewpoints. They enjoy spontaneity in the classroom and like the discovery method to understand complicated ideas. Chances are good this student will have tardies over the semester. Arriving late is connected to their reluctance to close down and finish a conversation in the halls. Homework is turned in late sometimes. Most of the time, homework is started at the last minute. There is often room for improvement in their work if only there was more time to pursue their latest thought. This student will always appreciate the teacher or administrator who changes it up, brings in some new material or adds excitement to the biology lab or traditional pep rally in high school.

Which of these two sounds like you?	
❏ **Judgement**	❏ **Perceiving**

Did you have trouble making a decision with any of the four? Let us remind you that taking the MBTI® with a professional or online can help with your indecision. But for now you can mark each of your four choices with an indicator of how strong you felt that the preference letter fit you. Was your choice a slight fit, moderate fit or a clearly defined fit? These descriptions are called Clarities. Write your preference clarity next to each of your four chosen letters in the box below. For example an ESFP would write: Extraversion - Clear, Sensing - Moderate, Feeling - Slight, Perception - Definite. It is okay to be just 51 percent sure of your choice. However, If you are truly divided between a pair, then select the preferences, I, N, F or P with a slight clarity so that you can move forward.

Extraversion (E)	Introversion (I)
Sensing (S)	Intuition (N)
Thinking (T)	Feeling (F)
Judgment (J)	Perception (P)

Now that you have your four preferences identified, circle your likely Personality Type on grid below.

ISTJ	ISFJ	INFJ	INTJ
ISTP	ISFP	INFP	INTP
ESTP	ESFP	ENFP	ENTP
ESTJ	ESFJ	ENFJ	ENTJ

You will find this same chart with each of the 82 college descriptions. If your selected preference is shaded then it is a college well suited to your Type. If your Personality Type is next to one of the shaded, selected Types, then there are considerable features at the campus that should appeal to you.

CHAPTER 4

THE EXPLORATORY TABLE OF MAJORS AND MINORS FOR PERSONALITY TYPE

In this chapter you will see the listing of majors described in this book that are compatible with your Personality Type. It is not an exclusive list. Students with high interest and passion can be and are successful in any major they choose.

The majors listed in these tables point to subjects and career fields that are historically proven to be selected by the Type. Each description is just a heads up, a hint if you will, to go to that college website and read what the faculty has to offer in course work and advising. Take time and read most if not all of the 50+ majors for your type. It could be a lens into the future, a hint of what you will experience while defining and earning your degree.

Personality Types and College Majors

ENFJ
Adolescents and Schools 68
American Musical Culture 173
American Sign Language 248
Anthropology 317
Archaeology 373
Architecture and Environmental Design 189
Art Conservation 109
Behavioral Neuroscience 133
Business Management 130
Chemistry 109

Chinese 301
Classics 377
Classics/History 157
Communication 342
Communication Sciences and Disorders 125
Comparative Literature 271
Computer Science 102
Critical Languages 377
Economics and Business 211
Education 365
Education Policy 365
Education Studies 88
English 52
English Communications 288
Exercise and Sport Sciences 181
Foreign Languages 238
Five College African Studies 59
French and Francophone Studies 63
Global Economics and Modern Language 178
Government 109, 333
Government and World Affairs 346
Health Sciences 165
History 297, 384
Human Development 113
Human Services 248
International Economics and Cultural Affairs 349
Language and Linguistics 84
Leadership Studies 153
Middle and Secondary Education 92
Modern Language 144
Museum Studies 219, 223
Peace, Justice and Human Rights 200
Plant Biology 148
Political Journalism 284
Preprofessional Studies 254
Principles of Education 276
Psychology 80, 137, 161, 262, 358
Public Policy 292
Public Relations 265
Romance Languages and Literatures 194
Science and Management 109
Science Education 305
Social Welfare and Justice 227
Sociology 141, 242
Writing and Rhetoric 116

ENFP

Advertising 305
American Studies 109
Anthropology and Sociology 287
Art History 373
Art Theory and Practice 251
Art/Sciences 305

Asian Studies 63
Big Problems 320
Business Administration 164
Business, Entrepreneurship and Organization 88
Certificate in Australian and New Zealand Studies 173
Chemistry and Biology 109
Child Psychology 308
Cinema and Media Studies 98
Cognitive Science 384
Communication 71
Creative Writing 129, 271
Early Childhood 291
Economics 51
Education 79, 199
Environmental Business 333
Environmental Communication and Arts 67
Film and Media Studies 137
Geology 124, 316
Geosciences 145
Gerontological Studies 103
Graphic Design 160
History 377
History and Philosophy of Science 95
Information Studies/Management 305
Japanese Studies 261
Jazz 153
Jewish Studies 239
Journalism 152
Management 312
Marketing 362
Material Science and Engineering 295
Metropolitan Studies 242
Music 103, 188, 300
Musicology and Ethnomusicology 354
Neuroscience 365
Nutritional Science 76
Peace and Conflict Studies 181
Philosophy and Religion 116
Philosophy, Politics and Economics 109
Policy, Planning and Development 342
Poverty 165
Psychological and Brain Sciences 207
Religion 357
Russian Studies 218
South Asian Studies 196
Speech and Hearing Sciences 169
Theater Arts 203
Urban Studies and Planning 231

ENTJ

Accounting and Marketing 337
Advertising 265
Aerospace Engineering 177

American Studies 348
Applied Mathematics 320
Arabic 309
Asian Traditions 238
Astrogeophysics 117
Biological Physics 211
Biomedical Engineering 149, 284
Biomedical Science 223
Botany 133
Business 358, 365, 370
Business Analytics 232
Chemical Engineering 96
Civil Engineering 102
Cognitive Science 262
Corporate Reporting and Analysis 71
Earth Systems Program 297
Economics 60, 153, 361, 370
Economics and History 354
Engineering Management Systems 130
Entrepreneurship and Management 207
Environmental Studies 280
Eurasian, Russian, and East European
    Studies 174
European and Mediterranean Studies 242
Film, Television and Theater 254
Geosciences 378
Global Health and Health Policy 272
Health Sector Management and Policy 325
Healthcare Management and Policy 330
History 236
Integrative Sciences 374
International Business 92
International Relations 276
Italian/Italian Studies 110
Japanese Language and Literature 169
Japanese Studies 236
Leadership 337
Legal Studies 110
Management Information Systems 248
Marketing 313
Marketing Management 305
Mathematics and Economics 79
Mathematics Specialty in Statistics 76
Mathematics-Economics 219
Neurobiology 196
Neuroscience 84, 317
Organizational Leadership and Management
    342
Physics 258
Political Science 56, 358, 370
Psychology 68, 99
Psychology and Linguistics 156
Public Health 385
Public Relations 227
Russian Area Studies 137

Russian Studies 186
Science, Technology and Society 110
Transportation and Logistics 251
W&L Student Consulting 365

ENTP

Astronomy 189, 316
Biochemistry 261, 300
Business Economics 67
Classical Archeology 137
Community Health 308
Computational Science 56
Computer Science 129, 173
Computer Science Sequence 110
Computing Technology and Information
    Systems 181
Cyber and Network Security 181
Earth and Planetary Sciences 370
Economics 64, 99, 231
Engineering Science 312
Entrepreneurial Studies 102
Entrepreneurship 325
Entrepreneurship and Emerging Enterprises
    304
Environmental Earth Sciences 370
Eurasian and East European Studies 79
Film Studies 125
Financial Economics 333
Freshwater Science 116
General Management 72
Geological Science 88
Geology 258
Government 132
Growth and Structure of Cities 199
Historic Preservation and Community
    Planning 120
History 291
History and the Practice of Diplomacy 271
Informatics and Modeling 373
Information Sciences and Information
    Studies 149
Integrated Sciences 251
International Politics and Economics 235
International Studies 358
Japanese Studies 102
Journalism, Ethics and Democracy 254
Language of the Mind 243
Law, Jurisprudence and Social Thought 59
Law, Letters and Society 320
Leadership Studies 337, 377
Literature and Creative Writing 186
Marketing and Communications 207
Mathematics 51
Mechanical Engineering 177
Middle Eastern Studies 169

Mock Trial 365
Natural Science 116
Pacific Rim 342
Physics 218
Polish 384
Political Science 96, 362
Politics 203, 365
Psychology 195
Public Policy 296
Rhetoric 358
Rhetoric and Communication Studies 337
Russian and Eastern European Studies 110
South Asian Studies 99

ESFJ
African Studies 210
Applied Mathematics 116
Art History 173
Biology 83, 165, 200, 300, 358, 377
Broadcast, Print and Online Media 161
Chemistry 52, 68, 141
Communication Studies 247
Communicative Disorders 333
Ecology and Evolutionary Biology 271
Economics 113
Economics and Business 203
Education, Schooling and Society 254
Elementary Education 56
German 181
Global Commerce 143
Health and Exercise Science 361
Health Promotion and Disease Prevention
    Studies 341
Health Studies 113
Human Performance 346
Human Resource Management 226, 275
Italian Language and Literature 239
Kinesiology 261
Leadership and Human Resource
    Management 284
Marketing 254, 350
Music Therapy 124
Natural Sciences 218
Nursing 287, 329
Nutrition Science 157
Operations Research 130
Organizational Studies 108
Physical Education and Health 153
Physics 196
Principles of Fitness and Wellness 239
Psychology 243
Psychology and Early Education 312
Real Estate 304
Religion 235
Religious Studies 108

Science, Medicine and Technology in
    Culture 316
Secondary Education 71
Sociology 291, 384
Sport Management 222
Sports Medicine 265
Statistics 88
Strategic Communication: PR and
    Advertising 91
Study of the City 384
Teacher Education 63

ESFP
Advertising 226
Animal Behavior and Cognition 190
Animal Studies 83
Arts Administration 91
Arts Technology and Business Innovation
    342
Biology 243, 378
Business Administration 334
Cell and Molecular Biology/Biochemistry
    113
Certificate in Design 251
Classics 378
Communication Studies 164
Communications 222
Convergent Journalism 222
Criminal Justice 275
Criminology 349
Dance 91, 239
Dance Therapy 239
Digital Retail Strategies 304
Early Childhood Education 287
Earth Studies 181
Environmental Analysis 108
Exercise Science 152
Health Science 75
History of Art and Architecture 88
Hospitality and Tourism Management 120
Human Biology 108
Industrial Design 178
Insurance and Risk Management 329
Marine Science Biology 346
Marketing 72
Music 124
Music Industry 247
Music Therapy 324
Neuroscience 51, 279
Nutrition 102
Public Health 168
Public Relations and Strategic
    Communication 55
Regional Studies in Asia 173
Retail Management 304

Social Work 283
Sociology 383
Sports Communication Marketing 160
Studio Art 144, 214
Theater 91, 116
Theater Arts 231
Visual and Environmental Studies 194

ESTJ

Accounting 70, 161, 165, 239
Actuarial Sciences 349
Aeronautics and Astronautics 231
American Studies 210
Applied Mathematics 196
Applied Physics 95
Biological Physics 173
Biological Sciences 251
Biomedical Engineering 308, 353
Business Information Systems 275
Chemistry 84
Civil Engineering 207
Computer Science 149, 279
Criminal Justice 338
Data Science 121
Economics 185, 321
Economics/Mathematics 384
Electrical Engineering 254
Energy Resources Engineering 296
Energy Studies 317
Ethics Sequence 108
Finance 361
Financial Enterprise Systems 346
German Language and Literature 169
Health Promotion 56
History 108
International Business 265
Investigative and Medical Sciences 284
Law and Society 214
Legal Studies in Business 313
Management 325
Mathematics 113
Medical Humanities 141
Molecular Biology 108
Neural Science 243
Neuroscience 59, 91
Operations Research 137
Physics 156
Plant Biology 251
Pre-Professional Program 223
Public Policy 177
Real Estate 227
Science Education 75
Scientific Computing 353
Selected Studies in Education 304
Sport and Event Management 153

Supply Chain Management 248
Translation and Intercultural
    Communication 271
Urban Studies 330

ESTP

Accounting 247
Advertising 75
Aeronautics and Astronautics 296
Asian and Middle Eastern Studies 137
Athletic Training 168, 275
Aviation Management 283
Biotechnology 160
Business Administration 349
Business Economics and Management 95
Cinema and Television Arts 152
Civil and Environmental Engineering 231
Civil Engineering 178
Computer Science 243
Computing and the Arts 383
Construction Engineering and Management
    226
Criminology 92
Dance 144
Economic Crime Prevention and
    Investigation 222
Engineering 95, 108
Entrepreneurship 255
Entrepreneurship and Innovation 247
Environmental Science and Public Policy
    194
Environmental Studies 185
Exercise Science 168
Finance 103, 239, 312
Financial Economic 107
Financial Markets 113
Forensic Science 304
Fundamentals of Business 349
Global Logistics and Transportation 120
Historic Preservation and Building Arts 287
Human Factors 308
Information Technology 164
Law and Society 55
Management 103
Management Consulting 255
Mechanical and Aerospace Engineering 271
Operations Management 72
Physics 357
Public Health Studies 207
Public Policy 214
Public Relations 324
Real Estate 342
Regional Studies in Africa 172
Sports Management 346, 349

Theater Arts and Dance 279
Urban Studies 129

INFJ
Administration of Justice 287
Architectural Studies 59
Art 140
Art and Visual Culture 63
Arts Management 120
Bioinformatics 369
Biology 182, 232, 235
Biophysics 341
Cell and Molecular Biology 261
Chemistry 125, 218
Chinese 235
Classics 305
Computer Science 258
Criminology and Public Policy 247
Culture and Politics 172
Economics 198
Engineering Sciences 382
Environmental Analysis 109
Environmental Studies 210
Geography 136
German 357
Health and Allied Sciences 357
Health and Human Biology 87
Homeland Security 311
Human Animal Studies 333
Human Rights, Genocide and Holocaust
  109
Interdisciplinary Studies 203
International Political Economy 67
Linguistics 128, 305
Management 337
Mathematical and Computational Biology
  109
Medieval and Renaissance Studies 242, 365
Middle Eastern Studies 189
Molecular Biophysics 373
Neuroscience 186
Neuroscience/Study of the Mind 202
Peace and Conflict Studies 116
Philosophy 316
Political Economy 378
Psychology 269, 300
Religion 157, 362
Religious Studies 51, 133, 320
Social Studies 195
Sociology 103
Sociology and Anthropology 99
Symbolic Systems 295
Theater 144
Theater Arts 164
Visual Arts 79, 148

Writing 291
Youth Ministry 160

INFP
African American Studies 63
Architectural Studies 88
Art 99
Biochemistry 218
Biology 260, 291
Chemistry 299
Communication of Science and Technology
  353
Comparative Study of Religion 194
Creative Writing 333
Drama and Theater Arts 128
Early Childhood Education 353
Education 51
Educational Studies 145
English 125
Environmental Economics 116
Fine Arts 199
Forensic Accounting 182
Geographical Studies 320
Geology 67
German Business 362
Gerontological Studies 103
Health and Humanity 341
Human Service Studies 152
Irish Studies 243
Jewish and Israel Studies 373
Language and Culture 269
Linguistics and Cognitive Science 109
Marine Science 189
Multimedia Design 265
Music 79
Neuroscience 140, 258
Nutrition and Dietetics 282
Philosophy 357
Physics 109
Psychology 149, 202, 316
Religion 160
Rhetoric and Leadership 265
Science, Technology and Society 231
Social Work 304
Studio Art 83
Theater 109, 378
Urban Studies 369
Yale Summer Session 382

INTJ
American Studies 235
Applied Mathematics 258
Architectural Studies 312
Art 109
Art History 103

Astronomy 373
Astrophysical Sciences 270
Biochemistry/Molecular Biology 186
Biological/Life Sciences 190
Biology 51
Chemical Physics 203
Chemistry 362
Cognitive Neuroscience 87
Computer Science 96
Digital Media Design 328
Earth and Planetary Sciences 206
Economics 55, 242
Economics and Engineering 109
Engineering and Architecture Studies 307
Engineering Physics 312
Environmental Studies 132
Financial Engineering 128
Geography 168, 235
Geology 120
Global Business 172
History 230
International Studies Concentration in
    Africa 337
Latin 300
Linguistics 148
Manufacturing and Design Engineering 250
Marine Science 324
Material Science 136
Mathematics 79, 291, 354
Mathematics-Computer Science 218
Military Science and Leadership 337
Mind, Brain and Behavior 194
Nanotechnology 316
Neuroscience 109
Operations and Supply Chain Management
    369
Philosophy of Mathematics 59
Physics 261, 320, 365
Physics/Computer Science 341
Political Science 99
Pre-Architecture 103
Psychology 63
Science, Culture and Society 156
Special Divisional Major 382
Theater and Performance Studies 295

INTP

Applied Design 190
Applied Mathematics 55
Astronomy 96
Bioengineering 329
Bioinformatics 312
Biology 186
Chemical Engineering 251
Chemistry 199, 354

Cognitive Science 99
Computational Biology 87
Computer Science 125, 203, 261, 270
Earth and Planetary Sciences 193
Earth Sciences 136
Earth, Atmosphere and Planetary Sciences
    230
East Asian Studies 258
Economics 133, 337
Economics/Math 156
Ecosystem Science and Policy 324
Engineering 300
Engineering Physics 103
Evolutionary Biology 148
Geobiology 370
Jazz 129
Jewish Studies 321
Mathematics 64, 110
Molecular Biology and Biochemistry 374
Neurobiology 172
Neuroscience 79, 218
Operations and Supply Chain Management
    342
Philosophy 110, 366
Physics 51, 59, 140
Physics and Philosophy 382
Product Design 296
Psychology 110
Theater 235

ISFJ

Anthropology 361
Architectural Studies 133
Art 383
Art and Archeology 270
Art History 357
Art Therapy 346
Asian Studies 214
Biochemistry and Molecular Biology 334
Biological Sciences 321
Biology 124, 377
Biomedical Engineering 178
Biomedical Sciences 226
Biophysics 59
Business 357
Business Administration 222
Child Studies 353
Communication Sciences and Disorders 91
Computer Science 152, 199
Criminology 160
Dance 108
Ecology, Evolution and Environmental
    Biology 129
Economics 140
Education Certificate 239

Education Studies 83
Fashion Design 370
Forensic Biology 181
Geography 152
Human Evolutionary Biology 195
Human Services 222
International History 172
Liberal Arts 264
Linguistics 108, 115, 295
Management 350
Marine Biology 279
Maritime Studies 377
Mathematics and Statistics 300
Museum and Society 206
Music 261
Music Education 304
Music Theory 164
Nursing 71, 157
Nutritional Biochemistry and Metabolism
   103
Occupational Science and Occupational
   Therapy 283
Organizational Studies 144
Pre-Medical and Health Professions 275
Psychology 144, 210
Public Health 239
Real Estate 328
Religious Studies 63
Science for Elementary Teaching 67
Science, Technology and Society 113
Science-Business 254
Secondary Education 286
Sociology 206
Studio Arts 337, 357

ISFP

Advertising Design 160
Agricultural Studies and Rural Life 189
Archeology 75
Biology 62, 80, 203, 334
Chemistry 144, 164, 291
Civil Engineering 349
Classical and Near Eastern Archeology 199
Classics 357
Computer Science 316
Education Studies 357
Elementary Education 279
Environmental Geology 247
Environmental Studies 247, 270, 361
Exploratory Studies in Business 91
Fashion Design 304
Folklore and Mythology 195
Health and Exercise Science 275
Health Care Delivery 275
Health Promotion 222

Japanese 300
Marine Biology 120
Mathematics 210
Near Eastern Languages and Civilization
   383
Neuroscience 113, 214
Nursing 102
Nutritional Science 265
Outdoor Recreation 222
Psychology 83
Radiation Therapy 283
Religion 140
Social Work 286
Special Major 108
Studio Art 67, 160, 222
Theater and Dance 124
Theater Studies 181
Theatrical Design and Production 152
Urban Design and Architecture Studies 243
Visual Arts 87

ISTJ

Accountancy 168
Accounting 120, 283, 336, 349
American Studies 83
Applied Math 178
Arabic Language 144
Archeological Studies 383
Biochemistry 258
Biochemistry and Molecular Biology 226,
   279
Biology 95, 361
Biotechnology 308
Business 159
Business Economics 124
Civil Engineering 251
Computer Informatics 156
Computer Science 210
Criminology 346
Economics 107, 164, 214
Education Policy Track 353
Education Studies 140
Electrical Engineering 129
Engineering Sciences 194
Environmental Analysis and Policy 75
Exercise Physiology 222
Finance 71, 247, 270
General Engineering 206
Geoarcheology 185
Geophysical Sciences 321
Geophysics 296
German Studies 373
Health Care Administration 274
Health Care Management 370
Health Sciences 91, 324

History 357
Human and Organizational Development 353
International Studies and Business 328
Justice 55
Legal Studies 83
Linguistics Modified Major 136
Literary Studies 235
Marine Science 178
Math Sciences 136
Mechanical Engineering 254
Molecular, Cellular and Integrative Biology 67
Nuclear Science and Engineering 230
Pre-Law 357, 366
Psychology 60
Public Policy Analysis 107
Russian 328
Science, Technology and International Affairs 172
Slavic Studies 133
Statistical Sciences 149

Medical Laboratory Science 283
Middle Eastern Studies 230
Music Composition and Technology 246
Physics 79, 214, 243
Psychology 107
Robotics and Intelligent Systems 270
Statistics 59, 321
Systems Engineering 168
Theater 287

ISTP

Actuarial Science 329
Aerospace Engineering 102
Air Force and Aerospace Studies 226
Anthropology 55
Applied Mathematics 140
Archeology 370
Art Practice 296
Arts and Technology 133
Audio Engineering 324
Biochemistry 99
Biology 156
Biomedical Engineering 312, 353
Biophysical Chemistry 136
Bulldog Bots 383
Business Economics 225
Chemical Engineering 128
Civil Engineering 255
Computer Engineering 308
Computer Science 83, 107, 185
Construction Planning and Management 343
Economics 95
Engineering Science 75
Environmental Engineering 383
Environmental Studies 366
Geological Sciences 72
Human Physiology 75
Jewelry and Metalsmithing 303
Materials Science and Engineering 177, 206
Mechanical and Material Science Engineering 195

CHAPTER 5

DESCRIPTION OF PERSONALITY TYPES IN HIGH SCHOOL

Each of the sixteen Personality Types is the focus of this chapter. The sixteen descriptions highlight how each one relates to the four core courses—math, English, science and history—in high school. You will see that the sixteen types react differently to the school subjects based on their preferred learning style. If you are slight on a particular preference, read both of those Personality Type experiences in the high school classroom. For example, read both ENTP and ESTP if you are slight on the Sensing - Intuition scale. Keep in mind that the teacher's own Personality Type has a lot of influence.

ENFJ Learning Style in High School

English: English is likely to be a favorite subject. A teacher who presents literary figures along with the reasons for their behavior in the novel is a favorite. This type can read between the lines and understands the motivations of the characters in novels like *Robinson Crusoe*. They often love to participate in class. They must have harmony in the class to feel positive and will actively participate in discussion where values are front and center. If the teacher plays favorites and allows the class to become divided for any reason, this type will shut down. The teacher who encourages study groups will appeal to this type.

Math: A teacher who assigns nightly homework in pre-calculus and covers the answers the next day in class really works for this type. These daily exercises will help this student meet their personal goals within the semester pre-calculus curriculum. The teacher who actually assigns a grade or a point value to daily or weekly work will gain their appreciation. Teachers will get a thumbs up if they offer markers or milestones that track completion and academic progress throughout the semester. Teachers who only give periodic tests will get a thumbs down because this type likes to know where they are at in the class.

History: This type will probably like history, but may not get the best grade because sometimes they let their personal opinions count more than the facts. The teacher who brings out the human interest in historical narratives really plays to their learning style. The teacher who devotedly follows the chronology or focuses on the objective reasons for a war may not get their approval. They might view the Pilgrims' perilous Atlantic crossing through the survivor's tales and emotional scars. They are much less interested in the actual year the Pilgrims landed than the drama of it all.

Science: The ENFJ will like a science teacher who assigns projects that require outside work with other classmates. They especially like anatomy classes because they are connected to human health. The "knee bone connected to the leg bone" makes for the orderly, structured way they prefer to learn. The teacher who acknowledges their skill and ability to be a team player will best develop this student's potential. The teacher who assigns technical lab reports that only require recording observations will be hard for this type. Daily or weekly quizzes centered on data will also not appeal to this type if it is the primary method for the final grade.

ENFP Learning Style in High School

English: English is likely to be a favorite subject. This type likes teachers who help them clarify their ideas. They will enjoy just about any novel, short story or poem the teacher assigns. They really like to have a personal relationship with their teachers. The English teacher is likely to appreciate this type's quick mind and solid ability to identify human emotions in the literature. As a result, the teacher might encourage participation by this type for help inspiring class discussions and ultimately become a friendly mentor or counselor. The ENFP will happily offer insightful comments if they actually read the assignment on time. Typically doing homework at the last minute, they may drag their feet on actually capturing those insightful comments on a paper. They are likely to get a B or a C in this subject if the teacher does not help them out.

Math: This type likes teachers who use humor and variety in the class, but also stick to the lesson plan and always explain the steps within each problem. This student gets the overall nature of the formula, but because they miss the details, the steps must be pointed out to them. This student is a big picture learner and loves the teacher who can teach with an imagination which stimulates the class. The teacher who scores big for this type makes time for informal problem solving and fun during class.

History: Teachers will get the best work from the ENFP if the homework assignment directly matches the information presented in class. The teacher who enthusiastically talks about Bismarck and Germany gets their attention and will get the best work from this type by assigning a paper that follows the classroom discussion to be turned in within the next few days. The teacher who speaks about Bismarck in class but changes the topic for homework that night will discourage this type. Variety in the assignment and extra credit projects are welcomed by this type.

Science: This student likes teachers who start with the adult insect to explain the process of metamorphosis in biology. The remaining steps in the process should have some fun and negotiation. A teacher who allows for a self-designed project will definitely please them. This type likes "minds-on" and "talking it out" with others rather than solo, pencil and paper, observational reports. They relate to the spoken word, especially if the teacher has developed a personal relationship with the class. Short answer, projects and verbal reports best reveal this type's knowledge in chemistry versus multiple choice and fill in the blank.

ENTJ Learning Style in High School

English: The ENTJ likes a teacher who is fair and rewards students who turn in homework on time and gives extra credit for lengthier reports. They are curious and like complex literature but also want it to be related to reality. They would like biographies and literature that explains how great minds and important figures came to be. They like a teacher who encourages a lot of classroom discussion. They like to speak up and will raise their hands to relay the continuous ideas that come into their head during class.

Math: This type wants to be right and often likes pre-calculus because there is a clear and finite answer to each problem. A math teacher who organizes a little competition between student groups will score a touchdown with this type. They like to do problems that others may not be able to complete. They like to invent their own way of working a math problem calling on their broad understanding of the formula. They will take the time to explore different solutions to get the same right answer. If the teacher is organized when presenting new material, the ENTJ will rise to the task.

History: This student will like history if the teacher can present the subject through class projects like dramatic reenactments, oral presentations and class discussions. A teacher who would assign team projects and offer a chance to lead a project would be a favorite. This type will not like a teacher who primarily uses a lecture format to teach history. At the same time, they do like an orderly, chronological march throughout the semester and appreciate a teacher who reminds them if they seem to be missing important details in their search for the big picture.

Science: The ENTJ likes the way chemistry, biology and physics teachers give the class a structured, sequential outline at the beginning of a segment or chapter. The ENTJ will be interested in learning facts and objective information about the brain if the teacher uses ferrets or gerbils to illustrate the application of that knowledge. They may dislike the physics teacher who passes up this type of experiment that offers the opportunity to use insight. Memorizing facts and cramming to cover one more chapter before the semester ends gains their dislike.

ENTP Learning Style in High School

English: This type likes the fact that literature is open to many interpretations. The ENTP explores the possible motives and reasons why a protagonist may act in a certain way. Poems are also something that trigger their imagination. They will like teachers who invite student discussion and include multiple points of view. They will not like teachers who do not deviate from a structured interpretation of book. The ENTP can deal with opposing points of view. When this type has an assignment, such as writing a book review, they are not likely to make an outline. They will like a teacher who gives multiple short stories or poems to read, as opposed to a teacher who stays on one novel all semester. Teachers may find that this student's original interpretation of a poem is not clearly supported in writing and find it difficult to assign a "C" to the most original paper turned in.

Math: The ENTP may have a hard time following the formulas and prescribed teaching in pre-calculus because there is little room for creativity. However, the teacher who shows different approaches to solving a problem will pique their interest. The teacher who gives an open-ended math test, such as "tell how you would build a bridge using math formulas" will be their favorite. If the teacher only offers one kind of math exam all year long, it could become the tedious, ho hum class of the day. The ENTP quickly tires of rules and could make careless, small mistakes. They tend to prefer conceptual math, where they can apply new ways of solving problems.

History: This student likes a fascinating teacher who ties in past events with today's world. They like to read and teach themselves. The teacher who speaks of the numbers of horses and soldiers and hours involved in the battle of Gettysburg will lose this type. The teacher who speaks of Lee's battle plan and Grant's hunches will have them raising their hands to join in with their unique opinions. On a test, they are likely to miss the starting date of the Phoenician wars but the reasons for it will be understood by them. For that reason, an essay test in history is preferable to a multiple choice test.

Science: The ENTP loves asking questions, figuring out how scientists discovered a new vaccine and knowing why milk is best drunk when pasteurized. Teachers in the subject of biology who really ask the "why" questions are favored by the ENTP. The teacher who makes them work hard to memorize the species and specific functions of cells is not a favorite. The teacher who gives students ten chemicals in the lab and rewards the student who made the most compounds brings out the best of their creative learning style.

ESFJ Learning Style in High School

English: This student will like the teacher who requires a chapter to read in the assigned novel and then follows it with a quiz, all the better if this is done on a weekly schedule that is predictable. The ESFJ does not like teachers who skip around and grade with different methods. They do not appreciate surprise assignments or quizzes. This student's written reports, however, will likely be well-prepared and reveal more insight into the material presented in class. If the literature is about values and compassion, their own passion for helping others will shine through because of their own, often deeply held values. This type will not mind a lecture on the various types of poetic cadence and will take detailed notes.

Math: This ESFJ likes to use graphic calculators because of the step-by-step sequences. Teachers who use this as a primary tool will be appreciated by this student. Typically very responsible and earnest, this student will remain on task during difficult algebraic explanations. The ESFJ could ask for clarification on behalf of the class. They are going to be a full participant in the classroom and could be very helpful to fellow students who are less willing to acknowledge their confusion. But no matter how far behind the class or an individual student gets, the ESFJ will be socially appropriate and not likely to disrupt the class or give up.

History: This type will often put forth their ideas in class discussions because they quickly recognize and appreciate facts. They will be well informed and freely share that information to help others in the class reach the same conclusions. They appreciate the teacher who gives them compliments and will do better when they receive positive comments about their work. Their clarity of thinking will shine when the teacher keeps the lessons concrete. They like that practical movement toward the knowledge expected for the coming tests and quizzes. They do not appreciate abstract, theoretical possibilities that require making assumptions about history. They will gladly help other students in the class.

Science: The ESFJ is likely to understand and appreciate the formulas because they can be demonstrated. In other words, this could be the favorite subject during the class day. Concrete concepts and application of those ideas is a favorite activity at which they often excel. Their lab work is very thorough and their lab grades may improve their overall subject grade. Mastering the individual concepts of meticulous lab work is their specialty, and they could earn the highest lab average in the class because of this. They like to work with their peers in a group in the classroom, preparing for the next day's lab experiment.

ESFP Learning Style High School

English: The ESFP is very social and often gregarious, and they may enjoy literature that describes social conventions such as *The Great Gatsby*. They usually support social traditions and may not appreciate literature with an abstract, philosophical bent. A highly detailed book that describes the social scene well will really bring the story alive for this type. Literature that defies social conventions may offend their sense of values. They could shine giving an oral book report on a subject in which they are interested. Their preference for step-by-step learning will allow them to give a sound, thorough report that other students may learn from and come to appreciate.

Math: This type does well with a structured math presentation, and they will especially learn well from applied math lessons that relate to a real situation. They will need those frequent spontaneous energy bursts sometimes to get through the semester in abstract algebra. If the teacher is organized and personable, the teacher will bolster this student's confidence in acquiring and mastering the math work. The teacher gets a thumbs up who regularly encourages discussion of the math problems while the class together works out the answer. Plotting, graphing and geometric designs make sense to them. Classroom management that discourages active discussion or allows one or two students to frequently provide the answers won't work for this type. Follow through with after class assignments and practice may be difficult for them because it is a solo activity and may not necessarily be fun.

History: This student will do well with a history curriculum that allows for hands-on activities like dramatic reenactments or interactive videos. Group activities, such as poster sessions for history day, where this type can study with others, will really bring history alive and pique their interest. They will prefer history taught through significant historical figures versus the traditional chronological time and events approach. They can be fascinated by the lives of people. They could become anxious if they are not encouraged by teacher and this could happen because they are typically sensitive. They are likely to procrastinate on turning in assignments unless they are passionate about the topic. Remembering specific facts and historical details is often a gift of this type who typically does not like highly abstract concepts.

Science: This type will like the teacher who presents the theory of radioactivity through Marie Curie's own research. Science must be connected with reality and purpose for this type. The hands-on nature of environmental science could be a favorite subject, especially if the teacher takes the class to the river to test water samples. They need a certain framework to assignments but also need some elbow room to test and try out their own ideas. The teacher who takes the lab outside of the classroom to identify rocks, collect and identify plants, find animal traces and monitor atmospheric instruments should make this student very happy. Group work and student pairing for class assignments is satisfying because of the personal relationships.

ESTJ Learning Style in High School

English: Papers will be written clearly in a journalistic style, handed in on time without any wandering sentences. The typical literature studied in the classroom, is likely to be somewhat mysterious to them such as *Beowulf*. Nevertheless, they will persevere and remain on task in reading the entire assigned list of books. They will also give their opinion in class especially if the book blends facts with a good story, like *The DaVinci Code, Nickel and Dimed: On Making it in America* or detective novels. The teacher who centers a reading list on books like *Beloved* by Toni Morrison may observe the impatience of this type because the story line is metaphorical. They will not easily suspend their disbelief to move along with a story line that intertwines fantasy with reality.

Math: Where order reigns and the teacher is well prepared and follows a predictable, sequential lesson plan the ESTJ will likely appreciate the class and the teacher. They prefer clarity in explanations of math work. They will want to be sure that they are right or present themselves well prior to raising their hands to ask a question or give an answer. Yet they will speak up even if they are alone in their opinion. They will not feel comfortable revealing a lack of understanding. They prefer tangible results so ongoing problems with answers the next day is not their favorite way to learn. They will appreciate being asked to mentor other students, if requested by the teacher. They gravitate toward finite math because solving the equations will yield correct or incorrect answers and their strong observational skills will identify small mistakes along the way.

History: Since these students are impressed by proven knowledge, history is likely to make perfect sense to them. This tradition-bound type likes the straight forward, historical records because they are factual events without hypothetical queries, and history may offer fewer opportunities for abstraction than some other subjects in high school. The ESTJ student can sit and learn from a dry presentation of the topic if it includes concrete examples. Clear expectations and homework assignments are preferred by this student. Conversely, abstract or opinionated teachers could possibly energize the student who would ask for clarification in a respectful and appropriate way. Typically, they will turn reports in on time, follow through with homework and take a leadership position in the class.

Science: They tend to like this subject because they are learning something useful and real to them. Opinions, interpretations and nebulous ideas are rarely interfaced in the high school science classrooms, so this student is more comfortable with this quantifiable subject. There is no room for argument on how mitosis occurs or at what temperature water boils. The ESTJ's attention for detail, conscientious approach and willingness to take charge helps them excel in the lab assignments. They respect the teacher who presents this subject traditionally, with a syllabus and well-organized. They also enjoy being publicly recognized for good work in the classroom because competence is an important milestone for them. The teacher who gives this independent learner the responsibility to lead others will find an enthusiastic student leader because leadership is a valued trait for them.

ESTP Learning Style in High School

English: This type will like literature which emphasizes, describes and is grounded in the physical environment, real things and people. The teacher who assigns reading that is primarily abstract and emotional in its story line will not hold the attention of this student. Hemingway's *Old Man and the Sea* and readings of Mark Twain are right up their alley. Homework that emphasizes variety in assignments and subject matter helps them stay engaged with abstract literature. Their contribution in class discussion is often summarizing or expanding on earlier comments so that the lesson can move forward. They're appreciative of the multiple points of view in literature and really enjoy the films and videos that illustrate the novel they are reading.

Math: The concepts involved in higher math such as pre-calculus can give this student pause and possibly stump ESTP who has previously done well in understanding discrete math and concrete problems. Their typical strength of collaborating with other students is not often seen in math. High math requires and rewards mastering the abstract concepts embedded within the formulas. The math teacher who brings in practical, real world examples of the math problems will make inroads with this student.

History: History may be the favorite subject of the school day if the teacher uses project-based activities such as documentaries, pictorial exhibits and dramatizations that liven up and add variety to this fact-based discipline. They could be strong contributors in class discussion because their recall of historical facts is a comparative strength in the typical history class. They find historical figures to be compelling if the teacher offers study methods that physically engage their senses. Curiosity is a very real learning tool for this type. Written assignments will likely avoid the 'would of, could of, should of' line of reasoning. They prefer instead to prove their understanding of the subject by revealing a logical thread without unnecessary theory.

Science: This student is likely to prefer the days spent in the lab verses the days spent in listening to lecture and preparation. They will be comfortable with lab partner assignments that include three to four students over the typical two assigned to an experiment because they are often gregarious. They are likely to be the enthusiastic member of the group and will move the experiment forward if it stalls, even if it requires a blunt direct comment from them. They prefer to experiment informally and explore with the least fuss and muss. The teacher who leans too heavily on book and lecture will garner their disfavor. Visible, concrete results, often a part of high school sciences, gives them a chance to excel through active, direct and assertive participation.

INFJ Learning Style in High School

English: This student could be quiet and unassuming about this subject that really speaks to their hearts, but they are shy about revealing this to others because they are private people. They do not like a teacher who would call on them, unless they raised their hand with a carefully thought out answer. They like a teacher who understands that they are listening and are on task, even if they do not speak out in class and answer questions. They may especially do well in a home schooling experience for a year or two because they need time and quiet to process their thoughts and prefer to teach themselves. Idealism and heroism such as is portrayed in *The Perfect Storm* by Sebastian Younger will appeal to this type.

Math: The INFJ prefers a teacher who is very well prepared. The teacher who offers a steady, even presentation of the big picture and the theory that underlies the numbers gets their respect. An equation will make more sense to this type even if it is not plotted on a graph because they can picture it intuitively. They thrive on careful analysis and the freedom to search for their own math solutions. They are independent learners and may need gentle guidance from a teacher to get back on the right track. They rely on their insights about math to be correct, but will ask a question of the teacher to confirm that they have the right answer.

History: This type is usually fascinated by this subject. They are excited to learn how the colonies came together to form a union. An assignment that required a full length examination of John Calvin would be right up their alley. Calvin is a complex figure and clearly impacted the pilgrim's motivation. INFJ would love to examine the puritan ethic. They prepare very well for all history tests even if the teacher doesn't teach to their style. This student loves to read and will do extra credit for the learning itself.

Science: They will do well in this subject. They will thrive with a demanding teacher who requires the students to be organized, good with time management and planning a semester projects and the accompanying papers, projects and reports. They will relate positively, through reason, to certain science issues like sustainability unless their personal belief system does not support that view. If they make a small error in judgment during a project or lab and the teacher calls attention to it, they will take it personally and be really hurt because of their high standards.

INFP Learning Style in High School

English: The INFP does well in class because INFP is usually interested in literature. They probably are avid readers of the Harry Potter series because it is richly metaphorical and depicts relationships and human values. They may also like science fiction books that stimulate their curiosity. They easily take on additional reading that is not required for class. They may find it hard to tear themselves away from a favorite novel. Their interests in literature range far and wide. They write their best papers when inspired and the topic relates to their own beliefs. They want the teacher to appreciate and compliment their work as well as coach and mentor them.

Math: In class, the INFP may be deeply invested in learning if math is taught in general concepts rather than preplanned, linear lessons and repetitive homework problems. For example, the INFP likes to know how the story of how Pythagoras discovered the Pythagorean Theorem, and how this can be applied to understanding how the universe works. A teacher who is always rational, objective and to the point, who doesn't let emotion enter the class discussion, may be upsetting to the INFP.

History: They like to use their inquisitive mind while working or studying solo. They typically like history if there is stimulating discussion in class and it is not abrasive or argumentative. Lectures might be considered boring, especially if it's a monologue by the teacher. INFP seeks to understand reasons for wars and is likely to look for a universal reason that explains all conflict. They prefer harmony in the classroom and will dislike a teacher who cannot earn the respect of the class. They may have trouble finishing their history report because the details can bog them down. The teacher who provides structure with some wiggle room does well with this student.

Science: This type sometimes gets bored with studying traditional biology or physics. They want science to relate to the human experience. The study of light and lenses make more sense to them if the teacher talks about people who suffer from cataracts. INFP needs broad concepts and big pictures first to spark the interest otherwise they may not incorporate the facts which they receive as too monotonous and boring. INFP would rather write about metamorphosis and life cycle in a short answer test rather than fill in a list of stages on a matching test.

INTJ Learning Style in High School

English: The INTJ loves the teacher who is competent and knows their literature. They would not like a teacher who accepts multiple interpretations of a novel. They want the teacher and class to settle on the best and most accurate interpretation that can survive the INTJ's analysis and critique. They do not like a teacher who moves from novel to short story to a poem in one lesson plan on a whim. They like an organized, logical review of each assigned reading.

Math: They challenge the teacher because they are quiet and learn privately. They often avoid group assignments and choose not to volunteer answers. They will complete math homework almost with resignation because the formulas do not give them freedom with the outcome. Sometimes they work so hard in trying to perfect the answers on their take-home pre-calculus exams that they get down on themselves. Generally, INTJ is comfortable in the math classroom. This subject utilizes INTJ's love for analysis. Solving a problem is like getting to the finish line, an important milestone for this type.

History: This type will challenge the teacher's position on the Vietnam War. They like a teacher who will allow them to ask pointed questions. They ask questions to learn about the subject. They risk being not liked by the teacher and possibly others in the class because they learn by challenging the views presented in history classes. A teacher who follows the textbook interpretations regularly is not their favorite. They like a teacher who presents history in conceptual frameworks that encourage student insight.

Science: This student finds that teachers who start with the big picture in chemistry or physics are right up their alley. They are okay with missing a few of the steps and details because they will fill in the gaps later. Some teachers may like it when the INTJ challenges a few of their statements. They like a teacher who moves quickly through the chemistry chapters verbally explaining and highlighting required concepts for the upcoming AP exam. INTJ has an inner vision of how chemistry composes the world. The teacher syllabus must interface with the INTJ's vision.

INTP Learning Style in High School

English: The INTP may be reticent to speak up although they have may have an opinion. INTP can get very absorbed in a novel if it interests them. If the short story or poem does not interest them, they are likely to get bored. If the novel includes puzzles, mysteries, riddles or science fiction it is a winner as far as they are concerned. They connect the unrelated hints and clues to find the solution.

Math: This student is often on the honor roll. They may shine in pre-calculus because they have the thinking power to hang in there and get the abstract theory behind the formulas. They are likely to enjoy the derivatives in higher level calculus. They really can tap in the coordinates and numbers on their hand held T-83 graphic calculator. For those who do not like math, their tendency to overlook details may trip them up on exams. Their uneven surges of energy could drain their overall effort. If the teacher negotiates with this student on the grading to include math problems that seem to be riddles, then INTP's impressive concentration kicks in.

History: Teachers that connect historic events with current problems and policy will really get INTP to pay attention. If teachers dwell on event upon event to build a chronological timeline, they are likely to lose this type. INTPs may not get appreciation by the teacher because they can become totally absorbed in connections between the past and future, with little bearing on current class discussion. History may be a favorite or a loathed subject depending on the teacher's approach. This type may come across as skeptical in their questioning as they explore and satisfy their exceptional curiosity.

Science: This type likes the pure science that teachers talk about in the classroom, and they can listen and learn while moving a concept around in their head. They may actually enjoy or not enjoy the lab experiments. They certainly don't care for the group and collaboration often assigned by the science teachers. They will shine at memorizing the formulas and enjoy the complexity of the problems in science. Sometimes they become so absorbed in their lab work that they lose sense of time and place.

ISFJ Learning Style in High School

English: The teacher who is clear and highlights the moral issues helps them figure out the various shades of gray in the story line. They will be comfortable reading Jane Austin's *Sense and Sensibility* because is pretty straight forward yet deals with common family issues. This author feeds the type's compulsion to make mental scrapbooks, rich with people details. ISFJ will be paying very close attention to everything said in the class so that they can be accurate in forming their judgments. They value the establishment and social conventions more often than not because it helps them know where they stand. Inferences made by students or the teacher in class may not be understood or accepted because they hear things literally. However, they are not likely to speak up and challenge the teacher or fellow students.

Math: Their usual mastery of the facts and their great work ethic will let them shine in the more sequential math tasks. The nature of abstract concepts in math may frustrate and wear them down so that test grades could be inconsistent sometimes. They complete all of their homework ahead of time even at the expense of play. They will like a teacher who applies the Pythagorean Theorem to figure out distance, which is a practical, hands-on concept for this type. They will like the teacher who offers a familiar routine to the lesson plan throughout the school year. They don't like to be rushed. The security of an orderly classroom that is evenly paced is very helpful to them.

History: Studying history through the social and human side is a favorite way to get into this subject. They can bring history alive for themselves by wondering what historical figures thought and believed at that time. They will even pass judgment on the morals or decisions made by those historical persons. Only when they ask will the teacher find out that the ISFJ has some unique and interesting insights. If a history teacher includes historical dramas in the course, they will make it easy for ISFJ to learn. Teachers who approach history in terms of facts, dates and events are less liked by this type, especially if the teacher calls attention to them in class.

Science: Mastering the facts in the sciences and then devising practical applications in the lab will be a natural and preferred learning experience for them. They will like the definite outcomes of experiments which leave little to guess about. Experimental teaching in the labs will work well for them if the teacher gives specific direction and identifies the end result of the lesson. ISFJ have their exceptional observation and retention skills. They are likely to be the best prepared lab partner and conscientiously accept responsibility for the exercise.

ISFP Learning Style in High School

English: The ISFP likes a teacher who is crisp and direct in discussing the story lines in literature and avoids shades of grey morality. What really drains this type's reserve is drawn-out explanations and hypothetical insights into what an author might have meant by a certain phrase or poem. In this high school class, ISFPs would rather watch a Shakespearian play on DVD first, and figure out the rest on their own. Usually, ISFP in English class hesitates before contributing opinions. They want to please the teacher. They are just as happy to observe rather than to propose an interpretation that they fear might be farfetched.

Math: This type appreciates the clarity of this subject. However, because they are not assertive and prefer to remain unnoticed, they could fall through the cracks if they don't have a caring teacher who coaches them along. They will put in extra effort if math interests them. They are cautious until they feel supported by the teacher at which time they can become energized in the classroom. Math teachers who don't seem personally interested in the students will not be their favorite. The pre-calculus teacher should give examples of practical nature when presenting formulas to this type. The teacher who injects humor into the class lesson or is willing to make a game out of learning math could be their favorite.

History: This student is likely to excel and enjoy history if the teacher encourages them to informally come up with their own interpretations of the facts and events. They appreciate a teacher who pauses and gives the class enough time to process new information and their individual thoughts. If the history topic really piques their interest, they will go all out and turn in a seven-page report. They will excel at a project that requires cut-and-paste historical mosaics. On history day, they will use posters to illustrate historical figures, complete with pictures and illustrations of clothing and dwellings. The teacher who notices them in a personal manner will be a favorite.

Science: They really understand and learn from those labs where there are animal samples and skeletons and specimens. Learning comes easier to them this way. They will learn from film or video presentations about the natural life cycles and the chemistry involved in those cycles. Sometimes the teacher does not understand their informal, impulsive interest in learning. At the same time, these students do not appreciate the big picture, relying instead on memorization of the facts. A teacher who pairs them up with another socially sensitive, down-to-earth student will get ISFP's best work.

ISTJ Learning Style in High School

English: This type will be suspicious of the many possible meanings to a metaphor. The inferential reasoning required to interpret literature could be a riddle to them. Deep inside they don't trust all the positions and interpretations because in their view, only one is correct. They will listen quietly, not complaining, and likely not reveal their discomfort with the open-ended and exploratory class discussion. They are likely to write clearly, with organization and free of flowery prose. They do well with book reports gathering factual information that would support a position. They could submit well-written papers and call on their previous knowledge of grammar and English structure that they learned and enjoyed via drills in earlier school years. ISTJs want to reach the learning objectives set by the teacher and if they don't get this in class they will sort it out later by themselves.

Math: They are able to grasp the theory and concepts in advanced math by building up their math knowledge sequentially over the years. Math takes advantage of their logic-based approach and so they can solve complex problems especially if the teacher is clear about the foundational steps. They will pay attention to formulas presented on the board with intense concentration especially if there are graphs, tables and illustrations involved. They will accurately pinpoint errors that they identify. On math quizzes and tests there will be no small careless mistakes. When they are solving equations they will remember to use the right laws of properties and numbers.

History: They will be accurate on dates and facts with reports they turn in on time. If the history teacher assigns a wide-ranging topic that is not broken down into a clear outline, they will not like it. They will like the class if the teacher offers the material in an organized fashion and sequentially leads to the big picture. The ISTJs make for very good students, carefully observing and following the teacher's directions. They don't want to call attention to themselves so they appreciate the teacher who acknowledges their due diligence quietly. They are keen observers of what is. Their excellent memory is like the hard drive in a computer. Group work is not their favorite way to learn because ISTJs will step in and finish what others did not complete. As a result of doing this heavy lifting, they become aggravated. When it comes to answering questions in class, they will be thoughtful with a planned answer. Sometimes the conversation will have moved on to another point and they will not volunteer that thought they were preparing. The teacher will often come to know this student's mastery of the subject through their written work.

Science: Biology, chemistry or environmental sciences are enjoyable because they allow for logic and reasoning to arrive at a definite conclusion. These sciences move toward the big picture typically after introducing facts and information followed by a building block sequence. ISTJ likes this approach. Hands-on lab work will provide them an opportunity to demonstrate their competency and awareness of safety issues. They will not blow up the lab. Through their senses, they are very grounded in the lab assignment. Occasionally, they will volunteer to do a demonstration, taking responsibility for carrying the experiment to the end and making sure it gets done. They won't forget to come back to the lab to shake the vial or check on the growth.

ISTP Learning Style in High School

English: This type will prefer literature that is in a journalistic style of writing: what, where, when and how. This satisfies their need to know what makes things tick. They will like clearly descriptive essays, short stories and novels about what is, in the non-fiction category. If the teacher prefers novels with high emotional content and allegory this student will likely be turned off. They are likely to find themselves out of synch with the English class during poetry study. However, they might like the haiku poetry because of its short, clear presentation with more concrete words. The teacher who is touchy-feely and highly creative will be a puzzle to them. This student is likely to be passive in class and if the teacher requires participation, the grade could suffer.

Math: They usually like this subject especially finite math like algebra I, statistics and geometry. They are often orderly, paying attention to detail and carefully print their numbers on the page so they won't make mistakes. They will adore math teachers who present lessons clearly. There are two types of answers, right and wrong, and this student is likely to willingly retrace their steps if they made a mistake. The short cuts in math formulas and most efficient proof to verify the correct answer is easy for the ISTP. They like the objectivity of math. The sequential, step-by-step teacher will keep the attention of this student. The occasional math teacher who gets lost in their own presentations is not going to work for this student because they crave clarity. Math helps this type understand technical material which is what they are really interested in.

History: The teacher who presents this subject with emphasis on facts in categories and logical classifications will be a favorite teacher and likely to get this student to raise their hand in class. A teacher who covers the chapter with multisensory learning tools like video, graphs, posters, maps and text will allow ISTP to look for that practical thread that pulls it together. For that reason it may take the teacher several months or perhaps the semester to understand what this student has to offer to the class discussion. A teacher who flavors their history with social, religious or political random threads will not be their favorite. If the history topic piques their curiosity, they will want to know the material clearly and objectively as it relates to their present circumstances.

Science: They are likely to shine in physics, chemistry, biology and earth science because these subjects impact their lives today. This type really enjoys the many hands-on experiments and learning assignments, like dissection, because these make practical things clearer and are basically like play. The classification and systems of science are very appealing to them. Enjoying and excelling in their observations of experiments, ISTPs are likely to become participants and leaders in this class. Their papers and written work will high-light the accumulative, factual nature of the sciences. It is likely they will be engrossed by class projects.

CHAPTER 6

THE COLLEGE DESCRIPTIONS

The reader will find our three powerful tools for finding the perfect college contained in each of the following campus descriptions. We suggest starting out by reading several of the 50 or so majors we recommend for you. It will not be difficult since their page number is found in Chapter Four. In this way you will become familiar with your preferred learning style. You will get a feel for many of the subjects taught in college with the teaching methods that work best for you. You will take a very large jump forward in self knowledge with this exercise.

Next pick out four or five colleges and read their entire descriptions including all of the major recommendations. It is important to realize that a college identified for your Personality Type preference lists 6 or 8 other majors too. The major we recommended for your Type is intended only to be a sign post. It calls attention to the overall college which has a good number of academic methods that fit your learning style. That is true because colleges themselves do not have Personality Types. They usually offer somewhere between 50 and 100 majors taught with all eight preferences. Their academic philosophies tend to lean toward four of these eight preferences and we selected those colleges that most closely associate with your four preferences. So please, if you are med school bound, don't get hung up with our major recommendation for a degree in Asian languages. Rather, if you are an ESFJ, take a close look at the majors we recommended for ESTJ, ESFP and ENFJ if they are shaded. In each case, you share three of their favored learning preferences.

As you continue to become familiar with the book, pay close attention to the bolded words in the Physical and Social Environment descriptions. They call out defining features of the campus. In the MBTI compatibility section you will see reference like (S) for sensing. Those letters identified within the sentence are predominant preferences on the campus in our opinion. The eight preferences listed below and their description are a quick reference to use while reading the compatibility section.

As you approach high school graduation, we hope you have a good feel for several new educational majors and will look forward to exploring them at the college you attend. We hope you will recognize your learning style and select educational studies and professors who are in tune with your preference. Most of all, we hope you will find direction to the perfect college through self knowledge.

E—Extraversion
Focus on the outer world of people and things

I—Introversion
Focus on the inner world of ideas and impressions

S—Sensing
Focus on the present and concrete information gained from the five senses

N—Intuition
Focus on the future, with a view toward patterns and possibilities

T—Thinking
Form decisions on logic and on objective analysis of cause and effect

F—Feeling
Form decisions primarily on values and on subjective evaluation of person-centered concerns

J—Judging
Prefer to have things settled and tend to plan and follow an organized approach to life

P—Perceiving
Prefer to keep options open and tend to follow a flexible and spontaneous approach to life

* Copyright CPP, Consulting Psychologists Press, Inc., 3803 E. Bayshore Road, Palo Alto, CA 94303

AGNES SCOTT COLLEGE

Office of Admission
141 East College Avenue
Decatur, GA 30030
Website: www.agnesscott.edu
Admissions Telephone: 800-868-8602
Undergraduates: 873 Women

Physical Environment

Agnes Scott College is in suburban Decatur, a nearby neighbor to lively Atlanta. The capital city jumps with energy and opportunities, all to the benefit of the "Scotties." The public metro line, MARTA, starts at the airport, travels through the city and then on to the Decatur station where Agnes Scott undergrads board it inbound for internships. A few blocks from campus there are quite a few small businesses and boutiques. Coffee shops make comfy study spots off campus. Lattes at Starbucks help students memorize formulas in Organic Chemistry before the final exam.

On campus, the 100-acre treed setting is quiet, cool and comfortable. The campus was established around the 1900s and is a mix of collegiate and Victorian style buildings. It has a strong **sense of history**. In 1886 it started as the Decatur Seminary for Women with a few buildings that now have a spiritual feel, especially Main Hall and Rebekah Scott Hall. These were the first buildings on campus. Some of today's students may still have future seminary aspirations.

The academic buildings sit on a long rectangular stretch of land that ends at the pond used for wildlife and habitat studies. Many women here are **ecologically-minded**. Five of the oldest buildings were retrofitted to reduce their ecological footprint. The weather in Atlanta is warm most of the year, and so swimming and tennis are two very popular sports at Agnes Scott. A lot of Scotties participate in Division III sports and the college fielded the first varsity women's lacrosse team in Georgia.

Social Environment

Undergraduates here expect to learn, search for the truth and make the world a better place for everyone. They accept the Honor Code which lets them schedule their exams when they want to take them. They are encouraged to think **honorably**. This is part of the Agnes Scott experience. The college takes in high school graduates and expects them to become a force in society. The administration seeks a wide variety of women. Many look for balance in their future and seek perspectives that combine career with traditional marriage and children. There is a quiet sense of pride in being a contemporary American woman. Students may join the meditation group, go to the dance studio for yoga or attend one of the lectures at the college's Bradley Observatory, like that given by Scottie Sarah Scoles '07 astrophysics graduate. Many Scotties are active in volunteer efforts, others join the women's business group. As a result, some are looking for that classic liberal arts education, others are headed into business, some for the pre-med and pre-teacher education, still others for the sciences that emphasize graduate school or research.

Scotties relate to helping others. Some undergraduates are members of academic honor organizations such as **Phi Beta Kappa** and Dana Scholars. Religious organizations, like the Baptist Campus Ministry and Jewish Student Association, are well received by the student body and include several Judeo-Christian denominations. Undergraduates are quite active on campus and like to join in **collaborative leadership**. It is valued as a good way to take a stand on current issues, from politics to ecology. Scottie clubs and organizations function to benefit the entire college campus. Undergrads make their views known in the school paper. The process of becoming is important along with the end goal. Scotties believe in themselves, and so they **speak out for the purpose** of making improvements, whether in their life, at the college or in society. They do this yet avoid the most radical of positions. Bright, competent, mindful women graduate from this college. Fulbright Scholarships mark the recent history of students graduating from Agnes Scott.

Compatibility with Personality Types and Preferences

The women here are outspoken in their approach to education. They come to this campus to secure professional skills and gain entry into the marketplace. The student body might define competency as subject knowledge with current day values and adaptability. Scotties go for competence, communication and persuasion to liven up new ideas (P) in a subject. Undergraduates look to traditions but also embrace change here. Faculty and administration follow a similar trajectory. Most areas of study are familiar, traditional (J) subjects found at liberal arts colleges, yet, there is a strong program to interface students with fast-paced Atlanta. Neither students nor professors back away from enterprise in this rapidly growing city. The new major in Public Health makes total sense with the Center for Disease Control and Prevention just a few stops away on the MARTA in downtown Atlanta.

Religious tradition and faith, originally the centerpiece in founding Agnes Scott College, have found their voices through study of current day American issues (E). This small, unique women's college in the 21st century seems to center on defining the role of today's women. Students are accepting of ideas that encompass the unknown (N). Graduates expect to become actively engaged with their communities. They anticipate opportunities to solve tomorrow's problems. They expect to bring talent and leadership to the table. Agnes Scott graduates are measured and confident at the same time.

Now read below about one of the majors that MBTI® research shows people of your type have selected since the mid-20th century. After, refer to Chapter Five for the 50 or so majors that can help you prepare for careers your type has selected. Most importantly, remember that this college description is a suggestion for exploration, not a commanding order. You can be successful in any major at any college.

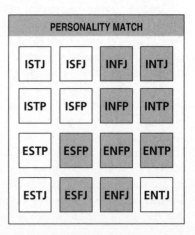

PERSONALITY MATCH

ISTJ	ISFJ	INFJ	INTJ
ISTP	ISFP	INFP	INTP
ESTP	ESFP	ENFP	ENTP
ESTJ	ESFJ	ENFJ	ENTJ

INFP likes to examine their own values and those of others. This habit is going to be an asset at Agnes Scott. The campus is a blend of modern day American social currents and traditions of past years. It is an environment in which social viewpoints are front and center. INFP will take notice and appreciate this. The minor in **Education** opens up discussion about the best ways to develop moral leadership for divisions found in our public school classrooms.

INFJ wants to follow their beliefs into a profession or work setting and often helps or cares for others. They have a passion for understanding people and themselves. The faculty at Agnes Scott College offers a major or minor in **Religious Studies** that focuses on the foundations of religions across the world. Spirituality often looks inward to the self. INFJs also like to mull their thoughts over with others. It helps mold their own personal beliefs. Never fear, INFJ is more than up to the challenge within the department's course offerings that reflect the smorgasbord of spirituality found in this major at many American liberal arts colleges today.

INTJ will likely enjoy the abstract nature of studying **Biology** at Agnes Scott. Students approach studies in this major by process, advanced technology and evolution. Very little is static in the course work, and facts are accumulated to find their way into the big picture. Courses in biology at Agnes Scott require a great deal of intuition plus sweat equity while figuring out the basic biological processes. The department offers a selection of courses across this growing discipline from evolution, genetics and ecology to botany. It is ideal for INTJ to study biology this way.

INTP is drawn to the impossible, well at least the hard-to-understand. The degree in **Physics** should suit INTPs for this reason. The labs and the intense logical reasoning within this science are comfortable for this type. The unknown, at least unseen, nature of physics requires abstract thought. This type can handle it. But that doesn't mean they like the lab's loud bangs, hissing sounds or clouds of unpleasant odors. Again, the department studies are just right for INTP who wants to focus on the how-it-happened. This is how you solve puzzles—the INTP way.

ESFP is often observant, specific and realistic. This is all good to have for study in the sciences. Agnes Scott's new major, **Neuroscience**, offers a good basis for many health-oriented careers after graduation. The labs in this major give ESFP the chance to learn in their favorite way: hands-on learning as you go. The practical nature of studying science to improve human health really could warm the soul of the optimistic ESFPs.

ENFP likes freedom and intellectual space to pursue their ideas. Business environments that offer this will bring out their entrepreneurial spirit. The degree in **Economics** at Agnes Scott lets ENFPs study economic theory and application through the big picture lens. The type's insight and creativity is very helpful with the abstract courses that center on distribution of scarce resources. Spontaneous and enthusiastic, with little patience for getting bogged down, they will be positive in college and on the job in the dynamic world of finance.

ENTP can look to the **Mathematics** major to take advantage of their strengths. Mathematics professors are actively connecting math with the power that it brings to society. ENTP is all about these kind of very large concepts. Given an inclination for math, they might declare one of the three math majors offered by the creative faculty in this department. Along the way, any number of interesting applications and careers will fly through the ENTP's active mind. It is likely to give them entry to important work environments and mathematical research at graduate levels.

ESFJ and the **Chemistry** major at Agnes Scott is a twosome that can work. The department is focused on practice and development in research design. It is a hands-on experience course of study that is very practical. The major prepares graduates for entrance into medical diagnostic specialties, teaching or pharmaceuticals. Each of these fields can bring ESFJs together directly with people in need. Agnes Scott regularly uses experimental research design in their curriculum. This often requires collaboration with others and conscientious follow through. Both of these are characteristic strengths of the ESFJ.

ENFJ could be quite happy with the quality and variety of course work in **English** offered at Agnes Scott. A broad study of literature is excellent training ground for understanding human motivation. Reading between the lines comes naturally for ENFJs as well as analyzing the written word. This ability could also come in handy at understanding social media's influence on the young children in our schools. Polished and decisive, they will likely move into the world of authorship with confidence and passion.

AMERICAN UNIVERSITY

Office of Admissions
4400 Massachusetts Avenue, NW
Washington, DC 20016
Website: www.american.edu
Admissions Telephone: 202-885-6000
Undergraduates: 7,386; 2,782 Men, 4,604 Women
Graduate Students: 1,334

Physical Environment

Located in the nation's capital, American University students get up close and personal with **Washington, DC, politics**, the media and socio-economic issues in our nation and the world. The campus architecture has many square and rectangular cement buildings that remind us of government bureaus. The lawns between the buildings are free of flower beds and other frills, except for the occasional bench. The university has an important connection with presidential history. The 2011 Campus Plan looks to preserve locations and buildings, such as the East Quad, where past Presidents Eisenhower and Kennedy gave policy speeches. Politics and history are really connected in the course work here. On this campus, undergraduates might start classes after 5:30 pm when adjunct professors in government, non-profits and world organizations are free to lecture. The nation's capital invites serious-minded students interested in **thorny issues**.

There are traditional, apartment-style and suite residence halls on main campus. Themed housing reflects the interests of the students and the university's curriculum. Residential Community Clusters allow 6 to 18 like-minded students to live together in the dormitory with **similar interests**. The McKinley building, completed in 2014, is home to the School of Communication with a modern media innovation lab. Since the Washington, DC, media streams fanciful stories daily, there will be no shortage of video to study for fact and fantasy in this new facility. With a full residential life staff and thoughtful activities, American University does not encourage undergraduates to leave campus for the pull of the city. The new East Campus, opened in summer 2016, has three residence halls and two academic buildings.

Social Environment

Students who fit in well at American University are **independently motivated**. They are not shy and usually take advantage of all that American University and Washington, DC have to offer. They attend happenings around the capital from political debates to demonstrations. Their goals are usually connected with journalism, government, political science and national and international politics.

Undergraduates often come with high school or community leadership skills plus international lifestyles from living overseas. Close to half of the student body identifies as a minority. They look to expand their network of friends with other undergraduates from around the world. Along with American's very strong foreign languages department, it is easy to find a native speaker with so many languages spoken in DC. A lot of students will also take courses in the international service programs or School of Communication while still majoring in traditional subjects. Plus there is a new undergraduate certificate in **European Studies** that is a good way to specialize without having to declare a major or minor in this important area. AU is for students who like to study democracy and most other subjects in a **practical way**, such as analyzing a system of ballot collection. They want to visit historic monuments, attend rallies and report on media events.

In the dorms, students create a home away from home as they forge relationships by introducing themselves to others on their floor. Sports at AU don't monopolize the social scene or define the school spirit. AU is in the Division I Patriot's League. It has no football but the Eagles basketball and volleyball teams are sufficient to keep fans entertained. Some international students have family connections in the nation's capital, be it taxi driver or **foreign embassy** staff officer.

Compatibility with Personality Types and Preferences

American University is adjacent to the strategic and cultural diplomatic neighborhoods of Washington, DC. For all educational purposes, there is a thin boundary between this university and the administrative offices in DC. Prospective students are alerted to the fact that professors might also be policy makers throughout the government. The faculty and staff regularly take advantage of their location in the nation's capital. The university has an established network which adds energy to the campus academics.

Happy students at American University can't wait to step foot in the office (E) of their first internship. Many of these positions are in the congressional offices but the city also has hundreds of national offices for business, the arts and the sciences. Students learn first hand of worldwide cultures by wandering into the city for entertainment or presentations. The American University curriculum is for those with a passion plus a driving need to accomplish (J). Those drawn to this university are likely to take a position on current day issues. Most desire a career track at international policy levels or within the U.S. government. Starting out as freshmen, they find the majors or minors that move them toward their interests in policy, politics, business, communication or the social sciences, etc. Students will define and likely settle on a career goal (S) like campaign manager or nonprofit executive. Before graduation day, they start to build a world view through the university's academic programs and courses that are policy-centered. The amazing international presence in the nation's capital also adds a level of current realism for a graduate with a government or political science degree.

Now read below about one of the majors that MBTI® research shows people of your type have selected since the mid-20th century. After, refer to Chapter Five for the 50 or so majors that can help you prepare for careers your type has selected. Most importantly, remember that this college description is a suggestion for exploration, not a commanding order. You can be successful in any major at any college.

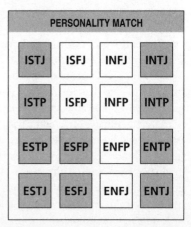

PERSONALITY MATCH

ISTJ	ISFJ	INFJ	INTJ
ISTP	ISFP	INFP	INTP
ESTP	ESFP	ENFP	ENTP
ESTJ	ESFJ	ENFJ	ENTJ

INTJ absolutely must generate new concepts and ideas by themselves. The Bachelor of Science degree in **Economics** at American with an emphasis in theory will be ideal for this type. The coursework is chock full of starting points to build an economic perspective. INTJs will take this as an invitation to develop their own ideas as they quietly connect information heard in class lectures with readings. This type can do both at the same time—if they read assignments before the class starts.

ISTP loves facts, details and information that have a practical use. The degree in **Anthropology** at American is based in reality which suits ISTPs who might otherwise pass over this abstract field. Looking a few layers deeper, ISTPs realize the major might be an excellent fit. Success in this field means searching for hard, specific clues that open up an ancient city or culture. The department also has several courses in archeology, a subfield of anthropology. Internships and work experience in national research libraries such as the Smithsonian and National Museum of American History offer ISTPs the reality base they prefer.

ISTJ is going to like the looks of the minor in **Justice**. They are practical in their work habits and attitudes. They want to go with fairness and following the rules. So the course in Justice, Morality and the Law will make sense to them. On this campus there is a special awareness of national government policy. So ISTJs, with their ironic sense of humor, will appreciate the American University prominent law professor, who in October 2015, dissected the Clinton email leaks that endangered national security.[1] It all gets stored in the ISTJ brain's data banks. They are dependable and conservative by nature.

INTP can be drawn to mathematics if a math formula could be used as a tool to solve problems. Considering this, INTP will like American University's **Applied Mathematics** degree. This type is always thinking, always defining and analyzing subjects of interest to them. Students in this major can follow their interests and bring the power of math analysis to their studies as an intern at national agencies—all within walking distance or a subway stop. The National Archives has tons of options for a research project. INTP would probably also like the rare, historical math volumes in the university archives. This collection will spark a few thoughts about the lives of those earlier mathematicians.

ESTP could go for the **Law and Society** degree at American University because this type has the ability to meet and quickly start a working relationship. ESTP will also find great internships at the nearby national government agencies. This type likes a fast-paced, trial-and-error environment that lets them scan the landscape, troubleshoot or negotiate a position on a lively subject. American University Conferences, like the Annual Eisenhower Symposium, just might bring talking heads to the stage with conservative cultural ideas that are opposed to progressive politics. This is fine for realistic ESTP. This type may also explore international legal careers.

ESFP is well suited for the 24 hour news cycle. The degree in **Public Relations Strategic Communication** at American University is chock full of arguably the best foundation courses. ESFPs need only to turn on the computer or TV to study the government releases moving across the airwaves in this capital. ESFPs live and work in the present day, the current week with much less interest in the distant future. Yet the faculty here can help them see that it is necessary. So as they pick up on what is going on today, they will learn to incorporate more for the future with enthusiasm and social finesse. This degree—at this university—for this type—is a stellar choice.

ENTP loves to look into the future with other interested students and a professor who is willing to listen. The degree in **Computational Science** offers the complexity that suits their style. Speculation is an ENTP passion and strength. So the larger the data field of a problem, the more the solution calls for computer modeling. The curriculum here requires creativity in combining computer models with the natural, social sciences or engineering. The nation's capital is a marketplace for organizational data problems and this is just the challenge ENTP loves.

ESFJ is most often the cheerleader for an organization and students love an enthusiastic cheerleader. The major in **Elementary Education** at American University is loaded with unique resources. Practice teaching in DC urban and suburban schools highlights America's different family backgrounds, histories and values. Here ESFJ can emphasize and promote what is held in common by their young students. This positive practice helps to deal with mixed messages from social media and national lobbies that often focus on differences among American citizens. Very social, almost always pleasant, ESFJs bring stability and caring to their classrooms, yet it will be their curiosity about others that might draw them into educational research.

ESTJ wants to live the responsible and sensible life—in the dorm, in college classes and thereafter. Order is a need and usually a talent of this type. Take charge ESTJs would enjoy the precise nature of the scientific courses in the medical health fields. The Bachelor of Science in **Health Promotion** has great internships in DC, sometimes with the Department of Health and Human Services. ESTJs will find the interdisciplinary nature of the courses helpful because the field of health is expanding. New discoveries in psychology and sociology are opening new career fields. The degree also leaves open the door for graduate work in medical research. The program has state of the art research in human performance focusing on diagnostic practice.

ENTJ with a political passion quickly recognizes that American University has several degrees for their own inclinations. The degree in **Political Science** has unusual courses like Ancient Political Thought. It explores Socrates, Plato, Aristotle and ancient Roman law from the political, civic perspectives. This is unusual because many liberal arts colleges study them through philosophy only. Metropolitan Politics covers the political nature of the city with its suburbs rather than the social nature of the city. ENTJs are power players themselves and would not shrink from the win or lose nature of political decisions in America today.

AMHERST COLLEGE

P.O. Box 5000
Amherst, MA 01002-5000
Website: www.amherst.edu
Admissions Telephone: 413-542-2328
Undergraduates: 1,795; 891 Men, 904 Women

Physical Environment

The Amherst campus spreads out over 1,000 acres, overlooking the Holyoke mountain range of western Massachusetts. Students notice the sweeping views and use the hiking trails. The landscape makes you think of the garden at nearby Emily Dickinson's home. Some Amherst students are attracted to this **literary setting** that calls back to early New England. The Book & Plow Farm, on Amherst's campus, is another call back to early New England with organic crops, seven acres and undergraduate interns pushing the shovels and rakes. The sloping Greenway helps to pull it all together with gardens and orchards. It all works to soften the heavy feel of traditional, red brick buildings that sit across the campus.

The new Science Center, opening in 2018, will be the exact opposite of gentle slopes. It will have sharp edges of glass rectangle shapes to form the outside walls. The inside will also be cutting edge. It will have the departments of biology, chemistry, physics and astronomy as you would expect. But it will also include psychology, neuroscience, math and statistics. The research and access for undergrads will be over the top.

With the charming, artsy town of Amherst right outside their door, a few undergrads would rather go for the buzz of social life at the large state university in town also. A few others take the shuttle bus to the other campuses for courses that cross register with the **Five College Consortium**.

Social Environment

Amherst College is an ideal setting for students who want to think about big issues and get their opinions heard. There are many **talented equals** on this campus, all are noticed, and about half of the student body identifies as a minority. As a group, they are interested in the national and international news items of the day. They might become involved through problem solving, demonstrations or taking public positions. They are very aware of events on campus also and easily pick up their tablets to voice strong conclusions for and against an issue. In Fall 2015 students staged a sit in at the library with a list of demands over racial justice.[2] The president acknowledged the sit in and its purpose, as a challenge to come together in the public square of free inquiry, expression and discussion.[3] So Amherst students have a great place to work through conflicting perspectives using their extra intelligence, energy and creativity in conjunction with committed administration leadership. Amherst is an open canvas so unity, undergraduate education and individual needs will take their place at the table for exploration. International perspectives show up in most if not all of the academic curriculum with faculty coming from around the globe.

The heavy academic demands for study on this campus channel the social life of the student body, composed primarily of high school valedictorians. Each has a faculty advisor, but there are no mandatory courses. Comfortable in the world of ideas, these bright and self-directed students form a determined and varied community of leaders. The Social Project Working Group is looking at starting Greek organizations in a trial period in Winter 2016. Amherst students can be super-studious and intense, even overly-invested in their studies. Reality is never far from their thoughts or this campus. Undergraduate students here arrived as freshmen with outstanding academic qualifications and individual accomplishments.

Compatibility with Personality Types and Preferences

With its orderly approach to offering a unique and wide ranging curriculum, Amherst appeals to personalities that are good with structure and accountability (J). At the same time, there is a wide, free range of choice within any particular major or course of studies. A personality that prefers to rationally analyze (T) will appreciate the foundation courses found in each discipline. They lay out the tools to tackle complex interdisciplinary subject matter in upper class courses. Students with a love of facts and details (S) will get plenty along with the sheer academic production that is required at this most selective liberal arts college.

Students on this campus learn by lively discussion and free exchange of ideas. They equally dialogue with each other and the faculty. They observe, read, discuss, observe some more, read some more and exhaustively review the foundations within a discipline. There seems to be a self-imposed requirement agreed upon by all who enter as freshmen, to astutely analyze the foundational facts. The point of that analysis is to drop into the depths, create new knowledge and synthesize an expertise in the subject.

The administration and faculty believe this process takes place primarily on campus. The libraries, coffee shops, dormitories, lecture halls and professors' offices are all fair game for learning locations. Basically at Amherst, learning occurs anywhere that is sufficiently free of distractions which could sidetrack the student. Undergraduates must master their own major as well as develop a significant knowledge base outside of their declared discipline. On the journey through this reasoned learning environment, students get sufficient, occasional reminders of the difficult world that awaits them on graduation. Their open, wide ranging academic experience at Amherst College mirrors cross cultural currents in unsettled, dynamic America.

Now read below about one of the majors that MBTI® research shows people of your type have selected since the mid-20th century. After, refer to Chapter Five for the 50 or so majors that can help you prepare for careers your type has select-

PERSONALITY MATCH			
ISTJ	ISFJ	INFJ	INTJ
ISTP	ISFP	INFP	INTP
ESTP	ESFP	ENFP	ENTP
ESTJ	ESFJ	ENFJ	ENTJ

*ed. Most importantly, remember that this college description is a suggestion for explora-
tion, not a commanding order. You can be successful in any major at any college.*

ISFJ likes an ordered, beautiful place. The new Science Complex will be in full
swing by 2018. Since it offers the unusual **Biophysics** track with efficient, light-filled
research labs, ISFJ must look seriously into this major. This track will take advantage
of their excellent ability to remember facts. Amherst faculty will smooth the connections between biology and physics because there are few walls on this campus. You
go for it ISFJ. This is a science major that you can learn to love.

ENTP will be attracted to the **Law, Jurisprudence and Social Thought** major.
They like to jump into difficult wide ranging discussions that sometimes start on
campus. In the course titled Law, Speech, and the Politics of Freedom, class members try to find agreement in the words "free," "speech" and "speaker." With those in
place they move on to identify dangerous, anarchic, politically correct speech in the
public square. It is all to understand critical components of modern day civilization.

INTJ who is down with math will probably make room in the schedule for
Philosophy of Mathematics. This course explores the three philosophies of math
that came about in the 20th century—logicism, intuitionism and finitism. INTJs
are great at mulling over the possibilities by themselves, in their mind, as they walk
to dinner. Maybe during dessert they will come up with experimental algorithms for
pushing math philosophy forward into the 21st century. Now INTJ will need to apply this to other disciplines.

ENFJ finds that no matter what major they select, their idealism will be honored
in the **Five College African Studies** Certificate Program. It goes together with any
major selected at Amherst. Diplomatic and ideal, ENFJs could happily work for organizations that coordinate services within African communities. At Amherst, ENFJ
might study the construct of mercy in Judeo/Christianity and Islam. Pope Francis
praised the national Ugandan government in Fall 2015 for taking in many refugees.[4]

INTP can become absorbed in the **Physics** major. Their courses go into the past
and recreate landmark experiments by masters such as Faraday. It is unique and allows students to discover the results and put those together with the current theories
in physics. New technology in laser application and photonics at the new Science
Center is on the list of things to do for this curious, flexible, deep-thinking type.

INFJ with an eye for design might like the **Architectural Studies** program that
is at the Five College Consortium. The design of our workplace buildings, neighborhoods and homes gets plenty of attention because of sustainability. INFJ will like
concentrating on the people who will work or live in their designs. They will have
little trouble defending and pushing for their architectural concepts. As spaces become smaller, we can use their creative vision.

ISTP might like the major in **Statistics** at Amherst. It will not have the social conundrums that they let others think about. Instead, ISTP gets to attend classes with
all the mechanical tools they might use for analyzing statistical distributions. The
department faculty thinks it is a good idea to take Probability/Theoretical Statistics
in the junior year. ISTP is okay with this if they can attach a metal part and move
that probability around.

ESTJ will be on time to make the required early declaration in the **Neuroscience** major at Amherst College. This type is good with preplanning. The elbow grease and interdisciplinary courses in this major work perfectly for graduate study in medicine, law and the sciences. ESTJs can see the sense in the well-structured, basic and some-what novel work required in this major. They could look objectively at the emerging neuroscience techniques used in counseling. They might not understand Attention Deficit Disorder, but neuroscience techniques in counseling are pushing ahead with real success for this brain hiccup.

ISTJ could find that the **Psychology** major at Amherst is going to work. They really like to get A's in their courses. They will find research in psychology pretty solid because of its scientific nature which fits into the scientific method so readily. It is not surprising that beginning, middle and end is explored at Amherst in foundational course work. After that, it's on to the study of memory, the psychology of leadership and more interesting human behaviors. New research across the nation's laboratories in biology and psychology finds its way to campus with the department's expanded facilities. This subject really requires a PhD to move into a career as a practitioner. ISTJ will have an excellent preparation to move forward with this degree from Amherst.

ENTJ will like the wide open curriculum in the **Economics** department at Amherst. From game theory to the economics of poverty to the nuts and bolts of micro and macroeconomics, the faculty and courses present a sweeping look at this complicated subject. ENTJs don't often back away from complexity or large concepts. In fact, they might do well with making sense of money and how it is used. Politics, people and policy are likely to fascinate young, bright ENTJs.

BATES COLLEGE

23 Campus Avenue
Lewiston, ME 04240-6098
Website: www.bates.edu
Admissions Telephone: 207-786-6000
Undergraduates: 1,773; 879 Men, 894 Women

Physical Environment

Bates College is located in the Lewiston area, about 35 miles north of Portland, Maine. Like many towns in New England, it grew on the river banks during the Industrial Revolution. Although most students stay on campus during the weekend, there are restaurants, malls and outlets within a short distance to buy brand name winter clothing and gear. Outdoor recreation is big and students like regional alpine and cross-country skiing. They also like hands-on experience and travel to the coastal **Maine environments** for chemistry and geology research, learning first hand with nature. The 109-acre Bates campus is in the middle of a residential neighborhood. The campus circles around a small pond called "**the puddle**." Warm-natured undergrads watch the **wintertime skating and impromptu hockey** on the puddle from inside the glass fronted academic buildings.

The architecture is a mixture of modern and historic buildings. The Dining Commons hall, a plain modern building, has three story windows with views of Alumni Walk winding past the trees. Plans are still on for historic Chase Hall, which used to be a comfy student center years ago, to take center stage again. Two new dormitories moved to completion in Fall 2016. Bates does a great job using their small campus with the outdoors in sight and mind. The Hedge-Williams Project changed up old historic dormitories into academic offices. The newest dorms have a Cluster Concept. This is pretty cool since you have suite-style and regular dormitory rooms all circled around the common room.

Creative students are drawn to the Olin Arts Center which has an art museum, theater, music and art studios. The sofas and lounge in the halls add a comfy feel to the stark, minimalist interior. The imaginative Bates students likely go for some spaces that aren't energy draining and that feature abstract art.

Social Environment

Bates students are somewhat **different from one another**. They arrive on campus like angular lines with a serious curiosity. They are seekers. They love the idea of leaving high school behind. They become socially and intellectually driven students. They probably were into Goth or Anime in high school. On the edge of being ironic, students here are okay wondering about the day-to-day stuff on social media. Undergrads might use **backwards humor** when they tap out a twitter opinion. Collegiate comedians, who are now turning down elite campus gigs, might consider Bates where the humor of laughing at yourself is okay, as long as you are learning and pondering. The English majors on this campus might take a course offered in Shakespeare. The Bard's deepest messages were in his tragicomedies, like *The Tempest*. In Winter 2015, the Student Government Association voted no confidence in the Bates administration and president because of lack of transparency.[5] The President's response leaned toward the nature of leadership and the holistic responsibility of decision making that affects the long term future of the campus.[6] Students responded their no confidence vote was not binding anyway. Look for irony and humor at Bates in the student newspapers and tweets.

The liberal arts curriculum mostly offers progressive thinking with less exposure to conservative cultural thought. Bates undergrads look for exciting, abstract courses that build and flesh out their beliefs and time on campus. Students like using their **fine-tuned writing** and computing skills. There is a certain sense of quiet and laid-back, comfortable in their skins. The multifaith chaplaincy on campus is a collection of organizations that identify with several of the world religions. Yet students here will probably **examine their purpose in life** through the broad academic courses. The majority of undergraduates are service-oriented and volunteer in local, state, regional and/or national venues. Bates undergrads voice their individuality from the get go with most of them opting not to submit SAT scores which are not mandatory at this campus.

Compatibility with Personality Types and Preference

Bates undergraduates are searching and bold. They don't use their Facebook or Twitter accounts to find the answers. But they will take positions on issues and interrupt their studies for the day. They are okay in their edginess (P). They will pick and choose from the traditional coursework for majors in math and the sciences. Other undergrads who search for career choices connected directly to helping people will find lots of courses that move in that direction. The faculty and administration support many service learning options (F). The campus environment seems devoted to the future (N). Bates undergraduates find time to build community, through fun and their own unique styles. They balance this with the academic work needed for careers and occupations at graduation. They hang on to the humor they brought to campus as freshmen. The administration and faculty are supportive of this successful mix. The whole Bates community centers the liberal arts education on learning and preparation for the future.

Now read below about one of the majors that MBTI® research shows people of your type have selected since the mid-20th century. After, refer to Chapter Five for the 50 or so majors that can help you prepare for careers your type has selected. Most importantly, remember that this college description is a suggestion for exploration, not a commanding order. You can be successful in any major at any college.

ISFP and the major in **Biology** move together nicely on this campus. This type likes to mix it up outside with activity and variety. There are many hands-on field studies in the

PERSONALITY MATCH			
ISTJ	ISFJ	INFJ	INTJ
ISTP	ISFP	INFP	INTP
ESTP	ESFP	ENFP	ENTP
ESTJ	ESFJ	ENFJ	ENTJ

open space and forests of Maine. The quiet and accepting ISFP will fit well into the unconventional ways. At the same time, this type has a real need to develop their deeply held values. The department just brought on line a confocal microscope that will let undergrads look at 3D images of neutrons. Pretty advanced for sure.

INFP might like the **African American Studies** at Bates College. The courses by subject are broad and include exploration across several traditional disciplines like English, science and math. INFP, ordinarily a deep thinker, will really notice the wide range of this major at Bates. On graduation, INFP would be a fresh viewpoint in the national conversations on CNN or Fox News about race relations or in the opinion editorials in the print media.

ENFJ is imaginative and goes for a challenge. The major in **French Francophone Studies** could work. So what does Francophone mean? At Bates it seems to mean studying north African countries where there is a history of French influence. It is darned interesting and that works for ENFJs, especially since it also includes other places like Quebec, Canada and the Caribbean. The degree mostly focuses on litera-ture of all the Francophones in these locations.

ESFJ is really ready for careers that help children and most children now are in the American public schools. The minor in **Teacher Education** is a great option for ESFJ who might like to teach in the sciences or math. These two subjects have the practical ways that they understand and value. ESFJ is always curious about others and genuine in helping them move forward in areas that are realistic.

ENFP likes to change things up. This will carry over to their career choices. Countries in the Pacific Basin, like China, Japan and Malaysia, make the news now pretty often. So a major in **Asian Studies** gives this type the background they would need to go into Asian finance, Asian retail products, Asian trade, etc. ENFPs are perceptive and versatile. With this major, they can look to China in 2025 using eco-nomic theories studied here at Bates.

ISFJ will notice the international courses available in the Bates **Religious Studies** major. Emphasis is placed on the culture and actual location of the faiths. Courses of ancient beliefs also fill the catalog like Medieval Religious Practices, Greek Roman Myths and Ancient Gods. Reflective and calm, ISFPs will sign up for this sampling. Then they might quietly collect their own spiritual and religious thought into a per-sonal, cohesive belief.

INFJ with an interest in art could look at the **Art and Visual Culture** major. The studies are likely to be dripping with symbolism here. There is a solid inclusion of European arts, thinly represented at some liberal arts colleges, but not at Bates. With this major, the INFJ might move into the world of visual design. This type's independence and creativity will be a strong asset for developing public and private events at galleries, museums, corporations and civic associations. On graduation, INFJ could spend a few years in the rural towns of Maine, struggling to hold on to their lifestyles and history. This artistic type could really capture Americana, Maine style.

INTJ will find academic roaming room in the **Psychology** major here. The re-quirements for the major are complicated with one class required in each of four areas, but other classes distributed over other different areas. INTJ is just the type to figure it out and also the one to connect neuroscience with psychology in their post-graduate degree. Whatever direction they move toward, it will be about the future.

INTP who selected high school math courses with a purpose should look into **Mathematics** at Bates College. The faculty presents this subject with excitement, interest and honest enthusiasm. Though this type doesn't need the extra motivation, the nature of unsolved solutions in math equations will keep INTPs busy searching for patterns. The course in Dynamical Systems and Computer Science is tailor-made for INTP.

ENTP has a pretty deep well of energy for their projects. With talent for numbers, this type will like studying **Economics** at Bates College. ENTP could sign up for the challenge in Big Data and Economics. Finding ways out of financial crises could become a career for this clever type. The larger the problems the grander the solution they will design. It sounds impractical but with this thinker on the job, it usually works.

BELOIT COLLEGE

Office of Admission
700 College Street
Beloit, WI 53511
Website: www.beloit.edu
Admissions Telephone: 608-363-2500
Undergraduates: 1,303; 546 Men, 757 Women

Physical Environment

"You don't voluntarily move to Wisconsin," says a Beloit student who comes from California, however, this is where she felt **compelled to come**. The college is on the Wisconsin-Illinois border and is easy to reach from the Chicago, Milwaukee and Madison airports. The city of Beloit is rather quiet, recalling its earlier paper and pulp industry which is now transitioning to artistic and niche small businesses. The campus is in a residential neighborhood near the town center. Beloit College was designed by a group of prominent folks from New England in the mid 19th century, so it has a northeastern look to its architecture. Close to Chicago and Madison, the college encourages internships and international studies overseas.

Some students live in **special interest houses** around the edge of the campus, mostly in old Victorian and Colonial homes. Usually about 10 students or less in each house, they become small friend groups connected by common interests. There are a few Greek houses as well, and they focus on community service initiatives. Most first-year students live in freshman housing. The state of the art science complex was designed around learning laboratories and promotes collaborative work. It is conveniently next to the living, fitness and academic areas on campus.

The **Beloit art and anthropology museums** offer students a real life experience as curators as well as exhibiting artists. The Hendricks Center for the Arts is a delight for musicians, dancers and artistic technophiles complete with a lighting design studio. These museums are open to the community. Very few small liberal arts colleges maintain regional museums. Here there is that extra intellectual layer and **artistic influence** for both college and city.

Social Environment

High school students who moved outside of the popular high school groups like Beloit College. Here it's perfectly all right to have your own sort of interests and to talk about them as you see fit. Undergraduates like subjects to study with a twist or a new direction. They mostly embrace a **very crunchy and artsy lifestyle**. Politically they lean to the left of center. The administration also budgets good support for human rights programs with exclusive progressive cultural perspective, such as the Weissberg Program. Beloit courses emphasize international perspectives and they are often directed at seeking knowledge outside of the national experience. Students accept that everyone is honored for their different talents here. A good number choose the vegetarian way.

Some within the community seek harmony and are less likely to strike out in nontraditional directions. They focus on their academic studies. Incoming students might declare a passion for molecular biology and research but quickly change over to political science. The reality is that many students here are change-oriented and proud of it. There is a strong desire to live and practice what they learn so they are attracted to advocacy clubs. They support activities like sustainable gardening or establish special interest housing such as the Interfaith House. Students at their core are **sensitive, caring and searching** for humanistic ways of building community. The smallness of this campus helps them try out and practice those concepts. Even though there are many different thinkers on campus, cohesion is a familiar concept. Conservative cultural views of American Judeo-Christian philosophy can find a place in the dialogue here.

The college supports the students' academic journey by reintroducing familiar ideas with fresh levels of interpretation. The interesting student personalities on campus also add their own spice to the educational studies. Graduates look to the world of employment and expect to be productive in their careers, well-equipped to support the arts and service organizations within their communities.

Compatibility with Personality Types and Preferences

Beloit College is dedicated to reasoned learning. While the faculty and administration remain open to many perspectives (P), students are expected to arrive at their own cohesive view of the world. There is plenty of encouragement to examine national and world perspectives. Students define their beliefs through their academic work and service to the community both on and off campus. Extracurricular events at Beloit College are offered usually with a service orientation (F). Some undergrads become socially active and follow their ideas through into clubs and events for that purpose. There is a hands-on, let-me-see-it approach to the course work. Students move through their educational studies by process, observing, collecting and arranging information into personal, meaningful understanding. The campus academic energy channels this type of analysis in a way that is intense, outspoken and caring. Conversations can be free-wheeling and oriented from many directions, but students are definitely reaching for a position throughout their academic studies that will lead to jobs within the helping professions. At Beloit, there is an undercurrent to an individual's purpose on campus, so that next semester's courses are carefully selected for graduation goals. Undergraduates tend toward the unknown, less understood subjects because they offer a new filter to observe through. The successful student at Beloit College is one who relates to the tension to add in an unexpected elective to their schedule. There is also a commitment to learning with and helping fellow students on their quest. Graduates have a sensitive, reasoned and reflective approach to life's work.

Now read below about one of the majors that MBTI® research shows people of your type have

PERSONALITY MATCH			
ISTJ	ISFJ	INFJ	INTJ
ISTP	ISFP	INFP	INTP
ESTP	ESFP	ENFP	ENTP
ESTJ	ESFJ	ENFJ	ENTJ

selected since the mid-20th century. After, refer to Chapter Five for the 50 or so majors that can help you prepare for careers your type has selected. Most importantly, remember that this college description is a suggestion for exploration, not a commanding order. You can be successful in any major at any college.

INFP should find the study of **Geology** works for their creative instinct. This subject is wide open for specialization and the department faculty nicely surveys all the foundational land forms within the four-year curriculum. This type is usually interested in concepts of human development as well. The Beloit campus is ideal for connecting this solid, observable science with human perspectives.

INFJ often brings compassion and idealism to studies. The major in **International Political Economy** suits them well. The curriculum requires a heavy math sequence. Undergraduates must reach their own perspective of world economies. They do this partly with mathematical analysis applied to international business, profit, non-profit and nongovernmental organizations. The department tends toward a holistic approach to international economies. INFJ is fine with this. They can be creative, caring and proud of their work. All three are pretty important for this type.

ISTJ will find the **Molecular, Cellular and Integrative Biology** major forms around testing hypotheses. It is an orderly, structured discovery. This is an ideal way for ISTJs to learn. This type goes for reasoned learning and Beloit is a fine collegiate environment for their learning style. Though they are usually not out-of-the-ballpark thinkers, ISTJ will benefit from the dialogue at Beloit. This major will give them a traditional preparation for graduate school in the health sciences.

ISFJ wants to express their beliefs in a low key way. This type is a real master of the facts with a fabulous memory for details. The major in **Science for Elementary Teaching** at Beloit College is a great choice for this type. Their course work in the biology department approaches learning by analysis of what can be observed. ISFJ's comfort with fine detail will be such an asset in this precise field. They search for personal meaning with quiet reflection and will be rewarded on this campus of searchers for life's truths.

ISFP will find the art department at Beloit College popping with expansive thinking. The **Studio Art** major is very connected to process learning. The process of communicating by art is a focus. Written and oral expression is part of the technical course work in drawing and design. Peer feedback is a regular part of this curriculum since it helps refine the artists' message. Well, that is fitting for ISFP who wants to be a loyal and cooperative member of the community. At Beloit, individual perspectives are encouraged, and feedback will be measured and supportive.

ENFP can keep the options open with the unusual major **Environmental Communication and Arts**. The requirements roam across courses in museum studies, history, English, journalism, dance and writing. Here is an example of the "twist" that Beloit faculty present with familiar subjects. ENFP can travel comfortably into the world of journalism with this foundation, especially since national and world media look regularly at sustainability practices.

ENTP could be attracted to the major in **Business Economics** at Beloit College. Typically, the core course work required of business majors would not excite ENTP. However, the department combines the fundamentals found in business with economic theory. The major adds in a survey of international courses and written communications for business analysis. ENTP's imagination will be fired up over the student managed Belmark Associates that consults with small businesses on market research.

ESFJ will really like **Chemistry** at Beloit. The department brings the abstract nature of this field into the labs for eyes/hands on observation. Much work is based on inquiry and experimentation using sophisticated instruments found in newer research labs. By replicating research designs, students at Beloit follow the chemical pathways through the reactions and behavior of materials at the microscopic level. It is a great companion and contrast to more experimental laboratory foundations. ESFJ will appreciate this practical, reality-based study in the somewhat unseen world of chemistry.

ENFJ has the supportive nature to work with today's teenagers in middle schools. The department devotes curricula and coursework heavily toward the **Adolescents and Schools** track. ENFJs will get the classroom experience needed in this field as well as theoretical practices that will impact motivation, theory and middle school pedagogy. Their warmth and enthusiasm will be an anchor in the topsy turvy school day of the average middle schooler.

ENTJ could really appreciate Beloit's basic foundation courses part of the interdisciplinary **Psychology** major. This field is growing by leaps and bounds as it studies human behavior in connection with sciences like biology and chemistry. Not likely to be spontaneous, ENTJ will calculate and leap across information along the way. The course Introduction to Cognitive Science would be a good choice since neuroscience in counseling is a hot research topic at grad school. It also takes advantage of ENTJ's natural ability to reason through patterns, ask meaningful questions and arrive at certain positions.

BOSTON COLLEGE

140 Commonwealth Avenue
Chestnut Hill, MA 02467
Website: www.bc.edu
Admissions Telephone: 617-552-3100
Undergraduates: 9,153; 4,189 Men, 4,964 Women
Graduate Students: 4,421+

Physical Environment

All it takes is just a walk through the campus of Boston College for most high school juniors and seniors to fall in love with this university. Mature trees line the way to the tower of newly remodeled Gasson Hall, the first classroom building on campus in 1913. "Recitation" is still in many course descriptions so undergrads here often practice up on the art of memorizing and public speaking. The collegiate Gothic architecture is prominent in buildings like the Burns Library that house rare manuscripts and antique books. The campus physically has a **spiritual feel** and the Jesuit priests, many of whom teach classes, offer Eucharist Mass services and interact with students.

The football stadium holds over 44,500 fans and is a popular place for these **sporty students** and alumni who go all out for their teams. Nationally, the football team is usually in a bowl playoff as a member of the Atlantic Coast Conference. The Flynn recreation center is the place to forget nearby crowded Boston, **keep fit** and get into intramural sports. A new residence construction project, 2150 Commonwealth, broke ground in winter 2016. It will add another 400 student beds. The Boston College campus is surrounded by a mature neighborhood of upscale homes and estates. There is public transportation just outside the entrance to upper campus. It's the last stop and turn-around for the T, a trolley that runs down the middle of **Commonwealth Avenue**. It is usually packed with students from other nearby universities on their way to the Boston Common, coffee shops or rental apartments in this popular college town.

In the past twenty or so years, Boston College has experienced significant enrollment growth in both its undergraduate and graduate programs. There are four distinct campus centers at BC, Newton, Brighton and Lower Campuses all with undergraduate housing. Middle Campus is strictly academic. The college provides regular bus service to get back and forth including a Grocery Shuttle. Getting around Boston demands foot, bus, subway and cars. Students will use all of these and often.

Social Environment

Students at Boston College were very high achievers in high school. They carry their ambitions into college and add an intense and lively feel to the classroom and social life. Achievement and professional goals are in the air that undergraduates breath. It's hard to get that admitted letter in May and students will be glad for their over-the-top qualifications when they tackle the academic work. Most are from a **Catholic** background and are comfortable here, and all will take courses in theology as part of the core classes. There are many students whose parents graduated from Boston College and not unmindful that one day their children might come to BC.

Students come to this college to **study and play hard**. Irish and Italian ethnic perspectives run strongly throughout the student body. Social life is active and plentiful. Students draw a direct line between their grades, a good job and a rewarding career. They **intend to be successful** at graduation. They take full advantage of the **hands-on career advising** by faculty.

The Jesuit faculty on campus sets the tone for tolerance with underlying moral foundation. Ethical conversation fits in easily and often here in the classroom. Some student activities are designed as ethical retreats. **Service to the community** is very important and no one graduates without volunteering many hours of work benefiting others. It may be why BC graduates remain a close-knit group of people who support one another up to and after graduation.

Compatibility with Personality Types and Preferences

Boston College has four undergraduate divisions—Arts and Sciences, Management, Education and Nursing. They separate the academic disciplines (T) in a traditional manner. Students have to declare admission to one of these four divisions on their application. This works for high school students who know what academic concentration they want (S). But, this is not the same as declaring a major and 'undecided' is okay to enter on the application for admission.

Although it might seem that the administration is pushing early career decisions on incoming freshmen, the opposite is true. Boston College offers a really great advising program. It leads undergrads to explore the career fields first and then discover which majors or combination of minors and electives will work. The faculty advisors meet with undergrads all four years. Advising for first year students is about professors relating their own experiences and knowledge. Frequent off campus retreats and programs help students connect academic majors and minors with potential careers.

The city of Boston plays big in the academic advising and career exploration. Undergraduates find the city noise and energy fills their college experience. Trips on the T's green line to downtown and the excitement of city life has to fit around the demanding academic coursework here. The successful Boston College student balances the city, the studies, spirituality and moral ethics. Students come with this in mind.

Now read below about one of the majors that MBTI® research shows people of your type have selected since the mid-20th century. After, refer to Chapter Five for the 50 or so majors that can help you prepare for careers your type has selected. Most importantly, remember that this college description is a suggestion for exploration, not a commanding order. You can be successful in any major at any college.

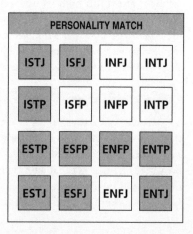

PERSONALITY MATCH

ISTJ	ISFJ	INFJ	INTJ
ISTP	ISFP	INFP	INTP
ESTP	ESFP	ENFP	ENTP
ESTJ	ESFJ	ENFJ	ENTJ

ESTJ could go with the **Accounting** concentration at BC. They are okay with accountability and responsibility so this field is a natural fit. They like to be ready for all things and the precise nature of accounting practices in public and private settings works well. The advising here and the curriculum really keep the list of unknowns pretty thin. On graduation, ESTJ will be comfortable with options for the next step. On the social scene, ESTJ can say "no" to enticing Boston events when studies are not finished.

ISTJ after college graduation will put on a suit and confidently present accurate, organized and timely work to the boss. The concentration in **Finance** offers the very business environment that ISTJ understands—the large organizational system. The Carroll School of Management expects graduates to understand risk, basic financials like stocks, bonds, derivatives, capital structure, mergers and the list goes on. Strong ethics discussions will pop up with required government regulations too. Relying on their sense of loyalty and fabulous memories, they are more than competent graduates.

ENTJ will make good use of the concentration in **Corporate Reporting and Analysis**. This type is naturally intuitive and reading quarterly report statistics will spark a few hunches. The business down turn in 2015, Twitter stock and other social media is fascinating. It gives ENTJ a starter for speculation and prediction. This major will prepare savvy ENTJs to read the monetary patterns in financial corporations. Socially, this type will want to be where the action is so catch them in the downtown Boston financial district during the day.

ENFP could find the **Communication** major at BC pretty attractive. The curriculum is solid and combines theory with practical course work. ENFPs are abstract thinkers that need variety but also a touchstone to stay grounded. The department subscribes to a lot of international newspapers and video news reports. It will keep this type far from routine which they find tedious. After classes, ENFP will be energized by places to go in the city, but will often stay on campus, too, supporting their friends' clubs.

ISFJ will warm up to the degree in **Nursing** at BC with so many top notch hospitals within subway distance. Internships at research universities might also include one-on-one contact with patients. The degree is strong in diagnostics, therapy and ethical issues. The ISFJ with deeply held personal values will really like the moral perspectives at this Catholic college. Off campus career advising retreats are perfect for this conscientious type. When time permits, they will step out into Boston life, but only after all other responsibilities are met.

ESFJ will probably look at the major in **Secondary Education**. Boston's ethnic landscape is very influenced by descendants of Ellis Island immigrants arriving from Europe in the late 1800s and the Atlantic Caribbean islands. The teaching practicum is great for these cultural viewpoints in Boston suburbs. Classroom management is so important for the teachers now since American classrooms educate many different ethnic groups. Finding cohesion is a dilemma and Boston College opens the discussion. A double major is required. ESFJ might declare science or math since our schools are short of qualified teachers in the subjects. Always a loyal team member, they will support BC through volunteer community service or cheering at the football games.

ENTP will like the flexible nature of the **General Management** program at BC. ENTPs can select two areas from accounting, information systems, finance, marketing, organization studies or operations technology management. Field research in the city's financial district is great. Their vision can be pretty clear when it is resting on accurate information. Their exciting, risk-taking nature also works well in the world of business.

ESFP will call up their outgoing, enthusiastic style for the **Marketing** concentration at BC. Students practice and study communication theory. Their talkative nature will be a natural asset. ESFPs have a cheerleader deep within, so connecting consumers with business services is a good bet. Totally thorough, Boston College is going to cover research, pricing, managerial accounting and retail buying decisions.

ISTP could go for employment or research with the **Geological Sciences** major at BC. Either way, ISTPs get to head straight for the labs and hands-on projects. This type will volunteer for that extra field study with all the instruments, set them up and live in a tent next to the gadgets until the data is recorded accurately. As far as Boston social life, they are likely to head into town with a few close friends and show up for the BC athletic games. Otherwise, catch them jury-rigging more gadgets in the dorm room.

ESTP and **Operations Management** is a good fit. Competition and fast-paced markets are good stuff for this type. They understand the goal and the fast pace. They are excellent at networking, troubleshooting and pulling together a deal among competing team members. The actual reading and lectures might bore some ESTPs, yet there are good chances to get out into Boston's business district for outstanding job training. While they are putting in a full day as an intern, they will listen up to join the office staff for after hour socializing. The line between learning, working and socializing is pretty thin for this lively type!

BOSTON UNIVERSITY

121 Bay State Road
Boston, MA 02215
Website: www.bu.edu
Admissions Telephone: 617-353-2300
Undergraduates: 18,017; 7,163 Men, 10,854 Women
Graduate Students: 14,095

Physical Environment

Boston University stretches along Storrow Drive mostly sandwiched between the banks of the Charles River and the Mass Pike on the south side. Commonwealth Avenue crosses the campus from Kenmore Square on the east side to Babcock Street on the west side by the university track and tennis center. This is a **very urban campus** and students who love it, **love Boston**. University shuttle buses are large, on time, cool in the summer and a better choice over walking in cold winter winds. The university is boxed in by the city neighborhoods and expressways. But the architects do an outstanding job designing new useful buildings, like the three-acre athletic field that will sit on top of the parking deck. Spaces like the Sergeant Activities Center cut off the city grime and congestion with six stories skyward. A new **integrated life sciences** and engineering research complex broke ground in 2015 and will be finished by spring 2017.

Undergraduates **learn to navigate Boston quickly**. Nearby Fenway Park, home of the Red Sox, Newbury Street and Kenmore Square call out to high school graduates who want to dress with flair and increase their city smarts. When it's sunny and warm, they go to the "beach," an area by the law school at the edge of the Fenway. With serious imagination, waves of heavy traffic substitute for ocean waves. At BU students live in different kinds of residence halls. First years usually live in the Towers which are classic cinder block dormitories. Then there are four city blocks of impressive brownstones which were renovated in summer 2015. Upper class students have first dibs on these. The student village is next to the sports complex and the ice-hockey arena. It's an 18-story high rise where about 2,500 students live in apartments. Some upper class students decide to live off campus in Brookline or other nearby areas.

Social Environment

BU students work hard and play hard. They **balance study with socializing** just about every day. All were in the top 10 percent of their high school class. They don't mind working with other undergrads on semester-long projects as long the plan is clear and the goals are doable. Students here are **self-directed** and manage their lives and activities in this busy, urban, mega city. They must develop city smarts quickly since Boston mirrors many large American cities with comparable crime statistics. Students must study the course descriptions ahead of time and select those that clearly interest them. Those who take several semesters to declare a major risk lengthening the time to graduate. Once their major is declared, they start to gain a greater sense of community at this **large** university. Students in the School of Arts and Sciences get into undergraduate research through directed study courses. They must turn in a proposal to the faculty whose research interests them and get approval. Students at BU are go getters.

At night students might go into the city with their friends leaving the dorm, yet the following night, they may join another group for yet a different adventure. They may not know everyone in the group by name but there is still a sense of camaraderie. The BU experience is a **smorgasbord of social activity**: living in a certain tower, exercising in the new sports center, cheering for the Terriers, watching a Red Sox game. All of these are part of this dynamic college.

Compatibility with Personality Types and Preferences

Boston University is for the high energy student who is pumped up by the city's fast pace. However, success takes a lot more than four years in this savvy city. BU students usually have the persistence and sharpness needed to juggle the consistent academic demands and extracurricular activities (P). At Boston University, the administration directs undergrads toward self responsibility with sometimes Byzantine administrative and academic policies. And it works. There may be a lot of instruction for major requirements but they are comprehensive and students leave here with superb current knowledge in their fields. They are realistic intellectuals. They recognize what is possible, and they are not inclined to charge into activist agendas. The true and valuable bonus of BU's academic philosophy is course content without prevalent political correctness. As a result, undergrads learn to work within public and private organizations that they will experience after graduation. Cohesion is understood as a value on this campus. They complete the requirements for graduation (S) in the required core courses and categories of divisional studies, concentrations and minors in the nine colleges.

College advising starts with students who must keep their Student Link page updated (S). Undergrads have appointments to the advising center for guidance throughout the undergraduate years. The faculty expect students to be confident and clear about their intentions. The student body grows this attitude within itself. Urban challenges add reality lessons and keep the undergrads here appropriately aware each day they leave the dorm room and head over to an administrative office about their degree or just out on to the sidewalks. Over half of the students identify as a minority with a fair number having lived overseas. For those who move through the academic system efficiently, there is the additional reward of acquiring sophisticated urban knowledge. Looking around the campus during any season of the year, you will find exactly these types of students. They are strong students, willing to take a risk, who know what they want in respect to fun and work. They are a bit like BU's Lee Claflin who provided most of the funds in the late 1800's for Claflin University. That legacy lives on in historically black Claflin University, Orangeburg, SC, on *U.S. News'* Best Colleges list for twelve consecutive years.

Now read below about one of the majors that MBTI® research shows people of your type have selected since the mid-20th century. After, refer to Chapter Five for the 50 or so majors that can help you prepare for careers your type has selected. Most importantly, remem-

ber that this college description is a suggestion for exploration, not a commanding order. You can be successful in any major at any college.

ISTJ makes a good choice with the **Environmental Analysis and Policy** concentration because it is a growing field, and loaded with details and government mandates. To help out with this, BU really buffs up their graduates' ability with lots of quantitative tools like computer modeling. This works well for ISTJs who will definitely drive policy decisions in the future. This type is comfortable with facts that go straight into their memory banks. They are sensible and realistic always relying on details with logic. Fortunately, this will work well at Boston University which is rule and policy-oriented.

PERSONALITY MATCH			
ISTJ	ISFJ	INFJ	INTJ
ISTP	ISFP	INFP	INTP
ESTP	ESFP	ENFP	ENTP
ESTJ	ESFJ	ENFJ	ENTJ

ISTP will make positive use of the major or minor in **Human Physiology** which is only offered at large universities. This degree will help ISTPs apply to graduate school especially since it has a good deal of anatomy and physiology in the requirements. Also BU offers an **Engineering Science** minor focused in the field of biomedical engineering. These two concentrations point to technical expertise and independent analysis of health data as a medical diagnostician. This type is comfortable with on-the-spot decisions of a technical nature especially if it involves machines.

ESTP who study **Advertising** at BU could be dynamite in a business setting. Adaptable and quick, they are perfect for this field. The required course in Fundamentals of Creative Development and the portfolio experience are part of the workshop that is similar to advertising agencies in the real world. But ESTP must be careful to balance their academic studies with the excitement of Boston's sidewalks.

ESTJ likes the facts and the tradition associated with teaching science. The **Science Education** program here prepares undergrads for jobs at all levels, elementary, middle, secondary schools and college too. This fits right into ESTJ views of the world. What high school principal wouldn't be happy with ESTJ always following standard operating procedures in the chemistry lab?

ISFP who works in the field of **Archeology** gets to play outside in the dirt and stick with the facts. In archeology they are called artifacts and they look like little bits of ceramic dishes. Leaving the abstraction and theory to others, this type will enjoy piecing together real finds, or getting most of the bones of a long extinct dinosaur. BU's department subscribes to international centers and research periodicals in archeology. So observant ISFP will search for other articles about similar dinosaurs or pottery. BU's minor in Archeology, not often available outside of large universities, is a hidden gem.

ESFP is a good bet for a career in physical therapy. BU has a strong undergraduate degree in **Health Science** for admission to competitive physical therapy graduate programs. This type loves to help others, especially if it involves repeating familiar, complex therapy moves. The degree also explores entry into emerging health specialty careers other than physical therapy. As medical treatment advances through technology, new careers are opening.

ENFP likes to be creative and the concentration in **Nutritional Science** at BU has a wide selection of courses. Nutrition in the 21st century is emerging as one of the factors in affecting specific diseases. In 2014, coconut sugar was identified to help with Alzheimer's treatment. Boston has many medical resources from Tufts New England Medical Center to Brigham and Women's Children's Hospital. Creative, fun loving ENFP will shoot for more than one internship and build a social network for post graduation.

ENTJ is going to reach for the stars with the **Mathematics Specialty in Statistics** program. They can blast through the stratosphere, so to speak, by combining this precise major with a minor in business administration and management. ENTJs have an entrepreneurial side to their personality that nicely mixes with professional positions. Boston will be more than happy to surround ENTJ with the high finance environments that demand the mathematical analysis that is the heart of this major.

BOWDOIN COLLEGE

5700 College Station
Brunswick, ME 04011-8448
Website: www.bowdoin.edu
Admissions Telephone: 207-725-3100
Undergraduates: 1,805; 902 Men, 903 Women

Physical Environment

Bowdoin College is located in Brunswick at the head of **coastline estuaries** leading out the Atlantic Ocean and about 26 miles from Portland, Maine. It is a quaint town of 20,000, with cobblestone streets and friendly restaurants and a 30-minute drive to Portland. The college's Coastal Studies Center on Orr Island is perfect for geology and marine research. Nearby Freeport, with its designer outlets, attracts students who want function with fashion in outdoor clothing that keeps you warm on near zero days. Bowdoin's 225-acre campus includes **forested areas** with walking trails where **athletic** students run or cross-country ski.

The landscape also invites wonder and spirituality. **The College Offer**, a 1906 purpose statement, calls attention to cooperation, nature, art, friends and the libraries of the world for knowledge. As the main campus is built around the 1855 Congregational Church, it follows that Bowdoin would move forward in 2013 and hire its first director of Religious and Spiritual Life. The museums of art and the modern theatre are usually in the weekly student activities schedule. Almost everyone on this campus loves the **visual and performing arts** even if they are not talented themselves. Student performances and talent shows thread in **literary and social meaning**.

Undergraduates live in green residential halls, built with recycled materials, using natural sources of light and heated by geothermal means. On top of that, dormitories save rain water to flush toilets. It all helps to call attention to reality and goals that the students support.

Social Environment

Eighty-five percent of students are out of state and bring a strong high school resume from public and independent schools. About one-third identify as a minority. They already are pretty good writers and speakers. Some of them will write for the **Bowdoin Orient**, the student newspaper that prints realistic articles on the campus happenings. The common denominator here is that students are willing to participate in and support **the Common Good**. The McKeen Center houses the Common Good program and coordinates student volunteer service and community learning. The ideas of cooperation and cohesion riveted the campus news in 2015. The faculty and administration sponsored a "teach in" of their own by inviting all on campus to join in a discussion of racism.[7] Students on this campus are not likely to make up a list of demands delivered to the college president.

Bowdoin students are **bright**, enthusiastic, curious and high achieving. They are thirsty for knowledge, willing to work hard, supplemented by intellectual conversation over coffee. Most dialogue will mirror progressive cultural views prevalent in social and news media. The Bowdoin Student Government is pretty robust. Education is student centered; faculty do not impose or take center stage. Learning tends to be **non-competitive and collaborative**.

There is off campus housing. The college does not officially sponsor nearby neighborhood homes. But close knit friends who might want to relax without residential programming can go off campus as juniors or seniors. Though there are no fraternities or sororities, many students belong to outing clubs and are skilled at outdoor sports. Some really identify with the house they were assigned to by Bowdoin in the freshman year. They continue to socialize with that house group. Others like to socialize through the clubs that organize primarily around sports, performance and culture activity. Students enjoy each other's talents and gifts whether they are modest or exceptional.

Compatibility with Personality Types and Preferences

Bowdoin College brings to mind the words "laid back" and "intense" at the same time. The Bowdoin undergraduate breathes in very large, sweeping ideas about society even though there is no fascination with 24/7 news broadcasts on campus. Their national perspectives on what is right and wrong about America are not likely to be formed by social media that pushes content on the iPhone and tablet. Faculty question students by asking for definitions of what "is" in the subject. Student answers could be more complex questions. Bowdoin undergrads have to deal with uncertainty and discover several paths to learning (P). It is okay to delay and get lost in the process before a good answer appears, maybe even more than one right answer will surface. This open, intuitive, approach (N) is nicely applied in the study of earth sciences where the interpretation of land forms and plate tectonics of the Appalachian mountains pops up through interdisciplinary study in other fields.

Students get use to purpose, accomplishment and outcome (T). They accept the role of change agent if they can do this with others and teamwork. The faculty and administration is active when it comes to reacting to chaotic societal changes in our society over the past few years. So look for student, professor and administration partnering on this campus to recognize the impact. Being connected with others (F) on campus seems to promote a large family, mindful of each others' value. To counter the outward focus, there is plenty of fun and stress relief starting on Friday night. Moving forward into their careers with confident expectation is a good description of the Bowdoin students on graduation day.

Now read below about one of the majors that MBTI® research shows people of your type have selected since the mid-20th century. After, refer to Chapter Five for the 50 or so majors that can help you prepare for careers your type has selected. Most importantly, remember that this college description is a suggestion for exploration, not a commanding order. You can be successful in any major at any college.

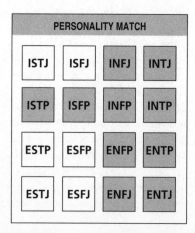

PERSONALITY MATCH

ISTJ	ISFJ	INFJ	INTJ
ISTP	ISFP	INFP	INTP
ESTP	ESFP	ENFP	ENTP
ESTJ	ESFJ	ENFJ	ENTJ

INFJ brings insight to the world of art. The **Visual Arts** major at Bowdoin is sitting pretty because it is within daily reach of Maine's coastline and rolling forests. There is a strong technical side to the major and also a good amount of self introspection in the course work. It will be natural for this type to pencil technical perfection into a landscape that pulls out an emotional reaction from the viewer. INFJ is always on the look out for meaning and fits in very well here.

ISTP enjoys seeing connection between movement, materials and force. Think robotics. The major in **Physics** at Bowdoin is ideal for this type. The major can also be easily paired with courses in oceanography. It gives ISTP wiggle room to stay in the laboratories and perhaps take a trip to Orr Island for direct wave observations.

ENFP may be attracted to the teaching minor in **Education**. The Bowdoin preparation for prospective teachers is precise and selective. The faculty require much introspection about the meaning of a purposeful life. The department is both practical and a bit idealistic. The underachievement in our public schools and the poor results in 2014 and 2015 of the Common Core government mandates are on the table for study and solutions. Schools are viewed as a national resource and the growing charter school movement gets a hearing at Bowdoin. ENFP will warm to this conceptual curriculum in education studies.

ENTP is fascinated with power and doesn't mind thinking about moving into power circles. The study of power is front and center after 2015, with Russia's Putin moving into the Ukraine and Syria. At Bowdoin, the **Eurasian and East European Studies** interdisciplinary major is a sweeping view of American withdrawal and inaction. Conflict—past, present and future—in this pivotal part of the world will be a worthwhile research study. ENTP will have many options for advisory or consulting positions after graduation.

INTP and **Neuroscience** is a good combination. This is a fast growing research field with lots of application in human health. The field is centered on the brain and outward behavior which also includes thought. Neuroscience counseling has developed treatment for PTSD, post traumatic stress disorder, for our military veterans returning from the violent Middle East. At the opposite end, young children with ADHD, attention deficit hyperactivity disorder, are getting therapy using discoveries from the field of neuroscience.

INTJ and **Mathematics** is a good major to launch into the world of graduate studies. At Bowdoin College, math is studied for its pure logic and for its use across all fields. The department is very active and practical because they have opened the doors for interdisciplinary courses in their curriculum. So INTJ might consider the degree that combines math with computer science, or maybe the combo with biology that is coming on board in 2017.

INFP with a good ear can devote themselves to a career in music. At Bowdoin the **Music** majors often follow one of four tracks: General Music, Music and Culture, Composition and Theory or Western Classical Music. Complex INFP might need the fifth choice: a self-designed music major. Don't be surprised if INFP writes a hit song that calls out to Americans to consider the Common Good. That message might go against American citizens dividing up by class and background.

ENTJ is a dynamite consultant in the business world. At Bowdoin, the interdisciplinary major of **Mathematics and Economics** will let this hard-charging type get hired at the most selective financial houses and consulting companies. The wide ranging conversations in coursework connect the linear lines of currency with math modeling. ENTJ smiles as they look into their consulting future with a Bowdoin degree on their resume.

ENFJ and **Psychology**. It makes good sense for this type who sees human potential in individuals and organizations. The Bowdoin College environment is also a good fit for this type. Their authentic relationship with clients in therapy will help individuals recognize their weaknesses and strengths. Bowdoin has really pushed into neuroscience and the practical connection with counseling. They are into research with memory and possibly retraining the brain.

ISFP often likes careers in the health services field. They are great at observing what "is." Diagnosing disease using scanned images and being observant naturally is a dynamite inclination for this type. The major in **Biology** at Bowdoin follows the college philosophy to add to the body of knowledge for the "common good." This works for ISFP since they really want to use their skills while working one-on-one with people. This major will allow ISFP to launch into any advanced medical training.

BRANDEIS UNIVERSITY

Office of Admission
415 South Street
Waltham, MA 02454-9110
Admissions Telephone: 781-736-3500
Website: www.brandeis.edu
Undergraduates: 3,711; 1,593 Men, 2,118 Women
Graduate Students: 2,216

Physical Environment

Brandeis is located just off the beltway surrounding Boston. The commuter rail stop is located near the Brandeis athletic fields on South Street and the university operates its own shuttles into Boston and vicinity. The campus is built on 235 acres of rolling hills, referred to as an **upper and lower campus**. All students get their exercise walking up and down the hills on this compact landscape. The buildings are modern, rectangular structures, with the exception of the circular theatre building and the **Usen Castle**. The Castle is a medieval, attention-grabbing structure and the most desirable dormitory. Just for the sophomores, it overlooks the campus below. It also houses Chum's coffeehouse with late night snacks so that all students have access to its sweeping views of downtown Boston. With a softer architectural contrast, the new Mandel Center for the Humanities seems to be purely glass and shining metal with neon light bars suspended in thin air. The Shapiro Science Center offers a sobering, geometric presence that complements the advanced national research laboratories inside.

There are three distinctive architectural **houses of worship** on this campus: Catholic, **Jewish** and Protestant. The academic calendar is arranged so as to permit students of all faiths to celebrate religious holidays. Although Brandeis is nonsectarian, it has a deep Jewish heritage. The dining room has a kosher section and signage to move you toward your choice. It is typical to see the interfaith chaplains joining students for lunch on this campus.

Social Environment

The university was founded in 1948 and is named after the first Jewish Supreme Court Justice, Louis Brandeis. It quickly came to be considered a top private research institution. Students easily participate as research assistants with faculty in the research labs. The Schuster Institute for Investigative Journalism sponsors student research in the area of **worldwide human rights**. It takes on a watchdog role, monitoring government policies around the world. Religious expression is a hot topic on this campus. Students are very tuned into religious topics in the media and the world political crises in the Middle East. In 2014, student positions on supporting Israel in the conflict with Palestine turned into a formal complaint between two undergraduates. The university administration verbally informed the accused student of a scheduled judicial proceeding and it was routine procedure that he would not receive a copy of the complaint. After a year back and forth over providing a copy of the complaint to the accused, the administration cancelled the proceeding and dropped the case when confronted by outside legal review.[8]

The Department of **Student Rights and Community Standards** highlights the Circle of Values: Citizenship, respect, civility, integrity, diversity and lifelong learning are the six values highlighted in curriculum across all departments. All students must reach the intermediate level of proficiency in a foreign language prior to graduation supporting the administration's commitment to understanding the international community.

Students who do well at Brandeis are **investigative** and **inquiring**, and a good number are intense. They must handle challenging academics and expect faculty to be outspoken in the mentoring process. Many students are interested in becoming medical doctors, veterinarians or lawyers. Half of the student body identifies as a minority. Approximately 75 percent of students come from outside of Massachusetts. **International** students bring their customs and perspectives to campus contributing to the global feel very much like suburban Boston. The college does not track the number of students who enroll who are Jewish but the general sense is that approximately half are Jewish.

Compatibility with Personality Types and Preferences

Brandeis University is over the top in connecting academic studies with student interest and exploration. The faculty is very active with their own independent research, but they do look for interested students to join in their particular research. There is careful, consistent and practical (S) advising for selecting majors, career tracks, advanced study and research after graduation.

Undergraduate students look to develop a personal **ideology** that includes spirit, body and mind. In fact that is part of the first year orientation curriculum. Students may become passionate about issues, and the full Brandeis experience shines a bright light on national subjects that are dominating American politics. Undergrads learn through traditional experience in the classrooms, where opinions and passion are part of the class discussions. It takes time to comprehend the academic complexity of this university (T). It also takes several dimensions of time and thought to graduate.

Extracurricular activities and clubs show the students' strong interest and study of humane issues (F) in the broadest sense. It is supported by the university's strong outreach across the globe. Brandeis admits international students to increase understanding between international cultures through its academic curriculum. Campus discussions point to the majority student view of discomfort with conservative thought.

Now read below about one of the majors that MBTI® research shows people of your type have selected since the mid-20th century. After, refer to Chapter Five for the 50 or so majors that can

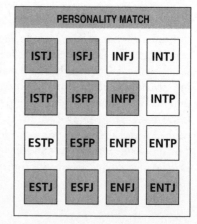

PERSONALITY MATCH

ISTJ	ISFJ	INFJ	INTJ
ISTP	ISFP	INFP	INTP
ESTP	ESFP	ENFP	ENTP
ESTJ	ESFJ	ENFJ	ENTJ

help you prepare for careers your type has selected. Most importantly, remember that this college description is a suggestion for exploration, not a commanding order. You can be successful in any major at any college.

INFP could elect to declare the **Studio Art** major at Brandeis University. Their personal vision is drawn out through the encouragement and sensitivity of faculty within this department. There is an underlying theme that requires students to look at art as an expression of their own motivation and to develop contemporary expressive techniques. INFPs excel at relating their beliefs through creative work. At Brandeis, both beliefs and creativity are expected and nicely combine in this major.

ISTP likes to be efficient with the resources of a student team or class project. The major in **Computer Science** at Brandeis requires coordination and efficiency. ISTPs like controlling chaos if their technical troubleshooting can save the day. Research directed at machine learning will definitely appeal to this technical type. The degree in computing here has a wide focus and ISTP goes with the spontaneity of this department.

ISTJ will like the historically-based courses in the **American Studies** major at Brandeis. The curriculum presents the American story through the evolution of the government, the culture and the people as a whole over three centuries. The curriculum tends to avoid using 21st century political and social trends as a filter for events of the 18th, 19th and 20th centuries. Rather, the department expects undergraduates to comprehend the foundation of the cultural American timeline. The minor in **Legal Studies** is a swell combo with this major. ISTJs will be headed toward a career in justice or law with these two courses of study.

ISFJ is often a natural leader in the field of education. This type has a comfort level with administrative procedure and attention to detail. Both are great for a major in **Education Studies**. The Brandeis degree prepares for graduate study in school leadership and administration. The department focuses on the ethical purposes of education. There are many "why" and "how" questions here for ISFJ to ponder. Kind and sensitive, this type will encourage cooperation in charged discussion.

ISFP has a thoughtful side to their daily routine. The major in **Psychology** at Brandeis really studies the current research in the field. It paints a clear picture of how the field is helping push forward practices in counseling and diagnosing human personality disorders. This type wants to offer immediate help to others in distress. So their practical side will like the Brandeis approach that highlights the best practices in current research.

ESFP more often than not has an affinity for animals. Brandeis has introductory courses that explore animal behavior. Perception: Human, Animal, and Machine is just one example. In the sophomore year, ESFP may elect to apply for an independent interdisciplinary major in **Animal Studies** that combines the fields of psychology, biology and sociology. Graduation may find them at zoological parks or wildlife preservation organizations.

ESFJ is usually conscientious, thorough and sympathetic. So this type might wonder why a Bachelor of Arts degree in **Biology** focuses on research. Yet it really sits well with a career goal that is involved with genetic counseling. This new field is all about sensitive, ethical requirements for decision. Graduate programs in genetic counseling are looking for skilled graduates open to applying current knowledge with sound understanding of the discipline to interpret emerging research.

ESTJ likes the idea of a solid, no frills undergraduate degree. The major in **Chemistry** moves easily into the job market and especially graduate schools. New twists like chemical fabric in the market place add jobs in industrial manufacturing. Careers in law and environmental sciences start with this degree also. ESTJ usually struggles to make career decisions early in the undergraduate college years, but once decided they are happy campers.

ENFJ with undergraduate study in **Language and Linguistics** could become a master at public speaking. Words fascinate this type because of the multiple meanings and possibility for persuasion. Some ENFJs are computer geeks. Brandeis offers just this very combination in the major. Graduate study could move into anthropology, sociology, computer science, psychology or pure research. Faculty in the department connect artificial intelligence with the mathematical properties of linguistics. It's abstract stuff, but ENFJs thrive on it.

ENTJ likes to use logic mixed with new ideas to solve problems. **Neuroscience** is a great major for these two ENTJ characteristics. Brandeis has the science labs, departments and current research of the brain through the nervous system. Check out this list of Brandeis labs: chemical, biological, genetic, computational, perceptual, memory, spatial and behavioral. ENTJ will be right at home with the huge scope of research at Brandeis.

BROWN UNIVERSITY

45 Prospect Street, Box 1876
Providence, RI 02912
www.brown.edu
Admissions Telephone: 401-863-2378
Undergraduates: 6,548; 3,150 Men, 3,398 Women
Graduate Students: 2,633

Physical Environment`

The city of Providence is a sophisticated and lively place for Brown students. It's like a mini-Boston minus the hustle and bustle. City streets like Thayer run through the university area adding beauty and **upscale atmosphere** with internet cafes, ethnic restaurants and street musicians in good weather. The campus sits on top of College Hill along with historical homes on the national register, like the very first Baptist Church in America from the 1600s. The federal style houses speak to social upper class living. The train station is within a few minutes of the university, and it connects students with Boston and New York. Students with artistic talent are drawn to the possibility of a dual degree from the Rhode Island School of Design, just across the street from campus.

Some of the Brown buildings keep the look and feel of the late 1800s, and undergraduates like New England's old customs and ways, possibly reminding them of a high school summer program in England. The large Life Science complex joins the "Walk" network of paths and parks. Following tradition, the Van Wickle wrought iron gate only opens and closes for incoming and graduating students. Lots of **crisscrossing footpaths** on the campus remind you of the **academic freedom** here. It is a bit romantic and the landscape points back to early European settlement of the late 1700s. The entire place speaks to a classy intellectual lifestyle. Students here want to be in the middle of it.

Like most recent college architecture, the new Granoff Center for the arts is filled with cubby holes for artistic production and reminds you of a toddler's attempt to square up three building blocks, but gets them off center. It is funny looking and delightful. The Metcalf Center for Research combines study for the cognitive, linguistic and psychological fields in one setting. The Faunce House Campus Center, with its minimalist design, is livened up by undergrads meeting over lattes and organic chemistry quiz questions.

Social Environment

Brown University's founding mission gave freedom to students to study what they wanted, to the level they wanted and without taking other "prescribed" classes. However, change is constant and today, the open curriculum is interpreted by the department faculty who develop concentrations by title and course content. After undergrads pick courses in conjunction with their advisors that meet the core curriculum, they go for electives that spark their curiosity. That is where the **Open Curriculum** plays out with reality and potential. It worked for a recent graduate whose major was 'Love.' It doesn't seem all that practical but in 2015, she became a very successful business woman.

Brown supports the idea that **knowledge is interconnected and relative**. Professors expect students to **learn from each other** and bring new ideas to the class conversations. In fact, it seems that faculty intend for students to be the trailblazers who will move knowledge forward and to start during their undergraduate years. Students come to see that they can and should contribute to the base of knowledge in any field, not just their selected concentration. They are likely to believe present day information is transient in nature. Faculty are primarily progressive and find much of American History problematic. Western civilization is viewed as a source of global difficulty.

The university calls out to thinking, bright students who are as comfortable with daydreaming as they are with accomplishment. Some are single-minded and can get lost in their dream. They are nurtured by professors and at times **treated as equals** with insights to share. Self-directed and pretty intense, they look for the niche, original material to develop their passions. A good number of those end up balancing their selected advocacy with the **heavy academic demands**. So with the future in mind they go through their day on campus. All are pretty much attuned to today's social media trending across iPhones. Some would have been described as "nerds with a social personality" in high school. Others are children of free thinkers who identify with their parents' ideals. Very few are conservative thinking on this campus. Sixty percent identify as a minority.

Students who take to Brown love the possibility of experimenting and the university obliges, at times with a solid dose of reality. In Fall 2013 they objected to the NYPD Commissioner and shouted him off the stage at a public lecture. The university president stated that the students kept the community from hearing and discussing important social issues. She cancelled the rest of the ceremony when undergraduates kept shouting and had the hall cleared.[9] In Spring 2014 graduates placed red tape on their caps demanding the university's policy on sexual assault be changed.[10]

Concentration, focus and intensity are in the air at Brown. Professors are equally this way. The recent publication of the faculty book, *The Pope and Mussolini*, is an exhaustive review of the Vatican Nation State's tragic political policy in dealing with Fascist Italy's Mussolini and Nazi Germany's Hitler. Aaron Rodgers' well heard advice, R-E-L-A-X, to Green Bay Packer fans in Fall 2014 is not in the air on campus. Students here look to their exceptional education as a foundation to address social problems. They often become quite successful. Others choose a path after graduation without any thought of practical, worldly concern.

Compatibility with Personality Types and Preferences

Brown University is a study in diffusion (P). Simply said, there are no hard lines or sharp edges within this intellectual environment. Instead, synthesis, discovery and expansion seem to rule. Students who find Brown a comfortable place are those who want to see beyond and to the side of what is presently known: the future with just a bit of the past and present. Their motivation may be intense curiosity, or they may be compelled to help others (F) as the best way to define themselves. These students are ready to jump into the unknown at some level (N) with the confidence that they will surface with positive personal abilities. They expect to nail down many important concepts in four years. They will find their own definition of "productive." They come expecting to find a campus that will welcome these very abstract questions. They are suspicious that their experience in American or international schools was too narrow. Yet, they will find progressive cultural thought at this university also wanting in basic foundational courses on the American Revolution and American government.[11] Nevertheless, undergraduates can request courses here and start the dialogue. Brown students devote their energy to learning through questions of all types. It is almost certain that the answers will expand the body of knowledge in their academic fields.

Now read below about one of the majors that MBTI® research shows people of your type have selected since the mid-20th century. After, refer to Chapter Five for the 50 or so majors that can help you prepare for careers your type has selected. Most importantly, remember that this college description is a suggestion for exploration, not a commanding order. You can be successful in any major at any college.

PERSONALITY MATCH			
ISTJ	ISFJ	INFJ	INTJ
ISTP	ISFP	INFP	INTP
ESTP	ESFP	ENFP	ENTP
ESTJ	ESFJ	ENFJ	ENTJ

INFJ might think the concentration of **Health and Human Biology** at Brown is a nice play on words. In fact, they might like the pair of words, health and disease, which is one of the required themes in the curriculum. This type doesn't always go for conventional practice. Their intuition will kick in as a first year student and they will not shy away from the huge health issues facing our nation. Their own idealism can translate into solid leadership when they believe in the work at hand.

INTJ is really the type where still waters run deep. Friends get surprised by the originality and depth of their ideas when INTJ chooses to talk about it. The educational philosophy at Brown is perfect for this type because they will be encouraged and rewarded for revealing their ideas. Although most undergrads like the process and evolving knowledge in their subjects, INTJ has the long-range detachment to find a definitive answer. Definitive answers are part of their larger-than-life visions. So who else to tackle such a revolutionary and intense concentration as **Cognitive Neuroscience**? The complex thoughts at free floating Brown University call out louder to INTJ.

ISFP will like the **Visual Arts** concentration at Brown since a sense of beauty is a part of their personality. This warm fuzzy type is good at communicating through the arts, especially hand-crafted, three dimensional pieces. ISFP is very good with the here and now, with what can be seen and touched. This is how and why they are so very good in the fields of design. At Brown, ISFP will find the encouragement they need to express well being and happiness. These are two reactions they desire for the viewers of their art.

INTP doesn't actually believe that problems can't be solved. It's not in their nature to give you that position. Naturally, they are pretty skeptical. Sometimes it's hard to get them to agree that the sun will come up tomorrow morning, clouds or no clouds. The concentration in **Computational Biology** will give them the math tools to be skeptical with reason. They are big, long-range thinkers who can deal with algorithms and data coming from DNA and genetic studies. Deeper in the data bits INTP might see a puzzle that needs to be solved. Statistics and innovation smooth right into their afternoon Coke break.

INFP admires art and design that also has a message. The concentration in **Architectural Studies** at Brown focuses on buildings and their design that fit into a particular setting. The department offers urban building design concentrating on daily use and how local citizens enjoy the neighborhood and how passersby react. Study abroad is darned helpful for urban studies too. The odd skyline in London with The Shard has originality for curious INFP. A few appointments with the Shard's junior architects and visits to the building will put a smile on the face of INFP.

ESFP could see the **History of Art and Architecture** concentration launching a career in Historical preservation. This type likes to entertain with good design. It's a good background for positions at museums of national history, like Thomas Jefferson's Monticello. This concentration allows undergrads to focus on critical interpretation. Since Jefferson used much of his political ideology in the function at Monticello, ESFP can lean on Thomas for support. Spontaneous and fun loving, they could put together history field trips to Slater Mill for local history teachers. Online American Revolutionary History for High School credit is also an option since older Millennials are complaining that they didn't get it in high school or college.

ENFP will find the novelty that they need in the **Business, Entrepreneurship and Organizations** concentration at Brown University. It puts the three fields of engineering, sociology and economics on the same plate to study. ENFPs will quickly pull their chair up to the table to figure it out. How about driverless cars? It could be the ever original ENFP who graduates Brown and lands a job at forward looking Ford Motor company, Amazon or Google.

ENTP likes to think Big. The concentration in **Geological Science** includes the other planets along with our earth. Now that ought to be big enough. The chemical process that forms planet bodies is a big part of this major. NASA's latest travel with the Dawn robots have just brought back buckets of data from Ceres, the dwarf planet in the sun's asteroid belt. Clever ENTP will have lots of big thinking waiting in the labs with this concentration.

ESFJ who has a talent for numbers will want to look at the concentration in **Statistics** at Brown University. Tender-hearted ESFJ is going to like this interdepartmental Bachelor of Science because it is in the School of Public Health. All undergrads must select a subject to apply the newly learned statistical tools. ESFJ will likely select a social science that can fit in with national and world service organizations. On this campus, statistics are considered an art and a science. That warms up those cold numbers and ESFJ wants their stats to be people-oriented.

ENFJ can see all sides of a conundrum in the **Education Studies** concentration at Brown. There are frequent conundrums in American education with students placing poorly among those from the advanced countries of the world. ENFJ has the skills to introduce new perspectives. They are good with leadership and persuasion too. The department requires that students focus on Human Development or Policy/History. ENFJ is a natural for the Policy/History track. But the emotional health of American students is also at front and center. Suicide in the teen years is ongoing. It is a sober subject for exploration.

BUTLER UNIVERSITY

Office of Admissions
4600 Sunset Avenue
Indianapolis, IN 46208
Website: www.butler.edu
Admissions Telephone: 888-940-8100
Undergraduates: 4,062; 1,636 Men, 2,426 Women

Physical Environment

Butler University is tucked inside metropolitan Indianapolis. In the last ten years the campus has changed from basic college era rectangle buildings to WOW. The Butler campus is triangular in shape with the White River at the base. The new parking garage helps with the cold, windy winters. But the wow part is the first floor retail shops and favorite local restaurant, Scotty's Brewhouse. You have to smile at the Zip and Uber cars on campus and the new BlueIndy car sharing. The administration jumps right on good ideas like these for collegians and Sunset Avenue Student housing opens for the 2016-17 academic year with the latest style living pods in the dormitory floor plan. Campus is less than a mile from Broad Ripple Village, one of six cultural districts in Indianapolis and a good place to find undergrads on a walk. The president's house is prominently located on campus and reminds one of the administration's focused, hands-on academic guidance.

Butler University is a lot like Indianapolis, energetic and forward-looking. The state of the art addition to the **Pharmacy and Health Sciences** building is front and center for the serious medical profession studies on this campus. In 2013, the Schrott Center for the Arts did the same for **theater and dance** also with undergraduate students headed for professional careers. The administration is a study in efficiency and concern in laying out the campus landscapes. Indoor passage from building to building during the winter months is the way to go. The Butler Field house with indoor football and baseball practice fields is like a huge aircraft hangar inside. Wintry wind and these buildings help undergrads meet and stay together. There is cohesion and purpose here.

Social Environment

While students like the classic collegiate environment, they really come for the practical academic curriculum. As high school juniors they tapped out searches on their iPad to find this unique liberal arts campus geared to training for jobs and professional careers. Undergrads really go for the **applied learning** and the internships in many of the majors. Faculty always keep career advising in the mix. Academically, students at Butler get freedom to explore within a clear structure of university guidelines. So both high school graduates who are undecided and those who know their future career get a solid education here. Students with learning differences also do well on this campus.

To help undecided freshmen and sophomores, the administration created the **Exploratory Studies Program** with advisors just for this purpose. They will likely graduate on time with an education that works for them. The very **competitive**

dance and theatre programs are for those who were in lessons since they were knee high. The professional environment, facilities and performances have more in common with Chicago's theater district than college theater. Graduates will go on to perform, teach, manage and take technical positions with professional theaters and stages across the nation. The professional currents at Butler really let the budding artists, musicians, doctors, CEOs and counselors dream and achieve.

The student body is wild for Division I sports. Their trophy cabinet holds 28 conference championships and the men's basketball went to **NCAA national championship** playoffs in 2010 and 2011. Butler teams received the top Academic Excellence Award for the conference in 2015. The **Fraternity** Homecoming Chariot Race each year and Butler Blue III, mascot and fine-looking English bulldog, are faves and lighten the spirit. Just about all students want to join clubs and events that draw them together for traditional collegiate activities. Many students come from the Indiana farms with about 40 percent coming from outside of Indiana. Politically, these students can understand conservative views. They are open for the discussion. They are likely to **value religion and tradition**. Their families have 19th century roots, Indiana family histories and more recently Ellis Island 20th century immigrant histories.

Compatibility with Personality Types and Preferences

Butler University prepares its graduates for the professional world of work and careers through four years of spirited advising and excellent courses in each of the six colleges. Students at Butler look to their professors for state of the art information (S) within their fields. The administration recruits professionals to serve as faculty on campus. They bring their expertise, excitement and reality to the classes. The performing arts faculty are usually retired from American or European theater districts. The natural excitement and optimism on this campus in sports and social clubs is great for the performing artists and these different energies build on each other. At Butler team spirit translates into community building, community strength and individual strength. Faculty advising combines the interests and talents of each student in their academic plan. It really opens up career exploration. Butler's exploratory course designations mean the content and purpose is wider than the typical introductory courses at liberal arts colleges. Generally, undergraduates here seek out and appreciate the majors that lead directly to entry level positions in the job market or admission to professional schools. This is exactly what the university provides. Administration philosophy is strictly oriented to academic disciplines, steering pretty much clear of political and social trends.

Now read below about one of the majors that MBTI® research shows people of your type have selected since the mid-20th century. After, refer to Chapter Five for the 50 or so majors that can

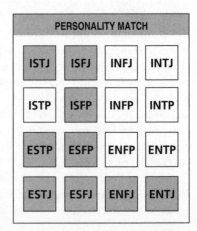

PERSONALITY MATCH

ISTJ	ISFJ	INFJ	INTJ
ISTP	ISFP	INFP	INTP
ESTP	ESFP	ENFP	ENTP
ESTJ	ESFJ	ENFJ	ENTJ

help you prepare for careers your type has selected. Most importantly, remember that this college description is a suggestion for exploration, not a commanding order. You can be successful in any major at any college.

ISTJ is sometimes sure about a career direction as a senior in high school. The Butler University **Health Sciences** major might be their choice because it can lead straight into the Masters for Physician Assistant Studies on campus. This type is usually steady, persevering and a master at the detail needed for admission to any of Butler's several professional schools. This carefully designed major can lead to several other health specialties too. Advising is practical, focused and ISTJ will appreciate it.

ESFP can juggle several projects at a time and the theater stage is pretty attractive to this type. With high school experience and demonstrated talent, the majors in **Theater** or **Dance** are a good bet. Classical ballet for the dancers and original productions for the actors are super fine here. Butler University is one of few smaller institutions offering an accredited Bachelor of Fine Arts. ESFP is all about the present and in this career field, they will be focused on the current season and production. The college also offers an **Arts Administration** major in theater and music.

ESTJ has the inclination to carefully preplan for a career. The precise field of Pharmacy definitely requires preplanning and the undergraduate minor in **Neuroscience** will be an asset on their application for graduate study at pharmaceutical schools. This new major concentrates on studying the brain and the nervous system. It also includes study of emotions in psychology coursework. It is a great background for pharmacists who always have to be aware of side effects in the prescribed medicines.

ISFP is a loyal, flexible and practical soul. In certain businesses, this type can anchor the whole organization. At Butler University, ISFPs can focus on the people side of the corporate and nonprofit business worlds. Encouragement and select internships by the advising professors will smooth the way into a worthwhile experience. This type likes to serve customers through their warm personalities. How about an events planning company? The **Exploratory Studies in Business** major could be a great choice.

ISFJ really might enjoy the therapeutic speech and language field. At Butler, the major in **Communication Sciences and Disorders** is designed for successful entry into graduate school. As a speech and language pathologist, ISFJs could help others directly and be a valued member of the school system or hospital rehabilitation department. Providing language therapy at the elementary schools will take advantage of this type's expertise at sequenced routines and accuracy with repetition. The curriculum includes critical emerging therapies for mentally-impaired youngsters entering school.

ESFJ enjoys the connection between business and the communities they serve. They could realistically shoot for an entry position in public relations between their employer and the customers or audience. The major in **Strategic Communication: PR and Advertising** at Butler University is all about hands-on learning, practice and developing a genuine approach. Very strong in recalling and using information, rarely getting their facts mixed up, ESFJ will be a fine spokesperson.

ESTP is curious and quick to react. A career in the criminal justice system could work. The major in **Criminology** at Butler University has a solid background in psychology and sociology. ESTPs enjoy interacting with other folks and being in the middle of the action. This type is observant and can also understand hidden agendas. After exploring many of the settings that require criminologists, they can settle on the one that suits their style. Maybe they will go for the forensics field which searches out the clues that must be presented at trial.

ENTJ will be impressed with the **International Business** major at Butler University. The degree requires foreign language proficiency, and this hard-charging type is willing to put in the study and wants to excel. ENTJs would enjoy financial transactions in a second language. They don't mind being a step ahead of the competition. The College of Business Administration has selected specific international business schools and internships for the needed global experience before graduation.

ENFJ will find **Middle and Secondary Education** ideal at Butler University. There is a ton of preparation for teachers here. Undergraduates spend days and weeks observing in the classrooms before actually student teaching. They are paired with master teachers at nearby Indianapolis schools. This type would find the advanced classes in high school rewarding to teach. American public school classrooms are tough environments and social media streaming across can skew reality. Responsible and diplomatic, this type might encourage high school students to rethink some of those messages.

CALIFORNIA INSTITUTE OF TECHNOLOGY

1200 E. California Boulevard MC 1-94
Pasadena, CA 91125
Website: www.caltech.edu
Admissions Telephone: 626-395-6341
Undergraduates: 983; 625 Men, 358 Women
Graduate Students: 1,226

Physical Environment

Caltech is an urban campus surrounded by the city streets of Pasadena. The neighborhoods really feel **small town**, almost quaint, lacking high-rise competition, and small vendors meet the retail needs of faculty and students. On this tight campus, students form **self-governing units** in each of the eight dormitories or Houses as they are called. They have enclosed courtyards, corridors and alley ways, offering privacy and independence. The residence halls are basic and look **well-used**. No frills or decor seem to be needed. Students serve the dinner meal at the tables in their dorms. Food is prepared by Caltech dining services, and the student waiters are paid. There is also Open Kitchen which is a lot like the kitchen in your home. Basic and utilitarian, open the fridge and pull out fruit, veggies and snacks, plop down at the table with your iPad to read about quantum physics and start thinking.

High school valedictorians and salutatorians get lost in the amazing Caltech laboratories. The labs in math, physics, astrophysics and geology are spectacular for our planet's geography and science. The tools, machines, robots, telescopes, microscopes and electron particle accelerators bring wonder to human accomplishment and a spiritual presence. Students at the top of their high school class smile at thoughts of Caltech's off campus **research facilities** in Hawaii and Peru. The Linde + Robinson Laboratory for Environmental Science is an eye popping renovation of the 1932-era astronomy lab. Researchers at the new Schlinger Laboratory analyze chemicals that were smashed together in unearthly vacuums and temperatures.

Back on firm earth, the Caltech **cannon** in front of Fleming house is a throwback to the 1950s—when it was fired for the first time to mark the end of a semester. Since then it has disappeared on occasion because other technical rivals steal it away. It actually made a long trip to Massachusetts once, landing at the edge of the Charles River.

Social Environment

Caltech has a small, very select undergraduate student body highly centered on the **physical sciences**. They spend a lot of time with the graduate students also. As freshmen, they take in the world's research on this campus and then in the second year they rub elbows with the grad students in courses and labs. Undergraduates are expected to step up their effort and learn at graduate levels of understanding.

Many of these exceptional students continue research in engineering sciences after graduation. They don't often want to become working engineers with jobs. Caltech only awards Bachelor of Science degrees at the undergraduate level. Techies would rather unwind a puzzling **theory** than demonstrate or sit out classes for a political conundrum. They are future-oriented students who prepare for grad school that is likely to be followed by working in national research labs. They will advance known science and will be called on to invigorate this nation in the future.

They socialize around research and solving problems, **slurping up a late night Boba** between 1000 and 0200 hours while **tackling scientific hypotheses**. Fun has to be involved somehow with technology. Be sure to ask about Ditch Day on the campus tour. They take pride in this tradition. They also like prankster humor—a throwback to the 1950s—when the cannon was fired for the first time to mark the end of a semester. Heat sensitive coffee cups were sent to the freshmen with their logo at a rival institution. When filled with hot beverages, the cups switched their allegiance to....Caltech coffee cups. The January 1, 2014, Rose Bowl fans were greeted at half time with a 2,000 square foot electronic sign that read "Caltech" in Rose Bowl red!

When not pranking, undergraduates are all wrapped up in their studies and discoveries; the campus energy is devoted to knowledge with just the required amount of energy given over to regular routine life activity. Caltech is unusual in many ways. The students are undemanding in how and where they live. They must use their imagination to roam, make connections and open up to unknown strands during **brainstorming** sessions. It is more demanding than some expect and the first two semesters are pass and fail for that reason. Students value truth and abide by a strong honor code whereby they can take un-proctored tests whenever they are ready. For the student who is fascinated by the uncharted areas of science and brave enough to follow their hunches, Caltech is perfect.

Compatibility with Personality Types and Preferences

California Institute of Technology is more than a university; in reality it is a national and world scientific laboratory resource that also has dormitories for young Twenty-somethings otherwise known as undergraduate students. Caltech does an admirable job working with these recent high school valedictorians and world-renown research scientists at the same time, on the same campus. Analysis (T) is always in this campus culture. It is hard to imagine how the extreme and fundamental nature of Caltech research could survive with emotions or feelings ruling the labs. Of course, innovation and the pull of the unknown (N) is nerve-wracking in the daily drill. There will be little welcome for undergrads who want to frame a current political trend with research. Passion is reserved for the truth here. The one exception being the Caltech professor who listed her cat as the coauthor of postdoctoral research in Fall 2014. Caltech's mission clearly states that human knowledge is expanded to benefit society by combining research and education, not animal knowledge. Their educational philosophy is more along the lines of a think tank that just happens to have young adults as participating members. It is an institution that prepares its graduates for the world of scientific discovery rather than careers and professions. The humans on this campus are prodigies and an underutilized American resource. They will have to step up in the not too distant future. But before that, they can celebrate with their parents at the classy Athenaeum on graduation day.

Now read below about one of the majors that MBTI® research shows people of your type have selected since the mid-20th century. After, refer to Chapter Five for the 50 or so majors that can help you prepare for careers your type has selected. Most importantly, remember that this college description is a suggestion for exploration, not a commanding order. You can be successful in any major at any college.

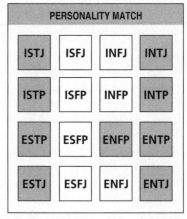

ISTJ will like the factual and fundamental nature of the **Biology** track option at Caltech. With emphasis on the basic life properties, the biology option includes current research in the department as a primary learning tool. ISTJ will set out to refine their research skills with a vengeance. This type is drawn to professional settings. Entrance to medical research universities will not be far from their daily thoughts.

ISTP is pretty good with numbers and will like the **Economics** option here at Caltech. There is a course titled Business Analytics. Students explore datasets that influence mega business choices. In the 2011 timeframe, McDonald's stock was down because of their mediocre menu, frayed restaurants and competition. Well that turned around in 2014. The economics option at Caltech studies these mega moves. It includes strategic behavior and asymmetric information in social/economic actions. Given that, here's a techy puzzle that ISTP might study. What did the Bill and Melinda Gates Foundation have to do with the turnaround? How, why and where is the 42 billion of the foundation portfolio directed as a power that shapes society? Not inclined to over worry, this type can snooze through marketing messages put out by public relations types about the strategic deployment of foundation power.

ESTP could like the **Business Economics and Management** option since it looks so heavily at strategy within the markets and financial networks. Undergrads use mathematical formulas such as binomial and Black-Scholes pricing models to study risky debt. This department expects graduates to understand how business and management change society. ESTP could take a second option in **Engineering** and be right in the middle of driverless cars or drones that deliver Amazon goods.

ESTJ who looks closely at the **Applied Physics** option will find practical stuff hidden within. As freshman they could set up test diodes, transistors and inverters. This gives ESTJ the immediate feedback they need to comprehend electrical storage theory. Since energy travels across locations through fiber optics, microwaves, radiation and X-rays there will be a lot more observable facts for this type to store away. And how about those gravitational waves that proved Einstein correct when two black holes collided and the waves reached our solar system in February 2016?

ENFP might be energized when we suggest selecting the **History and Philosophy of Science** option at Caltech. This broad-based study looks at how science helps human welfare. It is something that would attract an ENFP. The ironic course in Forbidden Knowledge is chock-full of foresight. It addresses cases in history where knowledge has been squashed, such as Galileo's experience with our sun-centered galaxy. Currently, NASA's Roy Spencer and his research questioning the validity of global warming will surely be reviewed as an example. Political movements of this decade push passionate agendas and the citizens as well as undergraduates are left to ponder.

INTJ could go for the **Computer Science** option here because it requires an original capstone project. This type creates vision with their ongoing thoughts but they don't often talk about. As powerful thinkers, they might want to study the limits of computing science theory in the course titled Decidability and Tractability. Algorithms will be flying across the screen in this option. INTJ's rigorous and creative thoughts will be chasing after the data too.

INTP could use the **Astronomy** option at Caltech as a stepping stone into basic research. The first year course includes a lab introducing astronomical measuring techniques. Within the last few years, Caltech faculty started measuring the universe in multi-terabyte and multi-petabytes. INTP goes for the theory and mystery of this field. And tinkering in the labs will help them get out of the Ivory Tower, aka favorite studying hole.

ENTP will like the **Political Science** option here because it includes predictive methods. Caltech brings their powerful analysis into this social science. ENTP is well suited to find the irony in the course option PS 126 which has changed its name in successive course catalogs from "Political Corruption" to "Business, Public Policy and Corruption" then to "Business and Public Policy" in 2010. However, the departments of anthropology and political science picked up the baton with An/Ps 127 simply titled, "Corruption." This type is a power player with little use for sentimentality. This option in Political Science appeals to their restless character.

ENTJ could like **Chemical Engineering** at Caltech because the department researches chemical reactions for energy as well as manufactured products. ENTJ will find the realistic connection to the future that they appreciate in one of the four tracks—biomolecular, environmental, materials or process systems. It is also possible that their entrepreneurial instincts will jump in to take a few course electives in the business, economics or management.

CARLETON COLLEGE

100 South College Street
Northfield, MN 55057
Website: www.carleton.edu
Admissions Telephone: 507-222-4190
Undergraduates: 2,014; 968 Men, 1,027 Women

Physical Environment

Carleton College is small and **quaint**, clean and friendly. Northfield's slogan "Home of cows, colleges, and contentment" is correct. It works for students who are looking for a safe, exploratory and artsy environment. Commercial shops wind along the river open for latte escapes, artisan bakeries, bars and restaurants. A former middle school was remodeled as the Weitz Center for Creativity. It has a monthly schedule of music, lectures and arts for those on campus and locals. Praise for Carleton for supporting your home town so well. Different faculty rotate their offices into this complex to meet and mix with each other for semesters at a time with fresh ideas. October 2011 marked the start up of the college's second wind turbine. It feeds wind-powered electricity into the local electric grid. This bold decision cost 1.8 million dollars, but it is projected to be paid off in 2023 from the sale of electricity it produces back to the local power company. Rural communities interested in "free" wind power can get actual production statistics from Carleton's experiment. That is an immediate benefit for the windy Plain States of the Midwest, courtesy of Carleton.

Carleton students especially like the **long connected buildings** and two new dormitories so that they can walk around in shorts and flip-flops in winter. The center of campus features the original chapel with surrounding buildings in comfy Collegiate Gothic style, architecture of the 60s and recent sassy collegiate architecture. Carleton has an active **Office of the Chaplaincy** that helps many Jewish and Catholic students survive the college years without losing their faith and God. Worship services and special religious holidays are posted in the monthly agenda. There are 15 special interest houses for like-minded people. We want to visit the Science Fiction House for an afternoon!

Social Environment

Carleton students arrive on campus excited to build on their strong high school academics at Carleton. Here history students can study American government which may have been dropped from their high school graduation requirements. Undergraduates are not wholly progressive or liberal and they are open to traditional or conservative ideas. Carleton students prefer **cause-related clubs** and want to include all on campus from the nerds to the alternatives and fun lovers. Clubs that have international outlooks like the local chapter of Engineers Without Borders go over big. Similar is the Fellowship in Christ student organization that hopes to bring different national and ethnic students together to study the New Testament. Other groups are out for pure fun like the Carleton Anime Society.

Students are **absorbed in their education** here. Undergrads are good at meeting with faculty and looking for that class or project that adds to their collegiate experience and resume for graduation. Carleton is one of a few colleges that offers three semesters. Sometimes undergrads feel they are overloaded with their trimester class schedule. But other times, they love their trimesters because they don't drag out the courses and the entire academic time on campus is definitely more than the typical two semester university.

Carleton students just **might challenge today's political correctness**. After all, this is a campus that was known for its non-conventional ideas. Carleton undergrads are okay with freedom of expression. They would accept an Islamic scholar who supports women's rights. In the classroom, they are comfortable with questioning and change is an answer they can ponder without immediately reacting in one direction or the other. Faculty and administration philosophy points to a welcoming campus that also encourages cohesion and civility. All in all, undergrads form fast friendships because of their similarities and the long winter months. The favorite winter pastime is broomball. Think hockey without a puck or ice skates. Students are athletic and participate in many sports; this tradition is not likely to change.

Compatibility with Personality Types and Preferences

The Carleton College environment is idealistic and emotionally safe. It is an imaginative place to learn (N). The mentoring between student and professors is almost like that of a family uncle who is helpful. The campus experience encourages the student to think outside of social media and twitter. Faculty and academic philosophy here want to connect the every day stuff with ideals (P). The educational philosophy moves toward critical observation (T) of American society. Carleton students get an intense, insular and individualized education. They step out smartly but with pause into messy big city, big issues America. This liberal arts college is likely to host discussions about the shrinking middle class and the removal of American history from American public high schools and too many American colleges. Carleton College brings together reason, introspection and humor that is ideal for their graduates who will move on to the scene of a nation in transition.

Now read below about one of the majors that MBTI® research shows people of your type have selected since the mid-20th century. After, refer to Chapter Five for the 50 or so majors that can help you prepare for careers your type has selected. Most importantly, remember that this college description is a suggestion for exploration, not a commanding order. You can be successful in any major at any college.

PERSONALITY MATCH

ISTJ	ISFJ	INFJ	INTJ
ISTP	ISFP	INFP	INTP
ESTP	ESFP	ENFP	ENTP
ESTJ	ESFJ	ENFJ	ENTJ

ENFP is often the fun-meister on campus. With an extra dose of emotions and drama, they could go for the **Cinema and Media Studies** major at Carleton. The course in Contemporary Global Cinemas says it all. From Hollywood to south Asia, this major covers 20th and 21st century films. Cinema is studied by nationality in the Film History sequence of three courses. The subtle humor on campus shines forth in this major.

INFJ likes to work with others in small teams to solve the world's problems. This works for a career in social science. The combination **Sociology and Anthropology** major is unusual in liberal arts colleges. It is like a gem discovered in an iron ore mine. The class in Anthropology of Humor, last offered in 2012, is still a good sign of the value in this major. Committed and conceptual INFJs will find the foundation they need to go on to graduate studies in Western Civilization and North America and possibly chill some of their laser-like passion with a few games of broomball.

INFP with talent in art finds a perfect home at Carleton College in the **Art** major. The studio arts include handcraft courses like Paper Arts that jump into dyes, colors and fibers now showing up in high end specialty shops, museums and big city boutiques. It really points back to the middle ages when Dyers were honored as professionals. INFP's originality and talent will fit well with Carleton's realistic look at contemporary America.

ENTJ will put practicality into the **Psychology** major at Carleton College. This department flexes between biopsychology and cognitive psychology. They are both valuable, but pretty different at this point in research directions. ENTJ with their faculty advisors should point their studies in one direction or the other. This type has the chutzpah of a chess master to negotiate the distance between the two and perhaps make that decision when applying to graduate school in a few years.

INTJ will find the major in **Political Science** at Carleton actually has courses on the politics of America including the huge divide between liberals and conservatives. There are few liberal arts colleges that so boldly put this subject in their course work. The faculty rewards strong thinkers like INTJ. American political history is surveyed with all its mistakes and limited successes. The department gets five stars for leaving out 2016 politically correct filters. INTJs can handle these cross currents in government service at national and regional levels.

ENTP likes to start up new projects. The concentration in **South Asian Studies** including India, Pakistan, Nepal and Sri Lanka is exciting and important as a region developing a strong middle class. A study abroad to the other side of our world will help fill up ENTP's bottomless curiosity and imagination. The major in **Economics** cuts across business, politics and regional cultures and might shed light on China's military strength and ambition menacing the South China Sea.

INTP might just like Carleton's concentration in **Cognitive Science**. The human brain is a puzzle that branches out like a Halloween maze. Carleton faculty explore the connections to each of the tunnels in the maze through language development. Some of these tunnels will lengthen considerably as DNA genetic studies advance. Careers in the cognitive sciences are cutting edge, especially at the graduate level. This type likes the precise approach and that will help with studies in this field.

ISTP can handle the precision and concentration needed for **Biochemistry**. At Carleton, students study both chemistry and biology as separate fields. But there are some exciting courses that pull them together like the Chemical Kinetics Lab. ISTP likes technical work so designing sensitive medical equipment will keep them in the labs. Heart disease is usually about advanced plumbing that is slowing down. You go ISTP, you will build the mechanical moves to step up that blood flow.

CASE WESTERN RESERVE UNIVERSITY

103 Tomlinson Hall
10900 Euclid Avenue
Cleveland, OH 44106-7055
Website: www.cwru.edu
Admissions Telephone: 216-368-4450
Undergraduates: 4,911; 2,247 Men, 2,664 Women
Graduate Students: 5,860

Physical Environment

Case Western Reserve University is in the heart of very cultural Cleveland, surrounded by museums, the Cleveland Orchestra's Severance Hall and the Institutes of Art and Music. It's easy enough for undergrads to catch a performance or visit a gallery show since they are within walking distance. In the opposite direction, students love the Little Italy neighborhood for the pasta and pizza. Downtown Cleveland itself surprises students with novelty and unusual places like the I.M. Pei-designed **Rock and Roll Hall of Fame**.

CWRU's campus is cut in half by Euclid Avenue which is the main thoroughfare. The north side of campus feels younger with newer buildings and the freshman and sophomore dorms. The architecture on north campus is ultra-modern. **Village at 115** is a seven-building housing complex for upperclass students which is essentially like apartment-style living. The Peter B. Lewis building for business management has rounded walls that look like they were melted and topped off with a huge metal bow on the roof. The whole thing reminds you of a boxed present left out in the rain. The whole campus is creative, and the **inspirational architecture** has a lot to do with that. As you go from one building to the next on a tour you realize the physical spaces are designed to leave previous designs and ideas behind.

The south side of campus is grander, definitely more classical and perched on the hill. More upperclass housing, **fraternities and sororities** are on this side. The hospital, engineering and science departments anchor the area in contrast to the north campus lighter architecture. The hospital on campus is ideal for many undergrads taking health-related majors. Taken together, these facilities put CWRU in the category of universities with **national research laboratories**. Students definitely choose Case because of the state-of-the-art scientific education in a cultural and artistic setting.

Social Environment

CWRU is great for students who want to know about **mega research, love technology** and wander into the big city cultural neighborhoods. High school valedictorians find a way to study, work in the labs and come to know Cleveland's artistic districts pretty well. Most will join a few of the 500 campus organizations. They tend to like the performing arts and will find a place for music on their weekly schedule. They come from all of the 50 states and, yes, it is a long flight from Alaska and Hawaii. Most international undergrads fly in on much longer flights from South Korea, China and India. All this variety feeds the imagination of the curious students on this campus.

Case students definitely expect to progress in their career fields by developing new knowledge. In their academics they are trendy, current day and future-looking. There is **exceptional openness** in departmental studies and research. Independent students find good rhythm on campus to develop and explore their thoughts. Competition is not the prime motivator. Nor is advocacy or focus on the social trends coming across on iPhones. The constant social scene in the city and the active Greek system on campus lighten up the heavy academic load. Many become **intellectually confident** through the research hours in the fabulous national laboratories and the nature of the academic philosophy on this research-oriented campus. Students are not out to attract attention to their views or positions on social issues. At Case there are more **traditional** ideas and political views that float through conversations than progressive trends.

Compatibility with Personality Types and Preferences

Case Western Reserve University and Cleveland are delightful, especially in warm weather. This university maintains the passion of a small liberal arts college for the humanities plus the intellectual rigor and commitment to advanced research in the physical sciences. The major foundation for Case educational philosophy is openness (P), with few intellectual boundaries. CWRU seeks to be a transforming player in America and the world. It is a world class institution that develops and maintains current scientific and cultural knowledge. Yet, the role of the CWRU graduate is to identify with everyday American enterprise and institutions. In this cooperative manner, the university interfaces the best of technology and research directions toward human diseases and medicine. The university is pretty fluid when it comes to required courses. Students can choose between a Bachelor of Arts or of Science, whichever best suits their plans after graduation.

The traditional academic majors are supplemented with a good number of interesting electives. There are 38 dual degrees that combine the bachelor and masters studies in one program. The academic philosophy brims with creativity (N). In 2016, the university made its third appearance at the International Consumer Electronics Show. What did they bring? They brought electronic Virtual Hugs (F), along with some other medical innovations. The Case culture is also fond of connecting logic (T) and free association of ideas. When you page through the academic bulletin look for novelty, fun and entertainment. In 2016, we found Crystallography and Crystal Chemistry. It sounded charming, but we're sure it has more objectivity than charm.

CWRU also steps up with confidence in their undergraduate students and the Greek System. Faculty and staff understand fraternities and sororities are another option for leadership and initiative as Greek membership is increasing in numbers across the nation's campuses. The administration is cohesive in their genuine optimism. It plays out in confidence and support for a healthy, structured, yet open collegiate environment.

Now read below about one of the majors that MBTI® research shows people of your type have selected since the mid-20th century. After, refer to Chapter Five for the 50 or so majors that can help you prepare for careers your type has selected. Most importantly, remem-

ber that this college description is a suggestion for exploration, not a commanding order. You can be successful in any major at any college.

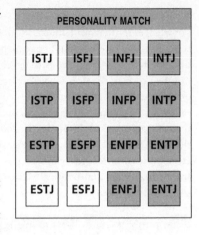

ISTJ ISFJ INFJ INTJ

ISTP ISFP INFP INTP

ESTP ESFP ENFP ENTP

ESTJ ESFJ ENFJ ENTJ

ENFJ might like the Bachelor of Arts in **Computer Science**. They don't usually do precise fields of study without connections to people but a warning system for tsunamis in the Pacific Basin would get their interest up. Case, with its openness, looks for those connections between people, technology and logic in the computer sciences. So ENFJ might go big for seismic detection by computer programming. It should fit into the department requirement to design and apply a new software program. Some of the Asian international students on campus can talk directly about tsunamis.

ISTP loves mechanical gadgets. Maybe America will return to the moon and the degree in **Aerospace Engineering** is mighty attractive to this type. CWRU has a good feel for space exploration since the only way to get there and do anything on arrival is with robots. The university has the research labs in heat and mass transfer to activate the robots here on earth in development. This is important stuff since the asteroid Ceres comes around to sun position every 4.6 years and the robots will wake up and perhaps take some commands. This will keep ISTP smiling.

ENTJ must have innovation and **Civil Engineering** plus CWRU can deliver. This degree is so versatile and ENTJ will take advantage of that in their career. But on campus in 2017, they might just go for the Construction Engineering and Management sequence. Case really wants its graduates and faculty to start businesses. It will be ENTJ who takes the latest ideas and technology out to the market.

ENTP is just fine with the strategic combo of **Japanese Studies** and a minor in **Entrepreneurial Studies**. Fast-moving international business works for ENTP since routine and structure tend to stress this type. However, there will be little of that in Japanese written characters and the curriculum starts off with elementary levels emphasizing the 50 kanji characters. The minor will help to get that entry level position at Samsung Japan. Think Android.

ESFP uses a toolbox of skills with a flair. The major in **Nutrition** lets ESFP help patients understand the connection between their disease and their diet. The research facilities add extra sparkles to this degree at the molecular level. Very few campuses can bring the molecular levels, technology and faculty to undergraduate study. Graduates get good encouragement to shoot for government positions in health policy. But Case will also prepare graduates to question bureaucratic policy. Centralized bureau policy really doesn't go well with openness and creativity.

ISFP is a tender personality and perfect for the **Nursing** program. This four-year nursing program is really excellent because of the Case openness and strength to question bureaucracy. In 1998, a Case graduate started the Hirsh Institute for best practices in medicine. Even in the last century, this university knew that every day medicine could get stale with standard practice.

ISFJ often likes to work in the health care environment. The undergraduate degree in **Nutritional Biochemistry and Metabolism** is a good choice. ISFJ, meticulous and reflective, will have the time and freedom to stay in the research labs. Case academic philosophy takes pride in their graduates who work directly in the field of their educational major on graduation. This type will probably move toward allied health fields and work one on one with their patients in medical clinics.

ESTP likes to pull solutions together with no notice. A **Management** degree and concentration in Finance could help out pretty well with some of those spontaneous solutions. This School of Management is loaded with all the analytical and logical studies that are going to help ESTP recognize entrepreneurial risk, waste and failure. Since they are good with risk taking, the curriculum will provide a judicious, balanced approach to management and ESTP can charge forward with both skills and chutzpah in the dynamic world of business.

ENFP will smile at the idea of combining two rather unusual courses of study while moving forward into a fun, rewarding career track. The double major is encouraged at this university and **Music** combined with **Gerontological Studies** is a distinct possibility for ENFP who likes to motivate others with their own sense of the possible. This type simply must have fun somewhere in their lifestyles and why not at work? Music fits in nicely with the elderly population. They are not as rushed and have the time to enjoy it. Can't you see the older faces smiling now?

INFP likes to reach out to others with services and programs. The minor in **Gerontological Studies** makes good sense with the growing numbers of elderly. Case Western is positive and optimistic at the core. INFP will find the freedom, intensity and individuality at CWRU to combine services for the aged within the expanding field of psychology.

INTP wonders about the laws of gravity when they crash with a skateboard or trip on the ice during a double axle. It is all related to physics, so the **Engineering Physics** degree and regional sports competitions just might fit together. In 2030, the Olympics may be using ice blades and skateboards with technology from Case labs and an INTP coach.

INFJ who decides to take the degree in **Sociology** at CWRU will study health policy and health decline of human life. This type is passionate about helping, but mostly through programs and services in community settings. The department is current with the hundreds of directives coming from the government about how Americans will receive health care. This is an important study because cultures in America are not cohesive and each has their own view personal healthcare. The Sociology faculty will lay out the nature of centralized health directives. There will be much to study with many Millennials choosing not to sign up for mandatory insurance policies, risking government fines.

INTJ plus imagination and a double major in **Art History** and **Pre-Architecture** is going to work. The city of Cleveland is a fabulous study in architecture. University Circle, a few square blocks, has just about any kind of entertainment or social service you would want or need. Both art and architecture thrive on the banks of Lake Erie. A four-year undergraduate degree will be about the right amount of time to understand it all. INTJ has the computing power and deep thinking to see all the connections.

THE CLAREMONT COLLEGES

Claremont McKenna College
890 Columbia Avenue
Claremont, CA 91711-6425
Website: www.claremontmkenna.edu
Admission Telephone: 909-621-8088
Undergraduates: 1,301; 673 Men, 628 Women

Harvey Mudd College
31 Platt Boulevard
Claremont, CA 91711
Website: www.hmc.edu
Admission Telephone: 909-621-8011
Undergraduates: 804; 432 Men, 372 Women

Pitzer College
1050 North Mills Avenue
Claremont, CA 91711-6101
Website: www.pitzer.edu
Admissions Telephone: 909-621-8129
Undergraduates: 1,076; 454 Men, 622 Women

Pomona College
333 N. College Way
Claremont, CA 91711-6312
Website: www.pomona.edu
Admissions Telephone: 909-621-8134
Undergraduates: 1,650; 812 Men, 838 Women

Scripps College
1030 Columbia Avenue
Claremont, CA 91711
Website: www.scrippscollege.edu
Admissions Telephone:
Undergraduates: 972: 972, Women

Physical Environment

These five premier colleges are the western version of New England's **small prestigious liberal arts colleges**. With 20th century innovation and a hundred years, the Claremonts were started with optimism that came with the 19th century California gold rush. Each of the five colleges has a particular architecture that shows its own character academically and socially. However, when we put them together, they become more than the sum of the parts.

The physical environment is **southern, warm California weather**. Outdoor sports go year round. How could you complain? Students get better at biking and skateboarding. They also walk, ride mopeds and balance on unicycles to get around. Summer wear in November works to get from one campus to the other. Because the colleges are **adjacent to one another**, it's common to see Pitzer students talking to Harvey Mudd students who are just across the street.

The Claremont Colleges are an hour's drive east of Los Angeles. The San Gabriel Mountains are directly north of the campus. Administrators at each campus compete to see which uses less water in this ecologically fragile environment. Students might pick limes and grapefruit on their way to class or maybe not if they are withered by the ongoing drought.

Pomona College opened the new Millikan Laboratory in 2015 with planetarium, teaching labs, classrooms, student research space, faculty labs, lounges and a machine shop. Large lawns, open spaces and an organic farm plot top it off.

Claremont McKenna has a fabulous interior courtyard where all Claremont undergrads can mingle at the snack bar or play Frisbee or lounge on the grass. Parent Field is large enough to be a **congregation point** and handles big social events for the five colleges. The Kravis Center with its fanciful design of glass, water and cantilevered wings reminds us of Frank Lloyd Wright architecture. The Mid Quad dormitories of the 1950s and '60s completed their update in 2015, now with air-conditioning for the warm, make that hot California weather in spring and fall.

Pitzer College is the most "**artsy**" campus with cartoon panels and vignettes painted on its walls. The 2007 **residential life project**, reminiscent of 1950s and '60s motels constructed along the highways of that era, has a green belt around the perimeter equal to the size of its footprint. Phase II, the East and West Halls, were completed in 2012 and received much praise for energy conservation design. The entire project, now completed and designed by committee, is comfortable for these sensitive Pitzer students.

Scripps College is located in the center, surrounded by Harvey Mudd, Pitzer, Claremont McKenna and the graduate university. Their dance studio, art museum and theatre arts center look out on Scripps' quiet courtyard. The dorms are furnished with antiques and rugs. Scripps adds a classy feel to the Claremont campuses.

Harvey Mudd fills up a narrow rectangle on the northern side of the Claremont campuses. The dorms are located at one end of the Mudd campus and students **skateboard** down to the dining hall, classrooms and library at the other end. New academic buildings have super efficiency plus lots of passive daylight strategies.

Social Environment

At **Pomona** undergraduates are **high-achieving**, talkative, fun lovers who like to **relax**. They are clean-cut and most of them are happy to be at Pomona. They have solid interests in non-academic activities, like ballroom dancing. What they wear is not important as long as it is comfortable. Sports gear and smart phones are daily wear. The student body is a mix of liberals and some conservatives. They all tend to be realistic, imaginative and some are bold. In Fall 2015 students delivered a list of demands to the President with initiatives to address racism on campus. He replied that undergraduates are actually frustrated over presidential candidate Donald Trump, unable to impact Trump's electoral bid which diverted their focus to campus policies.[12]

Harvey Mudd is the engineering college for the Claremont campus. The undergraduates here can't wait to get into the research labs in these broad-based engineering studies. Mudders and the faculty are team-based for the entire four years. They are **cohesive** and don't go for political trends that interfere with their science goals. Ultimate Frisbee is a favorite. High school students who might have spent their last four years behind a keyboard will become social groupies here at Mudd.

Claremont McKenna is known for hosting the most popular and well-attended parties. These undergrads don't fall behind social media and trends. They are pretty **polished** and sure of themselves. Sunday through Friday they are in their room studying intensely, maybe on iPads searching www.bloomberg.com. The college motto is "Leaders in the Making." In spring 2015, the Athenaeum scheduled progressive speakers marketing their books on tour. With a couple of exceptions, like the Athenaeum address on executive federalism, students must research with an investigative mind to learn of non-progressive political and social thought. In Fall 2015 students held a demonstration with demands by students, who identified as marginalized for accommodation of their special needs.. A few undergraduates also staged a hunger strike.[13] Three hundred undergraduates signed a petition that they do not condone the actions of this protest movement.[14] The dean of the college also resigned with an apology over one of her emails viewed as insensitive.[15]

Pitzer students are **sensitive**, some may be bold in appearance but there is a marshmallow somewhere in each of these undergrads. They want to be with other Pitzers and join causes like the preservation of the declining bumble bee population. But their second love is **food**. Pitzer has the best pasta on campus. Delightfully **unique** within the Claremont colleges, this campus encourages taking social chances, building friendships. In late Fall 2015, the Office of the President responded with an action plan that addressed a list of 28 demands presented by students on the campus diversity climate.[16]

Scripps attracts contemporary, **composed** women who express themselves with the dramatic arts, reading and writing. This is a group comfortable with humanistic values focusing on caring for others. Campus social life is richly supplemented by programs and activities in the Scripps residence halls. This college is the rare and enviable institution that promotes female perspectives within the context of impacting the whole of society as experienced by both female and male citizens.

Compatibility with Personality Types and Preferences

The five Claremont Colleges, collectively known as the Consortium, operate in five different environments with five separate admission offices. Their cultural environments seem to come from the time period each was founded, but they physically sit across the street from each other, sharing the same compact campus space. It is a great combination and it is not surprising that they have an educational fit for all sixteen of the Personality Types. Pomona College with its claim to being first, 1887, and the sponsor to the rest is also the wise granddaddy. Their founders embraced a leadership role and looked far into the future (N). Pomona has an intellectual environment that energizes the process between the student and Knowledge. Professors on this campus are facilitators, but not advisors in the classic sense. Pomona academic philosophies encourage intense independence. Scripps College, the women's college of the Consortium, was founded next in the roaring 20s with the liberated ideals of the times. Since then it has developed an educational philosophy that graduates competent (S) women who take their place in society with professional approach over protest. Claremont McKenna is a WWII baby, founded in 1946. While winning is not their motto, the triumph that came with World War II has seeped into CMC's culture. Leadership is a strong characteristic (T) within their student body. It catapults them into 21st century professions that call the shots in today's business, economic and regulatory worlds. Harvey Mudd, the unique engineering college, moved into a cultural open space at the Claremont institution. In 1955, America was struggling with ever increasing weaponry and technical progress that threatened to spin out of control; this is the turbulent vortex that Harvey Mudd competently filled. Their administration focuses on optimism for humanity (F) and they put it together with the technological disciplines. The youngest in the Consortium, Pitzer College, grew up in the 1960s counter culture and lovingly took on those ideals. Here it is more than okay to be uncertain (P); in fact, it helps Pitzer students dig deep into the meaning of souls.

Now read below about one of the majors that MBTI® research shows people of your type have selected since the mid-20th century. After, refer to Chapter Five for the 50 or so majors that can help you prepare for careers your type has selected. Most importantly, remember that this college description is a suggestion for exploration, not a commanding order. You can be successful in any major at any college.

PERSONALITY MATCH			
ISTJ	ISFJ	INFJ	INTJ
ISTP	ISFP	INFP	INTP
ESTP	ESFP	ENFP	ENTP
ESTJ	ESFJ	ENFJ	ENTJ

ISTJ can get ready for civil service positions with Pomona's **Public Policy Analysis** program. This type can be okay with authority and American government bureaucracy. There are eleven concentrations in the program. Workhorse ISTJ will get the data that they love in the **Economics** concentration. This type, often sensible and calm, can look for conservative views in the program's promised wide perspective on social issues. At the same time, Scripps College offers an approach to Economics that could work for the lady ISTJ. Intermediate Macroeconomic Theory looks at how economic models are created and managed by government policy.

ISTP works well at Pomona College, Scripps and Harvey Mudd. All three have the learning environment for this detached, confident type. **Computer Science** at Harvey Mudd mixes experiment, theory and design. ISTP goes for these three, especially the part about tinkering with data bits. For example, in Computer Science Clinic, two semesters long, they will work together on evolving techniques in software design with outside companies like Steelcase furniture. At Scripps, the **Psychology** major arrives at knowledge by observation, participation and experimental investigation. How about a career in forensic psychology that helps police officials develop profiles for certain types of dangerous criminals?

ESTP at Claremont McKenna is good with the optional **Financial Economic** sequence. The quantitative courses lead up to a mandatory oral defense of their own research on balance sheets, income statements or cash flow. This observant type is great at evaluating the quarterly financial report. At Harvey Mudd, ESTP learns about the physical world through trial-and-error. The Mudd Bachelor in **Engineering** degree puts juniors and seniors together with a faculty advisor to solve real problems for outside clients. For this type, who pages through the books only when necessary, Harvey Mudd has the 'show me' proof that they expect.

ESTJ at Pomona College could look to the **Molecular Biology** major. This type likes to study subjects by category and step-by-step. Mixing chemistry and biology, very different from each other, will require their dependable logical thinking. The two departments utilize undergraduate students in investigative research which helps ESTJ. The **History** major at Scripps offers a few courses on Latin America. With high numbers of Latinos in California and immigrants from across the Pacific basin, the department major looks at the origins of values and how they play out in American society today. Claremont McKenna offers an Ethics Sequence in 2016 that requires a course in government, philosophy and economics, but oddly none in any of the world's religious faiths which are all about moral perspective.

ISFJ who is interested in **Dance** will find a wide program at Scripps. The minor helps graduates enter a variety of other careers like arts administration, dance therapy, physical therapy and kinesiology where body awareness is so important. The growing field of linguistics could attract ISFJ as well. At Pitzer, the **Linguistics** major opens into several subfields. It will be this sensitive type of Eastern European immigrant ancestry that might choose to learn of the region's language and ethnicity. In the Ukraine, language will play a big role in resisting Russia's 2015 invasion and attempt to dominate the country. It would make for unique, relevant, independent research.

ISFP really goes for arts and crafts and is a good match for Pitzer College. Three dimensional arts can easily have an environmental slant. Private and quiet ISFP might design a **Special Major** with coursework like Mexican Visual Cultures, Sculptural Objects Functional Art and Environments and Art. As a graduate with this course of studies, they might start a career with the national park service, arts administration or nonprofit organization. Two of the three required advisors for the Special Major may be off-campus professionals in their fields.

ESFP will find a unique science major at Pitzer. The major in **Human Biology** connects physical science and the social sciences within the Keck Science Department. It could really talk to friendly, practical ESFP. The study of alternative medicines is encouraged and could lead to jobs with ethnic community health centers in the large Los Angeles area. The emphasis in **Environmental Analysis** at Harvey Mudd allows for a summer or year long research project. A Mudd engineering major could put a nice resume together with transportation engineering plus emphasis in sustainability. Realistic, observant ESFP will design that interstate cloverleaf with the least damage to wetlands, desert ecology or urban forests.

ESFJ will find a **Religious Studies** department and faculty at all of the five colleges. Together they form a cooperative program. Instead of spiritual direction or spiritual study, the major explores the history of people through moral beliefs established by humanism. ESFJ might also get a double major with **Organizational Studies** at Pitzer. So administrative positions with national or international religious institutes could be a realistic goal for this sociable type who supports tradition.

INFJ might go for the **Environmental Analysis** Program at Pomona. The curriculum includes field studies at the Bernard Biological Field Station where this individualistic type might direct their intense thinking on evolutionary biology. At Harvey Mudd creativity rules, and the major in **Mathematical and Computational Biology** has just enough mystery in it to attract this type. Graduate study in this major could lead to new health practices in occupational and physical therapies. At Claremont McKenna, the goal-driven INFJ can get prepared to find solutions to our most difficult societal problems such as terrorism and abusive, manipulative governments with the **Human Rights, Genocide and Holocaust** sequence.

INFP at Harvey Mudd can put their dreams to good use by majoring in Physics. The major concentrates on experimental or theoretical research and encourages students to follow their hearts. Pomona is the department chair for the **Theater** major offered by the five colleges. Theatre history, dramatic literature, design, technology and performance courses fill the curriculum. The introspective performance in dramaturgy and mime really speak to this type. A minor or major in **Linguistics and Cognitive Science** at Pomona connects right away to evolving career fields in psychology, computer science and sociology.

ENFP at Pomona College will find the big picture in the joint major **Philosophy, Politics and Economics**. It will stretch the imagination of all undergrads who bravely show up for the first day of class. The class Freedom, Markets and Well-Being hints at the conundrums hidden in the major. The **American Studies** major is a five colleges program. It points to the several cultures that dominate the national conversation and government policies. At Harvey Mudd, this type will want to take up the joint major **Chemistry and Biology**. Mudd research labs will be centered on discovering the narrow line where these two disciplines meet under the microscopes. It will fascinate ENFP.

ENFJ, often idealistic, could study **Science and Management** at Pitzer. They will relate to Pitzer's five core social values as a priority. At Claremont McKenna, ENFJ majoring in **Government** will bring their personal values to every course. Since this department promises a wide historical context, ENFJ could come across what happens when national corporations and U.S. agencies form policy together. It is a subject hardly ever covered by investigative journalism. Mudders in the **Chemistry** major can volunteer for the Science Bus to give a demonstration at local elementary schools. At Scripps College, this type could take the major in **Art Conservation**. With electives in chemistry and basic physics, ENFJ just might become an expert working for consulting firms brought in by our nation's museums.

INTJ wants a career field with room to grow for themselves and the discipline. The major **Neuroscience** offered at Pomona fits the bill. Twenty-first century research in this field is searching for the brain pathways that connect and direct our thoughts and behavior. At Claremont McKenna, this type would look at the **Economics and Engineering** program, a dual degree with Harvey Mudd. This five-year degree could challenge INTJ to connect the dots between courses in biology, chemistry, physics, economics, statistics, computer science and calculus. At Scripps, the visual resources library holds over 100,000 images available for those majoring in Art. This helps the INTJ find meaning in the hugeness of the visual culture explosion in 1998 and beyond.

INTP who wonders about personalities can go for the **Psychology** major at Pomona. The department compares theory with actual research on human personalities. As a result, this psychology degree offers an excellent stepping stone to professional schools in many fields. The **Philosophy** major benefits from Pitzer's own core values as a reference point for study and connection between philosophy and practical every day life. At Harvey Mudd, the degree in **Mathematics** reaches outside of the Claremont bubble and uses Matlab, a calculus sequence and series convergence. Praise for math Mudders who know that excellence lives across national boundaries and political trends.

ENTP often attracted to politics might recognize the importance of the **Russian and Eastern European Studies** at Pomona College. Those knowledgeable of the history and ways of the Slavic peoples are in demand. America and the western European governments in 2015 backed away from drawing lines that Russia's Putin would understand. ENTP can study this geographic area that was sleepy since WWII and now is explosive. **Computer Science Sequence** at Claremont McKenna is a strong set of courses that teach data analysis skills that this type can use in many fields. But you have to know that Harvey Mudd could also work for ENTP because the Humanities, Social Sciences and Arts program lives in the shadow of Mudd's optimism. ENTP is a number one optimist.

ENTJ will explore Pomona's **Science, Technology and Society** major for its practical use in business, politics or law. This type usually loves international subjects. At Claremont McKenna the **Legal Studies** might match up as a dual major between the two colleges and work well for the dynamic ENTJ personality. The major in **Italian/Italian Studies** is offered only at Scripps College. The major could lead to a number of interesting careers that combine creativity and consulting in the Italian culture. Think about the Vatican and the Pope's Jubilee of Mercy in 2016. The Vatican diplomatic corps, newsroom and massive archives are fascinating options for the typical ENTJ personality. A graduate study in Western Civilization might follow.

COLBY COLLEGE

4800 Mayflower Hill
Waterville, ME 04091
Website: www.colby.edu
Admissions Telephone: 800-723-3032
Undergraduates: 1,847; 868 Men, 979 Women

Physical Environment

Colby College is at the top of Mayflower hill that **overlooks the town** of Waterville. The industrial revolution and the banks of the Kennebec River combined together and formed the intellectual environment of Colby College that sits squarely in rural New England. The campus supports an **athletic**, energetic crowd, comfortable with the outdoors and snowboarding at nearby resorts. Undergrads love the Perkins Arboretum, Marston Bog and are **conscientious** about protecting natural environments. The dance majors like to practice on the lawn after the snow has melted and you can see the several shades of green grasses. In the springtime, the entire quad is covered with students looking to catch the beginning of a summer tan. On campus, red brick buildings line up neatly around the campus green which is also home to impromptu Frisbee throws and the like.

This traditional **Norman Rockwell** setting next to Waterville is a relief from steaming social media, CNN and Fox News. Downtown Waterville is a small city and students usually remain on campus. The unique BioMass electrical plant gets kudos from everyone. Colby stepped out here with a big vision. They use natural compost from surrounding woodlands to fuel their boilers. In this unique location with Maine's large stretches of forest land as a resource, the college is creative with its sustainable use. North America needs citizens and forward thinkers in each region to research practical initiatives like this. Although the adjective "practical" is still up in the air, Colby will be in the enviable position to host the conference and publish the findings a few decades from now.

Social Environment

Students here like Colby College and pretty much comfortably define the campus and its culture. Protestant work ethic and pride in the every day scene is strong. Colby College students are a smart, realistic bunch. They tackled some tough questions at their one-day student sponsored conference for national journalists in fall 2015. They asked about the role of reporters and technology posting news stories that cannot be verified in the "breaking news" moment. Ideas like this survive on this campus which open to exploring the negative impacts of social trending. The undergraduates are thoughtful **high achievers**. Relaxed and sporty, they study, study, study and play at least one club or varsity sport.

More than half of the undergrads come from outside New England although a sizeable group are "just outside of Boston." There is a metropolitan **perspective** on this rural campus as the college's Jitney that takes runs into Waterville for Starbucks refills. Faculty mentorship is okay with undergrads **taking academic risks**. Learning is **guided and structured** with the input by professors. **Student teamwork** is a favorite way to study. Study abroad is important for connection to the global nature of power within mega cities and dense population centers.

What about politics? Students at Colby are pretty clear about caring for the environment. They are tuned into the conflicts that come with many different ethnic views in America. They are mindful Millennials on a college campus within a very large American society of competing views. In Spring 2015 a small number of students protested police practices with unarmed black citizens. This sparked an anonymous social media comment to which the Colby President quickly replied that there was no place for bigotry and hatred at Colby.[17] Long active before this social media exchange, the college's own Multi-Faith Council seeks to bring faith and spirituality into campus discussions over division growing in America. The whole Colby College community works together with available resources and with present human understanding to reach for the possible.

Compatibility with Personality Types and Preferences

Colby College offers a consistent educational journey through four years of undergraduate collegiate studies. The faculty expects that students will gain "a broad acquaintance with human knowledge." The Colby College approach to learning seems sequential (S), orderly and often project-based or discovery-based. It is known as the Colby Plan. The administration keeps collaborative team work and principles in priority for all campus cultural events and academic studies. Colby undergraduates want to learn about the beliefs and values of cultures other than their own. Students expect sensitive, empathic views (F) toward world cultures and national ethnicities. They search for positive outcomes when the social tweets and news media run derogatory stories in the 24 hour news cycles.

The 360 Plan reflects Colby's broad presentation of American history and culture. The campus is moving toward a balanced representation of men and women undergraduate students. Colby College academic philosophy leans to objectivity maintaining distance from social currents trending on American liberal arts campuses today. Individual effort and belief is explored in contemporary culture. Government mandates and political pressure by nonprofits can be explored in classes here. American cultural missteps are studied in the context of the time and morals of the decade. The curriculum, academic practices and methods highlight the process of consensus, cohesion and majority agreement. The Colby community is optimistic that advocacy can become governance and regulation. Students want personal and career direction that builds American strengths and community health.

Now read below about one of the majors that MBTI® research shows people of your type have selected since the mid-20th century. After, refer to Chapter Five for the 50 or so majors that can help you prepare for careers your type has select-

PERSONALITY MATCH			
ISTJ	ISFJ	INFJ	INTJ
ISTP	ISFP	INFP	INTP
ESTP	ESFP	ENFP	ENTP
ESTJ	ESFJ	ENFJ	ENTJ

ed. Most importantly, remember that this college description is a suggestion for explora-tion, not a commanding order. You can be successful in any major at any college.

ISFJ usually is very organized. This type is perfect for research careers and would be a great curator in natural history and science museums. The major in **Science, Technology and Society** at Colby is a fabulous preparation for this important work that shows school children a different view of community than what they get on so-cial media. ISFJ is protective and will search for a caring answer to being human and swamped with technology in the 21st century.

ESFP often loves animals and a concentration in **Cell and Molecular Biology/ Biochemistry** could smooth the way into veterinary school. Optimistic, this type would be charged up to reintroduce endangered animals at animal reserves and zoos. Colby is right next to the Colby-Marston Bog. It is a great place to study animal habitats and this strong department at Colby is a major player in its preservation practices.

ESTP will like the looks of the concentration in **Financial Markets** at Colby. The department is balanced and innovative in this politically-charged discipline. The International System of Units uses a measurement called the Joule. It is used in all equations for energy. Colby undergrads get experience in finding and understanding neutral tools, like the Joule, to examine subjects like welfare, taxation and the gov-ernment interaction. On this campus feelings and emotions do not overlay economic studies.

ISFP often likes to help others. The concentration in **Neuroscience** at Colby College is a great preparation for addiction counselors and therapists. The disciplines of biology and psychology meet up in the course Biological Basis of Behavior. It is at the center of a huge research strand with the nervous system, including neuroscience in counseling. Colby's "four capillary DNA sequencer" is going to be a great tool for ISFP undergrads who are very observant and realistic.

ENFJ could go for a minor in **Human Development**. This type likes to work with regional groups like schools, churches, synagogues, businesses, etc. Colby is a great environment for this type to connect with students who are practical and fact-based. Imaginative ENFJ will get experience in speaking about their passions and the facts at the same time.

ESTJ will do well with a minor in **Mathematics** at Colby. They will probably become leaders on campus and beyond graduation. The department has both pure and applied math courses like Mathematical Reasoning. Faculty know it is critical for society to get better at using math. Here, undergrad mathematicians are expected to learn how to talk math to all citizens. ESTJ can pair this minor with a science major and head for national research labs.

ESFJ is a great cheerleader, and great at lowering tension and stress. Sympathetic ESFJs might look at an independent major in **Health Studies** combined with the **Economics** minor. The problem of health care in the United States is in the news every day now since national health care legislation passed in 2009. It has created problems with costs for the middle class and most Millennials dropping their health care plans. You go ESFJ, you just might reduce the tension created by government, big business and congress in the 21st century.

COLGATE UNIVERSITY

13 Oak Drive
Hamilton, NY 13346
Website: www.colgate.edu
Admission Telephone: 315-228-7401
Undergraduates: 2,875; 1,312 Men, 1,563 Women

Physical Environment

Colgate University is located in rural, central New York, in the small town of Hamilton. After students exit from I-90, they see farmlands, silos and cows. The Colgate campus is on a hill and the library seems like a castle surrounded by water and pasture. Weather-hardened students love the Trudy Fitness Center and the hikes up and down the hill. They make light-hearted videos of snow adventures on campus. Arriving first year students march up the hill led by faculty and the honor society with torches in hand. Four years later, graduates march down the hill with torches that are tossed into a huge bonfire. The senior class then celebrates one last time together. This campus community is **tight-knit**.

Students get an **international perspective** because over half of them study abroad. Financial awards apply to off-campus study trips and these students take advantage of it. Faculty-led research trips are important to Colgate's academic philosophy. The United States travel advisory warnings affect selection of location for the international trips. It is unfortunate that Eastern Europe and the Middle East are too unstable now since the withdrawal of Western European and American power in response to Islamic State, ISIS in mid-2015.

Social Environment

There are many outgoing, outspoken students on this campus which is an **incubator for leadership**, community service and cultural exploration. Colgate undergraduates juggle many activities while getting good grades. They are attracted to Colgate by the quality of **academic advising**. Faculty are involved in national research and may or may not hold current views on hot button subjects. Professors seem to represent a range of political thought on this campus. This is somewhat unusual at liberal arts colleges in America today. This variety in faculty perspective gives Colgate undergrads a heads up over the divisions within America.

At Colgate, **imaginative** students and those who prefer objectivity are equally attracted to sustainable practice for the environment. The new science complex is an incubator of ideas and faculty is open to new research directions. The astronomy and physics curriculum received national awards for its use of laboratories and technology. A professor and an undergrad, put together what looked like a few canisters and tubes and it recycled helium, never before done. Who knew helium was finite and got used up?

Campus enthusiasm tends toward optimism and responds to issues on social media. In rural America, students check in daily. In Fall 2014, several hundred students occupied the university admission hall citing intolerance on campus.[18] The administration and students developed a 21-point action plan in reply to those demands.[19] In the following two semesters, the student body answered with more leadership and more socials to match the administration's effort to protect students who feel marginalized.

There are about 200 clubs and about one-third of undergraduates join fraternities or sororities for more leadership positions within those chapters. Colgate students get together to have fun like the first ever annual gift exchange in 2015 at Christmas where they gave each other small stuff to survive finals. Undergraduates use Colgate as a lab in which to try out ideas that build cohesion. Football games are both athletic and social events where many friends cross paths.

Compatibility with Personality Types and Preferences

Colgate University is defined by and stands out because of its educational atmosphere. The relationship (F) between faculty advisors and students is central to the nature of learning on the campus. Here faculty encourage student originality, discovery and creativity. Administration practice at Colgate pushes independence and advising seems to build academic courage, so there is less need for learning centers and tutoring. Students select their studies and interests without an overlay of political activism by the administration. Faculty relies on students to precisely think and interpret what they experience. The Colgate education is characterized by this intensity, originality and modified risk-taking. In Fall 2015, the campus Center for Freedom and Western Civilization held a debate on campus about the Common Core required in the large majority of American public schools. The public was invited and heard from local high school faculty, retired and active. Colgate College practices freedom of expression for all, including average citizens speaking out on issues that affect our nation. It is an extension of the openness here. It leads to independent thinkers ready to function across national and global settings. It pushes each student to reach within and outside of Colgate, to build knowledge in their chosen major. In this way, the Colgate experience supports exploration (P) followed by analysis (T). Remember to ask your Colgate tour guide about the number the 13.

Now read below about one of the majors that MBTI® research shows people of your type have selected since the mid-20th century. After, refer to Chapter Five for the 50 or so majors that can help you prepare for careers your type has selected. Most importantly, remember that this college description is a suggestion for exploration, not a commanding order. You can be successful in any major at any college.

PERSONALITY MATCH			
ISTJ	ISFJ	INFJ	INTJ
ISTP	ISFP	INFP	INTP
ESTP	ESFP	ENFP	ENTP
ESTJ	ESFJ	ENFJ	ENTJ

ISFJ will enjoy the orderly nature of the study of **Linguistics**. The minor in this discipline at Colgate offers flexibility to study a specific language. Should ISFJ have East European heritage, family stories and genealogy will be valuable in reference to the spring 2015 Ukrainian crisis. Undergraduates will also write original computer programs to analyze verbal data. Meticulous attention to detail is an ISFJ specialty. A study of the military communications between the national Ukraine government and the Russian insurgent forces would be fascinating.

INFJ could select the **Peace and Conflict Studies** major at Colgate for its complexity. INFJ really goes for complicated subjects and this subject is a layered exploration of conflict and resolution. The major has includes research in three concentrations: collective violence, human security and international social justice. Working with others in harmony for the common good is ideal for this type.

INFP wants to follow their passions. If they are okay with math and passionate about natural habitats, the **Environmental Economics** major at Colgate is a happy find. Since our earthly environments are complicated, so are the best ways to understand them. This economics department chooses to lay a foundation for decision making with quantitative analysis. This major can keep INFP intensely busy reflecting on their values while juggling the limited supply of fixes for environmental problems.

ESFP is outgoing and will adapt to many kinds of entertainment in our communities. At Colgate, the major in **Theater** requires undergraduate patience and empathy to understand stories from Shakespeare to Christopher Durang of current day Broadway plays. The department has excellent design and stagecraft studies and this works for ESFP who is usually resourceful and spontaneous. Their playful side will mix nicely with performance careers.

ENFP might use the minor in **Philosophy and Religion** to get a solid background for a career in counseling. The study explores meaningful lives, natural law and conservative political thought. Speakers in Fall 2015 at Colgate's Center for Freedom and Western Civilization talked to these subjects. None of the scheduled speakers were marketing their own books as is the case at some very selective liberal arts colleges. Instead the speakers were bold thinkers of difficult subjects who covered threats to freedom in Russia, Ukraine and Iran. The Center is one of a few providing conservative intellectual content at American liberal arts campuses. Other speakers discussed government mandate and regulation in the Irish debt crisis and the Common Core requirements in American public schools.

ENTP in the **Natural Science** major will find that the faculty want undergrads to satisfy their scientific curiosity. Surely the emerging discipline of neuroscience which combines biology, chemistry and psychology will fascinate ENTP. Or how about the unusual combo of biology and geology in the **Freshwater Science** major? Either way, or another way, this type must have excitement and new stuff to think about.

ESFJ who has the math talent will like the **Applied Mathematics** minor at Colgate. Here, math is thought of as an art form. Okay this is unusual, but honestly, we think of math as a language. ESFJ is totally orderly and what can be more orderly than math? As a minor, undergrads can bypass the extreme abstraction of theoretical numbers. Instead, the ESFJ could use math formulas to bring order and meaning to huge data dumps by Google and Amazon.

ENFJ might consider the **Writing and Rhetoric** minor at Colgate University. Their gift of intuition will step up as they study the latest rhetoric offered up by American news and social media. Overwhelming to most citizens with a daily responsibility for work and family, ENFJ has Colgate support to investigate media visuals and sound bites. Trouble spots in Eastern Europe, Turkey and Greece just might catch the attention of this persuasive type, especially if they are headed for an international organization.

ENTJ who is willing to drive hours to see the northern lights might go for the **Astrogeophysics** major at Colgate. Logic in math, physics, geology and chemistry required by this major will explain the lights for sure. ENTJ will then move on to their long-range questions. Could it be about scientific exploration if America gets back to the moon in the second half of this century? *Star Wars: The Force Awakens* is a fave.

COLLEGE OF CHARLESTON

66 George Street
Charleston, SC 29424-0001
Website: www.cofc.edu
Admissions Telephone: 843-953-5670
Undergraduates: 10,440; 3,886 Men, 6,554 Women

Physical Environment

The College of Charleston is in the heart of historic downtown Charleston. It's within walking distance of 19th century palatial southern homes. The historic row of houses called "the Battery," overlook the sea and Fort Sumter in the distance. College of Charleston started as an independent college in 1770. It has long since been a public institution with all the bells and whistles on its very tight campus.

The center of campus is Randolph Hall while the Cato Center for the Arts has entire floors devoted to dance/theater, photography, visual art, music and exhibiting space. The School of Sciences and Mathematics wraps around a courtyard, so typical of historic Charleston. This urban campus is mixed in with city streets of historic homes and guided tours of visiting tourists are a common sight. It is difficult to know if you are on or off campus. COC also includes historic **Dixie Plantation**, a national archeological treasure continuously occupied for centuries before and after European settlements. Now it is a biological wildlife center just 17 miles distant from main campus. The college has a commitment to **historical preservation** and is bringing back the pre-industrial ways of simply and naturally caring for the wetland. Resources like the Grice Marine Laboratory point to practical innovation and commitment that stays so informed of our past.

A **state of the art library** offers many areas in which to study quietly or with others. The nearby Medical University of South Carolina helps undergrads keep their visions for careers in the sciences, research or medical school. Even though admission requirements are higher for out-of-state students, students flock to College of Charleston, charmed by the city's history and attracted to the **strong sciences, business and performing arts**. The nearby open air market delights visitors and students with ethnic Gullah basket weavers stringing sweet-grass into pleasing patterns. Similar to living museums like Colonial Williamsburg, downtown Charleston presents a slice of the 19th century American experience.

Social Environment

The undergraduate students are mostly from South Carolina with others from the southeastern states. Located on the Atlantic seaboard, they compete in the Colonial Athletic Association primarily with other mid-sized universities. The 2012 and 2013 coed sailing teams won best overall collegiate team in the nation. Campus dress is summer casual, taking advantage of the great weather most of the year. The social life is **light-hearted** and leans toward the arts.

Volunteer efforts support well known groups like Habitat for Humanity. The always rockin', never stoppin' **Dance Marathon** captures the hearts of the students who raise thousands of dollars each year for the families of medically at-risk children in the hospital near campus. The college has over 200 extracurricular clubs. They range from the campus democrats and republicans to crew and fencing on stage for theater performance plus the Anime Association. Students typically are focused on **careers** and their studies, however the confederate flag controversy in South Carolina brought out a protest against the Board of Trustees choice for new president in Spring 2014. Undergraduates objected to his support of the historical confederate flag.

Students who like to socialize and study with others do well at this campus. Most keep the call of Charleston's tourist atmosphere on low burner, focusing instead on socializing with each other on campus. **Imaginative** students who are future-oriented will enjoy the grounding in history, tradition and architecture. COC is forward-looking and practical at the same time. They put these two together well in how they develop undergraduate majors and minors. All undergraduates here are welcomed by the city's artistic and professional leaders. There is plenty of room for talented students in the city-wide performing arts.

Compatibility with Personality Types and Preferences

College of Charleston is remarkable for its emphasis on the cultural arts and its location. The impact of the port and the city's historic origination in the 1600s has seeped into the philosophy of the administration and faculty. The curriculum offers an element of practicality (S) that reflects today's specialized careers and the college's location on the Atlantic coast. Students attend courses taught by a faculty that is well informed of the American economy and entrepreneurial markets. The performing arts curriculum highlights the city's international reputation for beauty, charm and entertainments. At College of Charleston undergraduate students in the arts support and participate in the city's well known festivals like Spoleto as performers and stage managers. It provides that realistic thread that undergraduates here like so well. The port of Charleston is the background for the unusual, practical study in global logistics. Incoming freighters, offloading goods that must travel to America's heartland, bring the subject of logistics alive. The international port has also influenced the development of the solid international business school. The college archives proudly possess rare Jewish documents from the pre-colonial period. This campus wisely reaches to the past for academic and cultural excellence. Yet it is very obvious that academic studies include original, creative, risk-taking studies.

Now read below about one of the majors that MBTI® research shows people of your type have selected since the mid-20th century. After, refer to Chapter Five for the 50 or so majors that can help you prepare for careers your type has selected. Most importantly, remember that this college description is a suggestion for exploration, not a commanding order. You can be successful in any major at any college.

PERSONALITY MATCH			
ISTJ	ISFJ	INFJ	INTJ
ISTP	ISFP	INFP	INTP
ESTP	ESFP	ENFP	ENTP
ESTJ	ESFJ	ENFJ	ENTJ

INFJ will be at the top of their game in the business field when there is a lot of one-on-one conversation. The **Arts Management** major prepares undergrads for a career that really must focus on gaining support for the arts. INFJs are comfortable to the arts and will bring their personal stamp to original exhibits in regional and local museums. They are creative thinkers and will bring that to local Charleston internships and historic events in this destination city. COC requires five financial courses in this major which is great preparation for idealistic INFJ.

INTJ likes the responsibility and demands of leadership. They usually go for professional positions. The major in **Geology** at College of Charleston has one of the few national centers that give advice and preparation for environmental disasters. Their work is directed at the low country tidal lands off the coast of South Carolina. The department is heavy into undergraduate research through field experiences around the globe too. Many studies are global, especially in oceanography.

ISTJ will like the realistic course work in the **Accounting** major at COC. ISTJs love it all: accuracy, precision and diligence. With post graduate study, they could go on for certifications that look great on resumes. Certified public accountant, certified internal auditor or certified fraud examiner are great goals for this serious type.

ISFP is caring all of the time and cautious some of the time. They want to be out and about, doing work that requires attention to detail. The major in **Marine Biology** will take advantage of the Grice Marine laboratory, a national and state resource. The Atlantic Ocean and coastal low lands are a free laboratory that very few campuses can offer. Graduates of this major go on to become national and state resources themselves with advanced degrees.

ESTP sees what needs to be done to finish a project on time. They are a good bet for the **Global Logistics and Transportation** minor at College of Charleston. ESTPs can elect to declare this concentration within the business degree. High stakes decisions about moving company products across the globe work for this type who likes action to spice up their day. The port of Charleston is a natural for hanging out and learning about intermodal transport. Its all about logistics, so the goods have to transfer off the freighters onto other ships, rail or truck all within the scheduled time.

ESFP is good at positions in the service industry. The major in **Hospitality and Tourism Management** in Charleston is a natural for the ESFPs. Not too many liberal arts colleges offer it. But everyone knows that there are plenty of jobs around the country for at sports arenas, convention centers, Mardi Gras, Marriotts and Hiltons. ESFP is a natural at putting together good events because they are playful themselves. Sure enough, the COC business department is a member of the Walt Disney World internship programs.

ENTP wakes up thinking about the future. This creative type will like the futuristic focus in the major **Historic Preservation and Community Planning**. The College of Charleston combines these two in a strong, practical curriculum. ENTPs are strategic planners with their sharp vision and willingness to take risks. They can also be good at persuasion while they haggle over tight city funds needed for preservation. The downtown historic district of Charleston is a dream-come-true internship for this type and this major.

ESTJ is an ideal personality to pursue the new major in **Data Science**. In the last few years, Google, Twitter and Amazon have collected tons of information about us.

Together in one gigantic computer cloud storage, it is always in demand. But to actually use it, businesses have to "mine the data." Coming along as an afterthought are the social and natural sciences that have an interest in using the data for other reasons beyond selling. ESTJs are a good fit for this major and being organizational wizards they might look at a career with national defense and protecting us from terrorism. After all, the Citadel is just next door.

COLLEGE OF WOOSTER

Office of Admission
Wooster, OH 44691
Website: www.wooster.edu
Admissions Telephone: 330-263-2322
Undergraduates: 2,066; 926 Men, 1,140 Women

Physical Environment

The compact College of Wooster campus is surrounded by Victorian homes and small convenience stores used by the students once in a while. Downtown Wooster, with its 1970s mix of dated storefronts and businesses, is a contrast to the carefully designed campus upgrades of the last ten years. The COW landscape has massive trees, green lawns and **practical 1900s collegiate architecture**. The newly renovated Kauke Hall is the best bet for a meeting place with lounges and a coffee shop. With Kauke classrooms that remind you of lounges Wooster students linger for **discussions** after class. Kauke is the **intellectual meeting place** where topics for the Independent Study can start and develop. The new Scott Center for recreation is clever, cheery and classy. Its architecture of walled glass and light balances the heavier stone foundations of this campus. Students pretty much stay on campus with these great spaces. There are few places within an hour's drive that could compete. Undergrads find substitutes for the cafeteria trays of yesteryear and still barrel down the short hill near Bornhuetter Hall after a heavy snow dump.

Northeasterners find Wooster familiar. The new science facility, scheduled to break ground in summer 2016, looks a lot like those at liberal arts colleges in New England. The Underground dance club and bar, below the Kittridge dining Hall, is a favorite of all classes and host to the wry humor often in place on this campus. The Wooster chapel is also an underground structure. Its mid-century concrete architecture juts up out of the ground. Its a great perch to find family in the crowd below during convocation and other events. The Office of Interfaith Campus Ministries defines spirituality as a "balance of stretching and settling." Humor indeed does accompany irony here. COW has been recruiting overseas undergraduate students for decades and has a solid alumni network in third world countries.

Social Environment

The College of Wooster is for **individualistic** thinkers who want to look closely at where they will fit in the world after graduation. They each march to their own drumbeat. They want to be contributors and possibly make a difference. They are **heartfelt** and ready to discuss troubles in America today. Competition in class is pretty much absent because professors mentor each student individually through Wooster's signature program, the **Independent Study Program**. They become **resolute** in their IS topics over three semesters getting lots of input from their IS advisor. At the end, they start writing and it is pretty much a solo effort. Since most IS papers are over 100 pages of research, hypothesis and conclusions, **IS Monday** in January is a big relief when the paper is turned in. By the fourth year, COW undergrads know how to **write very well**.

Look for **humor** on this campus. How about the college's Fossil of the Week? The well known Atrypa brachiopod attached to a trepostome bryozoan edged out the competition for this prestigious award during the third week of January 2016. Undergraduates here tend to gather and socialize by their interests. **Music** is a big part of socializing. They make their own music in the dorm lounges or when they play in the ensembles, orchestras and choirs on this small campus. But socially, they really just like to get together and belong. The Greek system operates at the local level and serves up Saturday night gigs as an alternative or along with the Underground. All are invited and many attend sometime during their four years.

A lot of graduates in the physical sciences, political science and history go on to PhD studies. Others might step out their first year with a service job and take time to think over their next decision. Before 2006, this campus admitted an even balance of men and women undergraduates in each class. With the new president arriving in summer 2016, COW just might return to this healthy ratio.

Compatibility with Personality Types and Preferences

College freshman line up on the steps of Kauke Hall on the first day as curious students, unusually independent folks who were probably anonymous in high school. At Wooster, they slowly move into the educational limelight. After graduation, they go on to careers with optimism and confidence. They are all about the future. Wooster practices that successful educational mix of freedom (P) and expectation. It's a delicate balance that professors have fine-tuned. To some it might seem like indifference, but academic philosophy here is about patience. Students discover that the first years are open, light and exploratory. But it changes up during the last two years, when facts and conclusions are expected and narrowly defined (J) in the form of Wooster's superior independent study requirements.

Faculty, programs and policies are in a continuous exploration (N) of foundational knowledge. The sciences are over the top on this campus. In particular, the geology department has faculty of worldwide influence. Outside of the physical sciences, Wooster looks to new avenues of knowledge through international settings, possibly the heritage of the college's excellent third world outreach. The best bet for studies addressing pressing American issues will be in the Political Science department and Urban studies. Students here do not expect administrators to settle issues popping up on the social media feeds, but they do expect their studies to connect with solutions for America in some way. Wooster's educational climate runs on solid optimism and accountability for the world community (F). Faculty place great faith in the individual and society.

Now read below about one of the majors that MBTI® research shows people of your type have selected since the mid-20th century. After, refer

PERSONALITY MATCH

ISTJ	ISFJ	INFJ	INTJ
ISTP	ISFP	INFP	INTP
ESTP	ESFP	ENFP	ENTP
ESTJ	ESFJ	ENFJ	ENTJ

to Chapter Five for the 50 or so majors that can help you prepare for careers your type has selected. Most importantly, remember that this college description is a suggestion for exploration, not a commanding order. You can be successful in any major at any college.

ENFP could find it hard to declare a major because so many subjects interest them. **Geology** is good for this type because it is a very wide field. From physics to policy, ENFPs can decide where they want to work—in the field collecting dirt samples or in Congress advocating for the environment. The major at Wooster is open and laid back in that students are left to find their passion without too much direction from the faculty. Once they make the decision, though, it is time to step up their game and Wooster has the mechanisms in place to rein in freewheeling ENFP. On the academic move, graduates might end up on the Brooks McCall gathering samples at the epicenter of the Gulf oil spill, coring mud tubes in the Bering Sea for graduate study or teaching Geology 100 at community college.

ISFP is another freewheeling type and they quietly insist on being independent. This characteristic works very well in the **Theatre and Dance** track at the Woo. On this formative campus, art quickly translates to the written text in playwriting and performance. Its not surprising that Wooster took regional honors in 2014 and was selected to perform *Women of Ciudad Juarez* at the Kennedy Center in DC. The play has toured in the US and Canada at 14 locations. The physical nature of this major is perfect for ISFPs who likes performance and craftsmanship.

ESFP loves to entertain and the major in **Music** at COW would be good for any freshmen with high school musical experience. Undergrads can concentrate in performance, theory/composition or history/literature. The music therapy and music education majors would let fun loving ESFPs bring a light heart into their world of work. There are five ensembles, two orchestras, three choirs and one opera workshop at the small liberal arts college.

ISFJ could easily move into careers in the health sciences. But their day-to-day job would have to be about helping folks possibly in a clinical or medical setting. Professors give strong guidance in the **Biology** laboratories that help each student to find their passion in the field. Experimental design and hypothesis testing gets fit into the students interests through the Wooster independent study. This teaches ISFJ, not always happy with the unknown, to be creative in a step-by-step way.

ESFJ really shines in traditional settings like hospitals or schools. Wooster's degree in **Music Therapy** is a fit for this caring type. Woo hoo for Wooster since few colleges offer this major. ESFJ will smile at the thought of joining a professional group of helpers. Luckily, the Cleveland Music Therapy Consortium and American Music Therapy Association is just a car ride away. These national organizations set guidelines for service delivery that ESFJ will want and need in a therapy career.

ISTJ will go for the **Business Economics** major at Wooster because the faculty is right on top of complex financial environments. That is why Wooster is in a small group of colleges invited to compete in the Simon Graduate School of Business case study competition for undergraduates. It is a pretty select group of colleges that receive this invitation for their undergraduate majors. ISTJ can substitute two math courses for two in quantitative analysis, a particular strength of this type.

INTP is loving computers and we are not talking about visual social media feeds pushed onto iPhone. Woo's **Computer Science** major or minor is about tackling problems from a distance. INTPs like a good puzzle to solve. At Wooster, this major is located within the math department which bumps up the curriculum for this powerhouse concentrator. INTPs can basically be devoted armchair sport fans and smile at the 2016 Wooster Independent Study on Analysis of Game Theory and Baseball.

ENTP would understand a minor in **Film Studies** if you could show them directly how video changes culture. ENTP is really good at analyzing information for the sometimes hidden messages. You can bet their Independent Study will connect film studies with their major. Plus we know that their major could be in just about any discipline at COW since so many subjects interest this type.

INFP knows that **English** can be a complicated subject. How else do students show that they understand what Faulkner's *The Sound and The Fury* is about? In this department, undergrads can study and write about reflections from any perspective. They can focus on an author, an issue or a literary form like the short story. Now if they choose the short story, they must look at Flannery O'Conner, another powerful American writer of the 20th century who wrote of evil and mercy.

ENFJ will notice the complicated world of speech and language disorders. The degree in **Communication Sciences and Disorders** gets students prepared for the required graduate studies. ENFJ will study language evolution, human development and the cause of disorders. This type will naturally look to the emotional causes of speech disorders too.

INFJ likes to find new ways to help people. With the government health insurance plans going up in costs every year, alternative health care is getting more attention. Independent INFJ can see the wisdom in private, individual effort over state and federal programs. Wooster's degree in **Chemistry** with the impressive Independent Study program could be the starter soup for a local health movement in middle Ohio. INFJ with the major in chemistry or another science will want their career to benefit society and that may be as an employee of a health cooperative independent of the government.

COLUMBIA UNIVERSITY

212 Hamilton Hall MC 2807
1130 Amsterdam Avenue
New York, NY 10027
Website: www.columbia.edu
Admission Telephone: 212-854-2521
Undergraduates: 8,613: 4,536 Men, 4,077 Women
Graduate Students: 14,713

Physical Environment

Founded in 1754, Columbia University is located in **Upper Manhattan**, a lively and desirable section of world class New York City. With the energy and heavy traffic just outside their classroom windows, students carve out their favorite hangouts and their academic passions with delight. They develop **city-smarts** while walking the streets with a buddy at night. The ethnic restaurants, bookshops, theater, art, museums, music and the club scenes define different neighborhoods in the city. Columbia undergrads will visit them all. The university has 22 schools most of which offer only graduate level degrees. However, Columbia College has the liberal arts curriculum for undergraduates and the Fu Engineering and Applied Science School has undergraduate degrees also. Barnard College, the liberal arts college for undergraduate women, offers joint degrees, open courses and cross registration with all the undergraduate students at Columbia University.

High school students on tour will hear about the Manhattanville Project. The first buildings will be opened in late 2016. In the west Harlem neighborhood, the project will be for academic and residential use. Since the main campus is hemmed in by towering commercial real estate, this off campus 17-acre site will be open to university students and the public also. Within a decade, its name might be the Manhattanville neighborhood.

Housing is guaranteed for all freshman and students who accept the dorm assignment each following year. About 95 percent of students live in school-sponsored housing. There are Greek brownstones residences for those in sororities and fraternities. There are living and learning communities with faculty families, after-hours discussion and late evening imagination run wild. Undergraduates who like the **relentless intensity** of the city thrive on this campus. But most are attracted by the over-the-top resources within the university itself. The Northwest Corner building alone has **21 national research laboratories** and 250 faculty and students that find themselves daily in its **academic hub**.

Social Environment

New York City attracts people from all over the world and Columbia University reflects it. Students here want to learn in a global context. They want to fill their toolbox with international emerging ideas. These undergraduates are busy, motivated and already have their next goal lined up. They are **incredibly focused and ambitious**. However, despite the competition, students here are still friendly and willing to collaborate.

Each student arrives with a resume already filled with accomplishment. It makes for **searching conversation** on campus. Some of these conversations happen on the steps in front of Low Library. Social life is active during freshmen first days because each of the extracurricular clubs, fraternities and sororities are trying to gain new members. After these first weeks, many students start to go off campus with their new, tight group of a few friends. Social life here usually moves around **intellectual curiosity**. With just the call of a cab or quick walk to the subway, undergrads can haunt art galleries, music and theater performances offering trendy international culture. Humor wedges into campus life through the Varsity show. It is a Columbia tradition that makes fun of the administration in a campus satire. Most student clubs are academic on this campus, although anime and culinary clubs found their way into the mix.

Columbia students are **idea-driven**, searching for possibilities. They tend to come from very well-educated families with successful backgrounds. They have high expectations. All, including the want-to-be engineers, complete the Core curriculum. Students work with non-profit centers, design intranets for inner city public schools, learn about playground engineering and come to know about the New York neighborhoods. They have less time for demonstrations for a cause that put a halt to their studies over a weekend. Yet in 2014-15, the university had to respond to a campus sexual assault case stemming from undergraduate sexual behavior beyond the classroom walls. The accusation and denial of sexual assault between the two undergraduates was covered in the national news media. The Obama administration demands that universities and colleges investigate complaints of sexual assault with Title IX. Columbia investigated, held a hearing and cleared the accused of responsibility. It has prompted national attention to the legality of universities handling these cases.[20]

Compatibility with Personality Types and Preferences

Columbia University is the place for educational study (P) without limits. Undergraduate students are expected and expect to conduct research in the national labs. This goes hand-in-hand with teaching laboratories where students see (S) and learn in a place that is rarely constrained by budgets. Beyond seeing and learning, Columbia faculty predict that undergraduates will be generate discovery in their respective fields. It is a tall order and students are precisely (J) taught to develop their reasoning (T) patterns of analysis.

The faculty and administration is equally concerned with developing the moral standard (F) and aggressively inserts that perspective within their curriculum. The Core is a series of required studies for entering students that delves into the great books and texts of western civilization as well as fundamental scientific laws. Students are expected to develop a coherent belief system on the human condition and carry that forward in their future careers (N). Columbia may be remarkable in that it does not seem to actively push moral relativism. That may be why undergrads here are intent on their studies and shy away, if possible, from current day social trends and causes. Columbia University actively defines and completes part of the puzzle that is New York City.

Now read below about one of the majors that MBTI® research shows people of your type have selected since the mid-20th century. After, refer to Chapter Five for the 50 or so majors that can help you prepare for careers your type has selected. Most importantly, remember that this college description is a suggestion for exploration, not a commanding order. You can be successful in any major at any college.

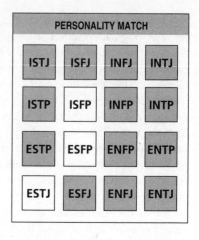

INFP will find the **Drama and Theater Arts** at Columbia abstract and analytic. The department offers courses in the crafts of acting, directing, play writing and staging. Theater of Nazi Germany is studied for the value it brings according to the faculty philosophy. American Theater is studied in the only course American Drama in the 1990s. All students will complete a project in their specialty or a written thesis. This works for INFP who writes expressing their values and views.

INFJ and imagination go together. The department in **Linguistics** at Columbia hasn't found a language they didn't like but faculty think that that 90 percent of the spoken languages might be lost by the end of this century. They really like under-grads to study a specific language, even hashtag and Tumblr on the internet. The course in Hungarian Descriptive Grammar would go nicely with a major in political science. INFJ is powerhouse at research and understanding complicated concepts. With a few days of effort, they will find a native Hungarian speaker in NYC where 300 or more foreign languages are spoken. The need for experts in Eastern European culture is great since Russia's Putin successfully invaded the Ukraine.

INTJ is going to find much that suits their learning style at Columbia. This type likes flexible ideas, far out concepts and freedom to mix and match with intensity. The concentration in **Financial Engineering** fits them well. Emerging mathematical theory and methods are developed at the Fu School of Engineering through research. INTJ who goes after the BS in Operations Research and this concentration will be right in the middle of it. Okay, we have to caution, it will only be after they master the calculus, differential equations, probability and statistics. INTJs who are private and skeptical by nature may benefit from the four-year advising system at Columbia.

ISTP will find a lot of facts to absorb in the **Chemical Engineering** degree. This type loves to build up their own knowledge base with factual data. Once they find a technical problem they, like faculty, will be open to check it out. ISTP will stay late in Northwest Building then be surprised to see the sun pop through the windows and their own consciousness. Engineering studies are only hemmed in by physical reality so advising is all about pushing the edges of the known reality. This demanding school is open to undergraduates who can declare the major. Before that students must prove they are able to handle the math and late nights.

ISTJ relates well to the direct nature of electricity—it is either on or off. The **Electrical Engineering** at Columbia is all about predictability and practicality.

Undergrad summer research is eye-popping. Always realistic, ISTJ doesn't check daily Twitter feeds, but they know that Google, Amazon, Microsoft and Samsung are in serious need of more internet bandwidth. The outstanding advising during all four years at Fu School will settle ISTJ toward their own interests. Maybe it will be fixing old network flaws captured by hackers. After all, on the internet words are data bits of 1 and 2. The Core liberal arts curriculum at Columbia will strike this type as being off the grid.

ISFJ likes to be in the middle of the facts, weaving a ball of string to be unraveled and used later. The major in **Ecology, Evolution and Environmental Biology** might just work. The course Saga of Life which sounds like a Disney attraction actually tries to tie together evolution with the physical sciences, social sciences and humanities. In 2004, the International Theological Commission, headed by Pope Benedict, held that science, not theology, must resolve the debate on evolution. Columbia University is working on it.

INTP graduating high school may already know about the history of **Jazz**. The music bounces around with random musical note and INTP likes the random data. This power thinker can listen to jazz recordings and with time pick up on the hidden emotions that travel the musical phrases. Leave it to the INTP to find patterns in the freewheeling instrumental play. The study of jazz is interdisciplinary and happily interfaces with all majors. Jazz is like the musicians who play it—intellectual, original, marching to their own drummer. This is the INTP. New Orleans is the destination for a summer internships—on the sidewalks with pick-up musicians whose family background wanders back to Son House, Robert Johnson or W.C. Handy. Or maybe more local with Diane Shuur.

ESTP wants lively action and New York City will deliver. This type loves to kibitz and they will scavenge the city for information on their research topic in **Urban Studies**. It will be the ESTP who attracts the curiosity of department professors to accept a two-semester project in Detroit. For the most part, the department would like this requirement to be about New York City. Yet as one of America's star academic institutions, the faculty might consider going outside of their immediate neighborhood. America has rich urban centers like New Orleans, Detroit and Los Angeles that have middle continental and Pacific Basin histories of intellectual wealth.

ENFP is such an emotional soul. The **Creative Writing** major is a study that might help them channel those emotions. This major studies literary masterpieces from the writers' point of view. Some of the most amazing written pieces find their way to the printed page, or iPad, through the short story. Authors like Flannery O'Conner cover human evil and God's forgiveness under layers of words like geranium, turkey and revelation. Quick reads, but not simple reads. The advisor will be important for this type. Personal relationships are highly valued by ENFPs. They look to their advisor to be an anchor for the chaotic NYC energy, as well as their own.

ENTP will like the **Computer Science** major since it has a lot of cool electives in the upper division courses. What will ENTP select for electives: artificial intelligence, computer communications, data bases? This adaptable, creative type is open to dabble in each of these and the others. Summer symposium topics will help narrow down the choice. And there is no reason why summer can't be fun too. How about a study of web-crawling techniques through anime graphics to look forward into the world of military space applications?

ESFJ doesn't often go for the pure sciences but **Operations Research** at the Fu School of Engineering has fabulous adaptability to apply to the health sciences. This type wants to make life better for people inside big organizations like professional researchers in medical technology. At the Fu School there are only two requirements for this degree: ability and commitment.

ENFJ is dead on as a speaker when armed with knowledge. The major in **Business Management** is definitely going to provide ENFJ with knowledge of large corporations. But this type will want more than the numbers. The department definitely looks at how psychology and sociology influence finance, marketing and management. This really works for ENFJs who are fine-tuned to relating with their customers. This type also wants their advisor to help with the tough work of defining career goals in a data and numbers kind of career field.

ENTJ is a leader. They can't avoid giving direction. The degree in **Engineering Management Systems** is about leadership that leads to results. The curriculum covers the concepts of risk and how to recognize it. Better yet, it shows ENTJ how to put numbers and formulas onto the levels of risk for current manufacturing decisions. Graduates of this major make tough decisions in worldwide construction and manufacturing. The faculty at Fu School of Engineering really specialize in operations research. Surprises, like China's decision to slow down economic growth, can fit right into the numbers formulas. This is an ENTJ dream major.

CONNECTICUT COLLEGE

270 Mohegan Avenue
New London, CT 06320-4196
Website: www.conncoll.edu
Admissions Telephone: 860-439-2200
Undergraduates: 1,992; 722 Men, 1,270 Women

Physical Environment

When you arrive at Connecticut College, you walk up the hill and overlook the Thames River in Connecticut. It is eye-popping pretty. The river is a rich biological resource for undergraduate students and central to all of the science departments and central to research in the 13 laboratories on this campus. The **Science Center** is a state-of-the-art facility that takes advantage of the surrounding **marine ecology**. Tucked between highways, residential neighborhoods and the United States Coast Guard Academy, undergrads take their rented Zip cars or the weekly shuttle to nearby big box stores, but for the most part stay on campus. The classic architecture of formal **gray-stone buildings** is comfortable for **traditional, studious** individuals who go for this charming, Harry Potter-like environment.

The **Arboretum on campus** is used for teaching and research. Along with the river inlets and estuaries, it points undergraduate studies toward nature. The college has an established plant collection and an Herbarium used for national research. Four specialized Centers have programs and certificates that combine with undergraduate majors. The Ammerman Center sponsors internships and colloquia that tie the arts and technology together. The Study Away program looks for the greatest academic benefit and is individually approved by advisors. Each activity and program on this campus is very well managed for the advantage and quality of study it can offer.

Social Environment

Conn College has many students that come from "just outside Boston," and if not that, then from Fairfield County, Manhattan or New Jersey. They are smart **thinkers**, outgoing and **realistically aware**. Undergrads take advantage of the rich programming within 23 residential halls. Each dorm has faculty and students in the **Residential Education Fellows** program to create an identity for each house. **Student planning** and leadership is key input to the nature the residential experience here. In Spring 2015 students joined faculty in a campus sponsored discussion of racist graffiti and student petition to condemn a professor over his position in the Israeli Palestine conflict.[21] The college president immediately called for this debate, cancelling classes for the day to assure all voices were heard.

Academic study is for goal-oriented knowledge. Some students gain research skills as assistants to professors in the sciences. Undergrads expect to become **accomplished** professionals after graduation. The administration supports this with funded internships that focus on career-enhancing life skills. It is unique and gives Conn College grads a heads up on sophisticated New York metropolitan enterprises and those along the northeastern seaboard. Athletics and fitness are closely tied. Division III basketball games bring in the alumni, fellow students and faculty. There are fourteen club sport teams and 75 percent of the undergraduates get involved with some athletic activity. Conn College is a great fit for those who plan ahead, are willing to step up to **demanding classes** and want their degree to be relevant to their future.

Compatibility with Personality Types and Preferences

Connecticut College very much delivers an atmosphere that appreciates and utilizes a student's logical thinking (T). On this campus, undergraduate academic success is encouraged and applauded. By investing in emerging technology and facilities, the college honors those who bring a futuristic, intuitive (N) approach to their learning. Anticipation and application work well here and, together, they direct students toward problem-solving research. Four Interdisciplinary Centers really expand the campus boundaries with nearby resources and adjunct faculty, lectures, etc. They also offer certificates to students with specialized (J) in-depth learning in several disciplines. The excellent science foundations on this campus are balanced by the Centers in public policy, environment, international study and art/technology.

Graduates find themselves prepared to enter America's business and academic institutions. Academic philosophy supports American concepts that have held up in the nation for over 200 years. The presence of the U.S. Coast Guard is a sobering reminder of the dangers for nations that do not remain inherently strong. Connecticut College is exceptional in keeping its eye on the American prize.

Now read below about one of the majors that MBTI® research shows people of your type have selected since the mid-20th century. After, refer to Chapter Five for the 50 or so majors that can help you prepare for careers your type has selected. Most importantly, remember that this college description is a suggestion for exploration, not a commanding order. You can be successful in any major at any college.

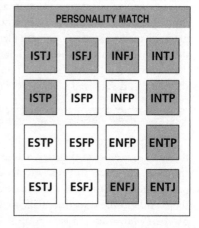

INTJ will love the solid looks of this campus. The **Environmental Studies** major has the science track that will suit their rational style. The department is right in tune with their location on the Thames river estuary, and INTJ will soon understand the importance of dredging and river bottoms. Conn College's hydraulic flume models river hydrodynamics and it could fascinate this type. INTJ's inner vision will be wide enough to look outside of the Thames, perhaps to the Mississippi river delta for similar research findings for their senior level seminar.

ENTP loves the wide-ranging, lively discussions at Conn College. The major in **Government** has a good grounding for this type. American Political Thought is a junior level course that studies the 1970s move toward self-importance and how it changed our national politics of the WWII era. At Conn College, faculty is right on top of current political trends that are once again changing the very nature of American government.

INFJ can weave their values together through academic study at Conn College. The major **Religious Studies** opens the door to faiths across the globe. The department tailors the curriculum based on individual student interest. It will include exploration of sects, traditions and religious practices. Insightful INFJ might select a topic like the mass expulsion and genocide of Christians from nations across the middle east. This directed type of study works for them.

INTP has a skeptical nature that is careful about taking positions. The study of **Economics** at Conn College has this same skeptical filter. Learning is pretty much around thinking by analysis and testing hypotheses. INTP can take honors study in junior year and do original research on one of the puzzles that keep their mind busy. Maybe how DirectTV and cable have competed and survived in the corporate world.

ISTP will love Conn College's research equipment and belief in original, hands-on studies. The science division's professional machine shop, electron microscopy suite and tissue culture rooms are a dream for this tinkering type. ISTPs might also tinker with visualizing sound or other visuals that come with a major in physics at Conn College. A certificate from the **Arts and Technology** at the Ammerman Center might push them to explore subjects they sometimes stay away from.

ENFJ with their great empathy will see the sense of neuroscience, an exciting research focus. The sciences are so strong on this campus. ENFJ should look at the **Behavioral Neuroscience** major which mixes up course work between biology, psychology and chemistry. The study of emotions will be front and center as the brain floods our nervous system chemically with anger, joy, shame, interest, fear, guilt, surprise and distress. Hopefully, not all at once.

ISTJ brings the facts and complete recall to roaming classroom discussions. It helps when your study is complex like the layers of Russian society. The major in **Slavic Studies**, not typically offered at liberal arts colleges, could be preparation for law school or a government career. This small department closely mentors undergrads who will learn advanced Russian. Study abroad in Russia under the direction of the faculty would be a worthy experience for their graduate resumes.

ISFJ is a natural at creating pleasing living spaces. They are sensitive souls and know the importance of **Architectural Studies** that speak to us as individuals. They have rich personal memories of friends and family usually connected to specific places or times. It is an advantage in the field of design, urban planning or historic preservation. Conn College faculty really go out to connect their undergrads with firms in NYC and that is good for this realistic type.

ENTJ can be direct, challenging and decisive. The unusual major in **Botany** is a possibility for that reason. Strategic ENTJ can see how the coastal estuaries and the scanning electron microscopes on campus make for engaging study. With a foundation in botany and graduate study in entomology, otherwise known as the world of insects, great professional careers open up. The many vacancies in this much-needed field fit right into ENTJ decisive strategies.

DARTMOUTH COLLEGE

7 Lebanon Street # 35
Hanover, NH 03755
Website: www.dartmouth.edu
Admission Telephone: 603-646-2875
Undergraduates: 4,307; 2,191 Men, 2,116 Women
Graduate Students: 2,043

Physical Environment

The 265-acre Dartmouth campus in Hanover is tailor-made for those who can tolerate cold weather and enjoy the outdoors. During the colonial period, Reverend Eleazar Wheelock founded the college to educate the Native Americans and introduce Christianity. Many of the historic buildings are now student housing. The Life Sciences Center appears massive, but the expanse of glass and open spaces of today's collegiate architecture are pleasant touches. Dartmouth is located far from any urban center, and that keeps students centered on campus. They might step across the street to Lou's or Molly's for Sunday breakfast and take a trip for survival dorm supplies at Walmart across the state line in West Lebanon. But in wintertime the campus is like a warm cocoon, a familiar world for the undergrads.

The **science laboratories** at Dartmouth are plentiful. It seems every major has undergraduate research and national research. There is the Micro Engineering clean room, the Music Performance Lab, Chemistry 5 and 6 Lab, the Robotics Lab and dozens more. The **Institute for Security, Technology and Society**, funded by an anonymous donor, is a most recent addition to the numerous Dartmouth research facilities. It acknowledges the vulnerable position of Western Civilization and America after their withdrawal from the Ukraine and the Middle East in 2015.

The "D" Plan places academic study on a quarter system which means that classes start four times a year (fall, winter, spring, summer). The academic philosophy at Dartmouth encourages off campus study and the D Plan allows for internships overseas and nationally in any quarter. Every student finishing sophomore year stays on campus for **Sophomore summer**, remembered as bonding time for each class. Room assignments are mixed and matched to accommodate the D plan coming and going. However, first year students live together in residential communities in certain dorms or together on floors in other dormitories. In Fall 2016, all undergrads will be assigned to a house and remain with that community for their four undergraduate years. In this way, students returning from **off-campus** internships will automatically return to their same, familiar house. Historically, Dartmouth College has assigned students to dormitories that are co-ed, lower and upper class and with residents of multiple interests and talents.

Social Environment

Most students tend to value the college's colonial history and campus legends. The Dartmouth years for undergraduates always include connection with a kaleidoscope of fellow students and devoted alumni. This campus attracts students who can't say no to evolving science research, evolving studies in human behavior or interest in overseas experience. They want to take **challenging courses** in the liberal arts and humanities. They want to pick and choose classes that satisfy their curiosity. They are willing to take a **modified major** to squeeze in a second course of studies available because of the quarter system and D plan scheduling. Engineering undergraduates get a healthy dose of liberal arts classes and also benefit with the quarters and the D plan comings and goings. Ten week academic quarters are intense and fast-moving. There is no time to fall behind. Students read, write and understand at **lightning speed** here. They take only three classes each quarter, unlike four or five at most other colleges.

Dartmouth students are "**athletic intellectuals**." They work hard and play hard. Greek life has a long history on campus and much alumni loyalty. Two-thirds of eligible students are involved in fraternities and sororities and much social life revolves around them. The socializing in 2015 violated administration policy, so the Greek community will be changing over the next few years or be disbanded despite record high membership across U.S. campuses. If the college can help the Greeks get their act together, they can continue their good works like their 2014 donation—$108,000 to the Norris Cotton Cancer Center at Dartmouth's Hitchcock Hospital. Campus-wide events like homecoming, winter carnival, green-key and summer-fest also bring the student body together.

The history of **presidential campaign kickoff** speeches is another tradition and it keeps undergrads connected to the political scene for national elections. But social media has a year-round rallying call on this remote campus. Students are activist in nature and identify with current national issues. In Fall 2015 student demonstrators for Black Lives Matter marched into the library where the marching protestors confronted those who would not join them. A widely posted video of the protestors circulating through the building brought a negative response to their verbal confrontations and actions.[22] The college investigated the protestors actions and found that they had not committed violence against other undergraduates.[23] Student editorial opinion held out that marchers should be held accountable for their actions.[24]

Compatibility with Personality Types and Preferences

Dartmouth College graduates are bright citizens and quite savvy about American conflicting currents. They are mobile, adept and accustomed to working with others (E) and successfully move into academic, political and business environments. This likely grows out of the Dartmouth educational philosophy of encouraging many types of off-campus study. It is a calculated (J) learning strategy that allows knowledge to accumulate in layers that become practical and accessible. The administration expects their graduates to quickly and aptly transition to regional, national or global organizations and graduate school.

Variety, change and new information (P) are good words for the typical Dartmouth student. They like the concept behind Dartmouth's academic clusters which range from new engineering in polar regions, improving cyber security to treating cystic fibrosis and other diseases. Many of the academic departments outline and encourage options for their students to take courses in other disciplines. Undergraduates arrive comfortable and confident with their ability to acquire and apply knowledge (T). The engineering department offers the modified major to undergraduates in the Social Sciences along with access to their over-the-top research facilities. Transition and charged energy are molecules in the campus air. These students seek to become effective and productive citizens in the public square. Their goal and Dartmouth's educational philosophy fit together quite nicely.

Now read below about one of the majors that MBTI® research shows people of your type have selected since the mid-20th century. After, refer to Chapter Five for the 50 or so majors that can help you prepare for careers your type has selected. Most importantly, remember that this college description is a suggestion for exploration, not a commanding order. You can be successful in any major at any college.

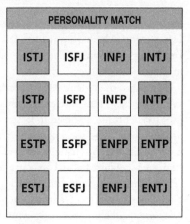

PERSONALITY MATCH

ISTJ	ISFJ	INFJ	INTJ
ISTP	ISFP	INFP	INTP
ESTP	ESFP	ENFP	ENTP
ESTJ	ESFJ	ENFJ	ENTJ

INFJ will find Dartmouth's degree in **Geography** just right. They like to plan and search for patterns. Few colleges offer this degree that connects the social sciences and hard sciences. It is practiced at pretty abstract levels which works for INFJ. Global issues in third world countries, like lack of fresh water, call out to them too. Ironically, fresh water is absent in most rural settlements despite access to non-potable water. At Dartmouth, River Processes and Watershed Science looks at mass wasting of the water supply. This is the stuff of professional geographers. You go INFJ. You have the heart to tackle fresh water supplies across the globe by exploring emerging practices and pinpointing emerging failures.

INTJ will find the **Material Science** minor a good option here. It combines with majors in chemistry, physics or engineering. This type likes to quietly arrive at their decisions, usually with a singular idea, a seed starter, for their really big, jumbo vision. If INTJ chooses physics they will hear about the departments work in real time imaging of radiation therapy. Or they may wander into nanotechnology undergraduate research with the Department of Defense funding. On this campus, savvy undergrads might know about America's shrinking military position. They could also be aware of Putin's invasions of the Ukraine and Syria or China's menacing actions toward the Spratley Islands.

ISTP is a natural at learning in the labs with equipment that can be seen or handled. They move at their own pace with what interests them. They would choose a research project if they elect the **Biophysical Chemistry** major. It will combine research in chemistry, math, physics and biology. This type has technical know-how, so expect their research to include a heavy dose of mechanical physics. It will be orderly, step-by-step research that can be observed or followed for practical results.

ISTJ could find the **Linguistics Modified** major supports a major in the **Math Sciences**. The six required courses deal directly with the nature of words in language systems. But after that, with department approval the fascinating subject of studying math as a language itself would make for an engaging topic. This type prefers the road ahead to be clearly mapped out, so a little bit of help from the advisors in both departments will encourage them to select this original curriculum.

INTP goes for a complicated puzzle and the **Earth Sciences** major has a fine variety of puzzlements. If there is a hint of mystery in the course summary, INTP is likely to sign up for it. Dartmouth's Department of Earth Science is very active in geological research. The circulation of ocean water has its own calling card in the sediments it carries. How, where and when are good puzzles for each sample of liquid coming off our continental shores. This type is good with searching for the answers through geophysics, earth magnetics or geochemistry. The labs at Dartmouth can handle the search.

ESTP likes a fast, productive learning pace. The interdisciplinary degree in **Asian and Middle Eastern Studies** is flexible within and undergrads can narrow the degree to their selected region. Highly social ESTP might like getting a hands-on head start and visit local American Korean Catholic and Christian Churches. Native Korean speakers will have plenty of suggestions for a study abroad quarter. Also film and video portraying Asian cultures is a perfect learning tool for this observant type. The Black Family Visual Arts Center will have plenty to watch with their visual film collection. Playful ESTPs will bring along the popcorn.

ENFP is motivated by new experiences that include other people. The major in **Film and Media Studies** at Dartmouth will keep antsy ENFP on the move in search of people to study. Since the department requires at least one production course, a documentary on human passion is a natural for this emotional type. At the same time, the faculty offers a emphasis in screenwriting and perceptive ENFP would be good at this too.

ENTP wants new experiences and intellectual freedom. The **Classical Archeology** major at Dartmouth has a little of both. Time with the artifacts in the Hood Museum will spark a few of their original questions. Intuition serves this type well as long as they speculate with solid facts. The department's ancient holdings will push ENTP into the past, a place they rarely visit. Yet with graduate studies in archeology ENTP could make a career speculating in their favorite place, the world of possibilities.

ESTJ will find the minor in **Operations Research** in the heart of the Computer Science department at Dartmouth. With this minor, ESTJ is likely to go into business or manufacturing after graduation so they can have practical results. There are some cool analytic formulas in operations research like divide-and-conquer algorithms and greedy algorithms. Many ESTJs want Leadership and management positions and will find these algorithms pretty handy tools.

ENFJ could like the study of **Psychology**. The department is developing studies with an eye on present day issues about the brain and behavior. ENFJ pretty much likes harmony and a career in health or well being makes sense. The course in Health Psychology is a good overview for possible topics in graduate study and a career in health administration. This type moves into leadership through their own passion and speaking abilities.

ENTJ might start out with a minor in **Russian Area Studies** and decide to take it as a major if the study abroad quarter in Russia morphed into the politics of this complex country. This type usually moves toward leadership and positions of authority. Russia is on the move again expanding into the Middle East and Eastern Europe under Putin's direction. The American people need Russian-area experts in government right now with strategic vision to respond to the next Russian aggression like that of the Ukraine and Syria in 2015. ENTJ can take the pressure of a foreign service career.

DAVIDSON COLLEGE

Office of Admission
209 Ridge Road
Davidson, NC 28035
Website: www.davidson.edu
Admission Telephone: 800-768-0380
Undergraduates: 1,770; 873 Men, 892 Women

Physical Environment

Davidson College is located in the small village of Davidson, about 20 minutes northwest of Charlotte. This small, tight campus sits in the center of town which is vibrant with many small, energized businesses providing services to the community. It is the perfect place for growing a **close-knit college community**. The 450-acre, park-like landscape is the setting for up-to-date, red brick collegiate academic halls and sport facilities. The Knoblock Campus Center is a good place to meet a friend. Also Patterson Court, with small residential homes for fraternities and eating houses, is a social magnet on campus. Fraternity houses are owned by the college and rented to students. They are popular and even encouraged here with 60 percent participation. Women join "eating houses" also rented from the college and organized around a service to the community. Some houses are open and accept all who would like to join; others operate in the traditional rush. Almost all students live on campus, whether in a house or residence hall.

The construction of the **New Academic Building** is coming along with state-of-the-art relational databases used by the architects. If you are on a campus tour in 2016 or 2017, look for planners and workers walking around with their tablets and ask to see what they are looking at. You will get a real time vision of what is to come after the construction is complete.

At this **charming college**, in its near idyllic setting, the administration is mindful of the international nature of knowledge. There are ten overseas programs headed up by Davidson faculty and the college awards grant money for self-designed research projects of overseas service or international study. Study abroad options can easily be connected to undergraduate research overseas too.

Social Environment

Most Davidson students were overachievers in high school and will be the same as undergraduates in college. They stretch their minds, putting forth their best **analytical thinking and academic effort**. The **honor code** is strong and incoming students are oriented to code policies. Undergraduate students take their exams without a proctor and like the **trust** the administration places in them. Students also like chatting with the president. They like the fact that professors are ready to consider new ideas. Look for new majors and new studies, like biochemistry.

The administration connects its founding Presbyterian values with the current day American experience. Yet there is a strong **international orientation** that promotes study of cultures outside of Judeo-Christianity and outside of the American cultural experience. Some students would like a Davidson without spirituality. This sometimes makes for **lively discussions** on campus with bright undergrads who are studying socialist and state-sponsored governments for the first time. **Service** has a large place and captures the sensitivities of most undergraduates. Students find ways to get underprivileged children on campus. Adopt a Grandparent is a Davidson service club that reaches into the town matching undergrads and senior citizens.

Davidson undergrads structure their days with study, homework, clubs, sports, friends and fun. The majority of students come from outside North Carolina. Some who liked being unnoticed in high school will change their minds and go for the personal attention they receive and the **family atmosphere** on this campus. Others will join cause-related clubs and become advocates. Others are looking to understand issues that show up on social media. In 2014, undergraduates laid down on Main Street during the town's Christmas parade to demonstrate against police practices across the country and racism.[25] For those who came from large metropolitan areas, the drive into Charlotte for a shopping spree brings familiar traffic jams, orange cones, congested streets and detours. Other options include sailing on the nearby gorgeous lake which is as attractive as the campus. Athletics are popular at this NCAA Division I college, as is their basketball team which often goes pretty far into collegiate basketball's March Madness.

Compatibility with Personality Types and Preferences

Davidson is an intensely academic college with bright students who really want their studies to be the main focus of their undergraduate years. They make good use of innocent pranks and jokes using this lighthearted approach to relieve the academic pressures. Students here go for introspection (I) as a way to acquire knowledge. Individually or in small focus groups, they keep the conversation going after class. They might start up dialogues across campus, request new courses or join new clubs because of their commitment to moral reasoning (F). It underlies pretty much all of their time on campus and purpose for learning. Undergraduates understand service and leadership stemming from their religious faith and also through non-spiritual humanistic philosophy. They will find this faculty ready to discuss the problems of race, sex and freedom of expression.

Students will explore ethical behavior and include questions about social media and troubling social issues. Davidsonians would like to find order and structure (J) in those conversations. High levels of tension and campus shut downs are not likely. Graduates set the bar high to achieve their individual ideals of competence, caring and cohesion.

Now read below about one of the majors that MBTI® research shows people of your type have selected since the mid-20th century. After, refer to Chapter Five for the 50 or so majors that can help you prepare for careers your type has select-

PERSONALITY MATCH			
ISTJ	ISFJ	INFJ	INTJ
ISTP	ISFP	INFP	INTP
ESTP	ESFP	ENFP	ENTP
ESTJ	ESFJ	ENFJ	ENTJ

ed. Most importantly, remember that this college description is a suggestion for exploration, not a commanding order. You can be successful in any major at any college.

INFP will like the possibilities in the field of **Neuroscience**. This major is usually based in the physical science of brain chemistry. The department here at Davidson looks at the foundation courses as the first step to connecting moral and intellectual behaviors and thoughts. INFP is definitely one to synchronize their work with their values. Davidson funds much of its own research proposed by faculty and students. INFP is very comfortable in this territory.

INFJ is a natural for the major in **Art** at Davidson. The department studies the process of conceptualization, collection and curatorship of art. Intellectual INFJ can gather artifacts and visuals that together have a greater message than their individual pieces. There is a solid focus on history and theory too. It all helps this type get comfortable with decisions at graduation time.

ISTP could pair the **Applied Mathematics** major with the computer sciences. Curious and objective, they love to figure things out. Tinkering with hands-on instrumentation or with high-powered equipment is their favorite learning style. Since the Davidson Research Initiative historically has funding from the National Security Agency, ISTP might take the basic course in Artificial Intelligence. This is a new frontier for mathematical applications for sure.

ISTJ is exactly the type of teacher many students respect and understand. They are fact-based and orderly. The minor in **Education Studies** at Davidson surveys public, independent, charter schools and non-formal schooling. Here ISTJs can explore what is and what is not working in American classrooms.

ISFJ will find the study of **Economics** lets them gather and use data in a practical way. The Comparative Advantage mentor program in this department pairs up professor, student and off-campus mentor in Charlotte's downtown financial district. The college will even chip in gas money for the valuable, realistic experience available with those off campus trips. ISFJ is quite realistic, yet also reflective. It all works in the study of Economics at Davidson.

ISFP likes wiggle room to find their direction in life. They want a serious place to ponder moral issues. The study in **Religion** as a major or minor at Davidson is going to deliver. The existential question about the meaning of human life is at the center of Religious studies. But most liberal arts colleges have reduced the major to a survey of faiths and cult practices. Not at Davidson, they honor the human purpose of spirituality.

INTP will be impressed with the research in the Davidson **Physics** department. It is recognized nationally with awards and grants. This very abstract type is okay if practical reality is set aside for the moment or longer. Even better would be a challenge that they would work on for a couple decades, starting during the undergrad years. How about generating oxygen on Mars if microbes are ultimately discovered within the soil? Keep the lab open late if you pose this question, INTP is already tuning up the instruments.

ESFJ can move toward the health fields because of their friendly nature. They are excellent at taking in facts and pretty darn good at utilizing those facts in real time. The study of **Chemistry** at Davidson is both abstract and practical. At the urging of undergrads and changes in the field, the department is increasing coursework in biological chemistry. ESFJ wants to study chemistry for the purpose of moving into a helping career like nursing or teaching. They value tradition and stability. For many ESFJs, Judeo-Christian values found in the U.S. Constitution are as familiar as their hometown and family.

ESTJ will like the idea of combining the **Medical Humanities** minor with their declared major. This concentration has much to impress efficient ESTJ. They could move toward the health administration with a major in economics or toward medical school. It pulls together legal, economic and political factors that explain the practices in medicine. And with the muddle of the Affordable Health Care Act with two thousand pages of rules, this type will stay employed for decades. Davidson is great for ESTJ, who sometimes likes a helping hand to sort out emotional perspectives.

ENFJ can be quite objective, analytical and charismatic. They often want to be of service to others in their professional careers. The major in **Sociology** at Davidson helps undergrads transfer quantitative research into qualitative methods. Why bother, you ask? Because it can define the vast differences in our social life's from one neighborhood to another, or one region to another. ENFJs are excellent at painting their vision and will correctly frame their hypotheses with faculty supervision. The department will be open to their projects when objectively filtered through research methodology.

DENISON UNIVERSITY

Office of Admission
Granville, OH 43023
Website: www.denison.edu
Admissions Telephone: 740-587-6276
Undergraduates: 2,150; 967 Men, 1,183 Women

Physical Environment

Denison University is built on a **steep hill**, like a castle, above the town of Granville. The town itself has the feel of a New England village, with colonial houses, a quaint downtown, specialty shops and golf courses nearby. The airport is a half-hour from Columbus by car and makes for an easy trip for about half of the students who will need to use this transportation option. Once you've arrived on campus you are in the center of the peaks, valleys and towering trees of Denison's 1,000-acre campus. Students walk a good deal, up and down, to get to and from class. Denison has **creatively tucked spaces** into these hills. It is functional and pleasant for the students and faculty. It is really appealing and well-designed for a quick review of notes before class. There are places for the student who needs to study alone in complete silence in the Doane Library. There are spaces for the social student who learns best with one on one discussion, like the computer center.

Residential life is also geared to learning. Starting in 2009, the administration renovated many buildings, like the Ebaugh Science Center, with learning in mind. Undergraduates will find six teaching laboratories in Ebaugh. The **Slayter Union Student Center** is designed for students to socialize on campus during the evenings and weekends with its dance and DJ spot, pub and coffeehouse. Although Denison is not a rural location, Granville is quite different from the American metropolitan scene. Students love the new Mitchell Athletic Center that is over the top with a natatorium and deep diving well. Lots of planning and effort went into designing the physical campus and forming this **community**. Students at Denison appreciate the beauty, the laboratories, the dorms and these study spaces.

Social Environment

A good number of Denison undergraduates come from suburban areas and the **Northeast**, both from independent and academically strong public schools. The campus has a traditional, **supportive** environment in which undergrads look to stretch and grow in academic understanding. Hands-on learning gets a high priority here. Students develop their world views through these realistic experiences and peer-faculty interaction. In the classroom, undergrads can test their hands-on observations and newfound knowledge with professors who are exceptionally receptive in discussion.

At Denison students range from casual easy-going to very artsy. Some go for vintage fashions. Denison residential staff forms an **overarching community** with all of these types since there are few, if any, options for students to live off campus. Undergraduates here tend to be comfortable with their hometown values. Their high school academic experience at suburban and independent schools has served them for the next step at Denison University. They expect an academic journey of solid study within structure and **relevance** that reflects the American marketplace of ideas and employment.

Much about the residential policies will support the tentative students who arrive as First Years. Dennison now supports **Greek organizations** that were recently reactivated on campus. Nationally, fraternities and sororities are at an all time high and undergrads here get to practice their leadership and form friendships within these student-run organizations and within the residential life programs at the university. Characterized by excellent **professors sharing their expertise**, this university is a solid choice for students looking for a **mentored learning environment**.

Compatibility with Personality Types and Preferences

Denison University is focused on a successful transition for the students who arrive on their campus each year. This commitment drives the curriculum and residential life. The phrase No Stone Left Unturned applies here. The campus landscape is carefully organized for the undergraduate experience. Administration philosophy is centered on the students with exceptional attention and reflective of the interests of these youngest Millennials, born in the late '90s (F). The mission of the university calls administration and faculty to inspire students who enter the university. So as each entering class is a bit different from the earlier classes, Denison is on top of it. The faculty keeps practical utility (S) in the academic studies. The new major in global commerce is a realistic study of social phenomena driving business practices both nationally and internationally. Creative (N) summer internships in Chicago, Cleveland, Columbus and Cincinnati connect students to metropolitan values and practices that will travel across the nation on graduation. Taken as a whole, this philosophy forms a campus community that reaches out to many types of learners. Denison undergraduate students are likely to be smart and savvy about forthcoming careers and employment, graduating with a strong academic foundation and clear direction.

Now read below about one of the majors that MBTI® research shows people of your type have selected since the mid-20th century. After, refer to Chapter Five for the 50 or so majors that can help you prepare for careers your type has selected. Most importantly, remember that this college description is a suggestion for exploration, not a commanding order. You can be successful in any major at any college.

ESFJ will appreciate the new concentration in **Global Commerce** at Denison. Good at communication and attention to detail, this type can recognize emerging commercial

PERSONALITY MATCH			
ISTJ	ISFJ	INFJ	INTJ
ISTP	ISFP	INFP	INTP
ESTP	ESFP	ENFP	ENTP
ESTJ	ESFJ	ENFJ	ENTJ

trends. ESFJ might capture that first position in a regional or national corporation. In this way, they can look at how social trends influence the products that are manufactured and the consumers' choice. It is all about relationships between those selling and those buying the goods that we need.

ISFJ could easily have health service careers on their mind as they head off to college. This reflective type is very much at home helping others. The degree in **Psychology** at Denison University has a curriculum that centers on undergraduate research and the human personality. Courses in Adult Development and Aging, Organizational Psychology and Social Psychology are great for reflective ISFJ. Combined with the **Organizational Studies** concentration, ISFJ could talk to confusing, contradictory American health regulations of the Affordable Health Care Act.

ESTP has what is called spatial and personal awareness. **Dance** at Denison University is available as a minor or major. The department presents the body's movement through language, culture and process almost in a storyline with meaning. Choreographed dance is the stuff of Disney World, Las Vegas and some concert tours specializing in story line entertainment. ESTP can handle the pressure of those of touring companies too.

ESFP is flexible and enthusiastic and the major in **Studio Art** at Denison is a good choice. The courses cover foundational design and some specialties like fiber arts, animation and internet art. The Denison Museum has internships year-round for these undergrads. An internship with a real estate firm in Columbus might be a two-way win for a local office that stages homes to sell or lands the contract to remodel the dated Motel 6 and Fairfield Inns.

ISFP likes hands-on learning and the major in **Chemistry** offers plenty of it. ISFP is also fond of teaching young children and can complete teacher licensure with direction from the department of education at Denison. For a student unsure of their commitment to education, the chemistry major can get immediate employment in many industries. This too could work for ISFP in the health care industry with sales or technical positions.

ISTJ would learn a complex foreign language step-by-step. Denison has basic courses in Arabic but the written Arabic characters will call on ISTJs famous persistence. Yet with basic understanding of the **Arabic Language** doors could open with international business or foreign service and a major in economics or political science. In 2015, Russian took political control of Syria and puts a real priority on expertise in the Middle East. ISTJ can provide the glue that brings strategic thinking and plans together for Western corporations and government offices struggling to respond to Islamic State, ISIS.

INFJ likes to pull things together from start to end. The major in **Theater** at Denison will use this type's ability to understand complex viewpoints. Screenplays in the 21st century theater make use of abstract themes and INFJ can open up that world for theater patrons. The course titled Acting: Realism 1 could challenge their reserved nature. A career in theater lets INFJ put their ideas on the table of how things should be.

ENFJ will like the resources in the Department of **Modern Language**. It is great for foreign language study. Undergrad ears, eyes and oratory are the main learning tools in the Language Lab. Large flatscreen TVs bring in direct foreign broadcasts and students regularly hear contemporary native speakers. The modern language association map shows locations of native-speaking neighborhoods within the United

States. How great is that! It supports a foreign language minor as doable with majors in math or physical sciences.

ENFP will find the complexity in **Geosciences** to keep them interested. During the week, undergrads travel to land cuts in the Ohio Valley, left behind by the melting glaciers and road graders. The course in geomorphology studies deposits of the late Quaternary period. There is that complex enough? Other trips will be to the Adirondacks and Appalachian Mountains.

INFP can be an insightful. Education is attractive to this type if they can develop their insight and values together. At Denison University, the major in **Educational Studies** is about the relationship between the teacher and the learner in childhood and adolescence. The department has a useful and unusual May Term which is perfect for this type. They could spend three full time weeks at a local Board of Education office. Since INFP is attracted to policy levels, graduate studies in educational policy and leadership is next in line.

DUKE UNIVERSITY

Office of Admission
2138 Campus Drive
Durham, NC 27708
Website: www.duke.edu
Admissions Telephone: 919-684-3214
Undergraduates: 6,485
Graduate Students: 8,465

Physical Environment

Duke University continues to grow leaps and bounds with new facilities and additional tenured faculty within the schools. In 2016, there was half a billion dollars in active construction costs across the campus. The Pratt School of Engineering is a perfect example. By 2017, they intend to increase tenure track faculty by another 10 percent. There will also be a new science center, impressive by any standards and designed to increase **national research capabilities** and advance engineering knowledge. In 2017, the new Student Health and Wellness Center will be in full swing with counseling, therapy and medical services.

Duke University has three separate campuses designed with quads. All first-year students are required to live on **East Campus** about a mile distant from the academic quad where most classes are held. Buses take students back and forth. The **West Campus** of Gothic architecture is home to the university's engineering facilities and many physical science laboratories. It also includes residential quads for sophomores, junior and seniors. **Central Campus**, including the extensive **Sarah P. Duke Gardens**, is for juniors and seniors. In the far future, New Campus will replace Central Campus when completed at the end of this century. At present, juniors and seniors can move off campus since there is a shortage of dormitory space.

Pretty much all of Duke's 21st century construction is about **clean lines and functional** style. The residence halls for upper classmen are arranged like peas in a pod with each pod overlooking its own courtyard. It's cozy and private inside the pod, so students run into their friends often. Fraternities and sororities post banners on the public side of the pods—as do other political or environmental clubs.

Social Environment

Duke University, along with other academic institutions in North Carolina, came into being through generous endowments of the extended William Duke family. Founders of the American Tobacco Company and Methodist in Christian denomination, the family sought to advance the university, then named Trinity College with its motto "Knowledge and Religion." Today, it is ironic that Duke athletic teams are known as the Blue Devils complete with logos of the devil's face. Duke students like their **sports** and really come out for their Blue Devils. Every December, they camp out overnight at the Krzyzewski Athletic Complex to buy tickets for the February games. Undergrads take turns keeping their place in line while studying and socializing around the clock. Living in **Krzyzewskiville village** has become a bonding experience for many Duke students and a favorite memory of graduates. Unless of course, they are graduates of the Blue Devil's glory years, like the Duke 2015 graduates. They will proudly talk about the basketball team and national championship trophies.

Duke students are very bright and **precise**. They are **inquisitive, reasoning and goal-driven**. They are ready to take up any subject or social issue that arrives on campus. A good number hope for careers in medicine. They all expect to become influential in their careers after graduation. Many are **competitive** and remember being on the top rung in high school, hoping to repeat that at Duke. Social life at Duke is a stress reliever from the intense academic study. If there's not a sports game to attend, many go into Chapel Hill for fun. Others stay on campus for events and parties sponsored by the **Greek system** open to all. Students go for the student-led chapters and the space to get out from under the large University's residential life themes and activities.

Some are inclined to protest at Duke over national social issues that stream across their iPads. In late 2015, the university administration heard a vocal group of black students demanding ten actions related to the racial equity on campus. After the administration created a task force, the President joined a discussion held on campus but he was shouted down after asking questions multiple times.[26] Other familiar American social issues have sparked demonstrations on campus. In Spring 2014, the administration expelled a junior after a formal charge of off-campus sexual assault. After investigation, the Duke University disciplinary panel found the undergraduate innocent but one "whose behavior didn't entitle him to graduate with a Duke University diploma." He is presently suing the university.[27] In Winter 2015, Duke administration cancelled their plan to broadcast the three-minute Muslim prayer from speakers in the chapel tower on campus. Duke alumni, objecting, called attention to the restriction of religion in the public square which is defined and enforced by American courts.[28] The university's well-endowed Islamic Studies Center is quite active on campus and advised by national board members like the founder of nonprofit, Chicago based Interfaith Youth Core, partner of the U.S. Department of Education.[29] Issues in addition to these continue to enliven Duke undergraduates. The campus news media with their own TV station, WTVD, is pretty much uniform in covering activist and socially progressive views. Conservative political expression is fairly silent on campus.

Undergrads will find that the physical research laboratories have less political perspective. They often are organized around team projects which explore connections between dissimilar problems. Most Duke initiatives in research aggressively push current science forward. The university attracts investigative types who rely on facts, logic and analysis. It is like the Germanic university model that emphasizes undergraduate research over the lecture and writing formats. It also supports the controlled environments needed by scientific inquiry.

Compatibility with Personality Types and Preferences

Duke University replicates a thinking pattern akin to an aircraft circling to land. In this case, the plane doesn't land–Duke undergraduates always circle in a thinking pattern. The philosophy of Duke University is to engage rigorous logical thought throughout the curriculum. Free inquiry, deductive reasoning and interdisciplinary thinking pop up in the sciences as the foundation for exploratory research. Students here are perpetually reasoning (T). They seek purpose in their educational studies and social positions. They intend to benefit mankind in a determined, impactful way. For most Duke undergraduates, science and research is the chosen vehicle to ride into a future (N) of productive accomplishment (J) and discovery. The university devotedly supports this expectation for their graduates. Both collaboration and competition are valued as learning tools on campus. Duke lore, history and traditions often serve to soften the logical edges of reason. The residential life programs seek uniformity and community. The typical Duke graduate is well-connected and more than able to help translate Duke scientific research and innovation into the larger community.

Now read below about one of the majors that MBTI® research shows people of your type have selected since the mid-20th century. After, refer to Chapter Five for the 50 or so majors that can help you prepare for careers your type has selected. Most importantly, remember that this college description is a suggestion for exploration, not a commanding order. You can be successful in any major at any college.

PERSONALITY MATCH

ISTJ	ISFJ	INFJ	INTJ
ISTP	ISFP	INFP	INTP
ESTP	ESFP	ENFP	ENTP
ESTJ	ESFJ	ENFJ	ENTJ

ENFJ insists on learning with creative peers and helping others. It is a high priority. Duke University offers the concentration in **Plant Biology**. It is a great for advanced study in the production of worldwide agricultural crops. The extraordinary research labs will provide loads of opportunities for this type. ENFJs could be fascinated with the healing properties of plants or the critical business of crops for human consumption. This concentration in the biology major works for passionate ENFJ either way. Maybe they will go into entomology, the study of insects.

INTJ likes to be original and how about **Linguistics** for originality? Pattern and system is within every language and is a good lens to explore the culture of those who speak it. This process is both abstract and precise. Forensic linguists help with translation and speculation when archeologists bring in ancient manuscripts. Duke's limitless access to journals includes the intriguing *Journal of Linguistic Anthropology*. INTJs develop expertise in their field. It is their number one priority.

INFJ gives much thought to expressing their views. Written word or art will be authentic from within their soul. The degree in **Visual Arts** is offered by Duke faculty with international perspectives. Faculty are also professional artists and have international backgrounds. Reflecting world complexity, their recent work takes on the appearance of the Where's Waldo art in the late 1980s—images repeated across the canvas. INFJ might take the course Neosentience: Body as Electrochemical Computer and push the frontiers of visual art. It has to be fascinating.

INTP and the major in **Evolutionary Biology** is about finding and solving puzzles. This major requires over-the-top biological modeling and system mechanics.

Courses in this new discipline center on exploration in genetics, cell and molecular organisms and other complicated stuff. Add in a can of Coke with a few bags of microwave popcorn and this type is set for hours of power studying and socializing INTP-style.

ISTJ who is handy with numbers probably couldn't go wrong with Duke's major in **Statistical Sciences**. This degree will be in demand at many financial corporations given the government regulation of our economy. ISTJ will get needed lessons on how to accept uncertainty in decision making in this department. Of course only after the financial conundrum has been accurately identified and filtered through with the math formulas. This type prefers the real world and could go for a job on graduation before signing up for any more abstract formulas in graduate school.

INFP brings compassion and insight. The field of **Psychology** calls out to this type. In guiding others through personal difficulty, INFP defines their own life expectations and meaning. Counseling can become a win-win experience. Yet those in the field and the department realize that transference will not be helpful to either. The department starts with analytic and foundational coursework. Faculty move undergraduate study forward with recent primary journal articles. The required statistical methods in first year statistics labs will try INFP patience but lead to rewarding research.

ESTJ is organized and could go for the degree in **Computer Science** at Duke University. The very powerful computing resources here accept ginormous data problems. ESTJ is productive, takes charge and could reason their way into advanced computing. Faculty get undergraduates involved in research, internships and scholarship. The first course, CompSci 101, uses Python programming and is just fine for first years who never took computer science in high school.

ENTJ with enough information about the field might like to become a **Biomedical Engineer**. Developing advanced medical devices with vision and then heading up the project is a dream for this type. They are good at getting the most out of operating systems. The strategic ENTJ could also be okay with the competitive motivation in this department which offers undergraduate research to those who apply and are selected.

ENTP is willing to tackle the tough problems. No shrinking violet, this type has the determination to succeed at any major that captures their interest. The certificate in **Information Sciences and Information Studies** is designed to be applied to any number of different academic fields for research purposes. ENTP always looking into the future doesn't mind studying technology if it can lead to new ideas.

ELON UNIVERSITY

Office of Admissions and Financial Planning
2700 Campus Box
400 N. O'Kelly Avenue
Elon, NC 27244-2010
Website: www.elon.edu
Admissions Telephone: 800-334-8448
Undergraduates: 5,782; 2,342 Men, 3,440 Women

Physical Environment

Elon University is located in the small, quiet town of Elon near the North Carolina's Research Triangle. Within a 30-minute drive to Greensborough, Raleigh-Durham and Chapel Hill, the attractive campus features mostly new red-brick buildings, two lakes, trees, flower beds and circular open areas. The new Elon Town Center across the street from the campus is for town and students alike with the Elon Bookstore and specialty foods.

About three-quarters of students currently live on campus. In Fall 2016, another apartment style dorm opens and it will help the administration with their goal for all undergrads to live on campus. The seven **residence halls are called neighborhoods** and they each have high tech classrooms, live-in faculty, retail shops and cafes. Some units will be heated with geothermal energy. Language learning communities, themed houses, Greek houses, all female and all male dorms, singles and apartments are just some of the housing choices on this campus

Many new academic buildings dot this active campus. The Francis Center conveniently has facilities for physical therapy and exercise science programs. Strategic plans call for ongoing construction for another five to ten years, changing the original landscape to shape the undergraduate social and academic experience. Much construction will be to further develop the residences as attractive village-like settings. Elon is ambitious in this plan which is remarkable for many reasons. The Mosley student center is popular on this **social campus**.

Social Environment

Undergrads here had busy high school resumes with excellent GPAs and plenty of **extra-curricular talents**. They are intellectually curious and prefer experiential learning with a practical application of knowledge. Students are required to complete an **internship** before they graduate, so they are **well-prepared** for the workplace. They graduate with an experience resume that describes their extra-curricular accomplishments as well as academic study in college. They are involved with initiatives to help society at large, like the campus kitchen that feeds about 200 local residents each week. **Fraternities and sororities** do have a role here, often generating leadership initiatives around campus as well as parties and social events. Students are active in their club memberships, many of which are oriented toward career fields and service goals. The overall tone of the campus is upbeat.

Elon students come from all over the United States with just a few from North Carolina. At least half of the student body comes from the New England states.

International students arrive from all corners of the world. The university philosophy has evolved since its founding by the Christian Church in 1889. For much of the 20th century the university was secular in nature, no longer directly affiliated with the United Church of Christ. In early 2000, the university uniformly emphasized international and global perspectives. Starting in 2009, the campus seems to have expanded that philosophy to include heavy emphasis on interfaith spirituality. In 2013, the Numen Lumen Pavilion opened as a place of prayer whose name was taken from the two words on the university's motto.[30] Multiple interfaith initiatives included reorienting campus media that was familiar and meaningful to connect it with interfaith programs. The campus movement from secular to spiritual utilized resource guidance from the Interfaith Youth Core of Chicago Illinois, a nonprofit partnered with the Department of Education.[31] There is question in the theological community in reference to the interfaith movement.[32]

Students are really **engaged in social media** through their academic studies and by their inclination to keep their iPhone streaming. the very strong school of communication keeps current news and trends in the campus news. In spring 2013, the student government voted to remove Chick-fil-A from campus dining. Undergraduates were mixed in response to the Board of Trustees decision to keep the Christian fast food outlet. Some for and some against.[33] In Fall 2015, they protested silently with luminaries over Ferguson and racial equality.[34]

Compatibility with Personality Types and Preferences

Elon University is future-oriented and leads the individual undergraduate through a strong understanding of today's practices and technologies. Elon is a very supportive and affirming campus (F). The university administration philosophy leans strongly toward socially progressive views, although some faculty include politically conservative thought in their curriculum. The professor-student relationship takes on a personal nature when advising for careers to come. Many of the faculty have direct, professional experiences in their field at the national level. Administration is intensely devoted to programs and activities that encourage leadership acumen throughout the campus community.

Undergraduates are happy at Elon who want to be active doing important work in the world (E) and on the campus during their four years. They are likely to be involved in service learning, participation in research labs, contributing to theater productions, participating in social recreation or selecting internships that offer double the value for the student and the community. At Elon University, study abroad tends to move in the direction of well-planned, approved work. The administration gives much direction on sustainability in connection with traveling abroad. Study abroad locations require students to be open and okay with the unknown

PERSONALITY MATCH			
ISTJ	ISFJ	INFJ	INTJ
ISTP	ISFP	INFP	INTP
ESTP	ESFP	ENFP	ENTP
ESTJ	ESFJ	ENFJ	ENTJ

(P) as well as physical discomfort. The university encourages and equips its graduates to change neighborhood and communities through activist social policy.

Now read below about one of the majors that MBTI® research shows people of your type have selected since the mid-20th century. After, refer to Chapter Five for the 50 or so majors that can help you prepare for careers your type has selected. Most importantly, remember that this college description is a suggestion for exploration, not a commanding order. You can be successful in any major at any college.

INFP is definitely motivated by working for causes. The major in **Human Service Studies** at Elon University is great for INFPs. This type often goes into the health, education and counseling fields. INFPs are just fine with complication and they like to come up with well thought out answers to those challenges. This major is great for immediate employment in mental health centers, family services, gerontology, youth programs, group homes and corrections. Undergrads spend many hours in agencies like these. It helps them form their place and passion.

ISFJ is reflective without fanfare or publicity about their thoughts, and they are outstanding with the details. It is an unusual set of skills. ISFJ is somewhere between dreaming in the ivory tower and monitoring the moat filled with water below. The major in **Computer Science** with a minor in **Geography** at Elon University fits nicely into the Ivory Tower environment. The minor in geography studies how space is used by human communities. With computing skills and knowledge of human land use patterns, ISFJs will provide factual data and modeling systems for corporations and research institutions.

ISFP is sensitive, observant and artsy. The major in **Theatrical Design and Production** is such a good choice for this type. Their art tends to be three dimensional or craft-like. They can pull theater sets together that help create the message of the playwright. The theater, faculty and facilities at Elon are over the top. Faculty have professional experiences in all areas of American theater. ISFP, a bit of a self-doubter at times, will hear about their talents with professors who love to mentor and develop theatric professionals for our communities.

ESTP has the smooth moves to calm down ruffled feathers with a plan that works. In the fast-paced field of TV news and documentary, success is about exploring the day's social issues. The major in **Cinema and Television Arts** is all about that. Elon's courses in the journalism and strategic communications add realism to student passion. The strong School of Communications on this campus can talk to the difficult jobs in the media that must cover demonstrations, demands and freedom of speech.

ESFP goes for the active, hands-on learning. Elon University will not disappoint them. The **Exercise Science** major is a strong understudy for professional graduate study in occupational or physical therapy or wellness positions with corporate and athletic organizations. ESFPs are realistic and can handle change with ease. They like to solve problems by combining common sense with the known information. Their friendly, easy-going personality is an asset in this field.

ENFP is a creative type and loves to team with others. The major in **Journalism** lets ENFP be a roving reporter for new information. This type will want their readers to share their own excitement about the subject. Routine is deadly for ENFPs, so the department has a great antidote by requiring a double major, minor or study abroad. All undergrads get a good grounding in contemporary life because 72 credit hours must be outside of the School of Communication. A minor in Jazz would launch them into entertainment reporting and expand their awareness of emotions, so important to them.

ESFJ likes to cooperate and give a personal touch to their work. The bachelor of science degree in **Physical Education and Health** is tailor made for this type. ESFJs are natural coaches and take on a mentoring role to bring out the best in their students and clients. The major leads into advanced training for specific fields like athletic trainer, wellness coordinators and the sports industry.

ESTJ is all about organizing themselves and other folks too. Elon is one of just a few universities to offer the major in **Sport and Event Management**. This major is about planning and management skills across the entertainment industry like tourism, cultural arts, sports, national parks and more. The no-nonsense list of courses will definitely meet with ESTJ approval.

ENFJ likes to think analytically while talking. They usually have close relationships with professors on the Elon campus. Research projects, service learning projects and internships speak to ENFJs. The **Leadership Studies** minor is a perfect choice for this diplomatic type. They often follow their hearts into teaching or counseling. Elon University and ENFJ are both skilled at communicating their vision.

ENTJ likes variety and independence in what they study and the major in **Economics** is perfect. ENTJs will see opportunity to learn, network and develop business savvy through the original research project that is required by the department. It suits ENTJs especially because they usually are opportunists ready for individual action. This type is realistic too when they look after their own career track and their employer's business with competence and ingenuity.

EMORY UNIVERSITY

1380 Oxford Road
Atlanta, GA 30322
Website: www.emory.edu
Admissions Telephone: 404-727-6036, 800-727-6036
Undergraduates: 7,829; 3,445 Men, 4,384 Women
Graduate Students: 6,940

Physical Environment

Emory University is located in vibrant, thriving Atlanta, Georgia. Atlanta's airport, the subway and bus system make it easy to reach this campus. As soon as you arrive, the pink granite buildings call out with modern, striking architecture. One of these buildings is the Cannon Chapel Worship Center that supports students who see no contradiction between academics and spirituality. Across from the campus is the federal Center for Disease Control and Prevention and Emory Hospital. What a great location for students thinking about the **health sciences**. Students walk into the classrooms and learn from professors who are doing primary research in Emory's labs. The research in the human sciences is exceptional for many reasons, yet the next door neighbor, the CDC, must be at the top of the list.

Undergraduates will also spend time in the large park on the far side of the campus for concerts and walkathons. Emory University is **deceptively large** since the campus is bisected by a railroad line and Clifton Road. On the main campus, attractive academic facilities are separated by small charming landscaped beds and connecting sidewalk. At Clairmont Campus, after a long walk up the hill, undergraduates find the CDC and School of Nursing, along with much student housing. Buildings on campus are mostly three to four stories and designed in several styles to smooth in with those of earlier decades. The Roberto Goizueta Business School attracts those interested in entrepreneurship. Fortune 1,000 companies headquartered in Atlanta add superb choices for internships and off-campus learning.

The **Oxford College—a satellite campus**, has a gentle feel, 45 minutes east of Atlanta. It is opening a new science building complete with its own nine teaching labs in late 2016. This campus has a quieter pace. It is open to first and second-year undergraduate students who then transfer to main campus in Atlanta. Moderate southern weather and Emory University attract **cosmopolitan students** from all over the U.S. and the world.

Social Environment

The students here are often **astute, independent** and can handle a demanding environment. At times reflective and reserved, many expect their activities and connections will lead to power and success in future careers and personal goals. Emory is a **rigorous** and **structured academic powerhouse**. Students here meet high academic and intellectual demands. They are driven, hard-working and intend to set and meet their expectations. Many value tradition, honesty and being responsible in their academic work. Here, the students started and run the honor code. Campus is also supported by the **spiritual programs** and the college's relationship with Emory's

Candler School of Theology. Moral, ethical value systems have a place in undergraduate course work. Fall 2015 brought black student demands for more support within the administrations policies and practices.[35] The President responded with continued reflection participation and action.[36] Emory leadership responded with reference to each demand and current offices and programs addressing each and planning for further dialogue.[37]

Emory works for **bright, resolute** individuals willing to tackle issues that cut across regional and national borders. They can assign fun to second place in order to reach a larger purpose. Socializing occurs around structured academic group projects, service learning and sports. Emory's intramural motto is "Athletics for All." As a Division III university, more than half of the students are active in intramurals. There is also traditional socializing within the many Greek organizations. The Greek life is well-supported and approved by the university in part because they connect with the surrounding neighborhoods through volunteer service. The November 2015 Veterans Day speech on campus had faculty, dean, staff and students in the audience. Veterans sat in all four sections. Service is common at Emory for all levels of community in America. Since bustling Atlanta is right outside the campus, they often go to a new restaurant, catch a game of the Braves or Atlanta Falcons, shop in eclectic stores or volunteer in the community. The substantial northeastern student population is right at home in the big city.

Compatibility with Personality Types and Preferences

Teaching here is devoted to developing critical thinking first and then passing on subject content. It's a tall order for four undergraduate years and Emory is aware of the critical nature of American society to skip ahead to the fun stuff. "Students who explore and expand upon the current body of knowledge with world class professors" is a good way to think of Emory's broad educational philosophy. Self-sufficient students thrive here. A healthy appreciation and comfort level (S) with the facts is a necessity and a given. At the same time, Emory demands interpretation and synthesis within the curriculum. Logical, sequential thought (T) is expected to lead somewhere—be it an end point or a beginning point. Introduction and foundation study rediscovers the previous brilliant minds in the established fields like electro-magnetism.

Intuitive leaps (N) are regularly accepted and expected in the classroom, although not as the primary learning tool. The administration and faculty at Emory are very open to creative students who want to propose a new line of study or a new location for an off-campus experience. The energy here is purposeful, directed toward productivity and accrual of knowledge. The School of Theology has a place and presence across the campus. In its own way, Emory is a very affirming, optimistic environment for undergraduate students coming of age in an underperforming economy with American bipolarization and social upheaval. This campus is judicious and contemplative as it develops concepts within their community and their outreach. At graduation, students are well-positioned for continuing professional studies and are likely to serve as ethical anchors in their communities.

Now read below about one of the majors that MBTI® research shows people of your type have selected since the mid-20th century. After, refer to Chapter Five for the 50 or so majors that can help you prepare for careers your type has selected. Most importantly, remember that this college description is a suggestion for exploration, not a commanding order. You can be successful in any major at any college.

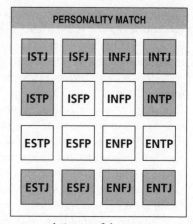

ISTJ will find the campus environment to their liking since it focuses on learning first and residential life later. Learning makes sense when it is the goal. The minor in **Computer Informatics** is a great choice for this type who wants to bring usefulness to uncorrelated data. ISTJ could go for a major in any other field and could/should pick up this minor. The Emory campus has clean lines and functional organization. ISTJs approve of it.

INTP is the curious, global type who understands quickly and gets intensely absorbed in their studies. They are an excellent fit for intellectual Emory. The joint major in **Economics/Math** allows this type to solve equations and/or puzzles, a favorite pastime. This degree is particularly for moving on to graduate study in economics or business study through quantitative analysis. Either one gives INTP the quiet space they like.

ENTJ will appreciate Emory's joint degree in **Psychology and Linguistics**. Brain development and awareness through language is a huge new research area. Undergrads get basic grounding in each of these fields and move on to studying cognition and language. The required Directed Study is about research with faculty advising and will take advantage of Emory's amazing labs in the health sciences. ENTJ is all about energy and enthusiasm, just like Emory.

ESTJ likes the regular educational model i.e. the teacher as the giver of knowledge and students as the eager recipient. With the BA in **Physics**, this type can be ready to enter medicine, law, teaching or business. ESTJs will want to narrow down the focus early and will get help from the great faculty in this department. Junior and senior year requires undergrads to keep a detailed laboratory notebook and that works well for this type, the organized note taker.

INTJ, ever the original, independent and skeptical student, will find that Emory applauds their style. There is enough wiggle room in the curriculum to explore emerging interests. INTJs might be challenging the wisdom presented in class but will do so quietly. After months, they could bring up their ideas with a few twists. Intense conversation in class is open and research can follow to check out those twists on the subject. The minor in **Science, Culture and Society** is tackling the likes of bioterrorism, race, addiction and well-being. Each of these is complex enough to take on INTJs twists.

ISTP is detached and seems "laid back." They might get some arched eyebrows from their hard-charging peers at Emory. Fortunately, ISTPs pay very close attention to the facts and steps in a process and will be appreciated by professors in the **Biology** major. This type will sign up for the department's summer undergraduate research with a faculty mentor. It is a great introduction to the ABCs of basic scientific inquiry and typical of Emory's focus on teaching.

ISFJ is a careful person who wants to serve mankind and soak up facts when learning in a stable environment. The department of **Nursing** at Emory's Woodruff School of Nursing considers it a privilege to care for the ill. ISFJ would agree. This type might find extracurricular programs offered by the school of theology for undergraduate students definitely worth exploring. The Farmworker Family Health Program really will connect sensitive ISFJs with hands-on health care for southwest Georgia farmers.

INFJ and the **Religion** major at Emory are a natural. The department is exceptional for its academic and moral foundation thanks to the Chandler School of Theology. The school, while remaining solid with its historical Christian heritage, offers extraordinary courses to the undergraduate. The curriculum addresses religious questions that we are familiar with, minus contemporary political agendas. The curriculum is distinguished for its absence of narrow courses in cult, myth and splinter quasi-religious practice now popular at many liberal arts colleges in America. INFJs will salute the complex nuances this department is willing to take on. There is emphasis on studying the Qur'an and its literal translations in connection with western civilization particularly in this century.

ENFJ likes to start with the people approach before the facts and details. The interesting joint major in **Classics/History** gives this determined type the tools to tolerate the facts with quantitative analysis of primary texts. This is a degree in critical thinking that translates well with graduate study and American enterprise. Emory undergrads get access to the best of faculty lectures and symposiums in the graduate and professional schools of Nursing, Business and Theology. Each of these three keep current day social and political trends from simplifying their academic curriculum.

ESFJ will like a minor in **Nutrition Science** because the four required courses are oriented to people throughout their life span. That makes for very careful and caring attention for the clients they will work with in the future. This type likes to work in traditional organizations, so ESFJ will look for internships in community health centers, schools and residential group homes. At Emory, the university is committed to quality internships and posts the requirements by the National Association of Colleges and Employers which describe the nature of good internships.

FLORIDA SOUTHERN COLLEGE

111 Lake Hollingsworth Drive
Lakeland, FL 33801-5689
Website: www.flsouthern.edu
Admissions Telephone: 863-680-4131
Undergraduates: 2,670: 987 Men, 1,683 Women

Physical Environment

Located half-way between Orlando and Tampa, Florida Southern College sits on the edge of a large pond just outside of Lakeland. Several buildings on this campus were designed by the iconic American architect, Frank Lloyd Wright. The chapel has long rectangular windows that shoot rays of light throughout the day, creating a mood and feel that encourages **spirituality**. Newer buildings such as the library blend in with **Wright's classic architecture** and call to students interested in **America's architectural heritage**. The Becker Business building, designed by architect Robert Stern of New York, squares well with Wright architecture and has a simulated trading floor, classroom, labs and cafe. Florida Southern is very well connected with the **business community** and the state of Florida. It is a great location for internships, just think ESPN and Disney. Yet, the national and international nature of **Junior Journey** gives each undergraduate a choice to travel with faculty of their major and that is quality competition.

The Rinker Technology Center has a cyber lounge and the latest stuff for seminars and work spaces. A campus tour through the performing arts facility speaks to students who are serious about **music and dramatic performance**. The pool and pond offer a **fun-in-the-sun** lifestyle with competitive water sports. Campus traditions like Steak and Shrimp night speak for themselves. Students who want more diversion drive to Orlando or Tampa and the gulf coast beaches. Florida Southern College draws students who want that residential, private college feel.

Social Environment

The majority of students come from Florida and prefer a community with **small town ambiance**. In 2015, while some campuses demonstrated against police actions across the country, students here walked to the Lakeland Police Department to show their support and appreciation. The successful Florida Southern student graduated high school with a good GPA and several extracurricular activities on their resume. Professors are open and very successful with undergraduate programming in several learning styles, for a range of interests and talents. This campus is calling out to students with traditional liberal arts expectations and goals centered on employment and career options.

Undergraduates at Florida Southern are **cooperative**, casual and friendly. Relaxing in the fall sunshine while peering into iPads or quietly talking over energy drinks, they settle in quickly on this well-designed campus. **Fraternities and sororities** receive good support here from the administration and the student body. Freshmen who like a **family feel** go for the First Year Halls that are either co-ed, all male or all female. Campus Ministries are student-led and many choose to grow in understanding their faith while at Florida Southern.

The college administration has a lengthy, cooperative relationship with the town of Lakeland. Since the 1970s, students and community leaders have pooled their efforts through a non-profit organization in order to benefit both town and college. Students participate in the many **service projects** for Lakeland families and seniors who are representative of solid **Middle America**. The Love Local project marketed and took orders on campus for fresh farm produce grown in the immediate surroundings. Winter 2016 found Florida Southern students showing their support at the Police Appreciation Day in town. Students here focus on their studies with daily attention, energy and a mind to service. They are proud of their academic and artistic work and expect to be successful and productive throughout their careers.

Compatibility with Personality Types and Preferences

Florida Southern College has a solid tradition of American social values which evolved on this campus community through decades of membership and affiliation with the Methodist Church. Florida Southern's ethical belief system is easily understood in the Cornerstone Concept of civil behavior expected of all students who enroll at the college. The honor code is a personal obligation of each student. The administration takes care to communicate it clearly (S). The standards in procedure and policy apply equally to faculty, staff and students. Academic philosophy leans heavily toward practical knowledge and skills. Much of the faculty in business has had entrepreneurial experience in the private sector.

The website is loaded with visuals that send a supportive picture of campus life. The Second Year Experience focuses attention on returning sophomores like that given to the first year students on campus. The entire community honors friendliness and contribution to others through service learning (F). From this foundation of strong values and helping others, the college promotes educational excellence. The innovative and unique Junior Journey is an overseas or domestic off-campus learning program that is individually tailored and organized at the department level. The sites visited directly correlate to the major and the world beyond the campus boundaries. At Florida Southern, there is much to be appreciated in traditional American perspectives.

Now read below about one of the majors that MBTI® research shows people of your type have selected since the mid-20th century. After, refer to Chapter Five for the 50 or so majors that can help you prepare for careers your type has selected. Most importantly, remember that this college description is a suggestion for exploration, not a commanding order. You can be successful in any major at any college.

ISTJ will get solid coursework with the **Business** degree and Finance track that emphasizes skills and management tools. The fo-

PERSONALITY MATCH			
ISTJ	ISFJ	INFJ	INTJ
ISTP	ISFP	INFP	INTP
ESTP	ESFP	ENFP	ENTP
ESTJ	ESFJ	ENFJ	ENTJ

cus on management helps ISTJs understand risk management. Often meticulous in what they do, ISTJ will respect and enjoy the excellent student-professor collaboration at Florida Southern. Commercial banking is a great option for this type.

ISFJ would rally to the call for help from juveniles in our youth detention facilities. On this campus, the degree in **Criminology** is well supported by the overall educational philosophy of service to others. Their reflective nature and ability to clearly see reality will be an asset in the career field. American youth are poorly served by both the national media and confusing policies in public schools. Mental health statistics reflect the need for quality programs in the early teen years.

INFJ has a mind full of impressions about the subjects they want to study. They hope those ideal impressions become a reality. The major in **Youth Ministry** at Florida Southern will help INFJ look at and create spiritual activities for youth in American churches. The required internship in senior year could connect ideals with practicality. This passionate type will be good at introducing biblical studies that bring meaning to today's teens that can be swamped by social media.

ISFP and art is a natural and likely combination. Visual art and design is hard to miss on this campus. The major in **Studio Art** with flexibility for concentration in sculpture, painting, ceramics, printing or photography is a good bet for this type. The department seeks to explore the relationship between art and emotion. The minor in **Advertising Design** will add a practical set of skills for job options after graduation.

INFP thinks about meaning and doesn't search for answers in facts or memorization. The **Religion** major at Florida Southern is a good starting point for their search. The department has excellent Judeo-Christian course work that explores the theological history. The McKay Archives Center is a treasure trove for American spirituality. Collegiate traditions, dating back decades, help students discover lost religious expression. Graduates of this department are accepted across America's seminaries and graduate schools of theology.

ESTP goes for action in the real world. The major in **Biotechnology** is all about the natural world. It is a wide open field that has research and job opportunities in surprising environments like biofuels, genetic research, agricultural crops and pharmaceuticals. The department requires a range of basic courses in chemistry and biology. ESTP will like the required original research study in junior or senior year.

ESFP who is interested in sports, whether playing or as a fan, might look into the **Sports Communication Marketing** major at Florida Southern. This campus with hands-on philosophy in business and communication is great for this unusual major. Florida spring training camps in baseball, college football teams and Disney's nearby ESPN center have good options for sports reporting and internships. Resourceful ESFPs will love using the HD video equipment to create their own sports broadcasts.

ENFP is going to find that the **Graphic Design** studies here offer a wide scope within the discipline. Admission requires an art portfolio. ENFP in high school can meet with their art teachers to focus and present their best work in the portfolio. This will help because once at Florida Southern, the faculty will make use of conversation and evaluation. That approach will help ENFPs, scattered at times, keep their eye on the goal of employment in specific sectors. On this campus there is no shortage of coursework that ENFP is likely to want to take.

ESTJ will move into the **Accounting** major or minor with ease because they are a pretty objective type. Their impersonal judgment is valued in this entrepreneurial study. Yes, accounting is now more than budget numbers. Today, accountants have to describe the current company position and predict future direction. The department centers its courses toward this. Undergrads will use audit software that simulates business activity.

ESFJ knows the art of sincere conversation. Their interest in others is also sincere and a distinct advantage when interviewing eye witnesses. Students in the News Media I, II or III courses will practice before broadcast cameras as news anchors and reporters. The major in **Broadcast, Print and Online Media** demands memory for detail and a versatile approach which ESFJ has in spades. This type might research in the McKay Center and bring some of the historical facts of those 20th mid-century decades into a background story for today's youngest Millennials born in the late 1990s.

ENFJ will find a warm, personal faculty in the department of **Psychology**. The curriculum emphasizes human behavior and interpersonal relationships which suit this type just fine. ENFJs will thrive on the personal mentoring within this department. Their right-on communication skills will be helpful to communities and individuals with new insights from their Florida Southern years.

FURMAN UNIVERSITY

Office of Admissions
Greenville, SC 29613
Website: www.furman.edu
Admissions Telephone: 864-294-2034
Undergraduates: 2,810; 1,208 Men, 1,602 Women

Physical Environment

Right on the edge of the Blue Ridge Mountains, this rigorous liberal arts university mixes colonial Williamsburg architectural style and red-brick walkways that crisscross the central interior lawn. The **landscape** is breathtaking and remarkable with its 18-hole golf course. The classroom buildings are modern and stuffed with the **latest technology**. Many are environmentally certified and designed with recycled materials for energy efficiency. Furman led the way among its college peers with the first environmental awards for new college construction in the south. The technology classrooms are designed to pipe in **fresh air and oxygen**. North Village, efficient with geothermal energy, provides all cooling and heat for on-campus apartments. The university PAC solar project sends unused electricity to the regional grid. The business office scours the financial exchanges for commodities like natural gas and ties down advantageous prices. Energy and facility planning on this campus is a study in **beauty and efficiency**.

Pretty much all of the campus has recently been renovated. The Bell Tower, a **6-bell carillon**, overlooks the small lake and amphitheater used for **outdoor concerts** and both point to the Furman music conservatory. New apartment-style residence halls and the conference center look out on this landscaped view also. Furman architecture functions for students who are lively, active and caring of the environment.

Social Environment

Most Furman students keep their family, hometown traditions and Christian values in mind throughout their days on campus. A Furman education is a family affair. During family weekend, everyone is invited, including cousins, uncles and grandparents. About one-third are actively involved in a religious organization. Influence of the university's Baptist heritage and Christian social responsibility is found across the curriculum and Furman's many outreach programs. The Chapel is a favorite for weddings, sacred concerts, weekly dinners, bible study and lectures. Students of the Judeo-Christian theology explore the eternal questions of "Why are we here?" and "What are we supposed to be doing?"

Undergraduates form a strong community that is civic-minded. Pretty much all of the **undergraduates' volunteer hours** of service or skills are in nearby Greenville. Furman students are environmentally conscious and politically interested. Well-known speakers are often on campus, scheduled by the university's non-partisan political think-tank that also funds student research. About half of the student body belong to Greek organizations, all of which get into volunteer activities like Relay for Life and Special Olympics. Palladin Division I athletics, club, intramural, wellness and fitness are all vibrant on campus. This university reflects conservative tradition that focuses on moral, prosocial community. The administration and student organizations invite speakers of differing perspectives. Students here actively blog their thoughts afterward.

Students like the liberal arts and dig deeply into their major. Professors are at Furman because they like to teach and are active in their disciplines with **research**. The undergraduate degree at Furman is really about a **four-year professional environment and experience**. Students expect this and support it with their own **skills, talents** and productivity. The Furman experience is about having fun, going off campus for internships, study abroad and scientific inquiries in the field. The academic **calendar is nontraditional** and it adds length and **rigor** to the collegiate workload. The great majority of students come from out of the state.

Compatibility with Personality Types and Preferences

Furman University purposely combines traditional religious values of the 20th Century with a trendy educational outlook of the 21st century. Faculty and administration create a lively social and academic experience for undergrads. There is a strong attraction to technology in use by today's generation. Furman embraces and uses it. Students use social media, text messaging and the ever present iPhone apps for collaborative projects. This experiential learning is a hallmark of the university's attraction to the future. Short travel classes are built right into the course requirements and funded with department budgets. Academic international travel is part of this administration's focus on cultures and ethnicities. Paladins look to gain academic competence and reject political trending that influences understanding toward socially progressive perspectives.

Students who have mastered the scientific method after first year courses are encouraged to join faculty in research. They will get academic advising during research experiences which are plentiful. Professors are tuned to the future and today's American practices in the public and business square. Service to others (F) is a common theme and volunteer events are organized and successful for both student and community member. There is a strong ethic for productivity. The pathways (J) are in place for undergraduates to double major and take additional coursework. Furman provides a creative environment through hands-on research and direct learning.

Students who like to get the facts and details (S) first and then move toward a general understanding of their subject will do well here.

Now read below about one of the majors that MBTI® research shows people of your type have selected since the mid-20th century. After, refer to Chapter Five for the 50 or so majors that can help you prepare for careers your type has selected. Most importantly, remember that this college description is a suggestion for exploration, not a commanding order. You can be successful in any major at any college.

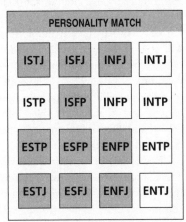

PERSONALITY MATCH

ISTJ	ISFJ	INFJ	INTJ
ISTP	ISFP	INFP	INTP
ESTP	ESFP	ENFP	ENTP
ESTJ	ESFJ	ENFJ	ENTJ

INFJ will find the **Theater Arts** curriculum at Furman University really quite thorough. One look at the current performances on campus each season explains why we recommend this degree at this university. Each undergraduate will be practiced in stage management, technical crew, publicity and acting. Introspective INFJ brings imagery and symbolism to theater. The department is ideal for its smaller size and mentoring. Original and introspective, the season production of *Arcadia* looked at time moving backwards and the choices that we make. That is right up the INFJ alley.

ISTJ might take a close look at the **Economics** degree at Furman University. It has much that appeals to ISTJs, especially the step-by-step survey of the economics and its connection to social policy. This sequential approach is how they want to master any abstract subject, including economics. The required capstone course in senior year, Empirical Methods in Economics, gets a set of financials ready for regression analysis software and other methods. This type of direct observational study leads to the best understanding for ISTJs.

ISFJ with a good ear for music will love the professional department of music at Furman. The major in **Music Theory** rotates performance requirements between choral, vocal, solo, ensembles and string quartet. The ISFJ is a sensitive person and quite aware of how others are feeling during any given activity. This type will bring a personal meaning to their musical composition and performance along with a precise, possibly understated performance. Auditions are required.

ISFP just might move toward a career in pharmaceuticals. The **Chemistry** major at Furman offers a track in biochemistry with the action and practicality that they want. Hands-on research in the labs and the detailed reports of chemical reaction is good stuff with this type. In 2015, a student/faculty research paper explored silver clusters in DNA strands that acted as reporters. This department shines forth with student faculty collaboration in research and learning through scientific inquiry.

ESTP could sign right up after scanning Furman courses in the **Information Technology** major. This major covers current application in software and programming for start up businesses. ESTP will benefit from the nuts and bolts in the course titled Project Management. With this practical collection of skills, they are quite ready for technology-intensive business environments. Undergrads rub elbows with community businessmen in some classes, and this is perfect for ESTP who loves to build a wide network.

ESFP is a natural at public relations. The major in **Communication Studies** will prepare this type for fast-paced social media news cycles. ESFP wants direct connection with people. Their social awareness is a real asset along with knowledge of communication theory. Undergrads at Furman will find there is support for social, moral responsibility in community but without faculty influence in progressive or conservative directions. ESFP's infomercials, produced at WFTV, would be filled with useful, factual information. The Furman student-run TV News has got to be a place to find a little fun too.

ENFP will bring their fun-loving style to Furman where optimism runs high. The major in **Business Administration** teaches the core principles of management through experiential learning and projects. This is good for ENFP to experience community and creativity in the world of business. The basic business block investigates accounting, finance, marketing and operations. With this overview, ENFP can then move into one of these career tracks and might select a minor that pulls at their heart, maybe Furman's unique minor in Poverty.

ESFJ should find the Department of **Biology** at Furman University loaded with options in experiential learning. ESFJs will approve of the read-study-memorize of most first-year courses too. Then it's on to the laboratories and field studies in the courses like African Ecology or the Galapagos. These are two of the "traveling" courses in the department. Students can bring 10 pounds of clothes to give to the local community clothes bank, that leaves eight pounds in the carry-on for them. Social responsibility and conservation biology go hand in hand at this university.

ESTJ is often a go-getter. This type sees their goal and efficiently pursues it. The major in **Accounting** prepares this conscientious type with a great background in the basic business core of classes. This realistic approach, tied to the reality of facts and numbers, is good for ESTJ. Undergraduate research is realistic like the study of foreign automakers opening up manufacturing within the United States.

ENFJ is going to be fine with the major in **Health Sciences**. The department approaches everything through the idea of wellness. ENFJ wants to get to know the whole person—their emotional health, spiritual health and physical health. There is a well-equipped laboratory for studying performance in running and anatomy. Since this type is exceptionally talented at speaking to large audiences, the message of well-being could easily become their prime career focus.

GEORGE WASHINGTON UNIVERSITY

212 I Street, NW
Washington, DC 20052
Website: www.gwu.edu
Admissions Telephone: 202-994-6040
Undergraduates: 10,740; 4,725 Men, 6,015 Women
Graduate Students: 14,873

Physical Environment

George Washington University's downtown campus, fondly known as the Foggy Bottom campus, is within blocks of the White House. When you walk the city streets E to J or 20th to 24th and admire the **tall buildings and Federal style houses** you are on the campus of GW. The location alone lends power and influence to this university's programs. Most of the campus buildings are in the area formed by the Avenues of Pennsylvania, New Hampshire and Virginia. Students walk to **DC museums and monuments**, from the Smithsonian to the Vietnam Veterans Memorial and the Korean War Veterans Memorial. Prospective visiting high schoolers are wowed by the history here. They may not notice the largeness of this environment and the impersonal nature of the campus.

The university master plan for development, completed in 2007, is redeveloping several blocks of GW's current real estate holdings. Square 54 has residential space, retail and commercial business. It is mixed-use and serves as a town center for students, faculty and DC residents. Square 55 has graduate level laboratories for the School of Engineering and the Physical Sciences plus the Biological Sciences, Physics and Chemistry. Square 77, to be opened in Fall 2016, expands residential housing and includes live-in-faculty residences. Each of the squares generate tenant income which is quickly budgeted into the university academic programs and research facilitates.

The **city hustle and bustle** is marked by ethnic shops and restaurants. The study of **Foreign Languages** is exceptionally fine here. Students who want to be near power find this university very appealing. The university and national government offices mix in a blur with professors recently retired or about to return to power with the next election. The housing options at GW are many, ranging from living and learning to residences for fraternities and sororities. The university tries to keep students busy on campus, although the city itself remains a huge draw. Each day there are dozens of on campus events ranging from debates to athletics to concerts to comedy. GW also offers a quieter location at its Mount Vernon Campus, fenced in with mature trees and red-brick buildings contrasting dramatically with Foggy Bottom sidewalks and vertical architecture. Students can take classes at either campus.

Social Environment

Students come from a considerable **variety of socio-economic** backgrounds. Some have parents in the diplomatic core. Others may be referred to GW by their country's embassy in Washington, DC. Home-grown U.S. students from across the nation regularly enroll for this unique collegiate experience. The worldly international students provide an open door to other cultures for the American undergraduates. U.S. students expect to secure **internships in federal offices**, political lobbies, corporate business headquarters and nonprofits. **International students** expect to enlarge their knowledge of American society and practices.

GW is a mega university and students gain bureaucratic skills simply by negotiating their own educational study and presence on campus within the first year. They learn to expertly navigate the somewhat tight rules of the university. To counter the **impersonal impact of the city** and largeness of the student body, the residential life staff plans **homey, fun activities** that remind undergraduates of the calmer lives in their hometowns. **Volunteer initiatives**, very familiar to the Millennial generation, are well-supported. Collegiate activities help resupply student energies to deal with the city and remain positive and self-directed. DC political, corporate and governmental soirees create a privileged setting very much unlike lower and middle class America. The university reflects the **progressive nature** of politics in Washington, DC. The degree in American Studies is marked by its absence of foundational principles, revolutionary history, European immigration in the late 1880s or American scientific contributions to western civilization. Rather this major is approached through American minority experiences of late 20th century and that is common at many American colleges and universities today. The university hosted the President's Community Service Campus Challenge National Gathering in Fall 2014. Students from across the country learned about interfaith civic engagement and using their local communities for learning experiences.[38]

Compatibility with Personality Types and Preferences

George Washington University takes much of its persona from DC, the nation's capital. GW echoes the nature of bureaucratic DC with practicality. On this campus questions within all academic disciplines are: What works? What is of value within the social sciences? (T) The university is a good neighbor. It is mindful of adjacent businesses, residences and corporations, including them regularly in university expansions that impact neighborhood activity. Students drawn to George Washington University want to experience it all, so their friends on campus and the student body in general must serve as the stable anchor.

Families of potential students understand that the campus offers a secure, predictable collegiate atmosphere within its buildings. The environment is fast-paced energy outside of campus and students want a safe place at the end of the day. Undergraduates are expecting to build and advance their academic skills. They want to learn how to negotiate the administrative lobbies, regulatory bodies, executive offices and national government. GW's curriculum is magnified several times over through its faculty and access to contemporary speakers.

Collaboration between the university and other influential partners, like Ford Motor Company, add to the intrigue of real time problems and solutions. Professors can be careerists who are also high-level civil service employees, policy makers, party officials, lobbyists and think tankers in the legions of administrators who work in DC. Above all else, students who are successful at GW must be oriented outside of their dormitory and outside of their campus (E), drawn into the movement of the city and happy to catch a last minute ride (P) for a wide-eyed day of learning.

Now read below about one of the majors that MBTI® research shows people of your type have selected since the mid-20th century. After, refer to Chapter Five for the 50 or so majors that can help you prepare for careers your type has selected. Most importantly, remember that this college description is a suggestion for exploration, not a commanding order. You can be successful in any major at any college.

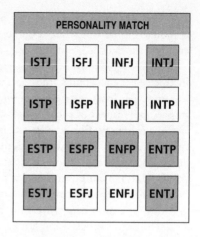

PERSONALITY MATCH

ISTJ	ISFJ	INFJ	INTJ
ISTP	ISFP	INFP	INTP
ESTP	ESFP	ENFP	ENTP
ESTJ	ESFJ	ENFJ	ENTJ

INTJ has the objectivity, vision and determination to deal with abstract ideas. The degree in **Geography** makes use of all three. The subject has evolved since the 1980s and exploded into other sub-disciplines like economic geography and political geography. Today's geographers highlight and predict land usage with their mathematical methods and ethical perspectives. INTJ will fit into this discipline which has philosophical foundations. At GW, the department uses spatial patterns as a starting point. The recent massive migration out of the Middle East, sparked by Islamic State, ISIS genocide and terrorism, into Europe is a perfect example of why and how geographers can quantify and study the effects on behalf of the European citizens undergoing radical social change.

ISTP can go for studying engineering techniques. The major in **Systems Engineering** is pretty much about this and coming up with software programs that predict productivity in big arenas like defense, management and manufacturing. ISTP in this program will take many classes in mathematics and modeling. In this large university, they will need to look for a spot to tinker with the engineering techniques and modeling software packages, perhaps in the computer engineering department.

ISTJ is going to like the looks of the Bachelor Degree in **Accountancy** at George Washington University. The business school provides programs to assure GW undergraduates will be prepared for the national certification. Lectures by well-connected faculty and the simulated stock market classroom anchor the department's approach. This type avoids risky activity, sticking with the tried and approved. Undergrads also have access to research projects through paid positions.

ESTP is good with physical fitness, part of their lively personality. The Milken Institute School of Public Health at GW has a great combination for this type. The major or minor is available in **Exercise Science** and **Athletic Training**. At GW, the undergraduates will intern in places like DC area Division I universities and colleges, high schools, medical clinics and other health settings. These opportunities will not be lost on ESTP who will build a personal network for job opportunities after graduation. The department is small and undergrads form their own small group on this huge urban campus.

ESFP is excellent at conversing with staff and patients in the health field. The major or minor in **Public Health** really fits well with this Type. The Milken School offers personalized educational study and it starts with the application to be admitted. It won't be a problem for ESFP to write up the public health issue that concerns them most. Generous and supporting, there are a lot of special populations that can use their sympathetic interest and concern. This is also offered as a 5-year program which leads to a Masters Degree in Public Health.

ENFP has a tender, fun-loving personality. The thought of working with children appeals to this type. At GW the **Speech and Hearing Sciences** major starts with coursework in biology, communication, psychology and linguistics. Later coursework introduces methods for diagnosing and treating disorders. GW has its own Speech and Hearing Clinic which is open to the public where undergrads might observe therapy. Advanced graduate study is required in this field and ENFP may also choose to minor in subjects that offer employment after graduation.

ENTP plus the unpredictable makes for a good day since they cannot stand routine. The major in **Middle Eastern Studies** during the 21st century is clearly many things, but routine is not one. This complicated political region offers clever ENTPs entry to business and government positions that operate at national levels. The major requires third year proficiency in foreign language. Independent, strategic and analytical, this type will not shrink from this degree.

ESTJ is especially good at being systematic, organized and efficient. The degree in **German Language and Literature** could introduce and launch them into a career translating professional documents. Critical translation that cuts to the heart of diplomatic treaties, technological papers or business contracts could put ESTJ in the driver's seat. GW operates a language center downloading television programming from around the world in native languages. This large department with over 50 faculty members provides access to global cultures through selected internships.

ENTJ will find that the **Japanese Language and Literature** major lives in two academic centers at GW: The Elliott School of International Affairs and the Columbian College of Arts and Sciences. Between the two, students get both worlds: art and politics. During four undergraduate years, this assertive, goal-oriented type will approach the courses with career thoughts of diplomacy, government, higher education, law or business. ENTJ can get familiar with the oral and written Japanese language by visiting DC's cultural centers and museums. The geopolitical nature of the Pacific Rim nations will not be lost on this type. They prefer to move in power circles.

GEORGETOWN UNIVERSITY

Office of Admission
37th and P Streets, NW
Washington, DC 20057
Website: www.georgetown.edu
Admissions Telephone: 202-687-5084
Undergraduates: 7,595; 3,418 Men, 4,177 Women
Graduate Students: 10,263

Physical Environment

The two tall steeples of Georgetown University stand over the Potomac River as they did in much earlier times, before **Washington, DC** became the capital of the United States. In the early 1800s the nation's capital moved from Philadelphia to Washington. On a strip of land between Maryland and Virginia, they formed an independent district named after Christopher Columbus. Today, Georgetown University sits on 110 acres of this very strategic property. The university has absorbed the culture of the nation's capital with its power centers and regulatory bodies.

Campus architecture is a mix of historic and 21st century structures. Georgetown founders, the **Catholic Jesuits**, offer daily Mass in the Dahlgren Chapel of the Sacred Heart, located right in the center of campus. The campus buildings have inclusive spaces for celebrating the spiritual life of students, **regardless of their religion**. Georgetown is replacing older, familiar dormitory-style floor plans with the suite-style **Northeast Triangle** Residence Hall, open Fall 2016.

Regents Hall houses biology, chemistry and physics. Chock-full of the latest technological labs and equipment, the facility bears a resemblance to **historic architecture** prevalent on the campus.

The university has a vigilant security presence on the campus to help undergraduates negotiate the unpredictable nature of the city. The Georgetown campus is not only a stone's throw from the **White House** but also a stone's throw from the nation's most important monuments and museums. When students need a diversion from the intense academics, Washington, DC offers many options.

Social Environment

Georgetown students use **abstract and concrete reasoning** to define their campus environment. They enjoy ethical and humanistic discussion and what it means to live in 21st Century America. They go for methodologies and models that predict outcomes. Many come from worldly, influential families. Approximately one-half of the students identify as minorities or international. Many students speak **more than one language**. The campus, true to its Jesuit tradition, embraces people of other religions and encourages appreciation of worldwide spiritual views. The university supports over 100 off-campus initiatives involving undergraduates serving the needy population in the nation's capital. They also maintain an active blog to increase student awareness of all religions. In 2011, the university hosted an intensive interfaith leadership training by the non-profit, Chicago-based Interfaith Youth Core, a partner with the U.S. Department of Education. University staff and campus allies from across the country attended.[39] The outcome of interfaith work is questioned by some in the theological field.[40]

Georgetown students work hard and play hard. This demanding academic environment finds students partying on the weekends. Other stress busters include rooting for the Hoyas, often nationally ranked in several sports, especially basketball. Georgetown Athletics boasts **Jack the Bulldog**, Hoyas mascot, available for private engagements as well as antics at the basketball games since 1964. With over 150 years of continuous performances, the student-led **Mask and Bauble Dramatic Society** at Georgetown University takes on a life of its own.

A number of majors in the undergraduate curriculum, such as in the **School of Foreign Service**, cover **unique disciplines** that are offered only as graduate study in other universities. They each have additional application requirements. As interdisciplinary majors they are designed and approved within departmental guidelines. Admission to Georgetown is just the beginning of landing the courses to fit an undergraduate dream. Faculty is **progressive in political view** for the most part as are most of the undergraduates. Conservative awareness and perspectives do pop up though. The American Studies major presents a balanced historical exploration of the revolutionary and 18th century American experience. In the School of Foreign Service there are emerging national research studies focused on 2015's cascading threats to the American nation.

Georgetown University is for those who want to secure policy positions within government, diplomatic corps, international organizations, think tanks and research. At Georgetown and in the capital, students **observe power and policy** at work. They see the government up close.

Compatibility with Personality Types and Preferences

Georgetown University could be thought of as an experiment in strategic engagement. This influential university is in a privileged position as it develops educational content with global perspectives. Looking over at the national capitol, two blocks from undergraduate housing lofts, provides a visual cue for the university's familiar coexistence (E) with power and leadership in our national government.

Much like the government itself, this university is organized by schools and colleges similar to a wiring diagram (J). The undergraduate schools and colleges are quite separate from each other. One can imagine the State Department with its own culture and mission as quite separate from the Treasury Department. In this way, Georgetown's School of Foreign Policy and the School of Business can be envisioned as existing quite independently of each other, yet part of the same university. Undergraduates get a full academic fire hosing of abstraction (N). An excellent example is the unusual Entrepreneurship Fellows Program. It helps students project

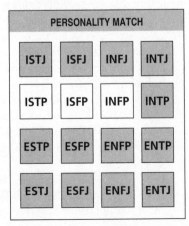

PERSONALITY MATCH

ISTJ	ISFJ	INFJ	INTJ
ISTP	ISFP	INFP	INTP
ESTP	ESFP	ENFP	ENTP
ESTJ	ESFJ	ENFJ	ENTJ

their own aptitude for success. Factual knowledge (S) is honored on this campus with emphasis in the sciences on analysis, methodology, systems and technologies.

Now read below about one of the majors that MBTI® research shows people of your type have selected since the mid-20th century. After, refer to Chapter Five for the 50 or so majors that can help you prepare for careers your type has selected. Most importantly, remember that this college description is a suggestion for exploration, not a commanding order. You can be successful in any major at any college.

INFJ desires an understanding of other peoples and their cultural values. They apply their insight to ethnic cultures with ease because of their own natural empathy. In the School of Foreign Service the major in **Culture and Politics** looks to understand how politics is formed by cultural practice and power. It is pretty abstract and the INFJ is particularly suited for it. With this major and a self-selected concentration, this type might see positions in international or national organizations that practice power diplomacy and political action.

INTJ looks at the majors available in the School of Foreign Service and says, "Yeah." They just might narrow in on **Global Business** because it is darn flexible for a lifetime of career productivity, and INTJ has very long-range vision and is already thinking about mid-career options. But first they can settle in on a basic business core with political and economics electives. Undergrads take business courses through the McDonough School of Business.

ISTJ likes to stay calm and consistently work toward the goal. This type is dedicated to accuracy and doesn't mind studying the fine details. All the better for the major in **Science, Technology and International Affairs** since there are so many details. The School of Foreign Service offers this major with a choice in concentrations. The perfect concentration for this type would be the Science, Technology and Security core. America needs this powerhouse concentrator to monitor the deadly incoming cyber attacks directed at the America. You go ISTJ, check in with the CIA. They fortunately started recasting investigative teams in spring 2015 to target Islamic State, ISIS.

ISFJ can be a deep soul on occasion, often pondering. The major in **International History** in the School of Foreign Service at Georgetown actually frames the question, Why did the world get this way? Answers will come often from the past as America struggles with the volatile Middle East, the unstable eastern European border states, Russia and China, The department asks students to select an area of interest. Meticulous, conscientious and pondering—this major is perfect for ISFJ.

INTP is intensely curious and quickly picks up on theories. The major in **Neurobiology** is really research intensive. This type will be okay with the hours in the lab peering down at cell and molecular structures. The DC power centers in the nation's capital are technologically connected and emerging research is in the Georgetown air. INTP will need to breath deeply because career direction after graduation could be an unknown with all those hours spent in the labs. Faculty advising will be important.

ESTP is often a confident type, looking for action and ready to move into unfamiliar territory. The **Regional Studies in Africa** at this university will supply them with methods and theory to survey the vast continent. In the last two years, they will select a topic, perhaps religions of Africa. Their application essay for approval of the topic will be a bit of a chore. Yet Pope Francis on tour to Uganda in November 2014, praised the President for accepting refugees into the country.

ESFP is practical and likes to study what is happening today. So **Regional Study in Asia** with its self-selected focus is a good choice. Did we mention this type is realistic? If you've traveled to this region you know just how difficult land, air and sea journeys can be. Now here is the connection. This type often goes into transportation. International and national corporations will be laying down transportation infrastructure across India with the Great Asian Highway Project and ESFP can be in the middle of it.

ENFP likes to keep their imagination well-supplied with new ideas. We think the **Certificate in Australian and New Zealand Studies** with a major in Science, Technology and International Affairs will work pretty well. These two studies really combine nicely for traveling ENFP who understands the rising importance of Pacific Basin cultures and enterprise. Their required paper can be on any emerging technology that has application in the southern hemispheric ocean-going nations. How about development of lightweight mechanical loading/off loading systems in smaller, regional harbors?

ENTP has many interests, all the world is a stage according to ENTPs. Yet they often can be found in the field of **Computer Science**. At this university, the department philosophy is about preparing for the future in the lightning fast world of data. The fundamental courses are taught with the principles that underlie the basics. ENTP will also get a complete instruction on multiple programming sets and learning how to program in several. This field works for ENTPs because they can be their regular theoretical, curious selves.

ESFJ has a successful day when they can support folks in ordinary life doing ordinary things. The stable and traditional study of **Art History** has been around for centuries and folks have been looking at art in museums for centuries. This is good territory for ESFJ. The location of Georgetown University in the middle of world class museums becomes the classroom for ESFJ. The study of art is so centered on humanity which, to repeat, this type needs for a successful day. Perhaps ESFJ will come across Brughel's medieval art. It is fascinating.

ESTJ can be a director for others in tough environments. The major in **Biological Physics** is a demanding study and will continue to be a demanding field as it moves into everyday scientific application. This type will probably pass up the research fields and move directly into law, medicine or business. The Bachelor of Arts has the extra room for electives in the McDonough School of Business or the School of Foreign Studies. Hard working ESTJ can jump between the three schools and not get lost or distracted.

ENFJ will sometimes take a leadership position. The degree at Georgetown University in **American Musical Culture** is unusual but can translate into journalism, arts management or entertainment law. America's gift to the world of music, jazz, is calling out for a New Orleans internship and will make for a great senior capstone project. A visit to the national WWII museum, near the French Quarter, will cinch the connection between American benevolence and American musical talents. Even Millennials smile at the snappy, optimistic tunes of that War.

ENTJ is happy to step out and conduct the orchestra. The certificate in **Eurasian, Russian and East European Studies** will just be another instrument in their band. Their entrepreneurial style will see the value when paired with a major in the School of Business or the School of Foreign Policy. Emerging markets or the invasions by Russia's Putin point to the importance of this major. ENTJ has the resilience and strategic thinking to contribute in both of these areas.

GEORGIA INSTITUTE OF TECHNOLOGY

22 North Avenue, NW
Atlanta, GA 30332-0320
Website: www.gatech.edu
Admissions Telephone: 404-894-4154
Undergraduates: 14,682; 9,715 Men, 4,967 Women
Graduate Students: 8,427

Physical Environment

Georgia Tech is a premiere public university located in **downtown Atlanta** right where I-75 and I-85 merge. The Georgia Tech campus is **enclosed, angular** with **mega laboratories** and bold architectural design. 'Enclosed' may be the reason this large university also manages to feel comfortably hometown even though Atlanta is just across the street. Athletes love the sports complex and natatorium. Techies like to exercise, swim and play on the club and intramural teams. Creative techies are right at home in the **amazing national laboratories** inside the huge modern architecture. The **concrete, aluminum and glass** structures on this campus are kind of like the manufacturing and research environments that most will enter on graduation.

Students attracted to innovative solutions come to study the environmental science and technology at the top research complex donated by the Ford Motor Company. In 2014, Ford and Georgia Tech developed the **first solar hybrid car**. In 2016, Georgia Tech, Ford and GE are researching drivability of electric with the Ford MyMobileApp. It is crazy how an app is doing research, but there you have it, technology in motion. Its about the design of chips in small devices that amplify and conserve power. Ask any ham radio operator.

The Georgia Tech School of Architecture has the **Digital Building Lab** that brings architects and civil/construction/computing engineers together to solve big time industry challenges. They get to play around in the **Digital Fabrication Laboratory** after they come up with a solution. There are PhD programs in the physical and engineering sciences moving the sciences into the future along with a handful other universities in the United States. Undergraduates are in the laboratories **pushing the state of knowledge** in many disciplines, and solar energy is just one of hundreds of research strands here.

Georgia Tech faculty responded with laptops a blazin' to the terrorism in 2015 and the strategic Russian takeover of Syria and invasion of Ukraine. As did other independent, private top research institutions in the country, this campus brought their resources directly to the problem. The first of its kind **Interdisciplinary Research Institute (IRI)** formed of resources of six colleges in one week and started operating on July 1, 2015. Western civilization and America's strategic place in the balance of world power continues to command respect and priority in the **200 scientific laboratories** at Georgia Tech.

Social Environment

Think **fun** on this campus. The Georgia Tech 2016 front webpage featured animatronic robots in their **Robotarium**. The four Robatariots. They are perfect for entertaining seven-year-old boys, 30-something+ nerd professors and all incoming freshmen. This campus speaks to folks who like **traditional school spirit** and strong competitive teams to cheer.

The majority of students come from towns and rural communities across the state, so there is a cohesive feel to social life. They escape the hectic city pace on this tree-lined campus. They are not turned away by the **study and work demands** of this unique public institution. Students keep good balance between fun and the books, but academic study is intense. Many join Greek life because of their sponsored social activities on campus. Some form networks through friends at the nearby colleges for other social outlets. There are 500 student clubs on this campus. As if that was not enough, the Braves, Falcons and the Atlanta Symphony add to the social calendar. Many students walk to Ponce de Leon Avenue over the connector to favorite local restaurants, clubs, galleries and shops.

Undergraduate students have an **intense affinity and aptitude** for the sciences and math. The all-consuming research on campus is anchored by the university's self-imposed demand to solve **mankind's problems**. Solutions move around inside the airspace on this campus, waiting to be snagged. These students form a strong can-do attitude. They see the future through the lens of **current technology** and emerging possibilities. Those who like practical, hands-on research are thriving. A fair number of students branch out from the physical sciences. The Ivan Allen College of Liberal Arts studies emerging manufactured systems, computing systems and technology for social application in third world countries. The college joined the Department of Education initiative, non-profit, Chicago-based Interfaith Youth Core to prioritize university activities that engage in community service projects with "interfaith" broadly defined to include people of all worldviews and traditions.[41] It is questioned by some in the theological community.[42] Most students, however, have little time to identify with causes and get diverted by advocacy. **Initiative, accountability and progress** are typical of Techies.

Compatibility with Personality Types and Preferences

On many Saturday mornings, a surprising number of students are out and moving around. Saturday morning sleepy heads catch up later. Students go through their day actively with a twinkle of humor. This campus is for the folks who like to see, touch, feel or listen to materials (S). They seek to understand the environment and its properties; they are comfortable with themselves, the temperature, the metal, the circuits and the physicality which is always present on this campus. At the same time they are fairly logical (T) folks who analyze and put stuff together for a purpose. The GA Techie faculty like their undergrads to dissect, step-by-step, what exists: whether in a theorem or in a piece of metal. The learning experience expects to move undergraduates into the future through the basics in each discipline followed by experimentation and research.

Educational philosophy is strongly centered on benefit for society. Sustainability concepts have long been part of Georgia Tech. Faculty and students agree that natural resources are used efficiently and applied with common sense. The laboratories on this campus have historically worked with national defense on fundamental research.

Human sciences are at the center of much biological research. Alert to the societal costs of emerging technologies, graduates become capable of making the tough calls between reality, ideals and politically correct agendas. Georgia Tech undergrads do not wear rose-colored glasses nor do the professors.

Now read below about one of the majors that MBTI® research shows people of your type have selected since the mid-20th century. After, refer to Chapter Five for the 50 or so majors that can help you prepare for careers your type has selected. Most importantly, remember that this college description is a suggestion for exploration, not a commanding order. You can be successful in any major at any college.

PERSONALITY MATCH			
ISTJ	ISFJ	INFJ	INTJ
ISTP	ISFP	INFP	INTP
ESTP	ESFP	ENFP	ENTP
ESTJ	ESFJ	ENFJ	ENTJ

ESTJ is an outstanding fit at Georgia Tech. The Institute's course catalog is exceptionally clear in setting out information about what a student will need to graduate. Course credit is awarded at Georgia Tech for top scores on the SAT Subject Tests taken in high school. The major in **Public Policy** starts with foundation courses in economics, politics, sociology and philosophy. The last two years move on to research and data analysis. Finally, undergrads work with an outside client on a policy issue. ESTJ will bring clarity and objectivity to the table during the meetings over two semesters.

ENTJ wants to take the natural matter in the labs on this campus and reshape it into something new, futuristic and maybe just a little beyond the truly practical. ENTJ might decide to focus on space applications. Aeroelasticity will be called into play with any vehicle starting in earth's atmosphere then translating to the vacuum of space. This is the kind of stuff ENTJ likes with their strategic, objective vision. The **Aerospace Engineering** degree at Georgia Tech is definitely into experimental design.

ENTP could like the **Mechanical Engineering** degree here because it is flexible and works across many fields. Inclined to be avid readers, albeit later in life, ENTPs sometimes like to be troubleshooters. This Georgia Tech department focuses mechanical engineering on the search for the best solution to an engineering problem. For instance, if you have a jet engine that throws out its fan blades on rotation at Mach 1, how to do you get this aircraft back in the air? What exactly is wrong? Could it be the physical grip between the rotating drum and the foot of the blade? The sorry manufacturing of the blade itself? You go to it ENTP, there are a few more possibilities.

ISTP is quite observant but not one of the vocal students at outgoing Georgia Tech. During their first week on campus, they will make a beeline for the Robotarium. But maybe one of the robots is malfunctioning because a composite part is unyielding at a connector. The solution could be in **Materials Science and Engineering**. In this major, they will learn about structure, processing and properties of metal, ceramic and polymers. Upperclassman work in teams to design, build and operate a process, component or material studied in the first years on campus. If ISTP has their way, it will be a moving component.

ESTP would find the **Civil Engineering** degree at Georgia Tech a good bet. The course work requires students to lead and collaborate on a senior project. This type goes for hands-on experimentation because they are very accurate in their observations. At the same time, they can smooth over ruffled feathers. How about Construction Engineering then? Architects, foremen, plumbers, HVAC, electricians, owners, carpenters—they don't necessarily see eye to eye on a construction project. ESTP will be the one to pull it together with this specialization available at Georgia Tech.

ENFJ will find the joint degree in **Global Economics and Modern Language** a thorough study in both economics and the modern language of their choice: Chinese, French, German, Russian, Japanese or Spanish. The department studies present financial mechanisms and economic theory as applied to third world societies. Courses like Health Economics will warm the heart of the ENFJ. This type is comfortable in courses that require sustained reading like economic theory.

ESFP is naturally persuasive and optimistic, just the type a business would assign to design a new product coming on the market. The Bachelor of Science degree in **Industrial Design** would give excellent training for the competitive nature of this work that primarily focuses on art. The materials laboratories and expertise on this campus will be the perfect resource for designers with a technical question. Since ESFP is socially savvy, resourceful and gregarious, they might wander into the Erskine Love building and ask away.

ISTJ has a dynamite combination of strengths that fit well on this campus. The Bachelor of Science in **Applied Math** with a business option works with their sense of utility and tradition. The degree in Discrete Mathematics might be another good choice. They are not likely to be fatigued by the intensity of these degrees as long as learning follows the step-by-step process of accumulated knowledge. They will start out with a core of mathematics, followed by formulaic applications and then move on to their subject of choice. Maybe it won't be business, maybe it will be a certificate in **Marine Science**.

ISFJ often believes learning is a serious business and is loyal to projects, classmates and assignments throughout lengthy research. The **Biomedical Engineering** degree requires mastering the life sciences and engineering plus the perseverance to live in these two different worlds. Demonstration, faculty guidance and feedback in the labs will help ISFJ, sometimes reluctant, to conquer the mechanics of living tissues, such as the heart, ligaments and muscle. This type wants to help others throughout their working careers.

GUILFORD COLLEGE

5800 West Friendly Avenue
Greensboro, NC 27410
Website: www.guilford.edu
Admissions Telephone: 336-316-2100,
Undergraduates: 2,137; 999 Men, 1,138 Women

Physical Environment

Guilford College is in university-rich Greensboro, NC. Guilford, with its own distinct flavor of education, was founded during the Civil War by the **Quakers** who took in wounded from both sides. Historical Founders Hall is the student center with a neat aquarium, dining hall and atrium. The campus buildings face inward to enclose a very large wooded garden where students walk and bike. The city of Greensboro has a lot of bike paths and greenways, so in good weather its an easy bike ride in to the lively downtown area. The college **Bike Shop** maintains a fleet of bikes and cycle repair for the undergraduates. The city provides buses for college students in Greensboro to **cross-register** for classes. There are two nearby historically black colleges adding to the cultural richness of the area.

Guildford College has a fascinating greenhouse, **The Farm**, that uses passive solar and tunnels to raise crops. In its fourth year, 2016, it is now 300 acres. Sufficient in quantity it now sells to the campus dining services. Without electricity but with **commitment and ingenuity**, the students on this campus are pushing into food production with very little beyond what the weather, soil and sun have to offer. The **Green Kitchen** is an intense study in efficiency, weekly keeping thousands of pounds of waste from going to the dumpsters.

Social Environment

Students who like Guilford College tend to **search, survey and ponder** and come to talk about it inside and outside of the classroom. The campus and undergraduates over the past five years have gone over the top on conservation projects. They are all centered on how to use the landscape and recycle materials. The search is on every semester to get greener. The Quakers are pretty active in the Division III athletic teams and the campus boasts both men's and women's rugby. Now for those who know rugby it can be pretty darn physical. Athletic action on the campus with club and intramural teams is another favorite break from the searching and pondering. The connection with the community is very active in partnership between the college and Greenville. WQFS is the campus radio station run by students and community volunteers. Their DJs primarily play independent labels with much variety. It has won national awards.

Reflection with observation is on the menu pretty much every day. Students are independent here. There is little inclination to look to the government for answers to familiar social problems. Fewer than ten percent of students on campus are Quaker and just under half of the students identify as a minority. Administration and faculty keep the strong ideal of inclusion consistent across the campus. The college also supports **emerging, ongoing research in conflict resolution** and mediation. About 40 percent of the undergraduates studying on campus are local citizens. Many are going part-time to pick up knowledge in emerging fields, some are going for second or first undergraduate degrees. They bring a practical thread to conversations and build awareness between the generations. This naturally follows from the Quaker philosophy of inclusion in society.

Guilford College is optional for ACT and SAT scores. Students can substitute a portfolio of writing samples in place of test scores. That is a heads up about the fact that Guilford is writing intensive. Yet, the liberal arts curriculum is moving toward **applied and practical knowledge**. The college is committed to the First Year Experience with faculty and resources. Residential living programs help freshmen take classes together and live on the same residential floors. The professors develop excellent mentoring and advising with their students because of the nature of this Quaker campus and the class sizes. This is an ideal place for those who would like to learn by **listening and practicing community** along with gaining actual academic knowledge and skills for future careers.

Compatibility with Personality Types and Preferences

Guilford College fits uniquely within small liberal arts colleges in America. Surrounded by southern cultural roots, it is a true meeting place for varied perspectives. The administration and faculty bring a profound sense of tolerance that translates into caring (F). The curriculum and the many activities outside of the classroom capture the quality of life students here hope to generate in their work and living environments. Service and volunteer initiatives are considerable and support the nearby neighborhoods in creative and long-lasting programs. Undergraduates have the full support of the campus resources and administration when they initiate projects for nearby residents. The administration supports many green, sustainable projects because they reflect the Quaker philosophies of community and peace.

Students here are going to be comfortable expressing multiple views (P). You could say that there is a common theme in questioning the status quo. But quiet observation and considered action is the path students on this campus like to take. Change directed by passion and political cause would go through several student-centered filters before it made it to the sidewalks with demands and posters. The undercurrents of Quaker philosophies promote sustained inquiry and community. It is the sensitive, individualistic student who is likely to find his way to the Guildford campus. The college educational philosophy strongly encourages experiential learning in off-campus experiences, internships, field studies and research, often in the local area. Graduates, regardless of their major, will be acutely knowledgeable of currents within America and how they are shaping and forming the larger nation.

PERSONALITY MATCH			
ISTJ	ISFJ	INFJ	INTJ
ISTP	ISFP	INFP	INTP
ESTP	ESFP	ENFP	ENTP
ESTJ	ESFJ	ENFJ	ENTJ

Now read below about one of the majors that MBTI® research shows people of your type have selected since the mid-20th century. After, refer to Chapter Five for the 50 or so majors that can help you prepare for careers your type has selected. Most importantly, remember that this college description is a suggestion for exploration, not a commanding order. You can be successful in any major at any college.

ENTP is just the type to cope well with fast change. The **Computing Technology and Information Systems** major at Guildford is pretty responsive to the evolving demands in computer science. The new major in Cyber and Network Security is also an option for this type. ENTP will get the basics in operating systems, networking systems and computer software. Students at Guilford will be expected to take a position on the ethical uses of technology, and ENTP loves to take a take a position. This type likes to get into a good discussion with gusto.

ENFJ might go for the Health and Fitness track in the **Exercise and Sport Sciences** major at Guilford. Improving health by exercise and activity makes good sense to ENFJs. They like the whole person approach to all things. The cultural environment at Guilford is energizing for this type who really seeks harmony. The overall sports industry in America is a big booster for health facilities in all our communities. ENFJ will likely look to these after graduation.

ISFP would rather show you with action than tell you through a discussion, college test or essay. Guildford's Theater Arts Department pulls actors, designers, directors and technicians together to put a script into action. ISFP will find out the nature of story telling through theater. The major in **Theater Studies** is especially oriented to serving others. The course Filmmaking Capstone can give this type a second avenue of expression through popular documentaries.

ENFP likes the complexity that is found in the unique **Peace and Conflict Studies** minor at Guilford College. The department offers a very realistic curriculum which serves as a needed background for those wanting to enter a career in mediation. The course in Pacifism and Just War Theory reviews two opposite stances on physical violence. The Quaker view of pacifism and the Catholic view of Just War is explored. Coursework also is aimed at the individual, personal level. Combined with any major at Guilford, this will be a very desirable skill to bring to a future position in the helping professions.

ISFJ goes for accuracy. They notice details and stick with a demanding job. These characteristics match up pretty well with the strong **Forensic Biology** major at Guilford College. The course in Forensic Chemistry is strictly about examining physical evidence at a crime scene. It makes good sense to ISFJ because they like to partner with others in the community of helping professions. Sometimes, they need a little cheerleading to recognize their contributions. At Guilford, faculty mentoring is likely to bolster ISFJ's confidence.

ESFP will like taking the intro courses in the **Earth Studies** minor at Guilford. It really works for this curious type because of the hands-on field work. This minor works well with majors in physics, chemistry and biology. At the same time, the optional course Images of the Earth: GIS and Remote Sensing can be perfect for professions in law, science and journalism.

ESFJ has what it takes to be an excellent translator and the **German** major at Guilford has much to recommend. Germany remains a big player in all the crisis' afflicting Europe. It has much influence within the international bodies seeking resolution. ESFJ with elective courses in conflict studies and a solid knowledge of this language will be well-situated as an international translator. This type has the backbone to accept irrational emotions without dropping it themselves. As the Islamic State, ISIS terror threat continues, work in this field borders on national service.

INFJ brings passion to their undergraduate years and the Bachelor of Arts in **Biology** at Guilford College welcomes their conviction. Precise thinking is their specialty, but that includes thinking about relationships and responsibilities too. The major in this department is designed for graduates to go into the policy arena like environmental law or conservation biology. Naturally this is a good choice for idealistic INFJ.

INFP has a good helping of insight and is self-directed. In fact, they are excellent researchers. The major in **Forensic Accounting** could be a good choice. They like complex systems and white collar crime and accounting fraud is usually deeply layered. INFPs could become crackerjack investigators. A nice companion to this degree would be the minor in Peace and Conflict studies since INFP will have to advocate or negotiate for the absent victims in white collar crime.

HAMILTON COLLEGE

198 College Hill Road
Clinton, NY 13323
www.hamilton.edu
Admissions Telephone: 315-859-4421
Undergraduates: 1,900; 920 Men, 980 Women

Physical Environment

Hamilton College is a bright, **educational laser light** in the landscape of liberal arts colleges. Namesake and Founding Father, Alexander Hamilton, would approve of the legacy and stable relevance in undergraduate education today. Campus overlooks the village of Clinton and sits on 1,300 acres near the Adirondacks. The facilities nicely fit the life and activities of today's student body even though architecture is from different historical periods and is assembled like a hamlet. Founded by Samuel Kirkland, a missionary to the Oneida Indians in the 1700s, it educated the children of white settlers and Indians in the rugged North American frontier prior to European settlement.

The Sadove Student Center has fun architecture that you might not expect. With its own **historic interpretation**, the administration avoided the large glass, concrete, steel architecture of 21st collegiate style. It pulls together Southern Appalachian extended porches with New England Salt Box design and multiple gables for shedding ice dams. The Kennedy Center studio arts building, albeit glass, metal and stone, brings musicians, dancers, actors, poets and scientists to together for **dimensional art in performance and structure**.

A lot of campus design keeps students indoors, walking from one end of the campus to the other in 15 minutes. The remarkable architecture of the Beinecke Student-Activities-Village, a **yellow rambling place**, also includes the Filius Barn. Here many concerts, lectures and parties take place. The connecting bridge, Martin's Way, brings students to McEwen dining hall and other residential and academic buildings on the south side of campus. The 1800 ELS house that is home to the Emerson Literary Society is on the docket for big upgrades along the lines of continuing the functional architecture on this campus.

The **outdoor education center** pushes students to leave behind their urban residences and experience life without red lights and traffic jams. The cooperation between the campus and the small town of Clinton is enviable. Undergraduates look for internships that bring together community programs and creative initiative in small towns across America. The university has a **Town to Gown** program that distributed 11 grants to Clinton and Kirkland in 2015. The Farm to Fork initiative brings local farm produce into the dining halls. The "**ultra-green**" science building is heated through geothermal methods and matches nicely with the excellent geological sciences on this campus. Students are actively drawn to the science majors which coincide with a strong **environmental stewardship** perspective like the unusual **Antarctic and Artic research**.

Social Environment

Students who want **academic freedom** select their course of studies without having to satisfy a set core of requirements. Now, more than a decade ago, the administration decided to let the traditional idea of a required core curriculum go the way of past history. With the help of **close advising**, students sign up for challenging classes. The college provides a strong safety net with the academic advisors and the mentoring professors. Throughout the courses, in all departments, students present their work by rhetorical speech. In sophomore year **students defend** their course selections to satisfy their academic plan which is similar to an independent study. The only required courses are three **writing-intensive** classes reminiscent of this college's past emphasis on rhetoric and elocution. Writing and public speaking are at the core of a Hamilton experience. In fact, writing and public speaking are at the intersection of precise thinking and knowledge.

Many undergrads choose an internship in Washington, DC and complete a thesis in senior year. Every year the college has nearly 50 graduates in the government major. Other popular majors are psychology, mathematics, public policy and world politics. Yet the sciences are developing as true gems in themselves with really innovative research that is interesting and valuable.

Hamilton students are **bright, ambitious**, motivated and **intellectually curious** enough to risk getting a lower grade to learn outside of their major course of studies. The college curriculum is bulging with research internships off campus, both for credit and with financial support. At Hamilton, the **internship as a teaching methodology** is spread across the curriculum. Rugged physical landscape builds resilience and discourages the "be careful" media messages of the 21st century. Hamilton is booster of undergrads who travel off campus to see differing community behaviors within the America whether it is a major power center like DC or a small, rural community.

Compatibility with Personality Types and Preferences

This college is quite interesting because of its long history and evolution with educational practices for students who like analysis (T) and thrive in an atmosphere that relentlessly seeks answers for problems. At Hamilton, these students can run with their ideas and innovations (N) and are not likely to experience much interference. The Hamilton undergraduate would not be satisfied with a midterm and final exam approach to grades. Speaking and writing, which allow for finesse and intellectual rigor, are king on this campus. The intellectual work moves toward order, productivity and accountability. Alexander Hamilton, revolutionary proponent of the national banking system, is both the namesake of this college and the guiding philosophical light for educational studies.

Not particularly doting or focused on their feelings, the Hamilton student is committed to intellectual exercise. Departmental philosophies exhibit and approve of intellectual courage among the students. Learning often centers on solving problems and collaborating with professors who guide student research studies. It can be a humbling experience with the bright undergraduate student body on this campus. In this way, students move forward with their personal beliefs while refining their ability to analyze and honor accountability. Tender-hearted sensibilities are reserved for socializing at Hamilton. The curriculum enhances interpersonal skills that will be used in the power positions that many on campus aspire to in government and industry.

Now read below about one of the majors that MBTI® research shows people of your type have selected since the mid-20th century. After, refer to Chapter Five for the 50 or so majors that can help you prepare for careers your type has selected. Most importantly, remember that this college description is a suggestion for exploration, not a commanding order. You can be successful in any major at any college.

PERSONALITY MATCH			
ISTJ	ISFJ	INFJ	INTJ
ISTP	ISFP	INFP	INTP
ESTP	ESFP	ENFP	ENTP
ESTJ	ESFJ	ENFJ	ENTJ

ISTJ will use their intellectual storehouse to capture and call back the names of geologic eras that are spelled with 10+ letters. In the unusual **Geoarcheology** studies on this campus, they will can work quietly and develop skills in this exacting science. The discipline is growing with increased use of geological methods to interpret the ancient sites. Undergrads are very active in research, recently tracking prehistoric stone tools back to their geologic source. Much work in this discipline seeks to further ground the biblical story. ISTJ will excel at the two semester capstone.

ISTP is going to fit right into the forward-thinking **Computer Science** department here. This type loves the independence to develop their own course of study and connect it to technical application. Instruction in the computer sciences is done with research in the labs, sometimes with case studies, other times tapping in code for new application. ISTPs with their wry sense of humor will sign right up for the course Secrets, Lies and Digital Threats. Focus within this discipline is sorely needed after the events of 2015 as both Syria and Ukraine found uninvited Russian troops on their soil. The downing of a passenger plane in Egypt and the Paris terrorist attacks were less obvious but equally sinister. It is the computer geeks who tie the source back to the terrorists and their national sponsors.

ESTP, always observant and always practical, will use those habits in the **Environmental Studies** concentration at Hamilton. The senior project gives ESTP a chance to employ newfound research skills with their natural bent for bringing competitors together. For example, this type would get a productive dialogue going between Save the Guppies Club and the employees of Bulldoze Construction Company. Don't you wish you could sit in on this meeting? The department focuses on policy with basic courses in the physical sciences followed by electives in the social sciences.

ESTJ will like the concentration **Economics** because of its wide survey of government practice in economic policy. The department leans toward understanding the social impact in the American community. Poverty and its connection with government safety nets is looked at closely in several courses. This type is a strong administrator who understands rules. Perhaps their Senior Project will be a study of regulations surrounding government safety nets. It's about accountably for ESTJ. As a natural leader they will encourage citizen resilience and individuality in economic policy that will support middle class America.

INFJ is ideal for the major in **Neuroscience** at Hamilton. Their inner vision calls out and demands attention. This particular major is focused on the biological basis of human behavior. This department is innovative and very current in its curriculum, so the coursework is kind of ingenious too. Since the discipline is about the connection between behavior and the brain's biology, Hamilton wisely developed a course for undergrads in Affective Neuroscience. This basic introduction could point INFJ in the direction of studying human emotion and its chemical basis in graduate studies. The super faculty here will be 100 percent behind that.

INTJ will not be discouraged by the string of impossible-sounding courses in the **Biochemistry/Molecular Biology** major. They are incise, intense reasoners. It will come in handy as they plow their way through organic chemistry, vertebrate physiology, cellular neurobiology and perhaps, geomicrobiology. This last is a new field and this type wants to be at the head of these emergent boundaries. Student research in 2015 was across the wide field of organisms at the molecular level. How about the student research paper on BPA and its use in our grocery products?

INTP could go for evolutionary puzzles, or any kind of puzzle for that matter. The major in **Biology** at Hamilton has a variety of course work, but the focus is the complicated stuff of evolution, so they will sign up for the Molecular Phylogenetics Workshop. You have to be an INTP or really like puzzles to sign up for this course. It looks at genetic sequences and best fit models.

ENTP has to try everything, more or less. Shakespeare's quote "all the world is a stage" is one that this type can live by. At Hamilton, the major in **Literature and Creative Writing** is superb. This department gets an A+ in the world of collegiate English Departments because of their emphasis on excellence. The selection of world literature and European literature, without the filters of 21st century pop culture, is an enviable exposure to human truths. This serious study of literature is clearly intended for thinkers who expect to take it to the next level with their own written pieces. From O'Connor's searing study of evil and mercy to Morrison's mysticism, there is little that will bore an ENTP in this Hamilton major. You go ENTP, writing should become one of your several careers throughout the coming decades.

ENTJ with a major in **Russian Studies** at Hamilton College will get a current, realistic curriculum. This department has quickly applied emerging content to coursework in reaction to the Russian invasions of Syria and Ukraine in 2015. It is a similar reaction that America's most advanced independent research laboratories took in refocusing resources toward cyber security immediately in summer 2015. The department is not shy in describing Putin's monumental changes in Russian strategy. Neither is ENTJ shy. This type is dynamite in political leadership positions. Think chess, think war games, they are often ENTJ pastimes.

HAMPSHIRE COLLEGE

893 West Street
Amherst, MA 01002
www.hampshire.edu
Admissions Telephone: 413-559-5471
Undergraduates: 1,376; 569 Men, 807 Women

Physical Environment

The idea for Hampshire College was put into practice with the purchase of 800 acres of orchard and farm land in the 1960s. The 1820 Red Barn was renovated in the 1970s by undergraduates and their professor. It is typical of the alternative ways that Hampshire College moves forward. The wide-open farm land and country setting push students to experiment with new ideas. Environmentally-friendly dormitories draw **eco-minded** students. The Kern Center, open Spring 2016, will be an exhibition space for teaching and multifunctional learning, The Hitchcock Center, open Fall 2016, is dedicated for public and college use in environmental study. Both Centers will entirely be heated and cooled by solar energy.

There are **eclectic students** on this campus who want to experiment as they learn. The Hampshire setting is a working farm and a living laboratory to test out their "**earth and animal friendly**" philosophies. Vegan and vegetarian students plant organic gardens, and some conduct research on the campus farm. In good weather, students use their bikes on the nearby dirt trails and cycle over to the other campuses in the **Five College Consortium** for cross-registered classes. Of course, this is Massachusetts, and December through April will come annually. All buildings on this campus are saving energy usually through their unique design. The two newest Centers will get energy saving through the latest technology and building materials like the triple glazed windows. Students who come with dreams of sustainability and lifetimes that honor rural practices will find a faculty and administration ready to explore the possibilities with them.

Social Environment

Hampshire College was established as a direct response to the 1960s feminist movements. During that short period of dramatic change college policies across the nation were dropped and social policies were changed, some innocent like the required knee length skirts and others not so healthy, like sexual experimentation. Over the decades, these 60s freedoms were open to question themselves at Hampshire College. The long running Re-Rad Club advocates for those freedoms and monitors the curriculum for restrictions. It is this tension between liberty and accountability that the Re-Rad club addresses. The campus still sports a large list of activist clubs and many are for community projects like Hampshire Food Advocates. The faculty and administration support **questioning undergraduates** who want to see how they can impact American social issues of the 21st century. Today, the college has the typical residential life policies and interdisciplinary academics found in liberal arts colleges.

Hampshire students are creative and quirky. More than half the entering students say they are going to study in a particular area but end up changing. It's part of the **Hampshire experience** to share ideas and be open to many perspectives. They evaluate and re-evaluate their point of view. They quickly get use to the unusual academic assessment and grading policy. They don't get grades, rather they receive **written course evaluations** from their professors. This encourages ideas, student/faculty conversation and ownership by the students. The departments do have required core courses and their advisors help select electives to meet student learning objectives. Hampshire undergraduates will receive letter grades though for any courses taken through the Consortium. Students prepare their own portfolio assessment at the end of the first year. It essentially functions as a final examination with their advisor's reading and qualitative review. The **portfolio assessment** stands out as the salute to the Hampshire founding principles.

Compatibility with Personality Types and Preferences

Looking out to the world, past the campus boundaries of the college, Hampshire students fuel the optimism of their own creativity (N). They intend to develop commitment for a discipline and discover its potential. Students here are attracted to the expressive forms of knowledge. Faculty are equally devoted to creativity and encourage reinterpretation of current knowledge. At this academically unorthodox campus, research in the social sciences springs up from current reality and is pursued through the committed lens of undergraduate individual study.

Internships and service learning are often used to explore options for change. This gives Hampshire the appearance of being radical at times. It keeps them exploring (P) and open to solutions of their own invention. The faculty and administration oblige by offering areas of study, rather than majors or minors. In fact, students spend the first year in Division I, exploring four of five content areas. The middle two years, Division II, are oriented to defining and securing knowledge in the chosen concentration. Division III, the last stage, is reserved for a two-semester project and internships. With this approach, undergraduates hold trust in emerging knowledge and they want to transfer those benefits into their chosen career paths. The ongoing practice of observation and synthesis drives the faith in human kind (F) and that lies at the core of Hampshire College.

Now read below about one of the majors that MBTI® research shows people of your type have selected since the mid-20th century. After, refer to Chapter Five for the 50 or so majors that can help you prepare for careers your type has selected. Most importantly, remember that this college description is a suggestion for exploration, not a commanding order. You can be successful in any major at any college.

ENFP is expressive plus creative. The **Music** area of study at Hampshire is about

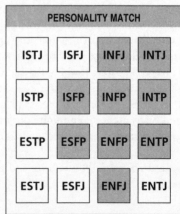

PERSONALITY MATCH

ISTJ	ISFJ	INFJ	INTJ
ISTP	ISFP	INFP	INTP
ESTP	ESFP	ENFP	ENTP
ESTJ	ESFJ	ENFJ	ENTJ

composition, improvisation and the courses in jazz and blues give good exposure to American musical heritage. Studies of Son House and Robert Johnson will point to the deep music and cultural roots that America boasts. This type will be comfortable with the Divisional studies and the nature of personal input and development of their course work. ENFP's Division III project might just move into vocal jazz stylistics with a study of contemporary vocalist Diane Schuur or 20th mid-century Billie Holiday. Always in touch with their emotions, ENFP will easily relate to jazz.

ENTP is often drawn to computers. They don't mind modeling problems a few hours ahead of time before they head to the computer lab. This is darned perfect for the study of **Astronomy**. At Hampshire College, undergrads will take advantage of the excellent labs and research within the Five College Consortium. On campus, the Hampshire faculty explores the social sciences and the wonder of the skyscape with courses like The Lure of the Paranormal and astrophotography projects at the Hampshire Observatory.

ENFJ enjoys suggesting change and often does with compelling reasons. Here at Hampshire, ENFJs will get scientific basics, like Building Physics through the Five College Consortium, along with the freedom to design their own concentration in **Architecture and Environmental Design** at Hampshire. They might look at design through human spirituality. On a study abroad trip, ENFJ could travel to Cartmel Abbey in England and decipher why so many visitors remark on God's presence in this medieval structure. Department faculty would likely encourage studying the emotional and mystical effects of architectural space.

ISFP can study **Agricultural Studies and Rural Life** at Hampshire. The campus has an organic farm and is probably harvesting their own seeds. But many folks and small enterprises must buy on the market where the government regulates the price and quantity of seed allowed to be purchased. It runs counter to small American farming life. Students at Hampshire College, and the other four Consortium Colleges, could research powerful corporations and the government offices that strictly regulate national agriculture. Undergraduates across the consortium might start a Five College Project that explores the pattern of agricultural purchases by Bill Gates in mid-2000. It would be a challenging project but his 2008 purchases of independent biomedical institutions that concentrate on researching genetics also fit into this picture. Okay , it would be a Masters degree at least, and more likely an PhD.

INFP is often committed and compassionate. The area of study in **Marine Science** at Hampshire College revolves around coastal regions in nearby New England and the Caribbean Sea. Much of the course work is offered through the Five College Consortium. At Hampshire, students look closer at management and policy in wetlands conservation. Electives courses from the Consortium include ecology, marine geology and oceanography. Caring, committed INFP might take the course in Ithacology and then explore best practices in small coastal fishing villages.

INFJ will find **Middle Eastern Studies** on this campus very relevant with faculty open to studying from different perspectives in line with student interest. With the 2015 change in geopolitics, member countries in the Middle East are moving in different directions to secure the survival of their state. Now is the time for a Student Project and INFJ is the type to wade into this complicated study. Insightful at their core, INFJs project might address the violence of the individual states directed at each other in the region.

INTJ likes to pull knowledge together by connecting different ideas into one larger concept. The study of **Biological/Life Sciences** at Hampshire follows this learning approach with survey courses that cross over into other fields like philosophy, religion and sociology. Fundamental sciences are taught through the Student Project. Those projects are very detailed in nature and laboratory intensive. This approach to the degree works well for those going into education or on to medical school.

INTP might wander into the Center for Design at Hampshire College and stay for a major in **Applied Design**. Across the nation, young entrepreneurs are setting up small shops and selling their own creations. The craft arts in blacksmithing, sewing, sheet metal, wrought iron and glass add value and depth to this degree. Faculty and training in each craft and use of the CADS and plasma torches are ready for students who sign up. This type likes photographic arts which could be combined with any of these other dimensional arts.

ESFP arrives on campus with impulsive energy and a willingness to try alternatives. The area of study in **Animal Behavior and Cognition** certainly offers a unique approach to studying cognition and awareness. The Hampshire Farm Center has flocks of sheep, goats and llamas. They are a living laboratory for animal behavior, cognition and communication. ESFP will delight in reviewing primate research by Dr. Penny Patterson with gorilla, KoKo. Starting her studies in 1972, she has interfaced communication, gorillas and cognition. Her work is very applicable to linguistic studies also.

HARVARD COLLEGE

5 James Street
Cambridge, MA 02138
Website: www.fas.harvard.edu
Admissions Telephone: 617-495-1551
Undergraduates: 6,694; 3,548 Men, 3,146 Women
Graduate Students: 18,453

Physical Environment

Imagine living in the same residence as Ralph Waldo Emerson or David Henry Thoreau. The **historic significance** of the Harvard University urban landscape is hard to miss. First-year students will live in residential dormitories reserved for their class located in the historic center of the university. Some Georgian-style residences were built in the 1700s while others are more contemporary, built in the 1970s. Most have been renovated in the past ten years with a few left on the schedule for remodeling. First-year students stick together and eat at Annenberg dining hall. In this setting, freshmen become accustomed to the city just outside their dorm room. They can guess whether the people they run into on campus are on the college tour or others just passing by. The nearby Campus Service Center helps out as first years adjust and learn to comprehend this **complex university** of 28,000 individuals studying at all levels of knowledge.

Rising sophomores know one another well and can put in a request to live together for the remaining three years. But most go through the lottery system as individuals and get assigned to one of 12-**balanced student communities** that essentially mirror each other in opportunities and resources. They learn firsthand of new cultures, political views and **international perspectives** with the other 300-500 residents in each House.

At Harvard College, the residential houses are designed to educate. There is a full residential staff of professionals who lead each of the Houses. Each has a House master, proctors and tutors. Each creates a **family-like setting** with the House master in some ways acting as parent too, socializing with students and evaluating their academic choices and concentrations. Some sophomores take tutorials with others in their House. In this way, the Houses become an extended classroom as well as a place for fine tuning artistic talents, from music to dance to sports.

The **scientific facilities, libraries, museums and resources** at the **university level** rival that of most third world countries. It would take years of residence on this campus and special invitation to comprehend the knowledge, wealth and power resident at Harvard University. But for undergraduate students, it is simpler. In their four years they become **loyal to their House**, attached to their friends and **respectfully awed by their academic departments**.

Social Environment

Students who are admitted to Harvard College have the **intellectual curiosity** and **emotional resilience** to pursue much of what the college has to offer. Freshmen have already achieved beyond that expected of most 18-years-olds and many have developed a particular skill or two in music, dance or sports. On occasion, **artists and well-known personalities** take a break from their career to finish an undergraduate degree at the college. Acceptance to Harvard normally is in the low single digits. In Spring 2015, the university received a formal complaint that quotas were set to restrict Asian American admissions.[43] Students who do arrive at Harvard are ready to soak up the knowledge that both the professors and other students bring to the table.

Intellectual intensity in the classroom is expected. Students set very high standards for themselves. They rarely power down—each waking moment is about intellectual inquiry. For those who want to study another field with their primary concentration, there is a program called Secondary Field. Undergraduates at Harvard can select one secondary field from an approved list. The list is one of the very few limits on academic study. Undergrads quickly begin to see the **relativism** of their own ideas. The college faculty and administration selectively present absolute truths and relative truths. It animates an environment where anything can be honored for some kind of truth. At the university level, where the actual academic departments reside, the research and faculty focus is on the scientific and social disciplines.

During the college's "shopping week" students test-drive classes, dropping in on any that interest them. Academic curiosity outweighs **academic risk** and some will design their own concentration. Passion for knowledge is strong among first year students. Students really search for that elective or concentration that fits their beliefs and career vision. There is advising and guidance for successful career paths and vocations from the college's progressive philosophical perspective. A good number of Harvard graduates will bring those cultural ideas forward into their active careers. A few will search out conservative cultural perspectives as the founding fathers would recognize.

What's for fun? There is everything and more. Some **social clubs** are officially recognized. There are also unofficial organizations that students join like the **Greek** social fraternities and sororities. Pretty much all undergraduates form tight **social networks** of some kind to negotiate this large, powerful place. Some networks will span the decades of graduating classes because of the loyal alumni. There are 41 varsity Division I teams, plus intramurals and club sports. There is a club for everything. With so much to do and learn there is **no uncommitted down time**.

Harvard College administrators hover very closely over the undergraduate student body with a descriptive website of acceptable and unacceptable behaviors. **The college** operates the residential houses with a philosophy that follows from the belief that all time on campus is instructive, in or out of the classroom. In Fall 2015, a college working group presented recommendations that address the Harvard culture and educational philosophies. If approved by the administration, some would be quickly accomplished. Photos of historical figures and events from the American experience prior to mid-20th century could easily be removed. They were identified in the report as creating a negative experience for minorities. Other recommendations reach into the **university academic departments** that have undergraduate concentrations. Suggested changes would come from the department's self description of their academic content or "canons" and their standards for excellence.[44] These suggestions point to what is currently taken into consideration when grades are given in courses taught by faculty in each of the undergraduate courses.

Compatibility with Personality Types and Preferences

Harvard is all things to bright students. Simply put, there is not a personality preference that cannot be accommodated quite well at Harvard. The educational philosophies are deep and wide in scientific scope. The structured students (J) who like to plan with defined objectives, practical rules and clear regulations will find it in the college's concentrations, tutorials and general exams. The faculty is widely divergent itself so knowledge is approached from a variety of avenues. A concentration in biology includes courses in all the physical sciences as well as anthropology and psychology.

The core course requirement at the college is fulfilled by choosing from among hundreds of entry level courses in the 40 available concentrations. These 40 are further expanded by options within each. This all really suits the flexible, free-flowing (P) students who will want, and maybe try, to sample most of the disciplines. For folks who like their facts and details straight up (S), observable, verifiable knowledge rules over the world class research venues in the School of Engineering and Applied Sciences. The faculty and student body are constantly reasoning with logical analyses (T). Undergraduates expect that their exploration, discovery and novel investigation will lead to extraordinary accomplishment.

Students preferring other ways of knowing, often intuitive or instinctual (N), will relate to the residential house system where students are expected to learn from each other. In fact, this house system helps the undergraduates who want frequent, close communication with others (F). Those students who are outgoing and expressive (E) will find the social contact they want outside of the classroom with club participation and house participation that is expected and extensive. Those folks who are quieter (I) will actually find some anonymity in the academic world which is very individualized and can be tailored so as to feel like a solo educational experience. Upon graduation, students hold a world view that prompts them to move aggressively and competently through their career work that should, indeed, increase the body of knowledge.

Now read below about one of the majors that MBTI® research shows people of your type have selected since the mid-20th century. After, refer to Chapter Five for the 50 or so majors that can help you prepare for careers your type has selected. Most importantly, remember that this college description is a suggestion for exploration, not a commanding order. You can be successful in any major at any college.

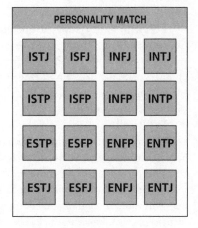

PERSONALITY MATCH

ISTJ	ISFJ	INFJ	INTJ
ISTP	ISFP	INFP	INTP
ESTP	ESFP	ENFP	ENTP
ESTJ	ESFJ	ENFJ	ENTJ

INTP is a good bet for the concentration in **Earth and Planetary Sciences**. This field has grown by ginormous data dumps from NASA's Keplar space telescope. In the Cygnus constellation there were 12 new planets identified. The department requires freshmen to take foundation courses in astrophysics, chemistry, biology and engineering. INTP, so fond of patterns and riddles, can search for them in the earth's oceans, atmosphere and solid core. The scientific facilities at the college could fill in that last missing piece to one of their riddles. Recent galactic exploration is finding evidence of water that would get INTP to sign up for geobiological or geochemical research.

ESTP is quick to sum up a problem and gifted with the ability to offer a solution. The concentration in **Environmental Science and Public Policy** could set this type up for ongoing troubleshooting after graduation. The foundational courses are clearly in the hard sciences. Students then specialize in one of the natural or social sciences. With advanced courses, they develop an expertise in their chosen topic then take that to the senior capstone project. This degree works for ESTP with no required thesis or written examination.

ISTJ goes for the tight academic structure in the first two years of engineering sciences at Harvard. Actually, this type will be fine with the suggested basic courses Math 1a and 1b. They demand accuracy and want a step-by-step, comprehensive mathematical understanding. The **Engineering Sciences** curriculum lets new concentrators take the four introductory courses that preview the five types of engineering degrees. With these, ISTJ gets to figure out which is the right one. This synchs with their motto—"Do it right the first time." Humor is one of this type's secret weapons and they will deploy it for the approved art decor that might be deployed in the residential houses.

INTJ is the perfect type for the **Mind, Brain and Behavior** initiative. It can be a secondary field or a track option for students declared to the sciences or philosophy. Outside of declaring a secondary field or track with their concentration, INTJ could simply attend the lectures and seminars of this initiative. The interdisciplinary work of tying together cognition, neuroscience and computers is the real stuff for INTJ. This type has superior inner vision and will really go for the intersection of cognition, neuroscience and computer science. Looking for patterns in the data bits, their goal will be to take their finds into the real world. Maybe it will be pathways in the brain's chemistry.

ENFJ absolutely enjoys an audience. At times, they can guide listeners to a really new interpretation. Harvard College and its **Romance Languages and Literatures** program lets ENFJ double their fun and charm audiences with knowledge of two languages and cultures. ENFJ really takes to their mentoring professor in this department. Tutorials are so important and a bit unusual in the college. They are a benefit of the RRL concentration.

INFP will take time and emotional space to find purpose for the four undergraduate years on any campus. Sometimes, it means looking at several options. How about the **Comparative Study of Religion** for a spiritual INFP? The nature of this concentration couldn't be more meaningful after the 2015 cascade of terrorist disasters in the Middle East and Europe. This area of study could quickly lead to a joint concentration in religion and computer science. Advanced research in national cyber security is critical now in the 21st century. INFP is a quiet participant who carefully considers all options.

ESFP sometimes is the entertainer in the crowd. They are spontaneous and will lighten up the room for serious discussion to follow. The concentration in **Visual and**

Environmental Studies has careers paths that are a natural for ESFP. Undergrads will take courses in photography, filmmaking, video art/performance, film studies, critical theory and environmental studies. The curriculum weaves in environmental studies as space altered by people. ESFP might go into film. Think about *Star Wars: The Force Awakens*. It is hard to forget that barren landscape. ESFP might spin their own personal memories into visual stories with the potential for another blockbuster movie on the horizon.

ENTP has intuition across the board and that includes intuition about people too, so the study of human personality is a player. As a concentrator in **Psychology**, ENTP would go for researching perception, memory or motivation. These processes are at the center of the studies at Harvard. The faculty and resources are over the top and research is about the study of age old human questions, like why we believe in religion. ENTP could get consumed by the junior tutorial with undergrad research on an age old question. In this perfect situation, they could also get overtaken by 'Happy.'

ISTP will be in high heaven with the **Mechanical and Material Science Engineering** concentration in the School of Engineering at Harvard. Building robots and designing experimental parts in these labs is a dream come true for this type. They will absorb the theories best when they can observe and tinker with the physical properties. In the school, each department has a learning lab. ISTP might just wander over to the Physics Learning Lab because they will find a dream come true—the machine shop. Observant, tolerant ISTP will bring their ways into the laboratory research.

ISFP and the concentration in **Folklore and Mythology** will be rewarding for both faculty and student in this small department. The curriculum has a methodical approach to other cultures and a lens to understanding relationships within the culture. Reserved ISFP will find much of the coursework very instructive for their own personal journey. Students can concentrate in a particular region and will take two years of language for that region. Oral and written myths will fascinate and inform. For ISFP, time spent in faculty offices with fellow undergrads might become home away from home.

INFJ likes complex subjects such as liberty. Of course, complete liberty can lead to anarchy or it could be viewed as a basic human right when defined as an Absolute Truth. The relativist definition of liberty opens doors for restriction and governmental tyranny. That is complicated stuff for high school students. Not to worry. Just know that at Harvard College, liberty is studied through intellectual philosophers such as Machiavelli who capture the reader with arresting logic. INFJ has the resolve to analyze primary texts in this chimerical discipline. Intense, idealistic and metaphorical, this type also has the ability to find value in philosophies other than the humanism featured in the **Social Studies** concentration at Harvard. This major is administered by interdisciplinary faculty who approve the student's course of studies and senior thesis. The concentration is a competitive, directive study with typically 200 undergraduates.

ISFJ will take to the detailed and step-by-step nature of **Human Evolutionary Biology**. ISFJ's excellent memory, love for facts and typical reflection make for perfect habits in this concentration. Research is encouraged and follows either a laboratory or field-based study approach. Most of the courses are held in Harvard's own museums of zoology, archaeology and geology and others are in life science laboratories. ISFJ will get a good grounding in all the methods used to interpret artifacts. They can also move into molecular research if they choose with this concentration.

ENFP is a cheerleader for harmony. The international events of in the Middle East and Europe in 2015 cut into their warm sensibilities. But the Pacific Rim Basin nations were a point of light in 2015 so the concentration in **South Asian Studies** fits in with ENFP's usual optimism. Their curiosity, imagination and versatile ways will point them in valuable directions inside the economic and political powerhouse that is Southeast Asia. There is the option to focus on Sanskrit and Indian studies complete with a language citation in Hindu-Urdu. They could also go for Honors in the concentration and write the senior thesis. It will be a first-class read.

ESFJ will find the concentration in **Physics** at Harvard College has a teaching option with eligibility for a teaching certificate. This type's need for order and responsibility are sure fire advantages for K-12 teachers. It will be appreciated by school administrators that are facing challenges in today's public school classes. There is no general exam, tutorial or thesis in this concentration. That is okay since ESFJ would rather use time to develop classroom skills and gain experience.

ENTJ usually likes the complicated stuff. The Harvard concentration in **Neurobiology** definitely fits this description. ENTJs are goal-oriented but can also catch unnoticed patterns in volumes of data. With advances in molecular science each month, the data banks available to the department are gigantic. The undergraduate research possibilities are huge too. It may be over the top and unappealing to some other personality types but certainly not to this type. Ambitious ENTJ might just join the scientists who are replicating the nervous system with software. Imagine how valuable this information will become in the life sciences.

ESTJ could go for the **Applied Mathematics** concentration at Harvard College. The department is both structured and flexible in how it directs undergraduates to move through the four years of study. Applied mathematics is exactly what it says it is and does. Students will gain spiffy mathematical modeling skills and then take that to their subject of interest. It could be in the physical or social sciences. Undergrads tailor their own degree with an advisor. This is a rather intensive degree and ESTJs are definitely up to the challenge. The department has a hidden focus within the coursework and that is maturity. The realism of applied mathematics has little time or space for immaturity or unaccountable idealism. Hey, that sounds just like ESTJ.

HAVERFORD COLLEGE

370 Lancaster Avenue
Haverford, PA 19041-1392
Website: www.haverford.edu
Admissions Telephone: 610-896-1350
Undergraduates: 1,205; 567 Men, 638 Women

Physical Environment

Located 10 miles outside of Philadelphia, Haverford College is a suburban campus with all the charm and mystery of a Thomas Kinkaid painting. The college belongs to the **Quaker Consortium** that cross-registers classes at three other nearby colleges. The actual Haverford campus reveals itself slowly with many pathways through the woods. Students feel comfortable here because of its smallness and charm. Centuries-old trees surround these Quaker buildings and add to a spiritual feeling of safety, both physical and emotional.

The Magill Library has a comprehensive collection of original Quaker books and students have access to rich historical documents. The Koshland Science Center has advanced research options like nanofabrication which is just the opposite of the historical presence in the landscape. Students who like the sciences and wish for strong pre-med advising come to this exceptional science center. The Gardner Athletic Center offers everything a student athlete or non-athlete might want to stay in shape during the college years. The college expects to open the new center for visual culture, arts and media in 2017. Fairly close to Philadelphia, about a 30-minute drive, students can breeze into town if the quaint landscape and studies close in.

Social Environment

Students come from New England and the Mid-Atlantic regions; they are typically excited and thoughtful at the same time. They believe that **tolerance** is the goal for a quality campus experience. Incoming freshmen became Fords for this very reason. As First Years, they are assigned to **Customs Groups** of 8-16. They live and socialize as a unit with upperclass mentors. In the first year, they discuss and explore the nature of their different backgrounds and the meaning of tolerance. As students from high schools of advanced placement courses, they like the non-competitive experience in the classroom. The faculty looks for each to become **observers**, starting with their own Customs Group. This is a characteristic of the historic Quaker meetings and will radiate through their four years of study.

With tolerance in mind, Fords cross over regular boundaries with each other's support and the administration honors this experimentation. Co-ed assignments to individual rooms were initiated in early 2000, yet, the majority of students live in single rooms with common spaces for bathrooms and gathering space. The new Kim Tritton dormitories were designed with input from the students, i.e. cubbies in the hall bathrooms. It offers both privacy and prompted togetherness for **tentative souls**.

The administration encourages discussion and exploration to form **a close knit social fabric**. Fords populate a really large list of clubs and activities. They have great options for fun and service on this campus of caring faculty. The Cancer Sucks club is a sympathetic support for all whose families are dealing with this disease. FAB, Fords Against Boredom, sponsors free social events without alcohol. The Nerd Club, our favorite, is about having fun, mystery-themed nights and all are invited along with students at the nearby Consortium campuses.

Students may come with an idealistic view of society because professors focus on a moral, ethical education for the individual. This **value-driven education** attracts some students who attended a Quaker high school. They add depth to the class discussions about community. Undergraduates here might also decide to protest the administration policies. In 2014, they demanded that their commencement speaker be changed out. Undergraduate students thought he was involved with a campus protest at Berkeley that ended with police enforcement. The former president of an Ivy League university, speaking at their commencement, pointed out that inviting only those you agree with can get boring.[45] All will get a **talk-discuss-argue education** regardless of their definitions here at Haverford.

Compatibility with Personality Types and Preferences

Haverford College offers an education that intensely seeks to understand other people (F) of the world. It is a high purpose and very true to the founding Quaker principles of the college. Undergrads are typically attuned to a humanistic perspective. They come to the campus eager to learn and expect to debate ideas with written and oral expression. They study humankind looking for positive qualities (N). Students at Haverford ask very difficult questions and look for answers among their own student body, along with the faculty. Some of those answers are found in the Quaker values and ideals for the human condition. It comes across in the curriculum through traditional courses and majors that were the foundation of the American experience. During four years of undergraduate education at Haverford College, students are going to discuss, search for, argue and practice living in a community searching for cohesion, knowledge and common goals. The faculty here is all about that because it speaks to the historical Quaker practice of "expectant waiting."

Now read below about one of the majors that MBTI® research shows people of your type have selected since the mid-20th century. After, refer to Chapter Five for the 50 or so majors that can help you prepare for careers your type has selected. Most importantly, remember that this college description is a suggestion for exploration, not a commanding order. You can be successful in any major at any college.

INFJ is persistent and penetrating, just the qualities needed to study and practice **Economics**. This type is caring and yet very private. INFJ will be on alert for theories in economics that contradict practice in economics. The department subscribes to a good

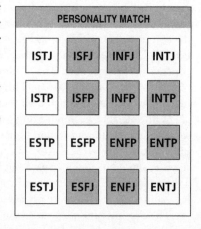

PERSONALITY MATCH

ISTJ	ISFJ	INFJ	INTJ
ISTP	ISFP	INFP	INTP
ESTP	ESFP	ENFP	ENTP
ESTJ	ESFJ	ENFJ	ENTJ

number of national and regional data banks that will help INFJ in their independent research project. Faculty bring statistical methods to human behavior and social practice in the economy. It is this penetrating approach that works for INFJ. It can lead to entry level positions at financial houses or grad studies after commencement.

ISFJ has a memory that won't quit. This type can take in facts and store them for retrieval like a researcher in the congressional library. The faculty in **Computer Science** designs coursework to search for answers to questions like Are there algorithms not presently known that can solve mega problems? In reality, the coursework is more down to earth. After all, computers are simply tools and realistic ISFJ just wants to get skillful and bring them out to the community. Software used by non-profits and international aid organizations like python and Linux Eclipse are covered in the first courses and then its on to Java and C++.

ISFP might go for **Classical and Near Eastern Archeology**. Its a natural fit for this type. The major takes advantage of cross-registration in the Consortium. ISFP's sense of design will be an advantage on digs. Active excavation starts again in future years, perhaps 2017 or so. Meanwhile the artifacts from recent digs have much to reveal. This type is a learner by sight, sound and touch. They are basically active academic souls searching for the freedom to reflect – a favorite ISFP pastime.

INTP will like the **Chemistry** major at Haverford College because there is an opportunity to complete required core chemistry courses at foreign universities in junior year. Since about 2010, chemistry courses really started merging into other physical sciences. Now INTP can cross-check their intuition with undergraduate research in any of the several labs on campus. Curriculum in 2016 and 2017 is going to offer up plenty of interdisciplinary approach to this science. This independent type will take advantage of both overseas study and interdisciplinary courses for the rewards of their own logical analysis.

INFP might find meaning in something simple like an ice cream cone on a hot day. They are searchers for meaning and could develop an artistic vision before the cone starts dripping. INFP will happily develop their own personal themes and look to express those through their art. At Haverford, the major in **Fine Arts** has experimental courses in the third year. Sensitive and introspective INFP might look to convey mercy and honor in their senior exhibition. Their junior or senior year was marked by 2015's terrorism. This works at Quaker Haverford.

ENFP will be welcome in the **Education** major for their emotional commitment. Yes, an ENFP teacher in the K-12 sciences can be downright happy with microscopes, rocks, plants and frogs. This major is quite strong with cross-registration at the Consortium campuses. Observing in classrooms, adult learning centers, online and juvenile centers really helps this imaginative type pick up realistic classroom management skills. The major also has the level of complexity required by ENFP to keep them focused and energized for their own creative instincts.

ENTP might like the major in **Growth and Structure of Cities**. It is unusual because planning for urban communities is studied through other fields like law, communication, the arts and health. Cross-registration courses use data collected by global satellites. It might just be the ENTP who decides to record the urban history of Detroit in the 20th century. Truly it is a complex city of cultural influences with the auto industry, 20th century Ellis Island immigration, 20th century southern

African-American migration and now the largest Islamic community outside of the Middle East

ESFJ is all about the community and the people in it. The Haverford Biology department offers a core program in **Biology** which is focused at the molecular and cellular level. The curriculum is unique with a taste of over-the-top cellular research at the introductory level. Traditional ESFJ may find it a bit too removed from the community. The sensitive faculty on this campus of Quaker heritage and the teaching philosophy of this department will help ESFJ move forward into the health sciences that directly serve the public.

ENFJ will find that the **Peace, Justice and Human Rights** echoes back to the founding principles of the Quakers who were practicing pacifism when the founding fathers were meeting to declare the Revolutionary War. Two centuries later, liberal arts colleges across America have the freedom to strongly endorse this concept. Graduate studies for this type might then focus on American Studies. Perhaps their future dissertation topic will explore reasons for ongoing immigration to the United States.

HENDRIX COLLEGE

Office of Admissions
1600 Washington Avenue
Conway, AR 72032-3080
Website: www.hendrix.edu
Admissions Telephone: 800-277-9017
Undergraduates: 1,358; 611 Men, 747 Women

Physical Environment

Hendrix College is the small town of Conway in central Arkansas and about a half hour from Little Rock. Familiar, traditional red brick buildings and roof lines marked by gables invite you to come inside. The campus has a mix of traditional and modern buildings that really look good together. The Student Life and Technology Center is considered the **"living room"** of the campus. It deserves that name for its mission and well-designed interior spaces on this forward-thinking campus. The large, rotating Hendrix theatre stage presents five annual theater productions. In 2010, the college and city of Conway opened a mixed-use residential and business setting across from campus. There you find the Hendrix Bookstore and 130 upperclass student apartments next door to neighboring Conway residents. There is a strong commitment between the town of Conway and the college.

The campus has a park-like setting with interesting nooks and crannies like "Pecan Court," a good location to chill out. The **Arkansas Garden** is a great example of Hendrix's commitment to the region. The garden is on campus and features a surprising collection of trees, shrubs, medicinal plants and a bog. It all forms a prairie that includes only species from the early colonial times of the region and helps cement the value of American community past and present.

Social Environment

Hendrix undergraduates were **studious** in high school and held positions at the top of their class. At Hendrix they continue those studious habits and gain clarity in subjects that influence **American community**. Undergraduates are imaginative thinkers, often with a good sense of humor that combines with **self-drive**. First year classes are **comprehensive**, demanding and require synthesis of large amounts of information quickly. Academic expectations stay high because graduates are expected to apply their major and minor studies to the enterprise of American productivity and culture.

Students here are interested in ethnic clubs, discussions and cultural activities. They attend presentations by many visiting speakers. The student organizations are balanced for fun, service, the arts, sciences, spirituality and service. There are 100-year old campus traditions that undergrads really keep active. **Shirttails** is a competition between residence halls that features live entertainment as students sport white oxford button down shirts, ties, and boxers. Along with **Campus Kitty**, the two traditions raise thousands of dollars for local charities.

The award-winning **Odyssey Research Program** is the premier and one-of-a-kind learning experience at Hendrix. All students participate in three Odyssey projects prior to graduation. They require petition and approval from the departmental faculty. All Odyssey projects and research are presented to the public. Many projects are local or regional and do not involve a budget. A few are supported with grant monies. Some are focused on the Hendrix collegiate environment. But most Odyssey projects are designed around service. That could also include actual coursework and field study with populations like the elderly. Regardless of the type of Odyssey, all students graduate from Hendrix with a wealth of community commitment and awareness. They are likely to become good neighbors and caring leaders in their choice of lifestyle and profession.

Compatibility with Personality Types and Preferences

Hendrix College and the study of social community is just about synonymous. Faculty and administration see huge value in learning through the perspective of others. Each department requires active student participation and interaction with the body of knowledge. Faculty and administration develop studies that encourage ethical inquiry and the value of helping others (F). Hendrix philosophy always points to idealism through sound objectives. Students learn to propose projects, perform social research and service learning. Their proposals can be quite sophisticated and they are mentored by professors who support one-of-a-kind learning experiences. The overriding purpose of student research on this campus is to encourage imaginative plans (N). Undergraduates come to campus with anticipation (P) of contributing toward the greater community after graduation. The curriculum combines the unusual intersection of practical, realistic and idealistic values. Graduates are prepared to enter the helping professions and careers that promote moral lifestyle and sound community.

Now read below about one of the majors that MBTI® research shows people of your type have selected since the mid-20th century. After, refer to Chapter Five for the 50 or so majors that can help you prepare for careers your type has selected. Most importantly, remember that this college description is a suggestion for exploration, not a commanding order. You can be successful in any major at any college.

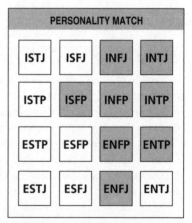

PERSONALITY MATCH

ISTJ	ISFJ	INFJ	INTJ
ISTP	ISFP	INFP	INTP
ESTP	ESFP	ENFP	ENTP
ESTJ	ESFJ	ENFJ	ENTJ

INFP likes to read by intuitive hunches as they page along on their notebooks. The major in **Psychology** at Hendrix starts freshmen with a survey human developmental stages. Throughout the stages there is potential for intuitive hunches that might lead to the advanced research course. The department starts all undergraduates with basic statistics and research methods. With these tools, this type will refine their intuitive hunches in the electives which offer a wide look at human personality. INFPs live in the larger world of idealism. With new information coming each year from genetic studies, INFP is likely to move on to graduate school to study the subfield that captured their hearts.

INFJ sorts out metaphors and concepts. The minor at Hendrix in **Neuroscience/**

Study of the Mind will deliver on both. The courses include philosophy of science, sensation and perception and cognitive psychology. INFJ will enjoy this study and likely apply for the **Interdisciplinary Studies** major. This minor and major will be an extension of their own values and beliefs. It will work well for further graduate study in the brain sciences.

INTJ is focused on turning insight into reality. Their careers often turn to research. The major in **Chemical Physics** looks at molecular interactions that lead to behavior and certain properties. Who knew that molecules had behaviors? In this department, undergrads join faculty in their ongoing 2016 research designs. It might be laser physics or molecular cluster ions and chemical process in high pressure water.

ISFP really enjoys working with their hands and being active. The Arkansas Garden is a gem of a resource for students in the **Biology** major at Hendrix College. The garden, planted in 2001, mirrors the Arkansas ecology of the colonial period. The large department has an extensive list of student research projects completed during the summer term. From paleobotany to genetics to marine ecology, the faculty expertly advises students with realistic options following graduation.

INTP will like the flexibility of the **Computer Science** major at Hendrix College. This small department goes for professor/student projects that explore current research papers. The team concept of professor/student carries through to designing and implementing software. The fun part is where they connect their software program to mini robots. Students can take their original research and present at the annual regional conference. This type may or may not step into this limelight, but they will certainly be in attendance.

ENFP should really check out **Theater Arts** at Hendrix College. It is practical and vocational. Graduates of this department go directly into community or professional theater. The required Theatre Production Practicum is comprehensive. It covers publicity, stage management, choreography and scenery, plus all the other pieces that make for performance as an expression of humanity. Students will write original plays for the Hendrix theater stage on campus. Faculty has a unique expertise in Irish Theater and rich Shakespearian foundations.

ENTP is going to like studying political science at Hendrix College. The major in **Politics** starts with the basic freshman course, Issues in Politics. This department directs students to study a single issue through the lens of political theory, comparative politics and American politics. It is a super way to comprehend this massive, all-over-the-map discipline. The curriculum is factual, historical and realistic of American political science without the influence of social media trending. ENTPs will complete the senior research seminar with scientific inquiry methods, but this type will need faculty advising for a cohesive presentation of their original ideas.

ENFJ who enters the business scene will like it if there is a direct relationship with the customer. They want the personal relationships that come with single product or a specific set of services. The degree in **Economics and Business** at Hendrix College is a good bet for ENFJ. It has the complex subjects of fiscal policy, trade and interest rates, yet it also includes the reality-based subjects of accounting and business law. This approach lets ENFJ discover financial institutions that value connections between employees, consumers and product. They are usually found in local, regional American markets and some smaller enterprises in third world countries.

JOHNS HOPKINS UNIVERSITY

3400 North Charles Street/140 Garland
Baltimore, MD 21218
Website: www.jhu.edu
Admissions Telephone: 410-516-8171
Undergraduates: 5,156; 2,696 Men, 2,460 Women
Graduate Students: 2,029

Physical Environment

Johns Hopkins University, in northern Baltimore, sits tightly on 140 acres punctuated by trees and handsome brick buildings. At the start of the 20th century, JHU laid the foundation for undergraduate and graduate learning, and gave America a host of industrialists and Doctoral scholars. In the process, Johns Hopkins laid out the template for the public universities across America. Following the German educational model of comprehensive physics and science laboratories, their century-long focus on medical research and graduate education is remarkable for outreach and continuing relevance for our nation.

The flagship building on campus is Gilman Hall, easy to recognize by its **huge ionic columns, stained glass windows** and indoor circular staircases. Named after Daniel Coit Gilman, the first Hopkins president, it is a 24-hour student-study area with an atrium that houses the university archeological collection. New **undergraduate laboratories** were opened in 2013 also with a dramatic atrium and comfort spaces for the mind and body. Johns Hopkins, always ahead of the scientific bow wave, has placed the departments of **Chemistry, Biology, Biophysics, Psychological and Brain Sciences** together within this new space. The field of Psychology is coming out from under the blanket of social sciences and getting a welcome into the physical sciences where it is more than appropriate.

The majority of first year students live in the freshmen quad. Alumni Memorial Residence, "AMR," has single rooms and is coed by floor. The campus also expanded on the other side of North Charles Street, where newer residences and a bookstore offer upperclass students more amenities right in the city. The Brody Learning Commons is one fine library and study space where undergraduate students especially spend a lot of time. This is an **intensely intellectual** university. Students benefit from calming, comfortable design while wrestling with concepts that most of us cannot recognize or spell.

Social Environment

Students themselves shape the essence of the Hopkins undergraduate experience. They create a peer culture that values intellect and collaboration. It's the highly **self-directed** and self-motivated student who does well at JHU. They came with high school resumes of leadership and strong commitment to a few extracurricular activities. They are okay with repeating the same at JHU. Students are not inclined to protest or demonstrate but rather to discussion and process. To that end in Fall 2015, the university Black Student Forum held a moderated panel with JHU President, faculty and students discussing racism and demands for change on campus.[46]

Undergraduates learn in the lecture halls and after hours by exchanging their views and discussing the **challenging material** presented by the faculty. Research opportunities are quite competitive and students independently petition for undergraduate grants. The enterprising undergraduate, given the nod for research, will join professors in **emergent research** within the prestigious Johns Hopkins labs. Many who come to this university for pre-med quickly realize they can take fascinating classes in other subjects that they want to explore. Hopkins has a strong reputation for pre-medical studies, yet many in the student body do not go on to major in the sciences. In fact, less than half go on to medical school. Undergraduates here secure **competency** in other fields, such as creative writing or international politics. Students say their **professors are simply amazing** since they direct state-of-the-art research and undergraduate teaching at the same time.

A few years ago undergrads sported Hopkins' T-shirts that read, "academics... social life... sleep...pick any two." Undoubtedly, life at Hopkins is about prioritizing and finding time for all that there is to do. The social life on campus depends upon the student. Those who seek it out will find it through participation in organized sports. Lacrosse is played at Division I level and generates much campus enthusiasm. Many student organizations combine service, fundraising and fun. Orientation for freshmen is a week-long affair that packs in JHU **talent and performance** like the a cappella and drama groups showcasing their enthusiasm. Others will join fraternities or sororities for leadership opportunities, philanthropy, friendship and social fun. The premier tradition on campus is the **Spring Fair** which is the largest student-run fair on American college campuses. Thousands come from off campus to attend. Undergraduate students participate, plan and direct it. They face-paint the little kids who attend with their parents, often professors at Hopkins. The Spring Fair offers light entertainment after two semesters of pounding the test tubes. Undergraduate **commitment to discovery** and collaborative spirit is all about the JHU student body.

Compatibility with Personality Types and Preferences

Johns Hopkins University is a research center of excellence that impacts our national economy. The administration and faculty consistently center academic study on invention and innovation (N). Activity in the research labs is driven to pursue, invent or discover new applications through scientific (S) properties. This university aggressively pursues generating knowledge and values scientific truth, primarily in the fields of human interface.

All undergraduates spend the first years coming up to speed in the highly technical scientific, behavioral sciences and social sciences (J). Upper-class coursework draws widely from expansive (P) current day societal problems in need of realistic solutions. JHU graduates are steeled in the art of "what is and what could you make of it" (T).

Faculty and administration are intense about emerging basic research in our technological society. Under the direction of a JHU graduate heading up NASA, American programs pushed space exploration through to landing on the moon in the mid-20th century. But in the 21st century, European initiatives have pushed forward into space. In 2016, JHU will contribute ongoing, fundamental research that can be applied to the cyber threats directed at the United States and western governments. JHU is all about fundamental research.

Now read below about one of the majors that MBTI® research shows people of your type have selected since the mid-20th century. After, refer to Chapter Five for the 50 or so majors that can help you prepare for careers your type has selected. Most importantly, remember that this college description is a suggestion for exploration, not a commanding order. You can be successful in any major at any college.

INTJ will find the major in **Earth and Planetary Sciences** is well-designed for turning their ideas into undergraduate research. This department covers basic concepts in the undergraduate years especially geared to ad-

PERSONALITY MATCH			
ISTJ	ISFJ	INFJ	INTJ
ISTP	ISFP	INFP	INTP
ESTP	ESFP	ENFP	ENTP
ESTJ	ESFJ	ENFJ	ENTJ

vanced research at the international level. It is a wide-ranging discipline about the processes that shape Earth and also planets in our solar system and beyond. The labs on campus are working with the reams of data coming back from NASA's spacecraft Dawn, a visitor to the asteroid belt between Mars and Jupiter.

ISTP will want to look into the **Materials Science and Engineering** degree at Johns Hopkins. Without a doubt this type will go for Johns Hopkins' focus on practical application. In fact, ISTPs can specialize with advanced courses in their last two undergraduate years. Energy research is currently looking at phase transformations during self-propagating reactions in multilayer foils. How about that for intense? ISTPs smile at the self-propagating words since they are all about efficiency. This type of advanced study can lead to industrial positions in research or application to graduate engineering programs.

ISTJ is one for knowing the rules and keeping track of the reasons behind the rules. A BA degree at Johns Hopkins in **General Engineering** could be the perfect preparation for law school and a career in intellectual property or patent law. There are several JHU programs and centers focused on the social sciences and humanities. The school is open to a student-designed degree with social sciences or a degree structured by the department. ISTJ is up for the tried and true and will look to departmental faculty advising after they select their concentration outside of engineering.

ISFJ can revisit the day from an hour-to-hour perspective. They have amazing dimensional memory. They do not miss much as the passing scene unfolds before them, so they are pretty good at understanding and preserving the meaning of our material world. The minor in **Museum and Society** at Johns Hopkins places undergraduates in museums to help preserve and interpret our artifacts and archival collections. This type is thorough and values much about the traditions of society. It is perfect for a museum curator with a major in **Sociology** from Johns Hopkins University.

ESTP often has a personality with pizzazz and with their skill at negotiating, they could put a bold face on health issues here in the United States. The major in **Public**

Health Studies offers preparation for the masters program in Public Health at JHU. With opportunity for specialization, this type might research rising health premiums and the Millennial generation's opting out of national mandated health care. ESTP prefers the real world and all of its messy, problem-generating practices rather than theories. The Affordable Health Care Act has provided a wealth of messy administrative requirements and ESTP is ready for this type of action.

ENFP will like the minor in **Psychological and Brain Sciences** because it surveys the emerging brain and nervous system research. The department specifically designed the minor to easily combine with a major in the social or behavioral sciences. This type will benefit from the introductory courses since it will likely help them settle on a major. It is a small department and faculty student advising is strong. It is quite possible that versatile ENFP will step it up to the major, also available in the department. It is ideal for ENFP going to graduate school in social psychology.

ENTP will want to check into the dynamic minor in **Marketing and Communications** at JHU. The curriculum was sponsored by the university's Center for Leadership Education. A career in marketing is often alluring to this entrepreneurial type. The track option in Integrated Marketing Communications could showcase ENTP's creative, clever ideas. JHU is an outstanding university for this type. Competence and truth reign on this campus. Political trends and social media are filtered and searched for value before they enter the undergraduate curriculum.

ESTJ often goes into professions that require administration and leadership. The major in **Civil Engineering** at JHU is a perfect fit. In this department, the emphasis is on the safety of our soaring modern buildings of glass and metal frame. Johns Hopkins is all about advanced research with evolving materials. The tradition-bound ESTJ can learn about the newest metals and techniques in construction. The faculty will guide and advise this cautionary type with first-hand proof from the advanced laboratories and eye-popping research.

ENTJ is not likely to regret signing up for the **Entrepreneurship and Management** minor in combination with any of the engineering degrees at Johns Hopkins University. JHU even allows students to take just three basic courses in this area or complete the seven courses for the minor. The three-course option is ideal for enterprising ENTJs in the engineering curriculum that is already packed with research and requirements.

KALAMAZOO COLLEGE

1200 Academy Street
Kalamazoo, MI 49006
Website: www.kzoo.edu
Admissions Telephone: 269-337-7166
Undergraduates: 1,461; 634 Men, 827 Women

Physical Environment

There really is a Kalamazoo College and it's in Michigan! At 183 years old, it's one of the oldest liberal arts colleges in America. The college history of the 19th, 20th and 21st centuries puts the campus in distinguished company with just a few other institutions. Comprehensive academics and cohesive culture make Kzoo special. The college takes advantage of its location in this working community by focusing on service in the nearby neighborhoods. Students walk together in **small groups** down the college hill to get to the shops in town. When college is in session, they volunteer weekly at the Douglass Community Association on the north side minority neighborhood. Kzoo excels in **service learning** by calling on its history of collaborating with underprivileged communities in many places. It also has one of the highest participation rates in **study abroad and internships**. Looking at the study abroad list reminds you of a textbook called *Nations of the World*. The energy often flows in and out of the campus by semesters as many are coming or going to internships.

Undergrads here bring an **ethos** of not being wasteful, a bit like the Dutch Reformists who settled along this southern Lake Michigan region. The Hicks Student center was created to bring students together outside of the classrooms and help those just returning from abroad. Built recently, there was a strong push to get green awards for the structure. Some students calculated the expense of certification as a green building. True to the college's reflective philosophies, Kzoo undergraduates recognized the downside to centralized, one-requirement-fits-all construction and inspection. This **efficient**, few-frills approach characterizes the students who put their values and action together in a thoughtful package.

The campus buildings hug a steep hill around a quad that acts as a wind break (sometimes) forming the campus center. It projects a **calm**, smallish space where students gather on steps in twos and threes. In early fall and late spring, it becomes the student center for this **reflective student body**. The commanding mural in the dining room reminds you of the magnificent Diego Rivera murals at the Detroit Institute of Art. It is an arresting mural of American historical significance and human productivity. Across the canvass, you see 1930s era rural Michigan farmers, Detroit's industrial workers, the creators of the manufacturing era and the academic life represented by Kzoo faculty.

Social Environment

Students who enroll at Kalamazoo were stoic studiers in high school. Here, they step out with confidence and **intellectual exploration**. Many were admitted to other selective colleges. They enroll at The Zoo because they want to build strong connections with their professors through a **values-driven education**. Students have free rein to explore what they want to study before they commit to the college's signature **K-Plan**.

The K-Plan is simply a tool that organizes their four-year course of studies clearly and produces a professional, experience-based resume. Undergraduates work on developing a plan for their **career** and complete extensive thesis-like research. They will study abroad for the most part in third-world countries in conjunction with objectives of their K-Plan. Kzoo is ideal for practical, hard-working students who care about exploring world culture and community. They visit India or Botswana to learn the local dialects, live with a family and integrate with that particular culture. Perhaps upon their return they continue with individualized instruction in that dialect as part of the Neglected Languages Program offered on this campus.

Kalamazoo College students often go beyond the required study in order to earn an above average grade. Students are **down-to-earth** and dress for comfort more than style. They really get into conversation about their beliefs or observations from out-of-country studies. They return with a strong **cultural knowledge** base which they feature in their K-Plan resume. These students follow an intellectual approach to their careers and their future. Fun takes on characteristic collegiate activity and loves to poke fun at The Zoo. Dances with light names like Haunted Hicks, Crystal Ball and Monte Carlo exist within the Zoo After Dark rubric, run by the student-led activities board.

Compatibility with Personality Types and Preferences

Kalamazoo College adopted experiential ways of learning decades ago when few other colleges knew about this type of education. The concept of learning by doing (S) is a basic building block to the academic curriculum here. Kzoo very much encourages students to select off-campus experiences that provide service for others. There are internships in Midwest and international profit and nonprofit research laboratories, businesses and communities. These field studies are honored as primary avenues of knowledge. The next level of learning is a hallmark of Kzoo philosophy also. The basic grounding in the principles of the students discipline goes well beyond introductory courses. It is followed by interdisciplinary study, expertly woven by the faculty into the undergraduate majors.

As a result, undergraduates encounter vibrant classroom discussion and considerable written work about people-centered (F) conundrums. Structure and order (J) is critical to this process as well as intensity. The experiential activities purposely reach to the outer edges of the familiar world. Kzoo students mix it up as they refine their beliefs and define. Their travel within the U.S. is to regions that are overlooked to explore the institutions that keep citizens in distress and poverty. Those attracted to Kzoo come seeking a precisely intellectual and utilitarian education. Kalamazoo College delivers exactly this.

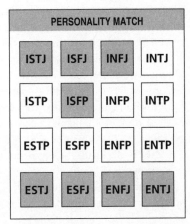

PERSONALITY MATCH			
ISTJ	ISFJ	INFJ	INTJ
ISTP	ISFP	INFP	INTP
ESTP	ESFP	ENFP	ENTP
ESTJ	ESFJ	ENFJ	ENTJ

Now read below about one of the majors that MBTI® research shows people of your type have selected since the mid-20th century. After, refer to Chapter Five for the 50 or so majors that can help you prepare for careers your type has selected. Most importantly, remember that this college description is a suggestion for exploration, not a commanding order. You can be successful in any major at any college.

ISTJ will probably like the Kzoo approach to **Computer Science**. The department approaches this evolving science with a practical bent. Software modeling is the guts of the expanding computer sciences, think algorithms, hurricane predictions or your flight cancelled without seeming reason. Students will first learn about central themes in computing technology along with required calculus and discrete math. Here at this college, ISTJ will get a good dose of the practical applications with the senior individualized project. This type might do summer research from home with the program through Google's Summer of Code.

ESFJ could select a concentration in **African Studies**. It is an extraordinary curriculum of continental exploration and the African peoples. The program was started in 1962, giving it 50+ years of depth and experience. The course titles point to the layered cultures of the continent and now include the Kiswahili language at intermediate level. In this program all subjects are on the table, Christianity, Islam, Ancient civilizations, slave trades, politics, Nelson Mandela. The department is generating newer African study abroad options in 2016. This avenue is appealing to ESFJs who will want Kzoo's expertise and structure before adventuring so far.

ISFJ might go into the field of **Psychology** as practiced in the public and independent schools. ISFJ could become a dynamite educational administrator or school psychologist. The department focuses on understanding research skills and techniques. Students also get a wide selection of human growth and development plus social cultural influences on human behavior. Undergraduates choose one of three career directions: graduate school, counseling or consulting in business and law. ISFJ usually drawn to teaching might take that middle direction.

ISFP will smile and reach for some of the joy that is resident on this efficient campus. The degree in **Mathematics**, kind of a calculating subject (okay you have to have a little humor) works for ISFJ at Kzoo. The department lends itself to the math courses you expect. ISFP can look forward to student-friendly support in the Math Physics Center and help from the Departmental Student Advisor. This type will want to use the degree to help others directly, perhaps at a regional service organization.

ESTJ may just like the **American Studies** concentration here at Kzoo. There are so many unique courses that are not available at liberal arts colleges. How about Culture and Society in Victorian America, U.S. Ethnic Literature, Black Religious Experience in the Americas? As a concentration it will supplement ESTJ's major selection who might go for interdisciplinary study of Public Policy and Urban Affairs. Both of these studies could open avenues for a career in management or executive positions. ESTJ is a natural leader in traditional environments.

INFJ is okay with the **Environmental Studies** concentration as a smart addition to their declared major. The concentration is interdisciplinary and the senior individualized project is mentored by INFJ's major department. This type is pretty darn good at initiating their ideas that reach for simultaneous goals. At the Kzoo, study abroad in the declared major can result in course credit in environmental studies too. This concentration and study abroad works just fine with a major in any physical science, as well as computer science. You go for any of these INFJ.

ENTJ gets interested in complex material and the major in **Biological Physics** will offer that up for sure. This emerging science came about from much of the DNA research completed in the last 20 years. After freshman level courses in physics, chemistry and calculus, ENTJ will start the search for upper level courses and the options for careers after graduation. Ever practical Kalamazoo College and the K-Plan will guide the search and likely provide the realistic career paths this efficient type prefers.

ENFJ is an excellent communicator in corporate environments because of their persuasive and polished personality. The Kalamazoo major in **Economics and Business** is about applying business principles in the world of finance. This type can bring presentations together easily with a Kzoo major in the field. ENFJ gets needed exposure to the tough problems in entrepreneurship through internships and field study. But before that, they study business problems, theories and economic policies. Quantitative tools plus actual business practice points to financial careers. This type is just right for leading the team meeting on business growth.

KENYON COLLEGE

Ransom Hall
Gambier, OH 43022-9623
Website: www.kenyon.edu
Admissions Telephone: 800-848-2468
Undergraduates: 1,662; 754 Men, 908 Women

Physical Environment

Walk onto the Kenyon College campus and be reminded of an **English rural landscape**. They have much in common. Kenyon's Quarry Chapel is on the National Register of Historic Places. The mature oak trees cast shadows on the **Gothic** stone buildings, creating a surreal feel, especially under an overcast sky. Ascension Hall was built in 1859 and casts a mysterious impression with a time-worn front door and original leaded glass windows. Students really identify with **haunting tales and ghostly traditions** associated with Kenyon. The fall colors and temperatures keep students outside in the evenings speculating about old campus rumors. The centuries-old cemetery on one corner of campus is fodder for Kenyon legends. It's not surprising that Halloween is a favorite holiday. The modernization of this campus has not taken away the **renaissance fair** aura. It definitely draws students who are okay with trying out fun social traditions from earlier times.

The new Gund Art Gallery and athletic center stand in stark contrast to Gothic architecture. The **Kenyon Athletic Center** is over the top for avid athletes who come from all over the U.S. and international locations. Kenyon students support their teams. They also use the Olympic-size swimming pool, the indoor and outdoor tracks and the Fitness Center with 200+ pieces of equipment. Athletes on Kenyon's Division III teams review their performance in last week's games and hold team meetings in the Athletic Center theater. Add in multiple ball courts with a spectacular arching glass wall and it's easy to see how accomplished high school athletes would be attracted to this campus.

The lovers of outdoors will smile in the fall after the first frosts. **Middle Path** which everyone uses to get to and from places is dreamy in its own beauty with an orange-red canopy above and green grass carpet below. The **Brown Family Environmental Center** is off campus, but open to the community, and a preserve for conservation research and those in Biology 101 scouting for volunteer frogs.

Social Environment

Kenyon College recruits are predominantly suburban students from across the country, as well as the major cities of the middle states. Out-of-state students far outnumber those who come from Ohio. Students attracted to Kenyon often have a full resume of extracurriculars. They look to continue those interests and try out others, including student leadership positions, on this campus. They are familiar with an active pace of life and seasonal extracurriculars whether sports or arts. The small, enclosed feeling of the campus promises an opportunity to **further refine their personal skills**. There are three levels of club sports on the campus. They accommodate the serious sportster who wants to continue competitive intercollegiate games, the sportster who wants to improve skills and get qualified instruction and the good old hoops gamer with practices and clinics on occasion.

Students read, review and practice their writing skills on this campus in a structured progression. They graduate with **clarity of thinking** and clarity of **written expression**. In Dec 2014, several student organizations sponsored a march and community discussion on race and minority experience in America. The underlying philosophy holds little value in acquired knowledge if one can't express it. The nature of the student-professor relationship is intense on this campus. Students have freedom to follow their interests. They may sign up to do an independent study or blend several majors and finish up with an interdisciplinary degree. Yet they must fit that passion into academic structure and requirements within the departments. Across the campus, the faculty goal promotes competent graduates with foundational knowledge and the ability to communicate it.

The **social scene** is lively, full and generates **sentimental loyalty** for Kenyon. Traditions like First Sing and Senior Sing historically mark the beginning and end of the four collegiate years. In between, there is constant activity, Greek Life, Homecoming, Late Night Breakfast, etc. Without a nearby metropolitan center, students finish each academic week with collaboration at Friday Cafe. It is all comfortable and familiar. They form a **close-knit** community together with the professors who live nearby.

Compatibility with Personality Types and Preferences

Kenyon College is very straight forward (S) in its dedication to teaching students. The faculty and staff provide an environment that is totally centered on individual student progress during four years of undergraduate studies. Kenyon students, in turn, passionately connect with the social and learning atmosphere at Kenyon. The campus community is unusually rich in tradition that keeps students emotionally attached to Kenyon years after graduation.

Undergraduates here enjoy and actively participate in building and maintaining the intellectual community through collaboration. There is agreement between student and professor to acquire and solidify personal knowledge (T). Learning at Kenyon College is greatly characterized by specifics, analyses and principles—in that order. There is a guided curriculum for each major which assures graduates enter professional studies or the world of work with specific skills. Students who find Kenyon attractive also very much appreciate the many programs supplementing residential life. Faculty and students devote much energy to the advising and learning process. Collaboration is a byword, whether its faculty/student or student/student.

Now read below about one of the majors that MBTI® research shows people of your type have selected since the mid-20th century. After, refer

PERSONALITY MATCH

ISTJ	ISFJ	INFJ	INTJ
ISTP	ISFP	INFP	INTP
ESTP	ESFP	ENFP	ENTP
ESTJ	ESFJ	ENFJ	ENTJ

to Chapter Five for the 50 or so majors that can help you prepare for careers your type has selected. Most importantly, remember that this college description is a suggestion for exploration, not a commanding order. You can be successful in any major at any college.

ISTP will find the major in **Physics** takes a broad survey approach in the first year courses. Since ISTP likes to collect, organize and retain facts this characteristic will come in handy. Next they will like the course in Experimental Physics I because students experiment and demonstrate classic mechanics of motion, rotation, electrical circuits and momentum. This is simply the best for ISTP who likes to tinker with stuff that can be observed. Space applications with roving robots calls out to this type as a career option.

ISFJ has a terrific, almost sponge-like memory for people and places. It works well for the **Asian Studies** concentration at Kenyon College. This reflective type will find a well-planned series of courses and study abroad options. The year of foreign language in Japanese, Chinese or Sanskrit can be fulfilled in the traditional semesters of language on campus or by an approved immersion summer program. Asian Studies becomes a very attractive addition to any other major that ISFJs might choose, perhaps art history or anthropology. The vibrant and strategic Pacific Basin also suggests a major in economics could be a good bet.

ISTJ will not shrink from the Senior Exercise in Kenyon's **Economics** degree. It is just right for this type. Undergraduates study economic models to understand the behaviors in society. It is not about personality though. Instead the department explores the reality of raising the minimum wage for, say, adolescents. ISTJs who are people-oriented, yet not all that touchy-feely, can build economic models that analyze and predict behavior. This type is very much attracted to facts and data, so the precise nature of the course work will be fine with them.

ISFP needs flexibility to sort out what will be their life's work. This type prefers to be doing things that are related to helping other folks. The interdisciplinary program in **Neuroscience** at Kenyon College offers a track in biopsychological courses that will take advantage of ISFP's astuteness in observing people. With a few years of additional training, ISFPs with this degree can move into professional health careers. It would also be ideal preparation for technical positions whereby kind-hearted ISFPs could "gentle" patients through the diagnostic medical procedures.

ESTP is quick to size up a social environment. Socially smooth, ESTPs will be in and out of the action at Kenyon with ease. The concentration in **Public Policy** has the action they love. In the last seven years, the United States government has introduced huge public policy programs across most areas of citizen and non-citizen experience. There will be no shortage of relevant policies to study. ESTP is not into theory or rhetoric.

ESFP loves to socialize and Kenyon College offers many ways to get attached to the Lords and Ladies community. The major in **Studio Art** is a fine foundation for careers in design or decor. Because of the flat economy and student debt, 20- and 30-somethings are looking to improve their living spaces on a tight budget. Courses like Painting Redefined have a large helping of fun and interest within the curriculum. ESFP will be delighted to create, market and sell affordable art.

ESTJ could be interested in the **Law and Society** concentration. It explores the connections between legal institutions and people's behavior. It has great value for the individual citizen. Increasingly, government agencies bring citizens, businesses and states into the federal courts to justify their behavior or be fined. Whether ESTJs go on to medicine, law or government, this concentration prepares them to deal with the conundrums that seem to regularly pop up in these fields. ESTJ is just the impersonal, practical leader to become a fine administrator, rarely allowing confusion to overcome the day.

LAWRENCE UNIVERSITY

Office of Admissions
115 S. Drew Street
Appleton, WI 54911
Website: www.lawrence.edu
Admissions Telephone: 920-832-6500
Undergraduates: 1,561; 706 Men, 855 Women

Physical Environment

Lawrence University is a liberal arts college located in downtown Appleton, Wisconsin. It overlooks the bank of the **Fox River**. Opulent mansions that now form "millionaire's row" line the banks of the Fox, formerly owned by 20th century industrialists. Lawrence University is the major attraction in Appleton. Beautiful art galleries, musical performance and theaters on campus bring in students and citizens for **cultural entertainments**. The **Wriston Art Center** on campus hosts permanent collections of paintings and exhibits the art work of graduating students. Often, students gather together and sit on the steps of Wriston to chat or play an instrument, except in the winter when everything is snowed under. They like to shop or walk together in groups to downtown Appleton, adjacent to the campus center.

The campus architecture is a medley of modern and traditional. The buildings are laid out with pleasing regularity on horizontal and perpendicular streets, Most students live on campus, and the dormitories include doubles with a few triples and suites. The **Warch Campus Center** is a modern, multiple-use structure with huge glass portals to view the sky and landscape.

Social Environment

Students here are **artistically inclined**, whether or not they are part of the **Music Conservatory**. They sing and play the pianos found throughout the campus. Academic knowledge is student-centered and incorporated by idealistic Lawrentians. In the Freshman Studies program, undergraduates read contemporary and classic texts. During both semesters, they discuss the nature of these reads together. They form a group of individuals who are focused on world social views. In this first year program, undergraduates take on tough questions, normally reserved for doctorate studies, like "What is the best sort of life for human beings?" Without benefit of chaplains or ministry on campus, the college received an alumna endowment in 2016 to hire a Dean of Religious Study. Perhaps undergraduates will find exploration of Judeo-Christian thought included now along with other world views covered in the 2016 and 2017 Freshman Studies.

One-third of the student population comes from the state of Wisconsin. About one-fifth of the students join fraternities and sororities. Some Lawrence students look a bit like the 1960s groupies, yet they fit in with the current grunge look. Most are comfortable in every day wear, not mindful of brand names. They are **sensitive to current day issues** that trouble the American community and will take time out to protest and to look themselves for answers. In Winter 2016, the campus held a community gathering with ten information centers staffed by offices responsible for managing the college's diversity initiatives with students, faculty and staff visiting each area.[47]

The annual **Lawrence University Trivia Contest** celebrated its 50th anniversary in 2015. Teams compete from across the country along with Lawrence University teams and local Appleton teams. It is a national and international Google Search Challenge to find the answers to arcane, amusing questions. The Music Conservatory focuses on theory, composition and music performance, but courses also include musical entrepreneurship and performance re-imagined. At Lawrence, all undergraduates who major in music are within the conservatory and must audition for admission. Non-music majors can take music coursework in the conservatory also. It adds another creative layer for idealistic Lawrentians. Although the weather is brutally cold here, students bundle up and go about their activities and student clubs which also center around "How to Live Life." It is one tough question to answer, but they spend a fair amount of time in the search.

Compatibility with Personality Types and Preferences

Lawrence University pretty much defines humanistic passion. Intellectual ideas come to the campus and freely float around for students to snag and incorporate for their own use. Searching for meaning is continuous, Academics form around that purpose also. Concepts reflecting progressive cultural thought that are retained by students, faculty or administration find their way into the curriculum and the Senior Experience. They are projects for the purpose of forming future knowledge (N). There is an undercurrent that seems to promote rational thought (T) at the expense of human spirituality on this campus. The academic program and extracurricular programs create an expectant collegial atmosphere. It is an intellectual place that defines excellence through idealism. Dialogue and conversation charge up an active, chatty campus (E). Student academic interests can become political passions over the course of the four undergraduate years. Their focus is on the future and contributing to their disciplines. Students want to become competent and they explore long lists of materials, ideas and texts to form their own ideals. Most look to graduate studies as an extension of the undergraduate studies. All this, to position themselves as decision makers and leaders in society.

Now read below about one of the majors that MBTI® research shows people of your type have selected since the mid-20th century. After, refer to Chapter Five for the 50 or so majors that can help you prepare for careers your type has selected. Most importantly, remember that this college description is a suggestion for exploration, not a commanding order. You can be successful in any major at any college.

INFP wants to get their studies in line with their values. They are organized and read everything available on a subject. Pretty much

PERSONALITY MATCH			
ISTJ	ISFJ	INFJ	INTJ
ISTP	ISFP	INFP	INTP
ESTP	ESFP	ENFP	ENTP
ESTJ	ESFJ	ENFJ	ENTJ

this is a solo activity with commitment and curiosity. The major in **Biochemistry** is all about tracking human disease back to metabolism and nutrition. Its easy to connect value for human life with this field. Let's thank the biochemists for putting us onto yummy blueberries and blackberries. The major points to graduate study and INFP will need to search out summer research which is recommended by the department.

INFJ might like the **Chemistry** major on this campus. The small department works for focused INFJ. The major leads into research, medicine, law or business. Faculty pursue their own research and students are invited to join and possibly for credit too. For INFJ, the course in Directed Study will polish off that last laboratory experiment that didn't fit in earlier studies. Perhaps INFJ will be a Lawrence professor in this very department in some future decade.

INTJ goes for originality. They look to the future of complicated subjects. They want to understand and to become an expert. They will surprise you with their knowledge. They use methodical study habits. The **Mathematics-Computer Science** major is about exploring and organizing large data dumps of information. Here's how it will go. INTJ captures the problem in numbers and then manipulates algorithms for the solution. They will need both the math and computers. That is why we recommend this interdisciplinary degree.

INTP will study the nervous system in the **Neuroscience** major at Lawrence. This field has plenty of unknowns and looks to understand human behavior through biology and psychology. So naturally it is about the Brain, the central director of human personality. INTP will complete the required Senior Experience with advising from the psychology, biology or neuroscience faculty. The degree leads to graduate study in research where INTP can find that hidden energy transformation that solves the puzzle. They like the What-If Game.

ENFP likes to wonder about the future. The events in 2015 with Russia invading the Ukraine and Syria will spark a thought or two from this perceptive, curious type. The major in **Russian Studies** at Lawrence explores the social culture and history of this pivotal nation. It is a small department with native speakers and connections with Appleton's sister city, Kurgan, Russia. The department encourages students to study for a term in Russia. Independent and energetic ENFP will need to design their senior-level independent study or request a tutorial to explore the political effects of Russian resurgent aggression in Eastern Europe and/or the Middle East.

ENTP often finds their way into the sciences. Analytical and clever, they like the **Physics** laboratories to see what is going to happen during a trial. The major on this campus starts with theory and then moves to hands-on experiments and investigation. ENTP is okay with the bigness of physics and its goal to explain the nature of the universe, and they wouldn't mind looking for the answers. It would keep boredom at bay, of which they have no tolerance. The department is all about learning experimental techniques and there are few higher priorities than discovery on the ENTP list of important stuff.

ESFJ could like the interdisciplinary major in **Natural Sciences**. ESFJ expects to contribute as an instructor in their career field. It could be in a museum, a science camp or through the National Park systems nature romps. The degree at Lawrence has good options for this potential career track. In fact, undergrads pick two fields from the list of biology, chemistry, geology or physics. How about Geology/Biology? We can see ESFJ now wearing their Park Service uniform leading an AP Biology field study from the local high school.

ENFJ will make good use of the interdisciplinary area program in **Museum Studies** at Lawrence University. It combines well with any major on campus. The courses are designed so ENFJ can pick up basic expertise in certain areas like the chemistry of art, ecology and other subjects exhibited in our museums across the nation. This is a swell study for ENFJ who likes to mingle and communicate as an instructor in public or independent organizations.

ENTJ might go for the **Mathematics-Economics** major at Lawrence University. The Senior Experience requires creativity and mathematics modeling. ENTJs could take the option to research the ongoing financial crisis of middle class families in America through mathematical modeling. This type is also very attracted to leadership and power. There could be advanced study in the political economy waiting after graduation from Lawrence.

LYNCHBURG COLLEGE

1501 Lakeside Drive
Lynchburg, VA 24501
Website: www.lynchburg.edu
Admissions Telephone: 800-426-8101
Undergraduates: 2,089; 842 Men, 1,247 Women

Physical Environment

Lynchburg College in the center of Virginia perches on a hill with views of the surrounding Blue Ridge Mountains. Red-brick buildings plus prominent white columns round out the Georgian-style architecture. Schewel Hall, with walls of glass behind traditional white columns, adds contemporary 21st design. Inside classrooms for the School of Business and Economics have current economic modeling software loaded and ready at the touch of a hypertext. The School of Communications sports the latest digital media equipment. Major buildings on campus circle a wide green lawn with crisscrossing sidewalks. Those sidewalks are thought of as the **Friendship Circle**. This campus gives off a sense of physical safety because of its familiar, predictable and cohesive architectural design. It all points to conservative cultural views of mid-20th century when America collided with nations controlled by dictators hiding behind political rhetoric.

The college mission is directly connected to the central and western Virginia culture of the Blue Ridge Mountains. The **Claytor Nature Study Center** provides an environmental laboratory of upland forests and wetlands. Education majors focus on lesson development for K-12 at the Claytor Center. Heated with geothermal energy and recently enlarged, Claytor is proof positive of Lynchburg's commitment to extend biological research through observation. It houses the Herbarium that stores botanical specimens of Virginia. Established in 1927, it has over 60,000 specimen plants. In 2014, the entire campus transferred over to 100 percent electricity generated by landfill methane gas. Now that is **sustainability, reason and faith**.

Lynchburg College was established as a **Christian**, liberal arts college by the **Disciples of Christ** in 1903. The college seal symbolizes the commitment to **faith and reason**. The Spiritual Life Center has a Chaplaincy that honors spiritual worship of Disciples, Jewish, Catholic and most Protestant denominations. The Chaplain's webpage recently featured a Jewish undergrad from New Jersey who participated in a Taglit trip to Israel. The Hobbs Science Center provides special labs for pre-professional studies in physical and occupational therapy, pre-dentistry, pre-optometry, pharmacy and veterinary science. Shellenberger Field, refurbished in 2011, calls to high school athletes who want to continue their sport in the Old Dominion Athletic Conference. Lynchburg is a **Division III athletic powerhouse**. Shellenberger Track field is also the location for serious **flag football** competition in the **annual November Turkey Bowl**.

Social Environment

Lynchburg is for those who want to learn and stay focused on learning in their four collegiate years. Academic classes are taught in an **interactive**, discussion-style manner. Students become hands- and minds-on learners as they pursue their major studies with **supportive professors** and **apply** what they learn. Primary source readings are included throughout the curriculum to develop students' speaking, writing and reasoning skills. The academic philosophy is about foundational study followed by experiential learning with internships and service learning.

Students who like sports and the outdoors will enjoy this college where physical fitness is both walked and talked. Most students find a place on a sports team of their choice and get to play often. The majors in athletic training and exercise physiology support the **fitness and sports** programs on campus with professional-level fitness facilities and equipment usually found in very well-equipped urban and suburban health centers.

Those looking for that classic college experience will enjoy the Greek **fraternities and sororities** that are encouraged on campus with opportunities for leadership and service. For those who marched in the high school band, the campus offers jazz, brass and percussion ensembles, hand bells, musical theater, orchestra, concert band and choral groups. They add to the traditional nature of fun at Lynchburg College.

Compatibility with Personality Types and Preferences

Lynchburg College has a solid understanding of the American Appalachian culture and landscape. Echoing Protestant work ethic, they have interfaced their business curriculum with service for decades. Religious and ethical perspectives guided Lynchburg College to reach out to regional communities. They established an historical understanding of the cultural values of European immigrants who settled this region, well before Ellis Island and without the cotton-producing cultures of plantation/slavery. This inclusive approach provides the student body with an optimistic, basic appreciation of regional productivity. In 2015, Lynchburg College President, as well as most other liberal arts colleges, actively questioned the purpose behind the administrations' intent to rank all of the colleges and that effort was cancelled when legislators refused to back this administration proposal.[48]

The Lynchburg curriculum is a cross between human rights, moral principles (F) and today's careers and occupations (S). The college is focused on helping students learn skills and develop their talents that are useful in today's society. It is easy to find internships that collaborate with local public and private businesses. Off-campus (E) study finds its way into the curriculum through Lynchburg's faculty, most with experience in their field of outside of academia. Undergraduates who appreciate a warm yet realistic approach in the classroom will find success here. Prospective students who seek entry into career tracks after graduation will find their preparation to be above and beyond. Lynchburg College is well connected in many human senses.

Now read below about one of the majors that MBTI® research shows people of your type have selected since the mid-20th century. After, refer

PERSONALITY MATCH			
ISTJ	ISFJ	INFJ	INTJ
ISTP	ISFP	INFP	INTP
ESTP	ESFP	ENFP	ENTP
ESTJ	ESFJ	ENFJ	ENTJ

to Chapter Five for the 50 or so majors that can help you prepare for careers your type has selected. Most importantly, remember that this college description is a suggestion for exploration, not a commanding order. You can be successful in any major at any college.

ISTJ will find the **Exercise Physiology** major at Lynchburg College falls in line with the meticulous ways they prefer for their own lifestyle. ISTJs are superb, dependable workers in these precise occupations. The department has great connections with local organizations that offer internships. With this major ISTJs will be helping athletes, patients and exercise buffs improve or recover their fitness, health and performance. The accredited department makes sure all graduates have the knowledge, skills and abilities. The major is good background for graduate study in most health-related careers.

ISFJ will find the **Business Administration** degree is focused on organizational goals in enterprise. The faculty in the School of Business is heavy on foundational knowledge. Hard-working ISFJ is all about reaching organizational goals, so this major at Lynchburg is perfect. Conscientious ISFJ will also like the business simulations that include ethical management. Student exchange is a possibility in South Korea or Austria in this major. It also requires a second major and ISFJ will find the one-on-one mentoring they like in the social sciences. This personal approach to the business workplace is very doable with a secondary study in **Human Services** at Lynchburg.

ISFP will find that fitness and well-being are a top priority at Lynchburg College. The minor **Outdoor Recreation** is right on for that reason. It combines with majors this type likes in health sciences or dimensional craft art. Two Lynchburg majors come to mind, **Health Promotion** and **Studio Arts**. ISFP, a gentle and observant soul, will want advising from faculty to combine majors in Health Promotion and outdoor recreation or Studio Arts and outdoor recreation. This campus is both practical and realistic. Graduates get quality career direction.

ESTP has been known to operate by the seat of their pants in an emergency. Actually they are acutely aware of the facts and see straight through to reality. The major in **Economic Crime Prevention and Investigation** at Lynchburg College is about investigating white collar fraud and corruption. So isn't ESTP with this degree exactly who you want? Faculty in this department have law enforcement and fraud investigative experience. Their credentials are the sad result of today's cultural, relativistic, compartmentalized reasoning. Without absolute truths in society, the slope gets slippery.

ESFP is a social being and pretty good in the spotlight. The major in **Communications** with an emphasis in **Convergent Journalism** is unusual and just might attract action-oriented ESFP. Lynchburg College is usually ahead of the curve in respect to careers and the academic curriculum. They have smartly recognized that journalists on the job with their cameras are creating the entire report. They take video, supply the spoken words, edit the story and must do this within minutes to support the 24-hour news cycle that has overtaken American media. The department has a solid ethical study within this curriculum.

ESFJ usually wants to be of service to others. In the world of business, this might mean sales representative. But it can also include management in the entertainment fields. The **Sport Management** major at Lynchburg College is a good choice as few other liberal arts colleges offer this degree. The Baltimore Orioles, Special Olympics Virginia and U.S. Marine Corps Quantico are internship locations. Hey, they look like fun, not courses for credit. The major works for immediate employment with professional sports teams, the Crimson Tide and community college athletics. Yes, one of us is from Alabama.

ESTJ goes for the no-nonsense approach in professions like law, medicine and engineering. This type can handle the pressure in high stake careers too. Lynchburg College has developed a system of advising for its **Pre-Professional Program** that is up-to-date in each individual field: dental, medical, optometry, pharmacy, physical therapy and veterinary. Faculty advisors are specialized themselves, so if ESTJ goes into working with animals, there will be an advisor who understands admission to veterinary school. Leave it to Lynchburg where confusion and wonderment is reserved for freshmen socials.

ENFJ wants to move folks along, so that they can be all they can be. ENFJs also want to be mentored and advised in one-on-one relationships. This type puts passion and cause together. Undergraduates signing up for the minor in Lynchburg's **Museum Studies** are in for such a pleasant experience. The college's Daura Museum is a treasure trove of Americana, but at Christmas there is a special collection of Christmas cards from one family, original artwork on the cards that were sent out from 1928 through 1972. They are Judeo-Christian scenes that in current day America are forbidden in public spaces by judicial rulings.

ENTJ has the professions in mind. The degree in **Biomedical Science** is ideal because it gives ENTJ a chance to sort out which direction to take for graduate study. This type does not have trouble with decisions, but they will want to know all the strategies surrounding each choice like medical research, medical school, pharmacology and physical therapy. The department is open to collaborative research which might work for ENTJ who is independent and creative.

MARQUETTE UNIVERSITY

Office of Admission
Marquette Hall, 106
Milwaukee, WI 53201-1881
Website: www.marquette.edu
Admissions Telephone: 414-288-7302, 800-222-6544
Undergraduates; 8,410; 4,008 Men, 4,402 Women
Graduate Students: 3,335

Physical Environment

The city of Milwaukee is a **vibrant** place to visit and attend college. It was settled by Eastern European immigrants who came across from Canada, probably via the Saint Lawrence Seaway and the Great Lakes. The streets are clean and not jammed with traffic. The **downtown skyline** shows sharp new buildings alongside old-world neighborhoods built in the 1900s. Marquette's campus blends with the city architecture. It is also tall and perpendicular with an inviting skyline of its own. The university encourages students to become familiar with the cultural and social traditions and also to join in volunteer projects in the city's neighborhoods. Yet "when the gales of November come hauling," to borrow the words from Canadian singer Gordon Lightfoot, students are inclined to stay indoors on campus. Those comfortable with the nature of American cities are attracted to this university. They bring their **city smarts** and openness to explore this city built along the shores of crystal clear, **turquoise Lake Michigan**. Should we add shark free, fresh water?

Approximately half of the student body lives on campus in the **tall rectangular** dormitories referred to as towers. Some upper class students move off campus to limited university-owned apartments. These residences next to the campus generate a waiting list each year because of the easy walk to and from classes. The Discovery Learning Complex is a spectacular engineering and science facility that was designed for student-generated research projects to explore fundamental science concepts.

Social Environment

Marquette University appeals to students who regularly work hard and produce results. This **work ethic** binds the city together as it does the university. In each of the schools there is a **rigorous curriculum**. Students get involved in serving the community regardless of their major. The university is a good neighbor for the city with frequent service, leadership and volunteer hours by the undergraduate student body.

About half of the students at Marquette come from traditional **Catholic** families. It would be a bit difficult to be an out-and-out atheist here. **Service learning** on this campus reflects Catholic doctrine in work productivity and spiritual centering. Students may not be leaders when they arrive on campus but they will almost certainly develop **leadership** acumen here. They will learn to transfer advocacy perspectives and practice into the Milwaukee community. In spring 2015 four students blocked traffic and were arrested protesting the slow work of the Presidential Task Force on Diversity and Inclusion.[49] In fall 2014 undergraduates also took positions on same sex marriage and families which led to one professor being relieved from teaching duties for expressing traditional Catholic teaching on marriage.[50] The faculty member has brought suit against the university for breach of contract.

More familiar social experiences that include fraternities and sororities have been an institution at Marquette for more than 100 years. They offer multiple ways to engage in **volunteer activities** and leadership. Student leadership developed **Late Night Marquette** which mirrors twenty-something entertainment on and off campus. **Sports** are very popular and games in the Bradley Center, especially their Division I basketball team, draw a big crowd. No matter which tower students live in or which organizations they join, they will develop a **wide circle of friends** from all over campus. Social life and parties are always at the ready here. Marquette graduates have a wide network of peers and the student body greatly benefits from strong **alumni support**.

Compatibility with Personality Types and Preferences

Marquette University has historically been quite orderly (J) and reasoned (T) in its educational philosophy. Analysis of ethical responsibility is ongoing. Along with focus on personal character, students are offered many opportunities that build leadership skills. All this is to encourage harmony (F) within the Marquette community as practiced by Jesuit tolerance and understanding of the current day American community. The university, with its realistically (S) oriented curriculum, graduates young adults likely to secure immediate employment in career tracks that are needed by society. Undergraduates are troubled by the minority experience on campus and across the country. They look to the university administration and most in the faculty of progressive cultural perspective to bring solution and harmony.

The undergraduates here don't often remain in their small, familiar circle of friends found during the freshman year. Programmatic and informal activities push students to enlarge their circle (E) on this campus. The advantage of this social programming highlights and builds many organizations and enterprises on campus and in Milwaukee. Students have a place for faith and religion within their values and lifestyle. They intend to have one heck of a good time in college and then settle down after graduation or post-graduate study, raise a family and make lifelong contributions within their selected discipline while actively supporting America, their state and city of residence

Now read below about one of the majors that MBTI® research shows people of your type have selected since the mid-20th century. After, refer to Chapter Five for the 50 or so majors that can help you prepare for careers your type has selected. Most importantly, remember that this college description is a suggestion for exploration, not a commanding order. You can be successful in any major at any college.

PERSONALITY MATCH			
ISTJ	ISFJ	INFJ	INTJ
ISTP	ISFP	INFP	INTP
ESTP	ESFP	ENFP	ENTP
ESTJ	ESFJ	ENFJ	ENTJ

ISTP is a maverick on occasion but in a quiet way, often with a wry smile. The major in **Business Economics** with a minor in **Air Force and Aerospace Studies** just might suit their efficient ways. The faculty is active in independent business consulting and publishing in economic journals. This passes the ISTP reality test. The hands-on orientation for selecting internships and the junior year mentor program opens up multiple career tracks. The minor in Air Force and Aerospace will move ISTP toward the large military industrial complex for a career. That career is likely to be satisfying for this very mechanical type who wants to be around metal and moving parts.

ISTJ is excellent at covering all the bases as does the natural science major in **Biochemistry and Molecular Biology** at Marquette University. It allows ISTJs to explore and analyze life-regulating mechanisms through two different "microscopes": biology and chemistry. This persevering type won't get discouraged with the precise and intense studies or the effort needed to retain and apply it. Naturally, these qualifications will work at research institutes across the nation. Yet, common sense ISTJs like having both of the options: work and/or advanced degrees in the field.

ISFJ with their strong work ethic fits in perfectly at Marquette University. The major in **Biomedical Sciences** has the hands-on curriculum for health care specialties, like dental hygienist and respiratory therapist. These are "like's" for ISFJs. They are private, but also gentle with people and very sincere while helping others. This major is solid in the sciences and designed for entry in the medical professions and health sciences. The department is well-resourced and quite up-to-date with advising for career options in this dynamic field.

ESTP is brilliant at pulling a team together with workable, on-the-spot redirection. This skill will come in handy as they manage construction projects nationally or internationally. The school of engineering at Marquette University has the much-needed degree in **Construction Engineering and Management**. Smooth ESTPs won't pause for reflection, but maybe lunch, as they work with electricians and plumbers. The required co-op helps this type recognize the best way to leverage their skills and knowledge. The department is focused on analysis and design capabilities for structures and systems. Graduates of this School of Engineering will have the financial smarts as well as the engineering credentials.

ESFP will find that Marquette University is one of a small handful of universities that offer the major in **Advertising**. This type is excellent at conveying messages. ESFPs with an artistic talent will like this active, design-oriented curriculum. Marquette University alumni networks have bunches of listings for internships. Students generate ad copy in the Mac labs on campus. Milwaukee's fine urban design and visual spaces provide plenty of inspiration. Sitting on the western edge of Lake Michigan, clear and turquoise, the cityscape is energizing if the weather is 32 degrees or above. Below this, find most everyone inside. Should we mention the salt and shark free again?

ESFJ occasionally will consider a career in business. To keep ESFJ interest, it must be heavy on customer service. The major in **Human Resource Management** is an excellent choice for this helpful type. Their loyalty and need for organizational structure will be advantageous in small and large corporations. At Marquette University, there is a solid integration of human values and community responsibility, and the business school is assertively pro-profit. Woo hoo for productivity and growth.

ESTJ is a solid bet for a career in **Real Estate**. At Marquette, students will get hands-on with transactions of current properties and the development of future properties. Commercial real estate transactions are well understood on this urban, desirable campus. ESTJ has the School of Engineering to turn to for realistic valuation when a property is sinking into the ground or the inspection report comes back with HVAC problems. The College of Business interfaces the studies with ethical frames of reference for graduates who will always be at the center of change and development. This major is almost an interdisciplinary degree.

ENFJ is frequently caring and sensitive toward others. They are promoters of well-being on the job and in the community. The major in **Social Welfare and Justice** at Marquette University is a good choice for this type. There is clearly a growing need for citizen advocates as ethical behavior is often snarled and devalued in legalistic renderings by bureaucracies and the federal courts. The department includes service learning where ENFJ can explore mediation practices that keep American citizens independent, solving their own problems without government direction.

ENTJ is cool under pressure more often than not. It's ideal for a career in **Public Relations**. The Millennial generation may not be aware of this growing career. The degree at Marquette gives entry to powerful positions within large business enterprises. First year students will study public relations principles, sophomores study media writing and advertising. Upper-class students take interdisciplinary electives. All of this prepares dynamic ENTJs to refine their analytic skills and move confidently to front and center on the public stage.

MASSACHUSETTS INSTITUTE OF TECHNOLOGY

77 Massachusetts Avenue
Cambridge. MA 02139-4307
Website: www.mit.edu
Admissions Telephone: 617-253-4791
Undergraduates: 4,512; 2,457 Men, 2,055 Women
Graduate Students: 6,630

Physical Environment

Massachusetts Institute of Technology is located on the edge of the **Charles River** in Cambridge. MIT students who need a break will jog along the banks. This 155-acre **urban** campus has an eclectic mix of buildings, from neoclassic to I.M. Pei design. Some buildings look like Lego construction, giving the campus a **utilitarian feel**. The buildings don't have names and are referred to by numbers. The "**infinite corridor**" connects buildings 7, 3, 10, 4 and 8, so that students don't have to walk outside. The university publishes construction updates just about every other month. The laboratories and facilities on this small land space are a **national and world resource** in every subject known to man and some that we don't know about yet. In fact, Mechatronic engineers were just discovered at MIT in early 2015. Mechatronic engineers are a hybrid of electrical and mechanical.

In reality, the undergraduate curriculum and students are the tip of the MIT iceberg. The university is very accommodating in focusing resources and support for those on the MIT undergraduate journey. That support will not likely include time off, but undergraduates will find access at all levels in the laboratories to join in world research and **discovery**. In 2018, **MIT.nano** will open its glass doors for, of course, nanoscale research. As best we can figure it means really, really small stuff.

More typical of the undergrad experience are the dormitories, more or less unadorned and simple as are the lawns and grounds. Maseeh Hall is an exception with trendy, uncomplicated design and Simmons Hall, which is fun to look at. They were part of the major building boom in early 2000 that erected many glass and metal buildings. All in all, bright students who like MIT also favor clean cut, angular design and practical spaces.

Social Environment

Students enjoy themselves here if they can balance intense study and a social life. They take in knowledge every moment. Competitive students are the exception rather than the rule. Most like to **collaborate** and work well on research teams. MIT students are creative in using their IQ. Each will wrestle with reaching for the A's, accepting mostly B's or tolerating an occasional C. They are the musicians who played instruments in and out of school. They are innovative in math and science. They expect to delve into the liberal arts and humanities. Most were the acknowledged math and science wizards of their high schools.

Undergrads ask questions that are perceptive and logical creating a **dynamic learning environment**. They speculate on programming possibilities with one another. Is Windows 10 a major step forward in operating systems or would you call that spyware? Where is Moxie Marlinspike when you have a question? Undergraduates here learn by doing research. Students quickly realize that there is a lot they don't know.

Undergraduates set about their own **humor** to relieve stress. Clever practical jokes and pranks bring them together. The MIT Hack club posts the Best of the Best each year. We liked the one about Pi Day which is every March 14th. But in 2015 the digits lined up like—3.1415 and three little pie-like people were plastered on the Lobby 7 skylight. Parties at MIT form around **food** with the students and clubs striving to create chef-like tidbits. MIT students dress for comfort and not trends. Undergrads fit in two or three clubs from the 450 available on campus. They leave campus for favorite foodie hangouts in Boston. About one-third of the undergrads join **Greek life** for another social outlet. Yet friendships often start out as a common interest in an academic subject or class. There are 33 varsity sports in Division III conference plus athletics at every level of skill.

Conversation may roam over to the realm of politics but it is not a dominant topic on this campus. When the news media breaks through their academic study by streaming iPhone, students take note. They are not inclined to protest or go active with time and resources diverted to passion related advocacy. As such there was a lively dialogue on campus over 2014-15 racial tension in America but without campus disruption.[51] Undergraduates come to campus expecting their contribution will be in the academic field.

Compatibility with Personality Types and Preferences

Massachusetts Institute of Technology is a powerhouse of technical invention. No surprise there. There are few universities of this caliber in the world. MIT remains true to its technical roots, decade after decade. That being said, MIT's School of Humanities, Arts and Social Sciences has broad courses of instruction. An undergraduate can declare a social science major and still be immersed in technology simply by living on this campus. The student body is powerful in intellect, commitment and energy. Both social science and science degrees lean toward objective, technical applications. On graduation students are likely to promote this technology at regional or national levels and, of course, use innovation (N) in their work places.

There are few universities that educate well in the humanities and provide their graduates interface to the most advanced technology of their discipline. MIT is one of them. Here there is little that goes unnoticed (S) in independent research or student collaboration. Those admitted are competent, objective observers (T) of their environment. Students come with a strong inclination to improve life's experience for themselves and society (F). They are only constrained by the physical laws of nature and common sense which actually finds a home on this campus. All technical discoveries get a thumbs up (P); the new knowledge will be quickly interfaced. MIT is a unique university with extraordinary national implications coming out of its technological efforts. Alumni are powerful and tend to observe, with a critical eye and doubting mind, many of the expansive pluralistic philosophies of the institute's peer intellectual institutions.

Now read below about one of the majors that MBTI® research shows people of your type have selected since the mid-20th century. After, refer to Chapter Five for the 50 or so majors that can help you prepare for careers your type has selected. Most importantly, remember that this college description is a suggestion for exploration, not a commanding order. You can be successful in any major at any college.

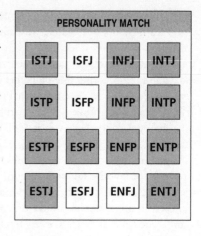

PERSONALITY MATCH

ISTJ	ISFJ	INFJ	INTJ
ISTP	ISFP	INFP	INTP
ESTP	ESFP	ENFP	ENTP
ESTJ	ESFJ	ENFJ	ENTJ

INTJ gets high marks when it comes to original thinking. Sometimes its hard for them to explain their never-before-heard-of ideas, yet given time, this type will reveal awesome work. The **History** major at MIT is pretty much about understanding the relationship politics, society and culture recorded in history over time. The department brings much focus to the 20th and 21st century. INTJ will be expected to select a theme, geographic area or historical period. Two terms will be used to write a thesis and present it to faculty for feedback. The thesis topic is wide open. INTJ may select American early history and government since many high schools across America have dropped this out of their core courses.

ISTP will look at the **Middle Eastern Studies** in this department as a chance to study outside of their favorite physical sciences. This interdisciplinary minor is a survey of culture, society, politics, economics, environment and technology in the Arab world. After the initial course work, ISTP will move on to their choice of country, historical period or current issue in the region. The catastrophic genocidal events of 2015 call out for research and study. Undergrads complete the language requirement at nearby universities. Always efficient with their time, this minor will have to make sense in connection with the major they declare at MIT.

ISTJ is just the type you would want to manage our national nuclear assets. They are all about accuracy and perseverance, perfect for this precise field. The nation's defense, with Iraq developing nuclear weapons, puts MIT's **Nuclear Science and Engineering** major in the spotlight. Although ISTJs don't seek the political spotlight that accompanies this field, they are drawn to the detail of operating nuclear reactions. The required undergraduate thesis might just be an intensive exploration of the possibilities for energy generation that are in research at MITs Tokamak fusion facility. The department research is across many fields including homeland security and human health.

INTP would be studying the past and the future with the **Earth, Atmosphere and Planetary Sciences** at MIT. This curious type goes for formulaic rabbit holes in global climate, tectonics, deformation and the solar system. INTP is intrigued by the impossible. In fact they are not sure that it is impossible. A good number of the courses have field studies. Undergraduate research in MIT national laboratories is open for INTP to join current work in geobiology, geophysics or oceanography. Or possibly, INTP could name their own study with faculty in the undergraduate research laboratory.

INFP could find their ideal double major in **Science, Technology and Society** at MIT. The degree will likely warm the heart of idealistic INFP. It questions what technology is doing to help humanity in the 21st century. The MIT Initiative on Cell Phones sounds intriguing. It could be INFP who joins this research thinking of a younger sibling at home The curriculum requires a second major in the physical sciences or engineering. This degree and the newly-minted MIT graduate will have insightful knowledge about the impact of global social media.

ESTP is right in the middle of people and processes. The **Civil and Environmental Engineering** degree at MIT is bang on for this type. Satisfaction for ESTP means carefully using resources, working with folks in a pleasant manner and solving problems. That is the exact description of Discover Course 1 in this department. For one fun-filled week, the first week of freshman year usually, undergrads of this major roam the campus in teams competing with a simple project. The whole week reveals all the areas civil engineering career fields, including newly emerging geotechnical engineers. ESTP's easygoing personality and passion for real life solutions will find a place to shine at MIT in this degree.

ESFP goes into the performing arts on occasion. They often have a sense of beauty and it comes in handy in this major. The major in **Theater Arts** at MIT is focused on performance so undergraduates in the program likely acted in or produced community or high school plays. The department seeks to connect theater with the world of science and encourages undergrads to join in their projects or start research in MIT's media lab. ESFJ will like Dramashop in this department run by the students themselves. This type's spontaneous, playful personality is an advantage in student organizations.

ENFP is good with studies that cut across several subjects. They are good with interdisciplinary degrees in college. The Bachelor of Science degree in the **Urban Studies and Planning** department at MIT has a study that ENFP might go for since it slices into sociology, business, geography, engineering, education and transportation. This type will scour the list of undergraduate research opportunities. This degree is offered as graduate work in most universities. Maybe ENFP will put their concentration together in urban education.

ENTP may find the details in the foundation courses for the **Economics** degree at MIT not so exciting. In fact, their enthusiasm may peak before they reap the rewards of putting their instinctive hunches into action. Yet they are a type who goes for big problems and this field has plenty of them. Development Economics as a concentration within this degree could work for them. It focuses on using economic tools that are designed to reduce world poverty. Notice "reduce" in that sentence. At MIT theology must recognize reality and ENTP will be rewarded for slogging through beginning micro and macro economics.

ESTJ will put their precise ways to good use in the **Aeronautics and Astronautics** degree. They want "prove-it-to-me" logic that is ideal for space exploration. Learning step by step about fundamental principles operating in unforgiving space environments is the preparation that ESTJ wants. After this, they are ready to move on to thermodynamics, fluid mechanics or signals and systems. This degree branches out quickly because getting man or machines into space is pulling from the most advanced knowledge across many systems. ESTJ must decide which system to focus on:

will it be propulsion or computing in the spacecraft? This degree has ESTJ written all over it.

ENTJ will not shy away from the **Business Analytics** major at the Sloan School of Management. The undergraduate curriculum is loaded with optimization, math modeling and other approaches to efficiency. The productive, quick ENTJ sees the reasoning and will stay on top of the daily inundation of systems science. They are motivated by competition and move toward taking charge. Upon graduation, this type will confidently enter the risk and reward side of enterprise armed with quantitative skills.

INFJ will find the degree in **Biology** at MIT studies live organisms and their chemical codes dictated by DNA. Oh, and about 100 other subjects. This major has considerable flexibility and undergrads can find themselves in courses with grad students if the topic interests them. The variety of research is over the top, like computational and systems biology, plus 13 more. INFJs are self-directed for sure and can shuttle between the test tubes and electronic data banks with ease. During the go-betweens, this is looking to push out of the amorphous box.

MIDDLEBURY COLLEGE

Office of Admissions
Middlebury, VT 05753
Website: www.middlebury.edu
Admissions Telephone: 802-443-3000
Undergraduates: 2,526; 1,222 Men, 1,304 Women

Physical Environment

Middlebury College is located in the north-central part of Vermont, about an hour from Burlington and three hours from Montreal, Canada. Although the location is isolated, the town has about 8,000 people. The average winter temperatures fall below the **freezing mark**. The weather plays a large influence here across the campus community. Ross Commons dining hall and dormitories are connected so students can walk the interior hallways. Students who make friends with the ice and snow head for the skating ponds, hockey rink and nearby **ski** slopes.

This beautiful campus, established in the 1800s, is a large expanse to negotiate. With Adirondack mountain slopes to the west, campus buildings are spaced across their own sloping landscape. **Interior space** is important and at the center of an undergraduate's daily experience. The literary connections to Robert Frost and other poets keep questions in the air about purpose and life. All in all, it makes for a **Romantic landscape** in several senses.

The **academic quad** is surrounded by the Mead Memorial Chapel, the McCullough student center, the main library and several academic halls. On the other side of College Street, the Freeman International Center and Atwater dining hall function as summertime hubs for students from across the country.

Middlebury's dormitories are referred to as **The Commons** and this is where first-year seminars are held. There are five separate residence halls in the Commons. Each has a Commons Head, Commons Dean and Commons Coordinator who live in the residence hall with their families. Together with the students, they coordinate events such as field trips, speakers and socials. Undergraduates identify with these residence halls living in the same one for the first two years. All juniors and seniors on campus are required to rotate out of their Commons to other housing options across campus. They usually elect to move with their Commons hall friends as a group to other places on campus. Plans are underway to open another dormitory along the lines of townhouses on the western side of campus.

Social Environment

Middlebury College attracts **super-academic** students, **serious** and determined to study and get the most out of college. Over 90 percent of the student body comes from out of state. They abide by rules, respect convention and look to their **residential staff to provide the foundation** for friend-making when they arrive. They tend to be quite different in their backgrounds and through discussion and common activities learn to become a member of the Middlebury community. About one-third identify as a minority or international resident. Risk-taking within the undergraduate student population tends to be about intellectual exploration and **pushing the**

edge athletically with winter sports like snowboarding. Opposing social perspectives have a place on this campus. In Fall 2013 students debated over a memorial placed to honor those who died on 9/11. At least one undergraduate strongly felt there was no honor due to those who died. Many others were shocked and voiced their disagreement with her.[52]

Sports are a way for students to get out of their heads and the interior spaces on campus. When they take a break from ongoing academic speculation, **harmless humor** works here. With assistance and support from the college, several recent graduates developed the first Muggle Quidditch competition. Now over 200 collegiate teams compete internationally. The campus has two new, over-the-top athletic facilities for indoor squash and intramural field house.

Did we mention Middlebury students are **cerebral**? The **foreign language study** on campus is excellent and the college hosts immersion study in each of 11 foreign languages each summer. There is always an international presence and currents on this campus. Many become aware of social issues, such as poverty and immigrant laborers, that are present in northern Vermont. Blessed with high intellect, graduates enter careers marked by research and service. They expect to take their place in quiet leadership positions.

Compatibility with Personality Types and Preferences

Middlebury College is rooted in historical literature. The academic environment honors the works of the early American poets with a philosophical thread. The developing American psyche of the 1800s combined with the poetic observations on life's meaning painted an ethical and responsible citizen in this literature. That ethic is studied at Middlebury College. It prompts the undergraduate to let go of self-oriented perspectives that might be considered intellectually inhibiting. Individual goals of the undergraduate student are likely to be interfaced with responsibility toward the world. This is a strong overarching theme at Middlebury College. Individuality and industry are less prized as a community value if they would reduce the nature of service to others.

By using multiple viewpoints, faculty ask students to find shades of meaning (N) and several answers emerge. Academic study is about anticipation and inspiration. Students must be okay with ambiguity at some level. There is optimism in the student body that a clear position will emerge. Middlebury students are inwardly (I) confident. They are expectant of serious and even tedious study to achieve their goals. They do not accumulate facts or skills to achieve expertise necessarily. They are more about an intellectual view of the world seen through their academic discipline. That viewpoint is abstract and graduates are often directed to social purpose on graduation (J).

PERSONALITY MATCH			
ISTJ	ISFJ	INFJ	INTJ
ISTP	ISFP	INFP	INTP
ESTP	ESFP	ENFP	ENTP
ESTJ	ESFJ	ENFJ	ENTJ

Now read below about one of the majors that MBTI® research shows people of your type have selected since the mid-20th century. After, refer to Chapter Five for the 50 or so majors that can help you prepare for careers your type has selected. Most importantly, remember that this college description is a suggestion for exploration, not a commanding order. You can be successful in any major at any college.

INFJ absolutely must look at the **Biology** major at Middlebury College. The department has state-of-the-art technical equipment and flexibility to keep vision-prone INFJs happy. These individuals are always dreaming about what could be, but they do not live in the ivory tower. They start with reality and a very strong need to know the basics of any subject that they study. Upper level students are expected to discover a topic of interest and complete independent research. Middlebury has a national program in languages which many from overseas attend in the summer. This expertise is at the ready for any undergraduate on campus. How about a minor in Chinese?

INTJ will find that the **Geography** major at Middlebury is about space coming together with people using it. This long-standing discipline is an excellent choice for INTJ who is original and digs deeply. The faculty is innovative and bold. With the course in Geographic Terrorism, INTJ may find answers for the relentless attacks on western civilization which have marred this century to date. The major may be nicely paired with the American Studies minor at this campus. Society needs a lot of bright young adults to enter this field. Fairly resistant to current political trends, the geography major has the long legs for use with intractable problems.

ISTJ is one for knowing the facts and keeping them straight. This type could easily become an archivist or librarian cataloging and retrieving documents for in a regional library. The major in **Literary Studies** would provide this type with a truly fine understanding of literary works. This department is exceptional in openness to literary knowledge. Thorough ISTJ will stay up extra hours, cataloging literary genius.

INTP has been known to develop complicated plans. The goal is important, but the process is the prize. The major in **Theater** at Middlebury is pretty much about the process. Faculty center the study of theater through by analysis. Undergraduates are required to focus their major on acting, directing, design, playwriting or production. After graduation, INTP might move toward performance or administration. Clever INTPs may also select internships on the business side of theater.

ENTP might get intrigued by the major in **International Politics and Economics** at Middlebury College because it is about issues that stream across the news media on iPhone and tablets. Second majors and minors are not approved. Yet this major is pretty interdisciplinary with coursework cutting across several other subjects. In this major, ENTP probably won't feel boxed in. Typically optimistic and confident, they will enjoy all the other undergraduate students in this popular major at Middlebury.

ENFJ will find that Middlebury has the long-term, grounded view of human history. It shows up in the amazing literary studies and, sure enough, it shows up in the major, **Religion**. In fact, this liberal arts college does not tack on the word, "studies" to the major. True to Middlebury's American roots, the department philosophy looks at worldwide religious views as they have affected the American experience.

Few universities or liberal arts colleges take this approach. Yet it is fundamental if there will be understanding and appreciation that all America's melding cultures offer. One culture, healthy, vibrant, not divided. ENFJ has the potential to see the future of America without the influence of collusion between economic and political forces.

ENTJ might go for complexity, challenge and even a foreign language to top off an educational major at Middlebury College. Most students who declare **Japanese Studies** take their first course in Japanese at Middlebury College. ENTJ is likely to move on to an international career with an MBA in mind. But first, they could declare a joint major in History and explore the U.S. and Japanese political alliance that was formed after WWII and is still in place today. Of course, this is not information that flies across social media. But strategic ENTJ will realize this important partnership and possibly schedule an internship in Tokyo.

MUHLENBERG COLLEGE

2400 Crew Street
Allentown, PA 18104-5586
Website: www.muhlenberg.edu
Admissions Telephone: 484-664-3200
Undergraduates: 2,440; 983 Men, 1,457 Women

Physical Environment

Located in the Lehigh Valley, Muhlenberg College feels like the middle ground between **Pennsylvania Dutch** country and the city of **Philadelphia**. Founded in 1848, the college is an Evangelical **Lutheran** campus. The campus has a picturesque rolling landscape and **doors painted in Amish red**. Seegers Union has inviting spaces for student collaboration. The newer **Trexler Theatre** encourages some to participate in the Broadway-quality productions offered by the drama department. The science building with its superb facilities draws in students who are interested in pre-med and pre-vet programs. The Life Sports Center is a combination of modern glass, winding architecture and the homey older brick and mortar left in place. It encourages the widespread **athleticism** on campus. Students' input was essential in the construction of the newest residence halls which encourage student involvement and a sense of community. As a result, East Hall retained its historical presence with modernization.

Social Environment

Students who want to grow in their spiritual beliefs will find open dialogue and encouragement on this campus. They value work that helps humanity, whether through research or active volunteerism in the Lehigh Valley or abroad. They appreciate the orderliness on this campus and seek to interface that with future careers. In some ways it reflects their hometown values. They often enjoy getting to know their professors and are usually confident in those **mentoring relationships**. Muhlenberg students are **very active** and vocal in the classroom and socially. They thrive on academic assignment, friendly competition and a challenge. They have a conventional sense of risk-taking, like pulling harmless pranks.

They are very active in club sports and support their NCAA competitive teams. The majority of students played sports in high school and enjoyed it, so they continue in college. They like taking the one semester of required physical education. Through these activities many become confident and find their academic niche on campus. Since 95 percent of students live in college housing, they form a loyal, tight-knit community. They are **high-achieving** and rank at or near the top quarter of their class. Many Jewish students and ethnic minorities feel quite comfortable here with a sizeable number of each at Muhlenberg. Students graduate with socially progressive perspectives. While mindful of the recession and the extra time it will take to land that first step on the career ladder, graduates have the resilience to attain personal and career success.

Compatibility with Personality Types and Preferences

At Muhlenberg, education has an undercurrent of dialogue and social perspective outside of the academic coursework. There are active centers, institutes and programs that seek to inform students and regional neighbors of the administration's philosophic views of society, primarily progressive. Considerable resources are devoted to the organizations and some departments and faculty use Center lectures in academic content depending on the field. In winter 2014, students held a sit-in on campus in response to racial incidents in New York.[53]

Academic guidance is clear and spelled out with detail in the course catalog. Here, friendly and frequent (E) conversation is welcome and one would likely find students conversing around the campus pretty much anytime. This carries over to the classroom where discussion is guided and encouraged by faculty. In this manner, students acquire content and knowledge. This educational philosophy prompts the individual student to accept responsibility, become productive and offer humane service (F) to others. Best Buddies is a popular club on campus where undergraduates form friendships with disadvantaged Lehigh Valley community members.

You can also find a simple efficiency in the academic course of studies and recreation options. Departments are well interfaced with the economy and the job markets that graduates soon will enter. Academic learning outside of the classroom is highlighted throughout the curriculum. Students expecting to transfer to professional schools find the same quality advising for this next step as those starting employment immediately on graduation.

Now read below about one of the majors that MBTI® research shows people of your type have selected since the mid-20th century. After, refer to Chapter Five for the 50 or so majors that can help you prepare for careers your type has selected. Most importantly, remember that this college description is a suggestion for exploration, not a commanding order. You can be successful in any major at any college.

PERSONALITY MATCH

ISTJ	ISFJ	INFJ	INTJ
ISTP	ISFP	INFP	INTP
ESTP	ESFP	ENFP	ENTP
ESTJ	ESFJ	ENFJ	ENTJ

ENFJ will find one of the eight **Foreign Languages** a desirable course of study. As a major, it would increase the audiences for this articulate type. The department keeps the Language Learning Center stocked with new technology and sponsors an annual literature volume in the foreign languages. There is an active calendar of speakers, events and socials. On graduation ENFJ typically would head toward communication, education or counseling for employment or graduate study.

ENTJ is going to like the idea of combining the **Asian Traditions** minor with their declared major. Both courses in Modern China and Modern Japan are realistic for 21st century careers in emerging markets. The five required courses are interdisciplinary and chosen from five academic fields. It all makes sense for this type who wants to make things happen. ENTJ will be good with the senior capstone course since they design it together with faculty.

ESFJ is definitely health-minded. Muhlenberg requires all students to take the **Principles of Fitness and Wellness** course. The one semester course takes advantage of the excellent athletic facilities on this campus. Travel and service are preferred activities for ESFJs. The minor in **Italian Language and Literature** could be ideal for career tracks in international tourism, language translation and the arts. Being sound and fit, ESFJs can handle the rigors of air travel.

ESTJ with a mind for numbers will totally like the Accounting Department. With an eye to the international nature of finances, the department encourages a study abroad at University of Maastricht in the Netherlands in approved business courses. **Accounting** majors can seek the certified public accounting credential with transfer into a Master of Science in Accounting degree at a nearby university.

ENFP might consider the major or minor in **Jewish Studies** at Muhlenberg College. Terrorist events in 2014-15 find their way into our national discussions very often. Yet many are unfamiliar with Jewish culture and perspective. This study is excellent background for ENFP working in the social sciences at regional, national and international levels. The courses are theological and historical in focus. They do not seem to overlay 21st century social, cultural or political perspectives.

ESFP finds the **Dance** major on this campus mirrors the college's philosophy for wellness as the building block of life. This type's energy and enthusiasm would be welcome in the professional dance and theater programs on campus. ESFPs are natural entertainers. Double majoring is an option with biology and ESFP may elect **dance therapy** for a career focus. Each year there are visiting artists in residence which expand the foundational courses in dance.

ISFJ might consider the major in **Public Health**. The courses review all the influences on health policy from a analytical view. This is followed by foundation courses in human behaviors, histories of world diseases and physical agents that carry disease across populations. The **Education Certificate** might be a good bet also. Moral responsibility for teachers of youth is definitely within the course dialog. The department is very realistic in exploring the several ways educational content is shaped along with the intended or unintended impact.

ESTP might decide to take the Portfolio Management course for a half credit in the **Finance** major at Muhlenberg. Undergrads study the current market and overall goals of the department's Investment Society. ESTP likes to like to learn by experience through internships or in this case, an investment club. Faculty provide undergraduates with a sound understanding of complex financial mechanisms. The department steers away from studying finance through social policy, the focus is strictly on financial mechanisms.

NEW YORK UNIVERSITY

22 Washington Square North
New York, NY 10011
Website: www.nyu.edu
Admissions Telephone: 212-998-4500
Undergraduates: 24,985; 10,744 Men, 14,241 Women
Graduate Students: 24,289

Physical Environment

The physical environment of New York City is basically the NYU experience. The 24,000 undergraduates at this university get a premier urban education. Urban University could be a second name for NYU. On the way to class students walk in, through and around tall skyscrapers, **negotiating the jumble** of streets, traffic and people outside the many NYU buildings. The campus is not traditional or self-enclosed. The university bus system and good old fashioned foot work get students between the **14 schools in six different buildings**. Students memorize the pathways they walk each day in the complex of **city blocks**. Campus stretches from lower Manhattan to Midtown, with Greenwich Village functioning as the unofficial campus center for students and faculty. All go to these retail shops for supplies and relax at the restaurants. There is so much going on all the time, yet the facilities are very functional and very comfortable. We think of it as Construction, Remodeling and Renovating @nyu.

There are over 400 student clubs on campus and of course, the city has about the same number of entertainment spots just outside the dormitories. NYU attracts **bright, independent, physically and emotionally resilient** students. Some like to take in operas at the Met or musicals on Broadway. Some are already "citified" from foreign travel and overseas living. The city acts as a research laboratory for the social science majors with its **over-the-top internship** opportunities. Depending on the department, faculty offer access to the amazing **physical science research labs**. Undergraduate students more often showcase their research in the annual Undergraduate Research Conference, much like students at smaller liberal arts colleges.

Many visiting high school students react the same way to the university and the city. They either love it or hate it, with nothing in-between. Those who enroll at this **cosmopolitan** university settle in with basic support in one of the first year residential halls. Some will explore the immenseness of NYC for the first time and like getting into the wave of people entering the subway. All can find that needed quiet nook in one of the numerous NYU libraries. Successful students quickly identify the **unpredictable nature of the city** once they leave their dormitory. They get help from residential staff on staying heads up about their personal safety. Even so, they engage the city, carve out their places and excitedly tour visiting parents and siblings. With all this going for NYU, the university still has considerable male under-representation in its student body that is found across American campuses. Where are the American guys?

Social Environment

The NYU name and academic **excellence** attracts students of many different personalities. Each incoming student finds friends and forms a stable home place in the dormitories. For some it will be a few months before they find that close-knit sense of community. Others will join the social life and activities with the NYU departments themselves. About a quarter of the undergrads do not live in university housing. They disappear into the city after classes or stay in department student lounges with friends. Students in the College of Arts and Sciences come across the greatest variety of individuals in their courses. Tisch School of Art has a very cohesive social scene with the fewest conventional-minded students. Stern School of Business students are likely to take more conservative views.

Advising at the university is a process that starts with website instructions on how to find an academic advisor. Remember, this university mirrors the city. There are hundreds of byways. Undergraduate students come from many **cultural backgrounds** with 65 percent identifying as a minority. On the whole, undergrads are fairly **assertive** individuals able to take advantage of the university's over-the-top academics. They are very **bright, preppy and funky**. For some students the social scene revolves around intramural and club sports, for others private parties and the local club scene keeps them so busy they need an extra semester to graduate. A few will engage Global Spiritual Life where religious faiths are identified as organizations or clubs.

Compatibility with Personality Types and Preferences

New York University may seem like an enigma. On a first visit the university can seem cold, distant and indifferent. The next visit changes your mind as you see the careful wrap-around services and academic attention given to the students by the administration and faculty. The university grew as the city's namesake and was always tuned to city needs and citizens. The resources of this world-class city extend into and throughout the university which offers 2,500 courses of instruction. NYU accommodates most personality preferences with a huge selection of learning options and degrees. The student who comes here already is, or wants to become, swanky in the current and classic sense.

The required list of core courses, as outlined in the Morse Academic Plan, guides students in expository writing, foreign language, scientific inquiry and contemporary culture during the first two years. Within each semester there are a fair number of courses that meet these four objectives. The curriculum and the faculty reveal what the limits of the objective approach can be (T). In this Plan, students explore how the written word of historical texts created and creates society (N). Both this study of objectivity and possibilities are highly abstract and not often featured in required core courses at universities. Similarly, the regional study of cultures around the globe expands the views of undergraduates beyond the American experience. The student who is most successful here will find those exceptional professors and enroll in their majors. All must cope with the demands of the city, however (S). After four years on this campus, their understanding of our nation may be greatly centered on urban culture and powers within. Undergraduates seeking study of middle class America, unique and increasingly fragile, will need to find those occasional courses and work direct-ly with willing professors.

Now read below about one of the majors that MBTI® research shows people of your type have selected since the mid-20th century. After, refer to Chapter Five for the 50 or so majors that can help you prepare for careers your type has select-ed. Most importantly, remember that this college description is a suggestion for exploration, not a commanding order. You can be successful in any major at any college.

PERSONALITY MATCH

ISTJ	ISFJ	INFJ	INTJ
ISTP	ISFP	INFP	INTP
ESTP	ESFP	ENFP	ENTP
ESTJ	ESFJ	ENFJ	ENTJ

INFJ can bring their insights to **Medieval and Renaissance Studies**. This major will oc-cupy INFJs as they ponder the decades of time between these two distinct periods. Their careful expertise in the discipline will be in demand if they pursue internships in archival work places, likely right in New York City. INFJ won't miss the interna-tional speakers or the university sponsored Spring Conference. Fascinating, wish we could be there. Seriously.

ENTJ may pursue **European and Mediterranean Studies**. The degree centers on 21st century politics, culture and society. With the Middle Eastern crisis and migration out of this war torn region, there is a lot to study. The department has an active and impressive list of notables who are speaking to Europe's immigration crisis in 2016. Diplomacy possibly interests ENTJ because of nature of national power and decisive, on-the-spot leadership. ENTJ would select the European language that makes sense for their intended career track and maybe add a second language too.

ENFP has the big picture that it takes for the curriculum in **Metropolitan Studies** at NYU. For those who sign up for this interdisciplinary major, careers might follow in the not-for-profit, public administration and city or regional plan-ning sectors. There is an internship rotation in this degree that takes ENFP to eight different locations in New York City. Then it is followed by a seminar that connects experience with theory. Now there's an idea to include a Midwestern, Southern or Western urban center rotation as an option.

ENFJ is very independent but also close in empathy with others. The academic discipline of **Sociology** is underappreciated. The department curriculum in this ma-jor focuses on contemporary culture and the complex events in our cities that stream across the national news media. NYU faculty and curriculum present both progres-sive and conservative cultural perspectives. We go for undergraduates here who reach their own conclusions without undue influence of either position.

INTJ and NYU are letters that work well together. The **Economics** major has speculation and data mines that power INTJ innovations. "Privatization" is a study of public citizens taking over state-owned products/services. It gets complicated very quickly. Should a nation have civilian military specialists who report to their em-ployer? Should the nation minimize reporting how many contractors are overseas, making it seem that there is less involvement in global conflicts? The economic department professors put these types of questions on the table along with the politics of awarding billion dollar contracts. A minor in History with an independent study of global mercenaries would shed some light on this complexity.

ENTP absolutely enjoys the idea of the Mind. Powerful thinkers in their own right, ENTP would do well to take pubic speaking electives to communicate those ideas. **Language of the Mind** at NYU is an interdisciplinary major, loaded with emerging concepts that must be explored and developed through, of all things, Language. It crisscrosses through linguistics, philosophy and psychology. ENTPs will puzzle at night, quietly, to merge these very different disciplines. Language is precise and linguistics can bring philosophy, words and thought together. The three are grounded in this major.

ESTJ can bring their quick, crisp decision making to the health field with a degree in **Neural Science**. This degree focuses on one of the new frontiers: the brain. NYU has the resources and the laboratories to develop ideas and grow biological cell cultures. Large, expansive NYU will sometimes challenge this type, but this major will provide structure with its scientific foundations.

ESFJ will be the lucky child who studies **Psychology** at NYU, committed to the science of the brain. Courses in the physical and social sciences are offered as tracks for undergraduates to follow. Research seeking to understand human personality is over the top at NYU. ESFJ might like to go into the counseling field and move on to a masters or doctorate in Psychology. Others might like to go into research and study the brain at the chemical levels that direct behavior. Either way ESFJ gets a choice.

ESTP just might decide the BS in **Computer Science** at NYU is efficient and practical. They like that. The degree is tailor-made for ESTP who might finish in three undergraduate years. This would leave a couple semesters to enjoy the Morse plan academic options and have fun in the city. ESTPs with 4 or 5 on their AP language exam may opt out of the foreign language requirement. Terrorism in 2014-15 points to the critical need of western nations to get ahead of the Islamic jihads. There is a strand of faculty research in Cryptography to support the global effort at containing this evil.

ESFP could select a major in **Biology** at NYU along with the track in Ecology. The field studies in open forests and the environment will keep ESFP moving and active. After upper level course work focused on disease organisms, ESFP might apply for summer laboratory research in this department. The alternate Biology track is broad and works for application to graduate schools in sciences or education.

ISFP could use their special talent in **Urban Design and Architecture Studies**. The course work at the elective level will delight thoughtful ISFPs who prefer to work with real services/products for people. These titles bring smiles to the face: Parks, Plants and People, Reading the City and Architecture in New York: Field Study. Careers in metropolitan planning and historical preservation would appeal to ISFPs as well as work in museums.

ISTP understands the value of a minor in **Physics**. They are so handy with physical and mechanical stuff. ISTP might change their mind in a year or so and declare a major after joining the Society of Physics Students. They put together lunches with faculty that talk about current research. There are lots of research positions open in the department for ISTP to join. They will just need to walk up and down the halls listening for the study with all the bells, whistles and moving parts.

INFP with the love of books might go for a minor in **Irish Studies** at NYU. Mythic Irish tales, the poetry and drama throughout their history could put a smile on INFP's face. Careers in archival artifacts or cultural specialist could spin out of this minor. The Irish diaspora certainly impacted the American settlement and could direct study hours and days in NYU's excellent archival collection in Irish Americana. The distinguished professors on faculty, specialists in Irish studies, will come to know and warm up to the INFP. Certainly a study of American President Ronald Reagan will require a trip to the Reagan library and a peek at the actual Irish pub brought from his ancestor's hometown.

NORTHEASTERN UNIVERSITY

360 Huntington Avenue
Boston, MA 02115
Website: www.nnortheastern.edu
Admissions Telephone: 617-373-8780
Undergraduates: 13,510; 6,688 Men, 6,822 Women
Graduate Students: 6,288

Physical Environment

Northeastern University is located in that part of Boston defined by the Huntington and Mass Ave intersection. It's reached from the airport and the far suburbs by the green line. Like most of Boston's subways, it is quite old and usually delayed in schedule. Distinction between the city and the university is thin with approximately 13,000 undergraduate students on campus alone. The main campus is **asymmetrical, like Boston**. It looks like an attractive business park with modern buildings, cobble-stoned walkways and high rise elevations divided by a busy avenue. Northeastern's new Science and Engineering research facility, open in Fall 2016, expanded the physical science curriculum and potential internships in the city. In January 2016, The university approved a 20-story dormitory which will help reduce the number of students living off campus.

The Curry Student Center for undergraduates is the hub of activity on campus outside of academic buildings and dormitories. **Residential complexes** are on the perimeter of this tight campus. The library developed a strategic plan to enlarge holdings and study spaces by 2019. On Northeastern's campus students expect to learn **navigating the crowded cityscape** and the real **world of employment**. They take to the **urban lifestyle** like the swan boats on the Lagoon at the Boston Commons. They come back to recharge in the evenings in the tall dorms, a bit cramped, just like the city on the other side of the avenue. A good number develop business and professional approaches to their academic studies. They look to catch those co-op experiences, internships, experiential learning and the latest cultural and technological trends in the city.

Social Environment

Northeastern University has re-invented itself many times over from its original start as Boston's YMCA in the late 1800s. Present day NU is all about productivity and **emerging entrepreneurial paradigms**. The College of Arts Media and Design sponsors an annual Global Game Jam where undergrads from international campuses compete at developing digital games with one common theme.

Most undergrads come from suburban areas of New England. One half of the students identify as a minority. Socially, they get involved in clubs, activities and sports. Some really jump into student government and leadership activities, honing their skills for similar positions after graduation. Many of the **clubs have a career focus**. The university hosts the **International Student Scholar Institute's** Carnevale as an event for students to learn about the religious faiths practiced across the globe. The university plays at the Division I level and students like to watch the Huskies basketball games. Personal fitness, intramurals and club sports have a good presence on the campus with four separate facilities and multiple classes and groups to join.

On this campus all undergraduates will explore their expectations and set goals in relationship to work and career. Students and parents are attracted by the extraordinary connection between the university's academic offerings and the cultural and business enterprise of urban America. It offers **focused job experience** and occasionally a paid position, often during the summer. Most students secure enough real work experience to successfully enter the job market in their desired field on graduation. Although with the extended weak economy, they may be underemployed like others of the Millennial generation.

Compatibility with Personality Types and Preferences

Northeastern University is true to its history of preparing students for employment and careers. The modern urban setting of this campus adds credibility to the college promise. Students and faculty are in agreement that emerging skills and capabilities are desired. These are acquired through a sequential learning (S) process, typically involving direct work experience. Bostonians, and Americans for that matter, are leaning heavily on smart phones for information and entertainment to get through their day. The lines blur between the two. NU well understands this and their entrepreneurial philosophy expanded its digital arts with eight separate majors in the field and several more interdisciplinary studies involving digital arts. The faculty and administration quickly adopt change and most undergraduate degrees are completed within four years of undergraduate study. Formerly known for their five-year degrees, only masters level study or options with co-op in the School of Business require extra time on campus.

The mentoring and advising relationship between the faculty and students (F) is darn near professional itself. Students at Northeastern enroll to acquire expertise and professors have this knowledge to provide. The advising is dynamic. It generates its own information set which reflects Boston's economy. The university is very much in tune with the city's financial fortunes. Energy flows between the students, faculty and city giving undergraduate days an outward feel (E) of productive, purposeful activity. Students are drawn to this energy and learn to manage studies, city internships, personal health and fitness with the persistent call of the vibrant Boston social scene. Productivity, productivity, productivity as they say.

Now read below about one of the majors that MBTI® research shows people of your type have selected since the mid-20th century. After, refer to Chapter Five for the 50 or so majors that can help you prepare for careers your type has selected. Most importantly, remember that this college description is a suggestion for exploration, not a commanding order. You can be successful in any major at any college.

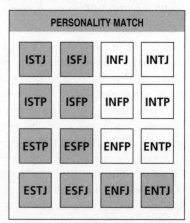

PERSONALITY MATCH

ISTJ	ISFJ	INFJ	INTJ
ISTP	ISFP	INFP	INTP
ESTP	ESFP	ENFP	ENTP
ESTJ	ESFJ	ENFJ	ENTJ

ISTP will be intrigued by the **Music Composition and Technology** program at Northeastern. It connects the aural tones of music with the logic of computers and sound equipment. ISTP takes in information through their senses and thinks with it logically. In this case, musical patterns, tones and rhythms are laid down with software. The degree requires music composition and this type could compose a cascade of notes with the one-on-one help from their instructor.

ISTJ often goes for the details found in business. The degree in Business Administration at Northeastern has seven valuable concentrations. The college encourages undergraduates to select two concentrations or add a minor from other disciplines. ISTJs could declare **Finance** which explores accounting principles, economic theory and quantitative methods in tracking money as it is acquired and distributed. This suits ISTJ who is thorough and knowledgeable.

ISFJ likes research combined with structure and predictability. The concentration in **Criminology and Public Policy** explores crime prevention through structure and predictability. The curriculum focuses on the institutions, organizations and communities that unknowingly enable crime. Equally important current social research in deviance, crime and predictability is in the curriculum. This major and career field are all about personal connection with others in a way that improves safety for the community.

ISFP is an active soul that enjoys the outdoors for the most part. The combined major in **Environmental Studies and Environmental Geology** delivers the outdoor life and career. It all appeals to ISFP's boots-on approach to learning. They are good at detailing the impact of human activity on the physical landscape. They have the technical inclination to be at ease in geology lab courses that use a good bit of instrumentation.

ESTP has a fine memory for details and they miss very few if it interests them. The business degree with a concentration in **Accounting** may seem a little dry on first pass. At Northeastern University the School of Business is very innovative with current courses and internships in the Boston financial district. ESTP likes to be where the action level is high and accountants often move into executive leadership. Another good option for ESTP is the concentration in Entrepreneurship and Innovation. As an accountant or business owner, this type is realistic with a sharp awareness of the issue at hand.

ESFP is a creative soul. The major in **Music Industry** at Northeastern is ideal for this type. The department has all the latest instruments and electronics to produce music in their labs. Internships highlight how music enters urban entertainment from concerts to sports. Emphasis in this major is on the Industry. Copyright laws, products, artist management and other parts of the business are in the curriculum. ESFP should bring their high school band instrument since the major requires two semesters of ensemble performance.

ESFJ will really approve of Northeastern's emphasis on community just outside the multi-story dorms of this tall, compact campus. This type arrives all about coordinating their work environment. Socially at ease with their attention to detail, they don't seem like fuss budgets when they redirect resources. The major in **Communication Studies** makes sense for this type because it is a springboard to organizational communication, strategic communication, production and entertainment and communication and health. These areas are newly emerging as positions in traditional business and regional public policy offices.

ESTJ is usually good with positions of authority. They tend to be natural administrators. The business major with a concentration in **Supply Chain Management** is a good choice for them. Advanced study and certification can lead to powerful positions within manufacturing enterprises. But before they reach this goal, they will study how to move the company's products, how much product to keep on hand and where to keep it. Oh by the way, they also need to know if it must have cold storage and at what temperature. Supply chain managers typically manage billion dollar inventories.

ENFJ is most enthusiastic when working on behalf of others. They also go for creative solutions with the big picture in mind. The dual degree in **Human Services** and **American Sign Language** could take advantage of the type's natural language ability and skill in communicating causes that they believe in. The actual course work in human services is a catalog of many issues troubling our communities today. There is a wealth of opportunity to help in this career field with this degree.

ENTJ will thrive in active Boston and on the Northeastern campus. They could take the concentration in **Management Information Systems** to get foundation in databases, digital media design and electronic business. Several years ago, this major was losing relevance, getting replaced by classic computer sciences. But now, with Google, Apple, Amazon and others, the discipline is coming into the limelight again. Some of the 2014-15 terrorist acts were created and directed through apps and iPhone, ENTJ could go for a Master's degree in Information Assurance. The need and the jobs in this area are exponential.

NORTHWESTERN UNIVERSITY

633 Clark Street
Evanston, IL 60208
Website: www.northwestern.edu
Admissions Telephone: 847-491-7271
Undergraduates: 8,405; 4,121 Men, 4,284 Women
Graduate Students: 11,931

Physical Environment

Northwestern University is located 12 miles **north of Chicago**, on the banks of Lake Michigan. The sweeping views, horizontal design and open atriums are part of a construction boom started in 2000. Opened in Fall 2015, the new home for the School of Music calls up the image of a cruise ship on the edge of the lake. Fun and inviting just to look at, it has 140 practice rooms for music majors. The Ryan Field House, at 23 million, will also perch on the edge of Lake Michigan. In 2018, undergrads will view turquoise Lake Michigan, salt and shark free, while they cycle the fitness equipment. Can you imagine the kinds of fitness equipment this budget will acquire?

Northwestern's fascinating research designs are best described as biggest and boldest. They capture imaginations and headlines. Also perched on an edge, the **Technological Institute Infill** sports analytic labs for **biomedical** research. As pedestrians walk by, they can peek into it and wonder about the potential for rich learning experiences within its clean room. Architects for Northwestern incorporate the "perching" concept. It makes for fun and gorgeous landscapes. The "**Rock**" is near and dear to the students' hearts and gets painted pretty much every night with promotional slogans or to announce an upcoming event. You can follow this century-old tradition by webcam. The picture is refreshed every five minutes. How about that for getting the word out?

Social Environment

Students accepted to Northwestern are attracted to the **well-resourced schools** within the university. Along with their degrees, many come to advocate for a cause, supported by the vibrant, outgoing faculty. Even the football team quarterback requesting union representation advocated for a cause. In Spring 2013, students demanded the university take action over the 1864 Sand Creek Massacre since John Evans was Governor of the territory at the time.[54] In Spring 2014, the university released a 100-page document clearing the name of John Evans,[55] **Northwestern's founding father**, and the namesake of Evanston, IL, founder of the University of Denver, the Illinois Medical Society. Jumping forward to current day advocacy, in summer 2015 the National Labor Relations Board rejected the Northwestern football players who were seeking to unionize.[56] The Black Lives Matter student group, in Fall 2015, posted a list of 19 demands and emailed them to President Shapiro.[57] At its founding, the university adopted the motto "Whatsoever Things Are True." In search of the Whatsoever, individual faculty members may be in the national news for research discoveries, and undergraduates are in the news for protests.

Most of the time, the student body is studying, active, energetic and optimistic. They want the **full college experience**. Along with the Division I athletics, the performing arts are a big part of the culture here. The **Greek life** is vibrant, raising over 14 million dollars for Chicago charities to date. Equally impressive, there are about 30 student-led Christian groups of faith at Northwestern including the Korean Christian Fellowship, Chinese Christian Fellowship, Adventist Student Association and Asian-American Intervarsity Christian fellowship. Irony often floats around sharp environments like Northwestern not affiliated with any religious faith at its founding.

Compatibility with Personality Types and Preferences

Northwestern University has an expectant feel to it. A walk through the campus reveals a very large physical facility. The open spaces between buildings are filled with purposeful students moving toward their next destination. That might be a class, research lab, social club or internship since rest and relaxation is probably allocated to the middle of the night and weekend mornings. These students are engaged (E) and interested in connecting with each other.

Educational study, casual conversation and academic discussion with other like-minded movers and shakers is common. The purpose is to gather up and digest (T) knowledge. This is to prepare the graduate for a professional position, preferably as a leader within their career field. Political passion within the school and department faculties at Northwestern University is very strong. It translates into firm positions on trending cultural topics that attract media attention. Information and facts are often presented through progressive social views. Yet most students who are successful at Northwestern select their major with a career in mind, not advocacy. The schools of engineering, journalism, communication, education and music are very visible and accessible to the whole undergraduate student body through introductory and elective courses. Undergraduate academic policies within each of these specialized schools reaches out and encourages the undecided student to identify and align toward their department or major. It's almost competitive. Students bring intensity to their major once identified. Northwestern University is mindful of their ability to inform the public square and they do so regularly.

Now read below about one of the majors that MBTI® research shows people of your type have selected since the mid-20th century. After, refer to Chapter Five for the 50 or so majors that can help you prepare for careers your type has selected. Most importantly, remember that this college description is a suggestion for exploration, not a commanding order. You can be successful in any major at any college.

INTJ will find a strong element of design in the School of Engineering. They could like the **Manufacturing and Design Engineering**

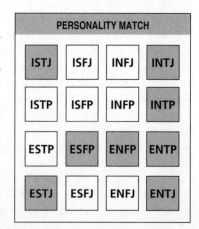

PERSONALITY MATCH

ISTJ	ISFJ	INFJ	INTJ
ISTP	ISFP	INFP	INTP
ESTP	ESFP	ENFP	ENTP
ESTJ	ESFJ	ENFJ	ENTJ

program because it expects and requires innovation. Product design courses work in the engineering projects sometimes start or finish at the Segal Institute of Design. Like how do you x-ray a 1,500 pound beluga whale? No, it's not a joke. The answer isn't even available as of early 2016, but undergrads here are working on it.

ISTJ, sometimes duty-bound, will find the **Civil Engineering** degree at Northwestern to be perfect. The department focuses on the pervasive problems of mega metropolitan centers like safe drinking water, dependable energy, efficient transportation and waste disposal systems. You go ISTJ, we need your talents, your leadership and your duty bound personalities in charge of our growing cities. Perhaps you will study the sad story of unsafe drinking water in Flint, Michigan.

INTP will find the degree in **Chemical Engineering** filled with the principles of physical properties in matter. This is just what this intense thinker might take on during undergraduate studies. Fortunately, the entire campus, including this department, is going to facilitate an understandable introduction to this tough discipline. Only in the upperclass studies will INTP get into research involving polymer science or nano technology. Read that as small technology.

ESFP and the **Certificate in Design** is a dynamic combination. Yes, this type is excellent at interpreting comfortable interior spaces and they will work in teams designing for real clients and develop their own design portfolio here. So what else could they study? A degree in transportation engineering just might catch their attention. The Segal Institute of Design takes its rightful place in Chicago's extraordinary history of architecture and design.

ENFP will enjoy the solid foundation in the **Art Theory and Practice** major. Talent and Type are separate to be sure, but the ENFP with talent will do well finding their way into this degree. But ENFP will have to stand in line with those who show up for the very popular introductory courses. Once a place is secured in the course, they will appreciate the fine foundational courses offered in this department. In art theory coursework, students present their art to peers for analysis.

ENTP is attracted to the sciences and the program in **Integrated Sciences** offers the big picture they look for when taking in volumes of knowledge. It is a very small, competitive program and the next step for all graduates is a Masters or PhD degree in the field of their research. ENTP is all about competency. How about a Churchill fellowship after graduation? This type could find a connection between Winston's values of freedom, fear of tyranny and belief in scientific research.

ESTJ will like the orderly way the Department of **Biological Sciences** presents this wide-ranging, evolving discipline. Students are first grounded in foundational knowledge, then emerging knowledge through exposure to current research studies. After this, they concentrate in one of five subspecialties. ESTJ may elect the Plant Biology track. Currently, few Millennials are entering Ph.D. graduate study on crop invasion by insects. With baby boomers retiring, this field is wide open.

ENTJ could select the minor in **Transportation and Logistics**. This type is comfortable in complex manufacturing environments. ENTJs would like their efforts to bring order to the jumble of transportation in our urban centers or emerging manufacturing plants like Tesla's Gigafactory in Reno, NV. The nature of this career field requires analytic thinking and a willingness to take calculated risks. Both of these are characteristic of ENTJ who will use it often and well over the long term.

NOTRE DAME UNIVERSITY

220 Main Building
Notre Dame, IN 46556
Website: www.nd.edu
Admissions Telephone: 574-631-7505
Undergraduates: 8,448; 4,417 Men, 4,031 Women
Graduate Students: 3,371

Physical Environment

The Notre Dame campus opens up to velvet lawns, tall trees and a straight path to the **gold-domed** administration building that can't be missed. It's a mystical sight, flanked by the **Basilica**, with pealing bells that ring throughout the day. No wonder Notre Dame students call themselves "Domers." Students are attracted to the grandeur of the architecture that seems to be devoted to the power of God more than the power of humanity. This campus has age and character with 1,250 acres. The substantial stone wall surrounding the campus points to the legacy of this American iconic school. Large numbers of influential alumni groups come into town for football weekends.

The university is a good neighbor and supports a number of programs with neighborhoods in South Bend. Yet undergraduates live in campus housing for the most part because the **Notre Dame campus facilities** are over the top. Two new dormitories opened in 2016. Notre Dame is at the beginning of a major building boom taking place across the campus. A massive interdisciplinary research laboratory will expand the curriculum in emerging sciences. A 10-year extensive renovation of the library started in 2016. The Campus Crossroads Project will add a whole new student life section. Of course it is right behind the football stadium which is also getting new premium seats. The football stadium is another signature facility that preserves tradition at this university. Each year ESPN speculates on who the Irish take on in what bowl game.

Social Environment

Most "Domers" are in the middle of the road with their political views. They are conventional, endorsing their **Catholic faith**, but there are also some liberal Catholic views on this campus. The ethos of Notre Dame revolves around **strong academics**, mighty athletics and thoughtful religious and service initiatives. The Notre Dame collegiate family includes students, fans, parents, alumnae, priests and the administration. **Well-connected and well-known alumni** in entertainment and media bring celebrity speakers to campus. They usually lean toward progressive social views predominant in American media. Controversial speakers and those with theological views other than Catholicism are invited to speak. In Jan 2015, the founding partner of non-profit, Chicago-based Interfaith Ministry Core spoke.[58]

There is little appetite for advocacy organizations that protest or make demands directed at the administration. Domers are **confident** in their abilities to impact America's social problems through knowledge, productivity and possibly by leveraging the powerful Notre Dame network. There are many service learning and service clubs on campus. Hundreds of student clubs communicate with a blizzard of notices posted just inside the halls on the way to the dining rooms. Quite a few are centered on fragile populations in our American communities. They are representative of the **social concern** prevalent in the student body. There are also plenty of student groups set up for fun and one of our favorites is Mechatronic Football which is about robots playing football. Maybe against leprechauns? **Notre Dame football** has a life of its own. On weekends, undergraduates play hard and wait for the next big athletic contest in football or basketball.

Students are comfortable joining this proud, vibrant and **well-established community** and find fun traditions within the 29 undergraduate residence halls joined by common dining and recreation space. Most live on campus for four years. The residences become part of a student's identity on campus which is fostered by the "stay hall" system. If a student lives in North quad he's loyal to the North environs and activities The majority of students come from public high school and 30 percent identify with minorities. The university avoids the troubling national trend of male under-representation on America's college campuses.

Compatibility with Personality Types and Preferences

Notre Dame is a reflection in reason (T) and community. The community takes on many layers of meaning at Notre Dame. At the most reflective level, it relates to mankind as recorded in the Bible from Adam and Eve through Jesus Christ. That is pretty reflective. At the most obvious level, community means the present day campus environment. At its core, education at Notre Dame means service to the community, and the purpose of the service is to support and serve those in need. When President Obama spoke at the university shortly after his first inauguration, his strong support for abortion became an immediate subject of controversy. The larger Notre Dame community of undergraduate students are in line with Pope Francis' intentions for strong families. Activities and clubs which align the university with radicalization are pretty much absent.

In respect to the daily educational experience at Notre Dame, faculty and departments are very much connected to the present day world of careers and vocations (S). Undergraduates find much academic depth and familiarity in the structure (J) of the curriculum. The First Year of Studies ensures comprehensive knowledge of Notre Dame's educational options as well as professional advising for all incoming freshmen. At the completion of the first year, students move into upper level programs and courses with confidence as a result of this professional advising experience. "Domers" are both academically and socially gregarious at Notre Dame (E) and beyond.

Now read below about one of the majors that MBTI® research shows people of your type have selected since the mid-20th century. After, refer

PERSONALITY MATCH			
ISTJ	ISFJ	INFJ	INTJ
ISTP	ISFP	INFP	INTP
ESTP	ESFP	ENFP	ENTP
ESTJ	ESFJ	ENFJ	ENTJ

to Chapter Five for the 50 or so majors that can help you prepare for careers your type has selected. Most importantly, remember that this college description is a suggestion for exploration, not a commanding order. You can be successful in any major at any college.

ENFJ tends toward a long view. **Preprofessional Studies** is a unique major here. It works well for those with long-term vision. ENFJ will select their course of study with the department chair or associate Dean of Science directly to tailored to their future profession be it optometry, pharmacy or any other in the health fields. The program also offers three sequences, science-business, science-computing or science-education with a little more wiggle room after graduation.

ENTJ is okay being the center of attention, especially if leadership is involved. The **Film, Television and Theatre** major at Notre Dame is open for innovation. The concentration in theater focuses on performance, production and design. Perhaps this type will switch to television with its direct connection to the business side of the entertainment industry. After graduation an MBA would also appeal to this type's appreciation for power positions.

ENTP will like Notre Dame's minor in **Journalism, Ethics and Democracy**. Notre Dame's Galllivan Program has connections at national broadcast news levels and connections to the power players who own the media. Courses like American Political Journalism and Media Ethics lay it out simply that electronic media is not neutral or objective. Rather, journalists face "ethical challenges they...must tackle on a daily basis." A review of the courses available point to the national media as a manipulative tool designed to shape the American scene. This competitive minor requires separate application for admission.

ESTJ often relates to cause-and-effect reasoning. The degree in **Electrical Engineering** is ideal for ESTJs because electricity is predictable. At Notre Dame, the curriculum explores new materials for circuits and algorithms to run future computer platforms. Calculus, algebra and physics are foundation courses for first years. It is optional, but undergrads could add a concentration in energy, nanotechnology, semiconductors, communications or biosystems.

ISTJ likes Notre Dame's expectation that engineering graduates will become technical leaders because this type is, above everything else, accurate and precise. The **Mechanical Engineering** is all about reaching for perfection. Critical operations on NASA's planetary explorers and defense aerospace platforms are heavily dependent on mechanical engineering. This all makes perfect sense to ISTJ. The department's summer engineering study abroad works for this type who is about work first and play second. The London Eye has plenty of high tolerance moving parts.

ESFJ can enjoy the business world as long as their responsibilities directly include serving clients and customers. The major at Notre Dame in **Marketing** is declared as a sophomore but only if ESFJ is preapproved for the Business School with admission to the university. They might also select the interdisciplinary minor in Education, Schooling and Society. It explores social values and business practices from an ethical view. They must declare for the ESS certificate in their freshman year, however.

ISFJ can prepare for a couple of work environments at once with the sequence in **Science-Business** at Notre Dame University. This type is often found in health care industry helping others with technical and practical information. The degree includes core courses equally in science and business. ISFJ might be on the sales force servicing medical centers, home and assisted-living care locations. The degree also prepares ISFJ to move on to an MBA and enter a career track in hospital administration.

ESTP may be interested in Notre Dame's **Management Consulting** major with a minor in **Entrepreneurship**. This combination puts emphasis on improving management leadership for business in rapid change and increased competition. That sounds like Sprint and Verizon IT network carriers. This is a risk environment and ESTPs are often okay with that. The College of Business operates many centers of study, like the Gigot Center for Entrepreneurship. Emphasis on skills and experience is ideal for this type.

ISTP is usually up for a contest in the physical sciences and will go for **Civil Engineering** at Notre Dame. The optional course titled Big Beam Contest is a definite must-have elective. The undergrads collaborate in teams, a natural activity for this flexible, passionate type. They are only passionate about technology, not life's issues. ISTP is also likely to assume the leadership on the team. This is a national challenge sponsored by private industry. ND took top honors in Fall 2015.

OBERLIN COLLEGE

Office of Admission
101 North Professor Street
Oberlin, OH 44074
Website: www.oberlin.edu
Admissions Telephone: 440-775-8411
Undergraduates: 2,912; 1,291 Men, 1,621 Women

Physical Environment

Oberlin College has a heavy sense of history portrayed in its architecture. Facilities were designed for a purpose and with efficiency in mind well before the current sustainable movement in architecture. There is red brick, yellow brick, stone, 1950s, domes, 1990s, 1980s design, it's all here, living together comfortably on this campus. All in all, the architecture points to **idealism and utility**. Students looking for this will not be disappointed.

There is strong collaboration between the college and the immediate region. The **Oberlin Project** is a decades-long business plan to reach 70 percent **sustainability** within the immediate geographic region. Geothermal wells and mechanicals operated by climate controls and solar arrays constructed on campus are impressive for energy conservation. The assessment objective of Project Oberlin covering 10 acres of land with solar arrays is to discover how viable the technology is for further development. The entire region and the local generations of Amish expect to become a **climate-positive city as defined by international standards**.

The **Allen Memorial Art museum** holds several rare collections in art and Greek statuary. These historic treasures expand academic study with one-on-one student faculty research. Students and the public both are audience to the group presentations of staff and faculty. The **Music Conservatory** is now bolstered by the Kohl Building, opened in spring 2010, which houses the jazz department along with a priceless collection of jazz memorabilia. Conservatory students form a tight knit group reaching for professional careers in musical performance. How about this? There are 230 Steinway grand pianos on this campus and 1,500 other instruments for practice and performance.

Social Environment

Oberlin students arrive with an interesting list of assets, both academic and personal. They have passion for **independence and efficiency**. They are **resolute** students and expect the long Ohio winters and student community to develop their own, unique lifestyle. Undergrads are **free-spirited**, mostly avoid big box stores and fashion labels. They strive to be accomplished, intensely academic, yet not competitive with one another. Popular causes on campus are **service and sustainability**. These two are the Oberlin ethic of this decade. Students run the Experimental College on this campus. It offers courses for credit focused on the art of teaching with student, staff, townspeople and faculty as staff. On today's campus, there is analysis of **progressive social concepts** practiced in the American community over the past 50 years. The leadership and faculty of this liberal arts college have historically supported these concepts which have reordered the American community of the mid-

20th century.

Students regularly absorb and reformulate ideas throughout their undergraduate studies. It may lead to activist causes on graduation, guided by a **unified vision** of how society should work. Some students on campus are comfortable with radical views for the American future. However, Oberlin's president took a crucial step in early 2014, disagreeing with a complex progressive agenda, supported by the U.S. Congress, that acted out across liberal arts campuses. His position made it clear that at Oberlin, radical speech, conservative speech and progressive speech get their allotted time on the soapbox. In 2015, student protests across America's elite campuses also came to Oberlin. The President remained steadfast with his open letter addressing black student demands that could undermine Oberlin community.[59] Most students, during these conundrums, go about their studies. But many sensitive, avantgarde types at Oberlin struggle with 21st century solutions to the daily homicides in nearby Chicago and Cleveland. A few also wonder about the health of the American middle class.

Compatibility with Personality Types and Preferences

Oberlin College brings to mind the word alternative, but not in the sense of fashion. Educational philosophy here is about shining a bright light on organizational practice that is viewed as wasteful of human potential. As a result, the range and approach to educational studies is wide open. This intense intellectual environment leans heavily toward a future orientation (N). Students here are very capable of dissecting a verbal argument in a precise way (T). This is certainly their inclination, and they favor learning in this manner. With background provided by their advanced high school courses, they arrive on Oberlin's campus ready to engage their passions. Oberlin undergraduates carefully study the present day body of knowledge in the field of their interests. This serves two purposes, the obvious reason being pure and simple knowledge. The second reason is to discern the shortcomings in the social sciences and promote discovery in the physical sciences.

Freedom of expression and alternative, conservative cultural concepts find a place on this campus because of faculty and administration leadership. Oberlin alumni form a strong philosophical community which supports critical analyses of the American social ills streaming across iPhone and tablets. Four years of undergraduate study at Oberlin in this decade serves to sharpen commitment for sustainable policy. On this campus, the coming decade may find the Oberlin community considering conservative cultural concepts to address intractable, growing social diseases. Oberlin College is all about leadership at many levels.

Now read below about one of the majors that MBTI® research shows people of your type have selected since the mid-20th century. After, refer to Chapter Five for the 50 or so majors that can help you prepare for careers your type has select-

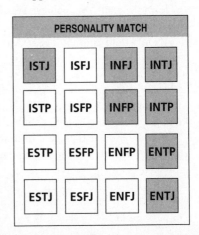

PERSONALITY MATCH

ISTJ	ISFJ	INFJ	INTJ
ISTP	ISFP	INFP	INTP
ESTP	ESFP	ENFP	ENTP
ESTJ	ESFJ	ENFJ	ENTJ

ed. Most importantly, remember that this college description is a suggestion for explora-
tion, not a commanding order. You can be successful in any major at any college.

INFJ likes the idea of development especially if it is developing goals to help community. The major in **Computer Science** at Oberlin defines this field as an art that seeks the most efficient solutions to theoretical or practical problems. During summer research or the academic semester, INFJ will jump at the chance to work with faculty in understanding learning and memory through computer simulation. This sounds exciting to us too.

INFP could be fascinated by 21st century emerging knowledge about the human brain. The major in **Neuroscience** at Oberlin College is about the foundation studies of human emotion, behavior and neuropathy. After those, it is on to original research work that will be comprehensive and penetrating for INFP. Faculty actively help undergrads find their niche among the several fields that this major crosses over into.

ENTJ can handle abstract **Physics** at Oberlin College as long as they can put the degree to practical use. The department is small and advising very helpful because physics is a gateway to many advanced research studies. Monthly speakers put a light on the degree and its potential. At Oberlin, students may also find courses in astrophysics and materials physics. ENTJ can propose experimental research in areas of faculty interest. Regional resources in northern Ohio are considerable and Oberlin faculty is creative in their use.

INTJ is a perfect fit for Oberlin College in our opinion. This precise thinker can look far into the future and develop a vision. INTJs sometimes seem like a freight train on a powerful, steady roll. The power of math reaches into many fields but this type might move toward operations research. It is a complex, unstable environment. Of course, this only makes INTJ smile a bit more. Summer research in Oberlin's CLEAR laboratories will bring analytical math formulas forward and give INTJ the foundation to move on to graduate study in **Applied Mathematics**.

ENTP is interested in so many subjects. The field of **Geology** has the variety and choice they are looking for here at Oberlin. The department is a member of the Keck Geology Consortium and geology majors in this department might capture one of their summer internships. There is an extensive collection of rocks, minerals, fossils and maps that ENTP can analyze for hidden abstractions or join in faculty research to "learn the trade" of geology. This field is wide open and has much of what keeps this type energized.

INTP could enjoy the **East Asian Studies** at Oberlin College. It is a popular major and for good reason. Decades of cooperation between Asian Oberlin alumni and current day Korean, Chinese and Japanese undergraduates really bring this study to life. With militaristic China and resource-constrained Japan at odds over islands off the continental Pacific shelf, there is need for economic and political research. Graduate study in economics could easily follow graduation.

ISTJ might take the major in **Biochemistry** right into the agricultural sciences, a traditional field that is critically important. Maybe not as fancy as human medicine, crop failures quickly grab center stage in third world countries. ISTJs will be pleased with the department's rigor in the field. The curriculum is solid. There are no trendy electives that divert energy from the tough foundational coursework in biochemistry. Don't stand in ISTJ's way walking to Quantum Chemistry and Kinetics class unless you are sharp enough to catch their wry humor as they circumnavigate you.

OCCIDENTAL COLLEGE

Office of Admissions
1600 Campus Road
Los Angeles, CA 90041
Website: www.oxy.edu
Admissions Telephone: 323-259-2500
Undergraduates: 2,117; 925 Men, 1,192 Women

Physical Environment

Occidental College is located in an area called Eagle Rock, one of the first towns founded near Los Angeles in the late 1800s. It is nestled between the **mountains of San Gabriel** and noticeable for its **Mediterranean architecture**. Characterized by many steps and hills within its 120 acres, its historic buildings are renovated and pleasant. The campus is in the middle of all **that is Los Angeles**, a bus ride away from numerous internships.

This whole area is gentrified with artists and people from various cultures who have settled in the small houses. Students are **relaxed and playful** in the welcoming **California weather**. Students walk to the Johnson Center, a popular meeting place and escape off campus during the hot, hot summers. Swan Hall holds one-third of the faculty offices on campus. Thorne Hall is the major auditorium used for the graduation ceremony and **musical** performances. Students are required to reside on campus for the first three years and are assigned to a dormitory by the first year seminar topic of their choice. There are 13 residence halls, all **governed by students**. The academic buildings and especially the extensive science labs are the settings for **experiential education**. The California Environmental Semester brings students into the Los Angeles sprawl and nearby national parks to study natural history and geography on several day trips.

Social Environment

Adventuresome, **spiritual and wondering** students enroll at Occidental College. They value the **relationship** that they build with their professors. Their college experience will center on "equality for all," "valuing diversity" and "change." Fifty percent of the students identify as minority. This mirrors Los Angeles and the curriculum explores the many cultural settings within the city. The administration regularly features **outreach with the city**. Third L.A. is a series of seminars held by local L.A. leaders on the Occidental campus. It looks at futuristic physical landscapes. They cover topics that follow from sustainability and progressive cultural views. Airbnb is on the agenda for summer 2016. Will it be a positive discussion since L.A.'s struggling middle income and lower income families supplement their budget by renting their bedrooms to vacationing travelers? Or will it be a negative discussion because the hotel industry is losing income? Occidental students will look to the faculty for guidance on this and other social and cultural conundrums.

There are approximately 100 social groups on campus that **affiliate around specific interests**. Some of the most active organizations are Hillel and Inter-Varsity Christian Fellowship (IVCF). The California State University system expelled the

Intervarsity Christian Fellowship, but here it is going strong.[60] However, the largest club is **Dance Production**. It is put on by the students with their own choreography and dance routines. Dance and music ensembles perform throughout the school year with many shows sold out. The Greek life at Occidental is pretty active in athletics, hosting open social mixers for the campus and rewarding academic study in the chapters.

The campus experienced a considerable disruption in Fall 2015 when hundreds of students and the Oxy United For Black Liberation called for the President's dismissal, presenting 14 demands and occupying the school's administrative building. Faculty also supported the demonstrations.[61] Administration reacted by pointing to Freedom of Expression and the Board of Trustees upheld the president's appointment.[62] This type of disagreement sets Oxy undergrads to further wonder about the nature of community on the campus which did not have a history of protest.

Compatibility with Personality Types and Preferences

Occidental College focuses much energy toward service learning experiences in Los Angeles' ethnic neighborhoods. Undergraduate students peer through the lens of these L.A. communities seeking world cultural knowledge. Students sign up for service learning in the city as easily as signing up for a required course in their major. Occidental College and Los Angeles have a blurred boundary line in respect to where the campus stops and the city starts. The nature of this expansive type of learning requires the Occidental community to search out, discover or develop innovative (N) social viewpoints.

The faculty supports the physical sciences with equal focus on innovation. New majors that have evolved from mega DNA research are solidly supported here. The robust curriculum in Kinesiology is unique since few other liberal arts majors focus on individual health at the community level. In neighborhoods across America, fitness centers and small health clubs understand the value and expertise that this degree offers. The undergraduate student body and its individual members would hope to see their successful initiatives find a routine presence and solid place (J) within the LA Basin neighborhoods. Students at Occidental College move toward personal goals with community in mind.

Now read below about one of the majors that MBTI® research shows people of your type have selected since the mid-20th century. After, refer to Chapter Five for the 50 or so majors that can help you prepare for careers your type has selected. Most importantly, remember that this college description is a suggestion for exploration, not a commanding order. You can be successful in any major at any college.

INFP likes the time with solitude. They can find it on Occidental's campus in the Moore Lab of Zoology. Once they declare

PERSONALITY MATCH			
ISTJ	ISFJ	INFJ	INTJ
ISTP	ISFP	INFP	INTP
ESTP	ESFP	ENFP	ENTP
ESTJ	ESFJ	ENFJ	ENTJ

their major in **Biology** they can head over to Moore and be amazed at the collection of Mexico's bird species from previous decades, 5,000 to be exact. With support from the faculty, INFP may start learning the intricacies of DNA research within this collection.

INFJ occasionally enters the field of health science research. The Department of Biology offers an emphasis in **Cell and Molecular Biology**. It is ideal for advanced graduate study. INFJ will want to peer into the DNA and cell physiology. This type prefers to study alone. The campus is chatty, but they will find those quiet spaces to pour over research on cell-to-cell communication.

INTJ sees far into the unknown and enjoys creating systems that might reveal new information. The major in **Physics** at Occidental College even has openings for qualified first years to start into research projects. But INTJ might want to wait until they finish studying electro and magneto statics in third year studies. INTJs like to learn through scientific research. Magnetic properties in geophysics and astrophysics could provide the key to INTJ's original hypothesis.

ISFJ will find the study of **Music** at Occidental College ideal because of its location. A lot of entertainment programming originates in L.A. with Hollywood and broadcast studios. This strong department offers many music courses and performances by faculty and undergraduates. Drop in on the occasional Music on a Friday Afternoon. For Oxy students who want music as a full-time career, the city showcases a lot of professional musicians at work. ISFJ will gain needed energy and build resilience through the hands-on, performing musical arts.

INTP will smile at the idea of a minor in **Computer Science**. This type who loves puzzles would not pass up a chance to give an old fashioned Rubik's cube a twist, or two, okay five. This minor completes the first two years of standard computer science undergraduate studies. Some upper level classes can be taken at nearby Caltech. INTP might major in biology, chemistry or history. Each discipline is wide open for statistical analysis.

ENFP loves to be with and around a wide variety of people. The major in **Japanese Studies** at Occidental will take this type off campus and into the city for conversation with native speakers in business and community. The department centers course work on the language, the arts, literature and film. This rich introduction will lead to other fields like journalism, advertising, arts or teaching. Asian culture in American society, with cultural gifts and perspectives comes forward into the limelight with ENFP's warm appreciation.

ENTP can be attracted to the sciences. The major in **Biochemistry** at Oxy has all the foundation courses in chemistry and biology. It also has exciting courses that center on experimental design and experiential learning. This hands-on, direct observation of physical organisms is good for ENTP. It helps them with their classic weakness—attention to detail. The department's approach to this physical science is perfect for ENTP who can be powerful innovators when they bring structure and discipline to their work.

ESFJ is an ideal candidate for the major in **Kinesiology**. This type is great at using their therapeutic skills in a conscientious way. This science-based degree is good for graduate study, employment in health and fitness centers and staff positions on many athletic teams in the L.A. basin. There are three instructional labs in the department at Oxy, anatomy, human performance and motor control/learning. ESFJ naturally takes to learning technical instruction and practice which is what this degree is all about.

ENFJ often enjoys careers associated with counseling. The major in **Psychology** in this department is rooted in classic foundational study. The field heavily relies on scientific methodology, research in physical sciences and theory. It is resistant to political and social trends that try to define its foundations. Faculty at Occidental understand these distinctions and provide a first class four year undergraduate study in psychology. ENFJ will pass the senior comprehensive written examination with their usual flair for communicating ideas.

ENTJ will go for **Cognitive Science** in this department which captures expression of thought, language and consciousness for formulaic filters in mathematics. It is an evolving scientific field that offers much challenge and opportunity. Faculty include the futuristic nature of this field with courses in Artificial Intelligence and data analysis/visualization. ENTJs are naturals at innovative thinking and leadership. This major calls out to them.

PEPPERDINE UNIVERSITY

Seaver College
24255 Pacific Coast Highway
Malibu, CA 90263-4392
Website: www.pepperdine.edu
Admissions Telephone: 310-506-4392
Undergraduates: 3,451; 1,514 Men, 1,937 Women
Graduate Students: 3,966

Physical Environment

Pepperdine students enjoy breathtaking **views of the Pacific Ocean** and the sunny Malibu beaches. The university is affiliated with the **Church of Christ** and the large majority of students are active in spiritual services of differing faiths. About one-half of the students are from California, with another quarter from the western states. International students mostly from the Pacific Basin nations are at about ten percent. The moderate weather and the hills on campus make for a physically active lifestyle. The university has NCAA Division I representation on men's and women's teams.

The physical presence of the campus outwardly speaks to **spirituality and stewardship of resources**. The university has a comprehensive, ongoing custodial plan that addresses the disposal of all unused resources. Heating, air conditioning and lighting on campus is centrally controlled. All dishware in the dining rooms and snack spots are reusable. Styrofoam is banned from campus. Dining options are not buffet style because of the waste typically encountered in help yourself venues. We outline these practices in detail because they speak to the ethos of the university. All within the realm of the campus environment belongs to God and is treated with spiritual respect.

This location is really key to **experiential learning** and **service learning** found in all the coursework. Undergraduates here find themselves in Los Angeles neighborhoods supporting communities through volunteer work. They are in excellent **internships** though the College of Business network developed over decades. The huge metropolitan complex with all its wealth is hard to wrap your head around. There are corporate and financial empires within a bus ride. Think Disney. Think baseball's Anaheim Angels and Los Angeles Dodgers. Think Lockheed Martin aerospace, and more.

Social Environment

Pepperdine was founded by a very successful Christian business entrepreneur. Students carry on his **Christian legacy** by **serving others** through non-profit management, service and fundraising. It all mixes quite well with Pepperdine's philosophy of helping others in a contemporary way through natural rights. They are not given by government or manmade institutions. It is the wellspring for service on this campus. Pepperdine is not for students who harbor doubts about spirituality, although not everyone is necessarily intensely spiritual. Most students live on campus. Residential dormitories are staffed with a professional Resident Director. Student spiritual life advisors and student resident advisors are assigned to each hall under the mentorship of the resident director. The student advisors provide program and peer support that prompts **holistic growth** within the members of their community.

Student-led ministry is very active with budget, facilities and communication services provided by the college. Students seek to **develop personal skills** and serve through these ministries. Undergraduates might travel with academic staff on service trips to impoverished islands in the Pacific Basin. But more often, undergraduates provide direct services to children and adolescents living in Los Angeles shelters, group homes and on the streets. They do this through cooperation with nonprofit organizations in the L.A. neighborhoods and they get into the city by public bus.

There's a strong emphasis on happiness though **spiritual wellness**, healthy eating habits, the art of dating and physical fitness. Students don't buy tickets from StubHub or Ticketmaster for the events in the city. They are inclined to put their own talents on the stage in professional level performances. The Pepperdine theaters, auditoriums, marketing and logistics are at their disposal. **Songfest**, an over-the-top **musical talent show** put on by the students, hundreds of them, showcases their performing arts. This show, with a professional orchestra, is always sold out, even with six performances. Optimistic, healthy and caring describe the campus environment. Pepperdine athletics are in Division I and Willie the Wave is their mascot. Well, that makes sense.

Compatibility with Personality Types and Preferences

Pepperdine University and Seaver College are exceptionally clear in communicating their educational goals (J). Even the website is easy to use and well-organized. A purposeful life is the outcome of education and Pepperdine students reach this goal through reflection, service to others, experiential learning and promoting values which are Christian-centered. The college campus environment is both consistent and caring (F). Practically all of the activities outside of the classroom (E) are driven by holistic concerns. The momentum of shared beliefs and cultural campus activities grows many friendships within the student body during the college years. The university predicts these relationships will be life long. Friendship and community is expected to serve as the guidepost for a turbulent American 21st century. There were no campus disruptions or demands made of the college administrators in 2014-15.

Students expect to bring change to the community through their professional careers and service orientation.

Now read below about one of the majors that MBTI® research shows people of your type have selected since the mid-20th century. After, refer to Chapter Five for the 50 or so majors that can help you prepare for careers your type has selected. Most importantly, remember that this college description is a suggestion for exploration, not a commanding order. You can be successful in any major at any college.

PERSONALITY MATCH			
ISTJ	ISFJ	INFJ	INTJ
ISTP	ISFP	INFP	INTP
ESTP	ESFP	ENFP	ENTP
ESTJ	ESFJ	ENFJ	ENTJ

ISFJ, often a reflective and thorough soul, could enjoy the degree in **Liberal Arts** at Pepperdine. This rather unusual degree also requires a concentration in the arts, human development, language, social science, math, science or sports. It is an inclusive course of study for a student who might want to become an archivist, librarian or teacher. The department includes three elective courses in student teaching. Faculty developed a unique Western Heritage Series that is integrated in the curriculum.

ISFP is good with collecting information that is practical. This is the right attitude for a **Nutritional Science** degree. The course titled Public Health has a service learning requirement where students plan, implement and evaluate through a community assessment. This type of learning-by-doing is perfect for the ISFP. The department is over-the- top with their post baccalaureate program designed to train professional dieticians and it meets national standards.

INFP hopes to express their inner thoughts but with distance between themselves and you. Art does the job nicely. If you put art and words together, you have a minor in the Fine Arts department called **Multimedia Design**. An option here at Pepperdine might be to pair this minor with a communication major such as journalism. **Rhetoric and Leadership** is another enticing minor available. All are appealing to INFP.

ESTJ is going to get an exceptionally fine **International Business** degree at Pepperdine University. Part of the philosophical core of this campus is to reach out and learn extensively about Pacific Basin cultures. The university has access to many cross-cultural currents because of its location on the coast and proximity to Los Angeles. The exceptional list of courses includes Ethics and International Politics. Internships in the Los Angeles basin of mega corporate enterprises or New York City financial houses cover both the world's great oceans for surfs up Willie the Wave Mascot. Okay you have to have a little corny humor to lighten this read. All students will complete a service learning project also. It all works for ESTJ.

ESFJ often enjoys people and it shows through their natural ease and curiosity about others. They connect easily with others, are supportive and uncomfortable if there isn't harmony in the workplace. The minor in **Sports Medicine** is a good choice for this type. The Natural Science Division offers a curriculum anchored in personal fitness. Courses in human physiology, anatomy, neuroscience and biomechanics round out the fitness-oriented courses. At the same time, it is also offered as a major and ESFJ might just change their study into the full degree and go for a career in the health/fitness industry where most patrons are anxious to reach goals and cooperate.

ENFJ can jump right into the **Public Relations** degree and find an outlet for their grand speaking style. The degree has both theoretical and practical courses. This type definitely puts harmony at the top of their priority list. It is a great characteristic for the public relations career field. ENFJ will study actual business problems to identify the real motive as well as the most ethical solution. Students at Pepperdine in this major write, direct and produce entertainment TV in the Pepperdine Studios.

ENTJ is usually quite the extraverted go-to-person. If they have talent in writing or art, the degree in **Advertising** could be right for this type. The Pepperdine campus TV and Radio stations are sophisticated in several senses. Undergrads create and broadcast their own advertisements, bulletins and sales pitches. ENTJ will want to join the Pepperdine Speech and Debate Club as another way to fine tune a message. The entertainment kaleidoscope in Los Angeles and Pepperdine's emphasis on ethical media really make for a good background in this major. Who knows? Maybe some of the fun commercials we see during the Super bowl are the work of Pepperdine graduates.

PRINCETON UNIVERSITY

Admission Office
P.O. Box 430
Princeton, NJ 08544-0430
Website: www.princeton.edu
Admissions Telephone: 609-258-3060
Undergraduates: 5,391; 2,759 Men, 2,632 Women
Graduate Students: 2,691

Physical Environment

Princeton is a town that plays host to its namesake university and suburban up-scale neighborhoods with shops that ring the university perimeter. The campus is a Mecca for intellectual activity that spills out onto the town through the arts, music and clubs. The town also hosts Dow Jones and Educational Testing Services who offer the SAT, familiar to most high school students. To take a break from the intense study, students head out to Prospect Avenue, which they refer to as "the street," for their favorite foodie place. Just about all students reside on campus or in school-sponsored houses for all four years.

It's clear to see why the campus architecture and the park-like setting are breath-taking with **castle-like residence halls**. There are Gothic and Georgian-style buildings, and the impressive Blair Arch. With over 500 acres, the campus transportation is by bus, foot and bike. Presently there are two large construction projects which somewhat mar the views on campus. The massive **Arts and Transit Project** will feature 21 acres with three **performing arts** buildings in a park setting with large expanses of green. It is projected to be complete in 2017. The Andlinger Center for Energy and Environment opened Spring 2015. This faculty will focus on sustainable energy, conservation and environmental remediation. These new modern steel and glass structures will sit in the middle of Princeton's old world structures and the later buildings designed by I.M. Pei and Robert Venturi. When construction is done, it will make for an impressive, **striking campus** worthy of the academics practiced behind the walls.

The **archives, research laboratories and libraries** at this university contain **human achievement throughout the centuries**. Princeton is home to scientific leaps in understanding and offered a place of refuge for Albert Einstein during his later years when doubt crowded onto his theory of relativity. Princeton must take pride in their history. At the very least, there must have been pride floating in the air at the astrophysics laboratories in Feb 2016 with Einstein's theory was confirmed conclusively with gravitational waves detected from two massive black holes colliding. It was a super day across the universe of mankind. Princeton has made **Einstein's Papers an open access site**. It is difficult to comprehend the university's entire range of collections. In the humanities alone, the Scheide Library is the archival home to 18 editions of pre-Luther German Bibles.

Social Environment

Assured and possessing **intellectual and social acumen**, Princeton undergraduates have near endless opportunities available for activity outside of class. Weekly and monthly dinners are designed to bring students together and foster **academic community**. Bi-monthly lunches are planned to give students and faculty a chance to communicate outside the classroom. Other social avenues build communities for like-minded students, like the **eating clubs**. There are 11 eating clubs, located off campus near Olden or Prospect Streets. Each eating club has a different theme and is run according to its own goals. Greek fraternities and sororities, along with the Eating Clubs, provide **leadership** opportunities, social activities and sponsor arts events and service projects. The majority of students join with one of these social organizations. Division I athletics is excellent with national ranking in 22 sports. More than half of the undergrads participate on one of the 38 varsity or 35 club sport teams. In addition, there are **200 clubs** that represent the arts, hobbies and advocacy. Students **look to clubs** primarily to round out their non-academic experience at Princeton.

Although some competition in class arises from the way the grading system works, the atmosphere is one of cooperation. Academically, in first and second year, students take classes to fulfill **distribution requirements** in seven to nine different areas of study, including **epistemology**—the study of knowledge, its limits and validity. Undergraduates select from 31 concentrations and 50 certificates. While they cannot double major, with advanced planning many get the certificate too. Students are required to **conduct independent research** as part of their **junior paper** and in conjunction with their **senior thesis**. This requires the approval of an advisor with whom they work one-on-one. This thesis could easily spin into a basis for graduate study or PhD program.

Students who want to study abroad are advised to do so during their first and second year of college, because the schedule is too tight for upper class studies. Princeton offers a **Bridge Year program** to admitted high school graduates who are selected and elect to volunteer service in third world countries for one year with most expenses covered by the program. There is also a formal group that offers support to any undergrads taking a gap year at anytime during the undergraduate study years. Princeton undergraduates typically come from independent schools or excellent public schools. They hail primarily from the eastern seaboard. Close to half of Princeton's student population identifies as minority. Sleep may be the only real down time here. Earlier in this decade, campus humor jestingly advised "get clones" as an answer for not enough time in the day.

In Fall 2015, the #occupynassau group, sponsored by Princeton's Black Justice League, occupied the President's office for 33 hours with a list of demands requiring his response before they would leave. The last demand assured there would be no academic consequences to the striking students. The President sent to a committee their demand to rename the Woodrow Wilson School of Public and International Affairs.[63] Many professors supported the students agreeing that the university's heritage promoted white supremacy.[64] Unlike other student demands at selective universities in Fall 2015, this demonstration did not garner attention from the administration as violating freedom of expression. However, 500 Princetonians signed a petition disagreeing with the President's actions.[65] It was a tumultuous time on campus.

Compatibility with Personality Types and Preferences

At Princeton, students enter the freshman doorway and proceed in any of 360° directions (P). It is a precise university that can be thought of as an infinite three dimensional grid of informational cubes. During their four years, undergraduates will traverse the infinite cube, a cerebral mind puzzle. They will rearrange those cubes of information each semester into a new assimilated whole. Princeton undergrads are always searching for the next (N) nugget that brings meaning to their understanding of a discipline. It is exciting, intense, rewarding and cautious labor. After all, one wouldn't want to get lost in the infinite cube of knowledge. One might miss dinner.

The Princeton student journey through the day, week and months matches up thought (T) with curiosity. The administration and faculty expect an independent search for knowledge. Academic courses and methods encourage students to research information (S) and occasionally present it as a formal lesson to others in Preceptorials. Some students reach for their understanding of a discipline through collaboration with peers (F). The Reading Courses are a type of learning experience settled upon by professor and student. At Princeton, students can put their own educational plan together (J) and propose it to the faculty. It is yet another avenue for the curious undergraduate with a desire to enter a particular cube in the infinite grid on this campus. Graduates of Princeton stand resolutely, move forward into discovery and precisely craft new knowledge for society at large.

Now read below about one of the majors that MBTI® research shows people of your type have selected since the mid-20th century. After, refer to Chapter Five for the 50 or so majors that can help you prepare for careers your type has selected. Most importantly, remember that this college description is a suggestion for exploration, not a commanding order. You can be successful in any major at any college.

PERSONALITY MATCH			
ISTJ	ISFJ	INFJ	INTJ
ISTP	ISFP	INFP	INTP
ESTP	ESFP	ENFP	ENTP
ESTJ	ESFJ	ENFJ	ENTJ

INFP is very satisfied when they can bring their talents to help others. The certificate in **Language and Culture** at Princeton allows INFP to move into the international arena. This certificate is paired with any other concentration. Passionate and committed, this type will take personal meaning from this study. INFPs can be valuable members of any team that needs a little vision, perhaps expanding the concept of cohesion on campus over individual needs.

INFJ will really take to Princeton's infinite pathways. This type is usually thinking about values that turn over and over in their minds. Princeton has a curriculum that talks to this conundrum. The concentration in **Psychology** is centered on the physical sciences and the social implications of problems in current day American society. The department organizes itself by studying the human personality with all its intellectual and metaphysical experience. This topic has segued into the work of psychological theorists such as Carl Jung and Christian apologists like Ravi Zacharias.

Okay, back to the real world. Current faculty research is focused on bullying in American middle class schools.

INTJ is most independent and private in respect to their ideas that can take months or years to meet up with reality. Very intense thinking is their specialty. The concentration in **Astrophysical Sciences** happily accepts these bold thinkers. Courses like Stars and Star Formation call out to their imagination. The facilities at Princeton are among the most advanced. With data bits streaming back to earth from the Keplar, Dawn, Rosetta and New Horizons space probes, the faculty is redefining space along with other international research teams. In this small department, INTJ will be right in the middle of it.

ISTP goes for little machines that move around on the floor. There is a child lurking within ISTPs. Therefore, the **Robotics and Intelligent Systems** certificate is likely to bring a smile to their face. In fact, ISTP wants to get their hands on the control stick. Better yet, ISTP wants to program the data commands and make this little machine do hip hop. This type might focus on any product, service or technical gadget that can become useful with application from pacemakers to space technology. The certificate centers around automation in manufacturing, systems for learning and understanding human intelligence. It's a tall order, but Princetonians do not back off.

ISTJ can catalog huge numbers of facts and have them at the ready for immediate recall. It is their specialty which is indispensable in many organizations. Princeton's certificate in **Finance** covers more financials than you can shake a calculator at. This very precise discipline is a good bet if ISTJ is inclined to math. The role of regulation and government requirements is ever increasing but this certificate is a heads up for any career in business or law that ISTJs typically go for.

ISFJ looks closely, sees what is there and commits it to memory. They do it with ease and ought to look into the major **Art and Archeology** at Princeton. This major mirrors educational philosophies at Princeton expanding in every direction, finding and using layers of knowledge, making realistic connections. It is also perfect for the ISFJ who fills their inner world with portraits of personal meaning. The department expects their graduates to be able to put linguistic meaning into visual art and artifacts. It's a big expectation and rather painstaking detective work is required. Undergraduates will create their own artistic pieces to communicate a message through historical interpretation and discovery.

ISFP puts a lighthearted, practical touch in conversation. It overshadows their deep-seated personal values. Many times, others are not aware of this. The certificate in **Environmental Studies** and the course titled Disease, Ecology, Economics and Policy explore the land with its inhabitants together. The department is flexible, so ISFP can take a generalist study, or they might go for the concentration in Biodiversity and Conservation as they are often in tune with animals.

INTP will find the **Computer Science** department at Princeton University full of very interesting options like artificial intelligence, bioinformatics, digital media and computational social science. After they finish the core requirements, INTP can go for advanced study in artificial intelligence. That certainly works for most INTPs always on the lookout for the unknown. This type likes to analyze and logic is their specialty. It is an ideal characteristic for a special study abroad at AIT-Budapest.

This program was developed for North American students of computer sciences and engineering. They will study computational thinking as applied to Hungary's rich cultural history. The importance of this region with Russia's invasion of the Ukraine is not lost on Princeton or INTP.

ESTP is a type that likes a little snazz in life. Sometimes that snazz is in the form of risk-taking. The concentration in **Mechanical and Aerospace Engineering** has got it all. In this flexible department, a student can get a mechanical or aerospace engineering degree, but with careful scheduling. ESTP will survey the research in the amazing laboratories and could go for the Senior Thesis. It is two semesters long but the chance to develop a new application with lasers and applied physics is too much to pass up for this active type. If they decide to go for this optional offer, they will be working at the edge of emerging science. Maybe walking in Einstein's footsteps.

ENFP might just be interested in the **Creative Writing** concentration, offered through the Lewis Center for the Arts. Students who take this certificate, about 25 or so a year, will write a piece of literature as part of the required creative thesis. ENFP is an emotional type and able to empathize with other's feelings. They will work with a faculty member to develop whichever they choose, a novel, screenplay, short story, poem or translation. There are several classes called workshops that ENFP will take to get prepared for this ambitious project. The advantage for this type is to learn how deeply they experience human emotions in comparison with other personality preferences.

ENTP finds it difficult to come across an idea or a topic in politics that isn't interesting. The concentration in **History and The Practice of Diplomacy** at Princeton will capture their attention. Students enroll during the sophomore year and learn together as a group for the rest of the coursework. They will take a summer internship in a government agency or international organization. Faculty advisors help with their thesis selection so that it is relevant to the program. It is also designed to introduce undergrads to the practice of diplomacy. ENTP will get some hands-on experience in softening some of their provocative chit chat.

ESFJ is a conscientious type and big supporter of traditions. The conservation focus in Princeton's **Ecology and Evolutionary Biology** could appeal to ESFJ. The department has a series of field studies in Panama where juniors study the tropical vegetation and animal life. They also spend a lot of time in the water with the course Biology of Coral Reefs. The last field course is back in the Panama Canal Zone searching out disease organisms. Professional guidance and logistics is provided by the Smithsonian Tropical Research Institute in Panama. It is the safe, first class study that ESFJ will require to wander this far off the beaten path.

ESTJ is often excellent at officiating. They can be a source of accuracy for others who do not have time. The certificate in **Translation and Intercultural Communication** focuses on revealing the meaning in written documents. There will be a lot of decisions within each paragraph, sentence and choice of word. Students take the first course in Thinking Translation: Language, Transfer and Cultural Communication. Notice all the words in the name of this course? ESTJ is likely to be accurate, observing and impersonal in providing listeners with the meaning.

ENFJ could select a concentration in **Comparative Literature**. This type, so comfortable with language, will delight in the use of the word, the turn of the phrase and the double meanings. They are also capable of bringing humane lessons found in substantive literature to the audiences of today. Empathetic, often with a tolerant perspective, comparative literature rewards their desire to connect with others. This concentration flows directly from the Princeton Board of Trustees' own vision. Essentially, Princetonians are to understand the world.

ENTJ is often right up front with their interest to organize and innovate. Princeton's certificate in **Global Health and Health Policy** is likely to catch their attention. The application requires a list of to do's that won't discourage ENTJ. The most important will be the essay on their interest in health. The program is focused on third world health concerns. A course in statistics and a course in basic science can come from ENTJ's concentration in science or engineering. But if they are Computer Science concentrators then they will go for disease patterns as a thesis project.

ROANOKE COLLEGE

221 College Lane
Salem, VA 24153-3794
Website: www.roanoke.edu
Admissions Telephone: 540-375-2500, 800-388-2276
Undergraduates: 2,050; 860 Men, 1,190 Women

Physical Environment

Roanoke College is located in downtown Salem, a small suburb of the city of Roanoke, within 20 miles of the **Blue Ridge Mountains**. Salem is a combination of suburban and rural Appalachian country, all within walking distance of the campus, it is easy to understand Roanoke's connection and heritage with the Blue Ridge Mountains. The physical landscape and buildings are very much valued for their **beauty and function**. They promote learning and personal development. Older campus buildings on the **National Historic Register** remind you of the pivotal place this region has played in American history.

There has been a building boom, no other words suffice, of construction on this campus since 2005. The university has also purchased properties in town, reaching out to enliven and support downtown renewal efforts. The new Kerr Athletic Stadium with eco-friendly lighting extends the hours for Appalachian fall track meets and sunsets that are hard to beat. The Cregger Center is about wellness and community engagement. The pre-orientation program for freshmen is **Journey**, basically a 3-day wilderness experience in the Blue Ridge Mountains.

Students appreciate this lovely campus as it often mirrors their home communities. This setting appeals to undergraduates who are looking for a campus where learning and undergraduate **socializing on and adjacent to campus** comprise a lot of the action. It is an environment with little social streaming or trend-setting distractions.

Social Environment

Roanoke College has spirited students who look to support conservative social views of Lutheran heritage. This is not a campus where a student can be anonymous, nor a campus where students are likely to protest or petition for personal benefits. Faculty and undergraduates throw their support and effort to **service** learning and volunteering in the region. It is an **outward direction** focused on others.

Undergrads are fun-loving, **purposeful** and actively engaged with each other. Life in the day of an undergraduate is impromptu. If it snows, they will be outside with the snowballs, trays and mittens. If it's hot in September, they rope swing into the pond. Greek life supplements the service throughout the campus with their own impromptu socials.

Roanoke is remarkable for its academic diversity that well reflects the undergraduate student body at most public state universities. It is all about **efficiency in academic study** too. One-on-one research opportunities are designed as student-faculty learning projects. Small stipends given to the professor's budget and the student's budget put the focus on getting bang for your bucks in this undergraduate research. At Roanoke, it becomes an academic, leadership and financial exercise. The faculty is well-tuned to emerging research and cultural problems within society. The social and **health sciences** give students a grounding in the causes and possible actions. The physical sciences are directed toward emergent knowledge. Affiliated with Evangelical **Lutheran faith**, the administration supports community with ongoing **outreach**. Their purpose is to **lift boot straps**, or as the Army would say **Be All You Can Be**. This philosophy forms the heart of this collegiate campus. Roanoke is about **responsibility, ethics and values**.

Compatibility with Personality Types and Preferences

The Roanoke College campus is for folks who are comfortable with reason and service. The faculty expects students to seek and apply that reason in their daily lives and upon graduation. The college easily puts together the expectation of being responsible with the independent goal of getting things done (J). High energy stands out and it helps build an active community (E). Balance is Roanoke's byword for emotional health. The interface between faculty and students is evident and purposeful in preparation for graduation and beyond. You will find experiential learning in many off-campus settings throughout the courses and the extracurricular programs. The educational philosophy nicely supports several technical and vocational degrees much needed by society. Academic philosophy here harkens back to the workplace and the current skill sets needed across America. Career trends that developed during the recession of the last eight years were brought into the curriculum for their relevance, advising and post-graduate direction. Roanoke College grows out of its Lutheran roots with both human caring (F) and a solid, realistic affection for American society.

Now read below about one of the majors that MBTI® research shows people of your type have selected since the mid-20th century. After, refer to Chapter Five for the 50 or so majors that can help you prepare for careers your type has selected. Most importantly, remember that this college description is a suggestion for exploration, not a commanding order. You can be successful in any major at any college.

ISTJ might take a look at Roanoke's unusual **Health Care Administration** concentration. The concentration offers immediate employment in hospitals, clinics and insurance companies. Many will go on to get the

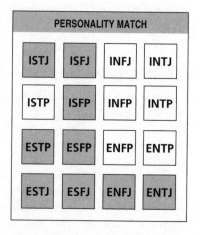

PERSONALITY MATCH

ISTJ	ISFJ	INFJ	INTJ
ISTP	ISFP	INFP	INTP
ESTP	ESFP	ENFP	ENTP
ESTJ	ESFJ	ENFJ	ENTJ

Masters degree in Health Care Administration. Either way, ISTJs, with this major, will have to explain conflicting health data in the Affordable Care Act to bosses and customers alike. Roanoke's business school gets top ratings for the student professor interaction. This type can handle the job with their computer-like memories.

ISFJ is good with organizing knowledge in the fact-based physical sciences like biology, chemistry and physics. The **Pre-Medical and Health Professions** program is excellent at Roanoke in advising and the art of being accepted into graduate studies. This type will have no trouble communicating their concern for others. They will have access to choice internships at nearby hospitals. Along the way, ISFJ may find that the Physician Assistant has much of the responsibility of medical doctors without the intensive personal demands. Their gentle, reflective ways will be more than welcome in stressful medical environments.

ISFP at Roanoke College absolutely must look into the **Health and Exercise Science** major, perhaps with the additional concentration in Health Care Delivery, offered in the Sociology Department. Roanoke's emphasis on reason and service squares up perfectly with ISFP. The magic in these two studies just might be that local fitness centers can deliver simple health routines that low income folks are willing to follow. Roanoke is all about the belief in their graduates who will influence health perspectives in their neighborhood, community, region and nationally.

ESTP will want to consider the **Athletic Training** major. ESTPs like to get skills and knowledge that they can use efficiently. In this field that means skills on the spot that reduce internal injury. It is a part of the course work in the major, but the major also focuses on preventative injury. The Health and Performance laboratory at Roanoke is going to give ESTP hands-on experience with the metabolic cart. Now, who is going to volunteer an injury?

ESFP is observant and oriented to the present day. The Roanoke major in **Criminal Justice** is chock full of present day realities. Foundation courses cover the impact of crime and methods of controlling criminal behavior. Roanoke is focused on practical knowledge, caring and correction for criminal behavior. They are also on top of the economic impact of immigration policies dating back to 2000. Incoming immigrants and American citizens alike would agree on this failure in national leadership. Alert, sociable ESFPs would do well to consider this major at Roanoke.

ESTJ would be interested in the Business degrees here. The department offers a concentration in **Business Information Systems**. Roanoke is on top of the curve with this major that almost disappeared under the weight of emerging algorithms in Computer Science. But in reality, information systems are pretty much about Google, Amazon and other retailers of products over the internet. Faculty in this department never lost sight of the relevancy of information systems. ESTJs are masterful at relevancy and can smile on the first day of class in E-Business.

ESFJ and the **Human Resource Management** concentration is a fairly good bet. Their curiosity about others often allows them to remember detailed information. ESFJ wants to balance the needs of the company with the needs of the employees. The department centers on practical knowledge in job design, recruitment, appraisal, compensation training and labor relations. Okay, you get it, this is an important leadership role in any corporation or medium-size business. ESFJ has that special persona to be loyal to the company and fair to the employees. ESFJ, we need your common, caring sense.

ENFJ who is interested in teaching will do very well to look at Roanoke's wealth of coursework and experience for wannabe teachers. This type relates well with children and adults. Roanoke explores the difficult issues surrounding American public schools in the course titled **Principles of Education**. In this department, students have instruction in classroom management at primary and secondary levels. As progressive social constructs have come to American schools through the Department of Education regulations and the federal court systems, children have struggled with the lack of common rules for classroom behavior. Coursework offered by this department is not about band aid approaches, but about establishing emotionally safe classrooms for all children.

ENTJ inclined to be in charge after graduation from Roanoke might look at **International Relations** with the idea of a graduate degree. ENTJ can focus on one geographic area or look at a topic like economics or history across regions of the world. This department taps into a valuable simulation of the United Nations Security Council that few liberal arts colleges offer. Leadership in Western nations during the terrorism of 2014-15 was unable to effectively deal with the invasion of Islamic jihads. That leaves few other options for action outside of the United Nations and other NGOs. Roanoke graduates will have first-hand experience in UN diplomacy.

ROLLINS COLLEGE

1000 Holt Avenue
Winter Park, FL 32789-4499
Admissions Telephone: 407-646-2161
Website: www.rollins.edu
Undergraduates: 1,932; 796 Men, 1,136 Women
Graduate Students: 1,275

Physical Environment

Rollins College was founded with the support of the Congregational Church in 1885. The church on campus stands as a reminder of this historic past, yet the **location** today of this liberal arts college couldn't be more cosmopolitan. Downtown Winter Park just blocks away is brimming with arts and culture. The Morse Museum has the largest collection of Tiffany glass, including his chapel interior from the 1893 Chicago Columbian Exposition. Downtown sidewalks are lined with fun boutiques, eateries and expensive fashion. The **compact campus** and town are tucked away in this **quiet, residential** area, amazingly just a couple miles east of I-4 with its massive traffic congestion.

Many of Rollin's buildings are soft, calming colors, pale pink and white, with terra-cotta tiled roofs. Newer buildings have brought a touch of the modern to old world charm. The Bush Science Center, opened 2013, has many lab spaces for student research in three fields: biology, chemistry and psychology. These three disciplines are at the center of emerging research on the human brain. At Rollins, the **accommodations are excellent** for these undergrad researchers. Students have the same-size offices right next to their professors' offices, complete with a mini lounge. It makes for a small unit of about 4-6 students in each pod who build academic community between the three disciplines.

Many students from the north are quickly taken by the warm climate, architecture and **lakes**. The Cornell Campus Center, the library and adjacent outdoor courtyards are filled with social conversation. The Bush Center has an IT lobby complete with snack shop. It is a gathering spot if you are in the physical sciences. Students appreciate being tanned, healthy and nattily dressed. The outdoor recreational lap pool is open year-round for students to swim and tan. The **architectural and natural beauty** of the campus is part and parcel of the Rollins attraction and college experience.

Social Environment

Rollins classes are small and the **faculty is dedicated and attentive** to the students. Students here like their professors who communicate **clear expectations** for class requirements. Undergraduates will find structured, sequential methods of learning used throughout the curriculum including requirements identified as rFLA, Rollins Foundations in the Liberal Arts. It prevents graduates from only focusing on their major and minor studies.

The college is committed to serving the **central Florida** community as well as out-of-state students. A good number of the students come from the north and graduated from independent schools and strong suburban schools in the Midwest and East. About half of the students are from Florida. There are also "non-traditional" students in the undergraduate Hamilton Holt School. These adult students bring maturity and experience to undergraduate classes during the weekdays also. Rollins is exceptional in these ways and others because of its location. It provides a place where views uncommon on other small liberal arts campuses come together. The realistic academics and realistic reflection of dynamic diverse central Florida keep the campus from becoming isolated and oriented inward.

There is a strong **Greek system** where approximately one-third of the students are members of sororities or fraternities. There are a total of 19 residential facilities with different options. The Pinehurst Cottage is coed and residents are focused on alternative learning experiences outside of the classroom. Students who are attracted to Rollins College like the extra programming in residential life. The **Arts at Rollins College** interface participation between Winter Park museums and the festivals at Rollins' own Annie Russell Theatre, celebrating its 100th anniversary in the coming decade.

Compatibility with Personality Types and Preferences

Rollins College students will gain foundational knowledge in the rFLA (S) curriculum with traditional competencies clearly identified for graduation. This curriculum requires all undergraduates to take five courses in one of four Neighborhoods. First term freshmen will declare their Neighborhood from one of these four: Cultures Collide, Mysteries and Marvels, Identities: Windows and Mirrors or Innovate, Create, Elevate. The Rollins College Conference courses are first year seminars that require students to analyze a particular topic. The RCC fulfills two purposes. First year students get to know a small group of fellow students. The topic studied in their assigned RCC is also the same topic studied in a separate course taken during the semester. In this way students can analyze (T) one subject from two different perspectives.

The administration has an attentive faculty which oversees the undergraduate student body on this campus. There are several programs centered on mentoring and guidance for the students. Undergraduates attracted to this campus appreciate the thoughtful recreational planning and emphasis on service options that the administration offers. The commitment to conservation is seen through the experiential learning and field study. Two-thirds of the faculty with international experience bring a global perspective to the conservation focus too. Rollins also supports regional organizations that are preserving the Florida geography in response to the ongoing influx of citizens to the sunshine state. They are drawn to the economic powerhouse that is Disney and Universal Studios just a few miles over on I-4.

PERSONALITY MATCH			
ISTJ	ISFJ	INFJ	INTJ
ISTP	ISFP	INFP	INTP
ESTP	ESFP	ENFP	ENTP
ESTJ	ESFJ	ENFJ	ENTJ

Now read below about one of the majors that MBTI® research shows people of your type have selected since the mid-20th century. After, refer to Chapter Five for the 50 or so majors that can help you prepare for careers your type has selected. Most importantly, remember that this college description is a suggestion for exploration, not a commanding order. You can be successful in any major at any college.

ESTJ is an excellent fit on this campus. They will understand and value the accountability required to earn a Rollins degree. Academic communication is efficient with the well-used campus intranet which continually evolves. R-net is the latest edition. ESTJs love to study information and form organized patterns, similar to algorithms. The software principles and capstone project in the **Computer Science** major are nicely organized and likely to meet with ESTJ approval throughout the four years. The Neighborhood Innovate, Create, Elevate will help this conservative type expand in their approach to academic subjects.

ISTJ gets rewards for their efforts in collecting and cataloging facts. It works great in the physical sciences which are so precise. The **Biochemistry/Molecular Biology** major is just such a degree. ISTJ may find the new digs in the Bush Center a little wanting for that private space they like and retreat to the library. Independent research is their favorite learning style when faculty provides structure, then ISTJ makes it happen. For their Neighborhood focus, this type could go for When Cultures Collide because of its global subjects. ISTJ is okay with taking in big volumes of knowledge.

ESTP will get appreciation from their peers when the lead doesn't show up for last rehearsal. They are naturals at reducing tension generated in the artistic process. The minors in **Theater Arts and Dance** at Rollins are excellent. This type is one for the action and they enjoy performing. In dance they will take six courses which include two electives of choice in jazz, modern, tap or history. In theater they take six required courses, plus two production courses.

ISFJ is also an excellent fit on this campus, near so many fresh water lakes in central Florida. The degree in **Marine Biology** is not often offered at small liberal arts colleges. But Rollins is perfect with its access to salt water ocean and inland lakes. ISFJ is a good caretaker and will like the conservation focus in this major. Their realistic side will get good vibes from the combination of classroom, laboratory and field study. The three bring meaning to the biological environment.

ISFP learns through hands-on participation. The major in **Elementary Education** at Rollins is a good choice for this calm soul. They prefer to support and encourage others. The practical courses offered by this department make sense to realistic ISFP. Social Studies for Elementary Schools and Integrated Arts will help when they must collaborate with others in team teaching. The team approach is ideal in elementary education because of its variety and experiential learning. On graduation, ISFP will be eligible for teacher certification in Florida. More liberal arts colleges should commit to this extra step.

ESFP might try the minor in **Neuroscience** at Rollins College. It is a great way to explore the different health-related disciplines emerging today as a result of DNA ground-breaking discoveries early in the 21st century. It must be combined with a major in biology, psychology, marine biology or biochemistry. Without doubt, this will place ESFP squarely in the middle of taking classes and spending time in the Bush Science Center. They will love all the social and academic stuff going on at the Center.

ENTJ will like the look of the **Environmental Studies** major at Rollins. The location is ideal with coastal estuaries, the Everglades and numerous fresh water ponds. Courses in biology will take advantage of the research projects in the Bush Science Center. This type is all about large systems and what could be larger than the Everglades restoration project? Started decades ago, the government's changes to the natural system caused much damage. It is only just within the last few decades that ecologists understood the problem. Now, all are working to restore the original within practical reason. This is just about the right size project for far-seeing ENTJ.

SAINT LOUIS UNIVERSITY

Office of Admission
13 Dubourg Hall
St. Louis, MO 63103-2907
Admission Telephone: 314-977-2500
Website: www.slu.edu
Undergraduates: 12,347; 5,062 Men, 7,312 Women
Graduate Students: 4,678

Physical Environment

St. Louis University, or SLU as students say, is located in mid-town St. Louis, near the art district and medical centers. This **Catholic** university takes up a square mile in the downtown area. The linear, inner city campus is connected by landscaped lawns, pathways and architectural spaces. It feels **self-enclosed and cohesive**. Students walk downtown to the restaurants and theatres and **readily volunteer** with Catholic Charities and other relief organizations. Local services for the needy and recent immigrants are a focus of the Social Sciences curriculum.

The Pius Library is remarkable for its **historic collections** documenting this institution from 1639 to 1966. Although it is fragmentary in nature, it is uniquely rich in its ability to inform culture through this period. The **St. Louis University Hospital** is located one-and-a-half miles from main campus. Recent urban renovation makes it very easy going by bike and foot traffic. Undergraduate internships are excellent in this beautiful facility. The hospital draws in students seeking **medical careers** in occupational and physical therapy, pediatric research, nursing and public health. The long-established Parks College of **Engineering and Aviation** is located on the other end of campus. It has a wind-tunnel and advanced technical instrumentation. NASA, the U.S. Air Force and SLU's Parks College launched the first Saint Louis University spacecraft in 2013. Have we mentioned the **really remarkable research facilities** at SLU?

Social Environment

Students **strive for excellence** in academics and in life, under an umbrella of ideals. They typically have a good idea about what they want to major in when they arrive here. Billikens are **career-oriented** and goal-driven. They are comfortable with their spirituality and having fun at the same time. They are motivated to transform society as viewed from the perspective of poverty and injustice. In Fall 2014, a small number occupied SLU's clock tower after a march with a large number of SLU undergraduates protesting the Ferguson jury results. After five days, they elected to leave clock tower. The president spoke with protestors, expressing his sadness over harsh words on social media about the demonstration.[66]

SLU offers a variety of on-campus housing options including **living-and-learning communities** which make it easy for residents to form a friend group of likeminded souls. Freshmen orientation runs for five days before classes start. **First Year Interest Groups** are optional. For those who sign up, about twenty freshmen in the same dormitory take two or three courses together in the fall, great for forming friendships on this urban, busy campus. Study abroad opportunities are over the top.

The **Billiken Club** is supported by the university's Student Life Division. It brings in loud, noisy bands with hashtag kind of names. Members of the 24 Greek sororities and fraternities engage in campus leadership, fun and initiatives that tend to be service-oriented. **Sports** have a very good presence on campus. SLU is in the Atlantic 10 conference. Undergraduates support their basketball team. Others take in a Cardinals game or smile with amusement as the city bemoans losing the Rams again. For fun, students enjoy visiting nearby Forest Park for picnics or long walks.

Compatibility with Personality Types and Preferences

Saint Louis University calls out and welcomes prospective students on their website in the familiar text and language of high school students. The university reaches out to students in a trendy way yet the message is clearly about service to the community, Saint Louis and beyond. Students are comfortable at some level with searching for truth and competence in God's world. The central theme of this philosophy is serving (F) the poor and disadvantaged. It supplements the educational curriculum with purpose and utility (S) in each major and minor. The university projects its deep optimism in mankind's ability through promoting stable culture in the American national community. To that end, the President issued a statement helping undergraduates with safety practices if they elected to demonstrate over the tumultuous Ferguson jury results in 2014. Students are focused outward.

Since current majors and degrees answer the needs of America's "help wanted," there is a lot of experiential and technical learning through the university's local, regional and national networks. The SLU campus in Madrid, Spain has strong outreach in the nearby Spanish neighborhoods for those studying abroad in international majors. Graduates contribute to their professional career fields at many levels over a lifetime. This sensitivity also translates into personal balance and students actively seek relaxation in athletics and the latest bands coming to campus (E).

Now read below about one of the majors that MBTI® research shows people of your type have selected since the mid-20th century. After, refer to Chapter Five for the 50 or so majors that can help you prepare for careers your type has selected. Most importantly, remember that this college description is a suggestion for exploration, not a commanding order. You can be successful in any major at any college.

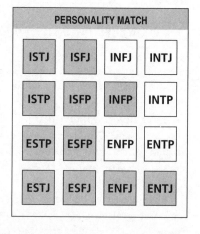

PERSONALITY MATCH

ISTJ	ISFJ	INFJ	INTJ
ISTP	ISFP	INFP	INTP
ESTP	ESFP	ENFP	ENTP
ESTJ	ESFJ	ENFJ	ENTJ

INFP always has a couple of dreams and possibilities up their sleeve so flexibility in course studies is required. At Saint Louis University, undergrads in the **Nutrition and Dietetics** degree explore several work environments in the field including personal nutritionist/chef. The facilities are over-the-top here. There is a gait lab for motion analysis, a culinary lab for food prep, a simulated medical office suite and exam rooms. INFP will complete requirements for registered dietitian nutritionist and certified chef on graduation. Like we said, over-the-top.

ISTP has the intuition and patience to use sensitive diagnostic equipment. The degree in **Medical Laboratory Science** at Saint Louis University requires both of these. Much of the course work focuses on biological processes and is for those who expect to go into medical specialties. The department features academic learning through hands-on experience and observation. ISTP will learn about early disease detection, diagnosis, monitoring and treatment. They will perform research and give presentations at conferences. Fascinated with technical equipment, this type may move toward diagnostic specialties using advanced equipment in research hospitals.

ISTJ is all about dependability. The field of **Accounting** has a certain appeal for this type. All undergraduates in the School take 44 hours of courses before they start into their concentration. ISTJ will then move on to upper level courses in analysis of financial data. Then to top it off, SLU has accounting internships. Now we don't see this too often, and it is excellent for bumping up confidence in this type who can be a bit of a perfectionist. The financial deals in 2008 between the pharmaceutical industry and the Affordable Health Care Act would be an ideal study in "cooking the books."

ISFJ likes to be directly involved, one-on-one, helping others. The degree in **Occupational Science and Occupational Therapy** is designed to lead right into the required Masters degree. The university's own hospital and the downtown medical centers in Saint Louis make access to clinical settings a breeze. ISFJ will like the department's clear guidelines, expectations, superior faculty advising and precise training. They are developing new practices for young adults with developmental disabilities and autism.

ISFP is the perfect personality to be interacting with patients receiving radiation. The undergraduate degree in **Radiation Therapy** at SLU offers technical training that ISFPs relate to. They are naturals at supporting those around them. This is a very technical degree, but it is also good for entrance to medical schools. During the undergraduate years, ISFP will get hands-on training with a radiation oncologist in treating cancer patients. Internships also in research facilities or even community hospitals are arranged through this department.

ESTP likes to be working with and studying how things really are. The Bachelor of Science degree in **Aviation Management** fits the bill and SLU is one of the few universities offering it. Upper level class work includes aircraft fleet management and engineering disciplines in aviation such as reliability, life cycle and project engineering. This type is a good troubleshooter and can excel at pulling together materials and people to get the airplane out of the hangar and back on the flight line. There is also a program in Flight Science that works for undergrads wanting a private pilot's certificate.

ESFP could go for the **Social Work** degree at SLU. The excellent internships and experiential learning are available within a quick walk to the St Louis neighborhoods which will prepare ESFPs for the demands of social work. SLU's educational philosophy and moral emphasis will also help with client conundrums for those living in poverty, illness or disability. SLU offers a realistic program about skill sets and practices that work to overcome obstacles in the client's lifestyle.

ESFJ can tailor a business degree at SLU with a concentration in **Leadership and Human Resource Management**. The emphasis of course work in the upper school curriculum is on developing productive business culture while upholding employment laws. But ESFJ won't even begin these courses until they have completed the 44 credit hours in the business core. With that under their belt, they are okay moving on to motivational concepts in business.

ESTJ is often good at collecting, finding and analyzing facts. What could be better than a major in **Investigative and Medical Sciences**? The degree has a flavor of intrigue added several years ago to meet the forensic science needs of our nation's crime labs. But practical ESTJ will be concerned about such a narrow specialty, so SLU designed the program for entrance to medical schools also, plus pharmaceutical research. Now if that still leaves ESTJ questioning, a minor in biology, ethics or health information management fits right into the curriculum. With one of these minors, employment right after graduation is probable.

ENFJ likes all kinds of folks in the work environment. They are at ease delivering a speech to the public, as long as the message is in synch with their personal beliefs. The minor in **Political Journalism** will offer this type practice in all of the above and the ability to put it into words. It pairs up with any major and especially fits well with a degree in communication or political science. ENFJ is a demanding disciplinarian on themselves. Certainly their moral vision will find a home at Saint Louis University.

ENTJ has the vision to work in **Biomedical Engineering**. It is a new 21st century field for the most part. You might think well, wait a minute, mechanical limbs have been around longer than 16 years, but how about tissue engineering? Or neuroengineering? We look at majors all the time and didn't even know about neuroengineering. There is much on the horizon for this type to look forward to while utilizing their crisp strategic planning and this degree. ENTJ is very much about business and perhaps there will be patents in the future for this entrepreneurial type.

SALVE REGINA UNIVERSITY

100 Ochre Point Avenue
Newport, RI 02840
Website: www.salve.edu
Admissions Telephone: 401-847-6650
Undergraduates: 2,121; 637 Men, 1,484 Women

Physical Environment

Salve Regina University is bordered by the **striking Victorian mansions** of Bellevue Avenue and The **Cliff Walk** towering over the Easton Bay inlet from the Atlantic Ocean. The university was founded in 1947 by the **Catholic Order of the Sisters of Mercy** who used the **historical buildings** in **resourceful ways** to build financial capitol for this campus. Historic Ochre Court is the first stop for visitors, the focal point and campus center of many ceremonies and performances by Salve music ensembles. The elegant architecture encourages students to wonder about the values and ways of the Gilded Age. Sophomores are housed in these historic buildings on campus, while first years are assigned to traditional dormitory style residences that support community building.

There is a defining relationship between the campus and this geographic location. Students will descend the "40 steps" to the huge boulders by sea. At times, sections of the walk are closed off after storms, yet they reopen eventually. It is an experience to walk the ocean's edge and ponder how this beauty came into place. The three-dimensional, mathematical sport of **competition sailing** is offered at Salve Regina. In Fall 2013, the Salve Seahawks captured 3rd place in three regional competitions. **Surfing** is legendary and Salve students definitely surf on Second Beach, a few seconds from campus. Traditional sports such as football, hockey, track soccer, tennis and more round out the athletic options on campus.

Quality internships are also at the ready because of this location. Rhode Island has relied on decades of federal benefit programs to improve their economy. Here there are impoverished, lower middle class neighborhoods that Salve undergraduates serve in as they study for degrees in the helping professions.

Social Environment

The Sisters and faculty immediately help first years arriving on campus with programs that emphasize responsibility to their class as a whole and the larger community of the region, the nation and the world. Undergrads arriving on campus will enroll in English 150: What It Means to Be Human. It sets the stage for many conversations and reflections in the coming years. Immediate friendships form quickly in the first weeks. Students of all faiths are taught in the **Catholic** tradition of harmony, **justice and mercy**. During the 1990s, the long-serving president of the university and the Order generated stability and diligence. She set the university community standard which continues with **Service Plunge**. It is a year-long commitment, starting with a leadership retreat followed by weekly service. There is humor on campus too. Salve students protested against themselves during Thanksgiving 2013. They stood at the entrance of the dining hall waving posters with messages like, Put Your Cell Phones Away.

The vast majority of students come from out of state. Students who may be concerned about their academic and organizational track record in high school will find **solid academic support** from the Salve faculty and staff. The curriculum is very much designed for **developing skills** to take into the workplace and to recognize human dignity in all walks of life. The male, female student population on campus reflects the national reality of lower numbers of young men reaching for a college degree. American boys are choosing to end their schooling after 12th grade or dropping out of college. Nationwide professional graduate schools also have noticeably fewer male graduates. Students at Salve have the background and the faculty resources to look into this imbalance.

Compatibility with Personality Types and Preferences

Salve Regina University is for students who like their education to be straight forward (S) in an evenly-balanced atmosphere. The entire feel of the campus has much in common with the words responsible, healthy and caring (F). The faculty pay close attention to the needs of incoming freshmen. The Student Government Association is active in partnership with the administration on academic policy. The comparatively safe and nearby city of Newport encourages exploration and undergraduates can find city sophistication if they want it. The university has developing curriculum that features the international port, the historical presence of the Navy and other DOD agencies. What is not common at Salve is students demanding individual rights for themselves during their four-year collegiate experience. On this campus, undergraduates are looking to serve others with practical support that leads to independence with human dignity.

Now read below about one of the majors that MBTI® research shows people of your type have selected since the mid-20th century. After, refer to Chapter Five for the 50 or so majors that can help you prepare for careers your type has selected. Most importantly, remember that this college description is a suggestion for exploration, not a commanding order. You can be successful in any major at any college.

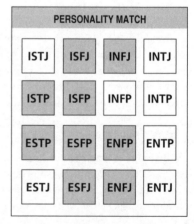

PERSONALITY MATCH

ISTJ	ISFJ	INFJ	INTJ
ISTP	ISFP	INFP	INTP
ESTP	ESFP	ENFP	ENTP
ESTJ	ESFJ	ENFJ	ENTJ

ISFJ will really appreciate the historic and elegant architecture at Salve Regina. This orderly, structured environment gives a hint about the quality program in the **Secondary Education** major. ISFJ will select a second major in the area they would expect to teach—biology, English literature, French, history math or Spanish. There is an active Student Education Association on campus that has a mentoring program, special events and casual monthly meetings. This works for ISFJ who might receive valuable feedback on their conscientious, considerate teaching style.

ISFP may look closely at the **Social Work** degree at Salve Regina. There are a good number of nearby federal, regional and state programs that will serve up internships in this field. Interaction with young children or the elderly is naturally appealing to ISFPs. The department keeps a good number of community-based service learning projects in the curriculum. This gives ISFPs the opportunity to increase confidence in their future career field.

ESFP is lively and spontaneous. The major in **Early Childhood Education** would put this type into optimistic settings with new parents and their young children. The course in "Authentic Assessment" helps identify areas in a child's development that can be improved with early intervention. The course Parents/Teachers/Community is a realistic course which helps young educators understand all the stake holders in decision making for a young child. Who better to play with the kids, yet notice both the strengths and weaknesses of each child entrusted to their care, than fun-loving ESFP?

ESFJ relates to the Salve Regina ethic: relieve misery and address its cause. The **Nursing** degree is centered on experiential learning in densely populated Newport. There is also a good amount of service learning in this degree. Rhode Island has a growing population of citizens who need support. There is also strong coursework in the mental health field. Ethical philosophy at this university is an asset to carry forward after graduation. Much government-mandated health care policy is contradictory to Judeo-Christian faith, although the Supreme Court has upheld those government mandates.

ISTP is just about always comfortable with technical stuff. The major in **Theater** at Salve offers a technical theatre concentration. This skill set brings job options along the eastern seaboard in New York, Washington, DC and Disney World. Salve's historic Stanford White Casino Theater is brilliant and takes the audience back to theater before streaming media graphics. ISTP will gain a lot from the program called Vital Studies for Whole Life Design. The six courses are centered on imagination, humor, humility, intuition and ethics. It requires application and taking the course Speaking Wisdom in freshman year is a head start. We'd like to take that course!

ESTP likes to work with real things. The major in **Historic Preservation and Traditional Building Arts** is new and one-of-a-kind. As 20th century structures are preserved there will occasionally be complete reconstructions. Those reconstructions should be done just as the historical craftsman of the original period. Laboratory courses in this major are on location at preservation projects in Newport. On occasion, coursework will involve archeological digs and ESTP's fine observational skills will shine in the dirt.

INFJ will take to the history and the purpose behind the **Administration of Justice** degree at Salve Regina. Mercy, in all its senses, is the go-by for the Salve Regina administration and faculty. INFJ will explore the meanings of mercy, harmony and justice. Internships are at the nearby U.S. Secret Service office or tutoring delinquent youth in the Rhode Island Training School. These internships work as service learning projects for youth coming from broken families receiving multiple subsidy programs. Mid-20th century author Flannery O'Conner will be a good source for papers on the word Mercy.

ENFP goes for the big picture and change. The combined major in **Anthropology and Sociology** certainly has the big picture with Salve's focus on global collectives. That is Human Collectives, third world populations caught in the middle of political, religious, ecological, economic and cultural rigidity. In many places these are regions of dictatorship. As western nations lose their robust middle income families and abandon their faiths, so to do they open their lives to these human collectives. ENFPs bring their intense emotional passion to those in need, but they also bring enthusiasm and creativity to their workplace. This is all consistent with Salve Regina's educational philosophy.

ENFJ and the **English Communications** degree jump into place almost immediately. The coursework is excellent for literary ENFJ who just might have a few ideas for a book or two. Graduates are prepared to join staffs on newspapers, magazines, book publishing and new media. Combined with the Christian ethical perspectives, this curriculum offers both the complexity and service perspectives that are attractive to ENFJs.

SARAH LAWRENCE COLLEGE

1 Mead Way
Bronxville, NY 10708-5999
Website: www.slc.edu
Admissions Telephone: 914-395-2510, 800-888-2858
Undergraduates: 1,437; 491 Men, 946 Women
Graduate Students: 324

Physical Environment

You won't find big bold signs announcing the location of Sarah Lawrence College as you exit the Hutchinson River Parkway north of New York City. The pale green signage for the college is barely noticeable as one drives onto the campus. Located 30 minutes north of the Big Apple, Sarah Lawrence welcomes the visitor with sudden silence, tall trees, green lawns and English **Tudor-style** buildings. Modern buildings have been added to one side of the campus; they are covered by ivy. Below the canopies of fir trees, students can imagine the tales of Robin Hood and the **enchanted forest**. It's a place that invites you to think of the day and the perfect life. You want to set up an easel right away or get down to **exploratory conversations** with other students. SLC was established as a liberal arts college in 1926 and became coed in 1968.

The Tudor-style dormitories contain faculty offices, classrooms and conference rooms where morning meetings with the Don (student advisors) are held. Professors' work spaces are close to the student residences and that supports easy interaction and communication between the two. These dorms characterize the nature of Sarah Lawrence where **learning and living** take place together in a lot of residential spaces, cottages and houses. Ninety percent of the students live on this campus that is designed for self-expression, thus there is a psychological symmetry between the park-like setting, the work of these undergraduates and SLC's invitation to discover talent with the help of an individual tutor.

Social Environment

SLC students merge their private world with that of others on campus by **sharing observations, sentiments and beliefs**. They seek out conversations for the benefit of the process, not to arrive at positions, but to learn about self. They like to study what is meaningful to them. Students should really **commit to their chosen area**, be it Humanities, Social Sciences, the Arts or Natural Sciences in the first year. This will secure all the advantages of a Sarah Lawrence education and why would you want to miss out on any? The successful student is attracted to the idea of writing and interested in the wide range of liberal arts. Written evaluations are extremely helpful in each course and grades are recorded only for the graduate's transcript.

The curriculum and the mentoring system keep these students on track as they enroll in **three year-long Seminars**. One of these Seminars will also have a **Conference** where a professor, called a "Don," becomes a mentor in the academic subject. Students select which professor to work with. The Conference has many features of a tutorial since the undergraduate student meets one-on-one with the Don several times a week throughout the semester. The Conference is the distinguishing academic feature and at times the social jewel in a SLC degree. Students dig deeply into their selected areas of study. They write **extensively in the Seminars**.

SLC undergraduates are **supportive of each other**. For the most part, they tend to form strong ties and become a closely-knit community. They are not over-the-top on athletics, more often taking enjoyment from their own performances in the arts, community service and each other's company.

Compatibility with Personality Types and Preferences

Sarah Lawrence is a campus for those who like to imagine and deliberate (N). They are caring folks (F) in a casual but compelling way. They accept responsibility for designing their curriculum, but are also very grateful and cooperative with the faculty support. Here undergraduates must choose coursework that is tailored to their interests, so most students arrive on campus without a favorite subject in which to major. If they did favor one subject over the other, it may only serve as a spring board to move in another academic direction. Yet students who do not declare their interests in the first year find some features of the academic study have moved past them.

SLC faculty expects students to develop a perspective that will give direction to their conference study. A student might read *The Sound and The Fury*. That student may decide that William Faulkner understood mental illness better than most literary figures of the 20th century. Therefore, the student decides to concentrate in the field of psychology. A realization like this may evolve over two to three years on campus. Actually, one year is required just to read that book. There is tension within the individual student over which opportunity to take and which opportunities to pass by. The ideal world also has limitations because of the nature of making choices. Undergrads here may not always be passionate, but they do take on the shades of conviction. With that in place, its not a giant step toward declaring their Conference studies and careers upon graduation.

The student body at this university flexes in academic interest, is somewhat restless (P) and attracted to novel interpretation. What could be better to these students than this educational approach that demands introspection and reflection? Here students will be able to spin a strong thread between individual interests, curriculum and future careers.

Now read below about one of the majors that MBTI® research shows people of your type have selected since the mid-20th century. After, refer to Chapter Five for the 50 or so majors that can help you prepare for careers your type has selected. Most importantly, remember that this college description is a suggestion for exploration, not a commanding order. You can be successful in any major at any college.

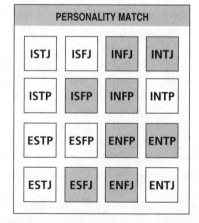

PERSONALITY MATCH

ISTJ	ISFJ	INFJ	INTJ
ISTP	ISFP	INFP	INTP
ESTP	ESFP	ENFP	ENTP
ESTJ	ESFJ	ENFJ	ENTJ

INFJ and introspective speculation go together like hand in glove. There will be no shortage of speculation on this campus. The Conference System pairs student and professor, biweekly, to discuss the most meaningful way to complete the course. The INFJ who often explores in depth will find the first year course in **Writing** perfect for this. The course titled Visible and Invisible Ink: How Fiction Writing Happens will make sense because so much of what INFJ ponders is invisible to those outside their thoughts.

INFP can be quiet and passionate. On this campus, they reach to personalize their academic subjects through discussion with other students. Two nicely organized semesters in the General Biology Series fulfill all the requirements for medical school. After that INFP can take any of the interesting courses in the **Biology** department exploring the limits of human health and the limits of specialists who choose these careers to help others.

INTJ who is analytical and future-oriented will want to take advantage of the Conference Courses for advanced students. The major in **Mathematics** opens up INTJ's options for tackling big problems. This type can process knowledge in two modes, a fuzzy hunch or clear definition—both support their passion to find solutions with mathematical concepts. The course in Topology is about order, continuity, configuration, boundary and dimension. Funny but this sounds perfect for problem solving. Perhaps INTJ will bring this to some of the social issues streaming across our news media.

ENTP thrives on wide-ranging knowledge and tension in the debating scene. This logical type will bring definition to the conversations on campus although sometimes with abrupt explanations. The typical interdisciplinary work here meets ENTP's need for variety. **History** courses like France and Germany in the 20th Century could really work with their interest in laws and principles. The current immigrant crisis in these two nations because of 2015 Islamic State, ISIS terrorism gives this course relevance. Future ENTP career direction could come out of this study.

ENFP might get the greatest benefit from the Don system at SLC. The Don can deliver the structure needed by this free-roaming intellect who is also warm, enthusiastic and caring. SLC's **Early Childhood** Center will fire up ENFP's imagination. Interaction with the children comes naturally for this fun-loving type who might be majoring in one of SLC's social sciences.

ISFP will enter debate at SLC when the subjects are centered on serving others or nature. They believe in community partnerships that include service learning. The **Chemistry** department at SLC combines course readings with volunteering in the surrounding community. Action and hands-on activity bring personal worth during life's travels for this type. The department relies on laboratory experiments as a primary tool in upper class courses and the hands-on works for ISFP.

ESFJ is usually orderly and down to earth. This type may be surprised by the ideas that float through and around conversations at SLC. The concentration in **Sociology** studies several subjects dear to ESFJ's sympathetic heart. Faculty focus on how current social issues affect the individual. Recession economics and political power within the Affordable Health Care Act could be explored in the course Health Policy/Health Activism. The Don will be instrumental in the approach of this study whether through progressive social ideas or conservative social ideas.

ENFJ is another good bet for this campus. This imaginative idealist expects harmony but likes open, flexible environments. They try to weave these two ideas together with objectivity and caring. The concentration in **Public Policy** at SLC covers difficult societal themes like promoting peace, workers' rights and health services. ENFJ will have to advocate for internships and field experiences that provide a balanced view of these growing issues in the American middle class.

STANFORD UNIVERSITY

520 Lasuen Mall
Stanford, CA 94305-3005
Website: www.stanford.edu
Admissions Telephone: 650-723-2091
Undergraduates: 7,019; 3,704 Men, 3,315 Women
Graduate Students: 8,732

Physical Environment

Imagine 8,000 acres in northern California, eye-pleasing Spanish architecture and a lake with walking, biking and hiking trails. Stanford appeals to students who like the outdoors and the **moderate climate** south of San Francisco Bay. **Bicycles** are the vehicle of choice for those who want to make the most of their time. That is virtually everyone at this very selective institution. Moving bikes create vehicle jams along with the skateboard crowd and other wheels at the rotunda, jokingly dubbed "the death circle." We personally know it's good to stay out of the way.

Students typically live on campus. They are not required to live in any house system for their undergraduate years. They can live in any of the resident halls and plan to room with friends. Stanford avoids shaping undergraduate students with residential life policies and residential staff. The nature of **independence and chance** is part of the university's **confidence in their undergraduate student** body. Sorority and fraternity houses offer residential options for those who want to identify with a social organization within the Stanford collegiate community.

After room assignments and first day move in, students **study and study** here. They look forward to the day they will be in the research laboratories. In early 2016 Stanford researchers developed a process using carbon dioxide and agricultural waste to manufacture a product used as an alternative to plastic bottles. Environmental concerns often drive innovation and research here. The Institute for Research in the Social Sciences uses computational methods and big data to study contemporary American issues. Stanford libraries house **invaluable research collections** in the humanities and social sciences. Did we mention the bicycles?

Social Environment

Stanford students look **together, sporty and sociable**. They dress on the preppy side, and ride their skateboards with iPhones in hand. Sixty percent of students who attend Stanford come from states other than California. These students are **serious** about their studies and their future. They understand the **research culture** that prevails here. After getting accepted, they must get focused on joining research either with ideas of their own or helping professors with their research. This may be why students are up at two in the morning discussing an idea, whether or not it will ever see the light of day. For Stanford undergrads, it's important to get these **ideas out in the open** and subject them to light of other bright intellects in the dorm.

Students mix and match various classes to define their major here. **Connective thinking** links theory and course work with research results at Stanford. If their idea is beyond the current interest of faculty and ongoing research, they work through the

Hasso Plattner Institute of Design that serves as an organized, accessible platform for undergrads who want to participate in IDEA. Bravo Stanford—and the other 20 universities in our book that elect this approach to educating tomorrow's leaders. This type of interface with international citizens of power and wealth is typical of selective universities. Undergraduates of this university are privileged with a faculty that is not one-dimensional in their progressive social views of culture. Undergraduates expect to show up for visiting speakers like Condoleeza Rice. They are okay with hearing conservative social ideas. They are open to social ideas outside of progressive policy.

Stanford admissions looks for the **independent, creative** high school graduate that can smile with a dorm assignment and show up in class wondering about undergraduate research. Students at Stanford would judiciously look at taking time out of their studies to protest against a campus rule or shortcoming. In Summer 2014, that process met their judicious test and found a good number of undergrads confronting the administration's decision to retain a student accused of sexual assault.[67] Stanford's Title IX office which upholds federal gender-equity law found all three complaints brought against the accused were accurate. Consequences for the accused were viewed as administrative in nature.[68] This federal policy requires investigations of sexual assault be conducted by universities. There is question why they are not referred to the civil authorities.

Compatibility with Personality Types and Preferences

As juniors and seniors in high school, Stanford undergraduates were incurably curious. Now, they actively jump into the chance to experiment, study and load up their minds with knowledge. The university is a superb educational institution for the undergraduate student on a mission (J) to excel. Since all students on campus seem to fit this definition, the determination in the air is pretty considerable. Fast-moving undergrads on wheels mirror the precise, linear thinking on this campus (T). The typical freshman has a well-developed passion for a special topic or subject. With that idea, they ask "How does this happen?" and "What next is important?" As students on this casual but also intense campus, they are likely to be open and excited about exploring (N) while collecting a solid foundation of hard facts (S) in their chosen field.

Who fits in well here? The bright student who tops off the day's studies with roomie dialogues on that last lecture of the evening. Flexibility and individual choice highlight residential planning by the administration. Stanford loyalties are to the ideas and the knowledge forged within the student body or campus organizations, not to the residence hall.

Underlying the campus energy and productivity is confidence. Students do not second guess their interests, commitment or ability. Professors welcome the interested, prepared undergraduate who inquires about their emergent research. At the same time, there are seemingly endless options to imagine and execute mini-research with the curriculum of the undergraduate degree. Research grants and other resources are available at Stanford for the motivated undergraduate. Independent, confident learners can cram as much as possible into their four short years.

The university takes the mini-research a step further with the co-term program. Co-term lets undergraduates apply for graduate school and take grad course work during the last semester of their senior year on campus. The advantage is flexibility and freedom (P) to immediately move into advanced levels.

Now read below about one of the majors that MBTI® research shows people of your type have selected since the mid-20th century. After, refer to Chapter Five for the 50 or so majors that can help you prepare for careers your type has selected. Most importantly, remember that this college description is a suggestion for exploration, not a commanding order. You can be successful in any major at any college.

PERSONALITY MATCH

ISTJ	ISFJ	INFJ	INTJ
ISTP	ISFP	INFP	INTP
ESTP	ESFP	ENFP	ENTP
ESTJ	ESFJ	ENFJ	ENTJ

ENFP with so many interests could like the freedom in **Material Science and Engineering** major. The department offers choices of eye-popping research for the undergraduates. ENFPs are passionate about their sense of the possible. They apply their gut instincts to just about any subject. This department especially concentrates on nanotechnology calling up the need for dreamers and brainstormers. One such undergraduate in early 2016 was being guided by a PhD candidate in the labs toward discovery of lithium battery shutdowns before the battery burns downs. It sounds ordinary but it is revolutionary not to mention safer.

ISFJ can mix factual memory and ability to accurately recall social activity. The **Linguistics** major will use both skills. The language labs use many sensory options like computer-assisted instruction and audio/visual presentations. These are ISFJ's fave learning tools. Students take classes in sociolinguistics, psycholinguistics and computational linguistics. It is fascinating how language crosses so much of what we know. These courses introduce undergrads to the amazing research in linguistics labs and help ISFJ find the concentration that works for them.

INFJ wants to jump into complex projects that benefit others and the major in **Symbolic Systems** at Stanford fits the bill. This major is packed with abstract possibilities, but grounded in the disciplines of language, mathematics and objective information. INFJs will pull out meaning from language systems and creatively transfer those meanings into computational theory and utility. This type is competent and comfortable crossing boundaries into new territory. After the foundation courses, the labs are waiting with research in artificial intelligence and human-computer interaction. Count on INFJ to sign up.

INTJ with high school or community experience in theater could find the **Theater and Performance Studies** very compelling. It covers theory, critical study and production. INTJs who declare this major must also complete a Senior Project from one of eight areas. This type likes the freedom and integration found in the Directing. They will bring the interpretation to a screenplay through the actors' performance. This is a large project even for commanding INTJs, but three undergraduate years of study in production, staging, performance will set their fertile minds flying.

ISTP could find the **Art Practice** major at Stanford calling out to the maverick side of their personality. ISTPs have loads of creativity when it comes to their interests. The artistically-talented ISTP working with metals, glasses and solid materials will use advanced equipment available on this research campus. They might use rare earth elements in their sculptures. Stanford's engineering, geology and chemistry labs stand at the ready for the budding ISTP three-dimensional artist. The new studio arts facility, McMurty, opened in 2015 and will likely see some ISTP heavy metal.

ISTJ looks with appreciation at the objective major in **Geophysics** at Stanford. The curriculum is arranged so that graduates can directly enter the work force or move on to graduate studies. The discipline will make good use of their spectacular memory for details and powers of concentration. ISTJ will gladly show up for supervised research in the Center for Computational Earth and Environmental Science. But it takes ISTJ's wry sense of humor to sign up for Rock Physics though. Others might mistake it for a study in 1970's alternative rock.

INTP has patience and insight with technical problems and a lot of the advanced curriculum in **Product Design** is about patience and insight. Stanford offers this unusual major within the School of Engineering. The course work is an interesting blend of art, psychology, math and mechanical engineering. The department views this activity as an art in several ways because of the creativity, craftsmanship, personal expression and brainstorming. Products in this sense can be revolutionary; think of LEDs. INTP is just the type to get absorbed and come up with a winning patent.

ESTP has a set of skills ready to use. Although the major in **Aeronautics and Astronautics** will require a focus on the future, the day-to-day work environment is stimulating and all about observable events. Dilemmas such as how to recycle life-sustaining chemicals or how to move around in light gravity on a planet surface are the stuff of this study. These "how" questions are a specialty of Stanford's approach to education and a favorite ESTP word. Graduate study follows on completion of this degree in a ton of research options like aeroelasticity, applied aerodynamics and more.

ENTP with an interest in politics will jump right into the problem solving offered by the senior seminar in **Public Policy**. This major appeals to ENTPs because of the high stakes decision making. Stanford's curriculum intersects with bay area policy issues through analyses and experimental practices. Undergraduates get firsthand experience with success or not so successful analytic problem solving. Biosecurity and Bioterrorism is a fascinating course in the program. The course deals with the U.S. capability to defend against biological threats. With 2015's Islamic State, ISIS terrorism and the ongoing development of Iran's nuclear program, quick, strategic ENTP will recognize that this course is a must-have in this degree.

ESTJ will bring their strong reasoning and practical thinking to the curriculum in **Energy Resources Engineering**. Stanford searches for energy production through evolving engineering methods. The department looks to alternative energy sources and explores their social and physical limitations. First world economies thrive and survive on oil and its byproducts. It will take Stanford graduates in the social sciences and the physical sciences to find lifestyles that can circumvent the agenda of wealthy corporations, powers that are determined to keep their economic position by selling oil consuming products. Perhaps Public Policy graduates can see past the media fog and put the spotlight on the current cooperation between the U.S. government and wealthy corporations. Some call it crony capitalism.

ENFJ is inclined to gather up large views of history and the causes behind it. The Stanford degree in **History** is a three-dimensional look at time, geographic regions and a specific topic. The amazing social science research archives at the Green Library will be very useful. ENFJ will likely develop a friendship with librarians at Green. This is a fussy degree and a bit of a fussy department. We admire that. History is subject to folks who want to change it. We need courageous, objective faculty in charge. Idealists at heart, ENFJs will need to pay attention to the details and realize that faculty guidance is objective, not personal.

ENTJ will probably like the **Earth Systems Program** that is chock full of complexity and relevance. Stanford shapes this degree with the critical question, "What should be measured within the air, land and organisms of the planet?" Undergraduates will spend their first two years answering this question. The faculty follows with "How to measure and gain relevant meaning?" This question will launch ENTJ on a quest for the last two years. They will take the course Atmosphere, Ocean, and Climate Dynamics: the Ocean Circulation. So, yes, there are a lot of words in that course. Always pondering the big picture, ocean circulation around the planet makes sense to ENTJ.

SWARTHMORE COLLEGE

500 College Avenue
Swarthmore, PA 19081-1390
Website: www.swarthmore.edu
Admissions Telephone: 610-328-8300, 800-667-3110
Undergraduates: 1,542; 754 Men, 780 Women

Physical Environment

The Swarthmore campus is located within a beautiful **arboretum**. Collegiate buildings call out to their Quaker foundations with **clean lines and simplicity**. The college takes advantage of this setting with an outdoor amphitheater and white Adirondack chairs placed across the lawns and in nearby woods. At Swarthmore, endless discussions about **life and injustice** take place. This liberal arts college is doing a good job of recruiting young men and avoiding the unhealthy national trend of imbalance between women and men on campus. Swarthmore's experimental programs in the physical sciences speak to the guys and gals who remember high school chemistry classes that focused on reading, a few lab experiments and a dose of social drama. Now all get to practice innovative with full support of the faculty.

The Swarthmore campus is almost a nesting spot for undergraduates who come to think and advocate for improvement. Students eat together in Sharples Dining Hall. Dining services caters to undergrads who want to picnic before the weather closes in with delightful, delicious-looking picnic baskets to go. Almost all students live on campus or in school-sponsored housing. The **Tri-College Consortium** doubles the course offerings available through cross-registration with two other similar colleges in the area. Indoors or outdoors, **observation/discussion/consensus** are pretty much ongoing day and night. When students want a break, the nearby train runs to the Philadelphia, where some volunteer with initiatives to benefit the inner city.

Social Environment

Students here write well and write quite a bit. Even students enrolling for engineering, an unexpected major at this liberal-arts college, write a great deal. Public speaking surfaces throughout the curriculum. The Peaslee **Debate** Society is well-known for winning many parliamentary debates. Swarthmore students must have or develop the ability to think on their feet and come up with a reply to an argument as it is being made. Students here are **absorbed in soaking up knowledge** and focused on sharpening their minds.

Undergraduates generate **intense investigation** so that they can impact contemporary society. They are highly motivated to join **cause-related clubs** like the Democratic Socialists of Swarthmore and Students for Peace and Justice in Palestine. The Swarthmore Students for Liberty is a smaller group for moderate, conservative and libertarian students. There are many typical collegiate clubs on campus for fun too, like the Boys Meet Tractor which is a sketch comedy troupe. With the Quaker ethos in its founding, there are a larger number of progressive clubs than at many liberal arts colleges of this size.

Some service projects, emanating out of political activism for change, reach into local underserved neighborhoods. But the students put most of their efforts into **their campus environment**, supporting a daily campus newspaper and a campus radio station with simultaneous webcast. It is a huge task and responsibility as the content includes both entertainment and political news. Students are also likely to strike for a variety of causes. In Spring 2015, undergraduates and alumni staged a sit-in on campus demanding that the college cut ties to fossil fuels.[69] In Summer 2015, students came prepared to discuss the issue with Board of Trustees, the entire assembly achieved a consensus not to divest fossil fuels from the portfolio.[70] It goes without saying that students are up for academics and advocacy at Swarthmore. The relationship between student, professor, administration and alumni is like an intense bright light. Students take the intellectual risks inherent in pursuing a challenging course of study.

Compatibility with Personality Types and Preferences

Swarthmore College is thorough in dialogue on education and social positions within society. These conversations among faculty and students evolve and reform within the whole student body. The college environment places high value on humanistic concerns (F) by connecting citizenship to advocacy within society for a common good. This layers on top of the curriculum and activities on the campus. Random activity has little use at Swarthmore and spontaneity is measured (T) and judged by its outcome or product. The minds of the students are frequently in overdrive as a result. Education is truly the winding path that you travel (P) and knowledge is information that you gather along the way to advocate for change. Swarthmore educators really fine tune the art of the question. In fact, there is a sequence of courses offered that center on the process of interpretation (N). The campus is a very functional environment that avoids activity outside of the Swarthmore philosophy. Directions and expectations are clear and simple in reference to curriculum requirements and major advising. Residential life is quite community-oriented and intimately connected with learning. Relationships within the college culture are key learning vehicles also.

Now read below about one of the majors that MBTI® research shows people of your type have selected since the mid-20th century. After, refer to Chapter Five for the 50 or so majors that can help you prepare for careers your type has selected. Most importantly, remember that this college description is a suggestion for exploration, not a commanding order. You can be successful in any major at any college.

INFP has iron will and iron values to persevere in the tough courses of **Chemistry** at Swarthmore College. They will need to apply some of that iron in Physical Chemistry: Energy and Change. Bright INFP can handle

PERSONALITY MATCH			
ISTJ	ISFJ	INFJ	INTJ
ISTP	ISFP	INFP	INTP
ESTP	ESFP	ENFP	ENTP
ESTJ	ESFJ	ENFJ	ENTJ

it along with an outlet that is non-academic, perhaps volunteering in an animal shelter. Upper level courses are taught seminar-style and this is excellent for this type who likes to discuss and exchange ideas with professor.

INFJ is thoughtful, reserved and quite aware of others. The major in **Psychology** at Swarthmore covers the largeness of the human personality from feeling, thought, relationships and physical viewpoints. In respect to just one of these, feeling, all experience happiness, depression, joy and anger. You can see how large this major is now. On this campus of political activism, INFJ only has to take a walk along the beautiful campus pathways to encounter these emotions in passing.

INTJ has the determination to study a language that few speak. The study of **Latin** when combined with advanced degrees is a possibility. They are original, novel thinkers and will pull plenty of meaning out of Roman-carved inscriptions during study abroad to Italy and Greece. If the minor is switched over to a major, advanced work in Latin is required.

ISFJ especially likes the facts and can handle a lot of information. The major in **Mathematics and Statistics** at Swarthmore is an orderly approach and the department naturally focuses on the use of statistics in what is understood now as Applied Mathematics. Using math and statistics together ISFJ and others can move on to many other professions. Recall those mathematical formulas, no problem.

ISFP can get lost in the study of the **Japanese** language on this campus. The department offers chat hours with native speakers and language tables for this highly visual language. Just think about those black and white ink slashes on white paper. This type is good with visual space and sometimes can be found in design careers. ISFP will enjoy study abroad and relate well to the calming, contemplative Japanese gardens.

INTP is likely to enjoy the degree in **Engineering**. The course in Truss Bridge is a competition and a tradition that this type can relate to. Using wood and glue, prospective engineers build small scale bridges that are put to the test. It is a nice break from the typical intellectual work that comprises much of the engineering focus. That is just the type of extracurricular activity for INTP.

ENFP usually has a soft spot for the arts. The major in **Music** here is a good bet. There are several ensembles and a Swarthmore favorite is the jazz ensemble that performs on campus. Beyond the practiced faculty instruction, the department also includes teachers from New York City and the Lang Center has practice rooms open all the time. We recommend an internship to New Orleans and a study of Son House or Robert Johnson to check out the contemporary jazz roots.

ENTP will like the study of **Biochemistry** on this campus. After the sound training in the basics, ENTP gets excited for the upperclass work which switches over to seminars. In these later studies, exchanges and discussion take over between student and faculty in the campus laboratories and could lead to an optional research study.

ESFJ may enjoy the **Biology** major here. The curriculum teaches students observational skills while they design and perform their own experiments. ESFJ will enjoy working in the local fields and streams, maybe to think about future high school lesson plans if they go into teaching. The faculty is focused on students reading, critiquing and understanding research articles and students writing their own papers with standard professional procedure.

ENFJ is a bit of an idealist and could like the interdisciplinary major in Asian Studies with a focus on **Chinese** language, history and culture. A fair number of courses will be offered through the Tri-College consortium where this friendly type can meet even more friends. It is a sure bet that they will use the database of Chinese movies to learn about the culture before studying abroad.

SYRACUSE UNIVERSITY

200 Cruise-Hinds Hall
Syracuse, NY 13244
Website: www.syracuse.edu
Admissions Telephone: 315-443-3611
Undergraduates: 15,224; 6,959 Men, 8,263 Women
Graduate Students: 6,268

Physical Environment

An aerial view of Syracuse University shows a large campus within greater Syracuse, New York. Chartered in 1870 by the Methodist Episcopal church, there is a **functional** element in design across the campus. At times, it feels like a large, state university. The renovated residence halls are **multi-story towers of brick** and cinderblock built in the 50s and 60s. Undergraduates have the **stamina** to walk back and forth to class in heavy blankets of snow, but also use the shuttle **transportation** around campus.

There is much outward enthusiasm and a **charging spirit** at Syracuse University evident in the **Carrier Dome**. The largest physical structure on any college campus it seats 50,000 fans indoors. Basketball, football and championship playoff games are the starter for the social life here. Most intramural and fitness sports sign up for a reserved time in one of several gyms. The administration prefers to keep these well-used and no-shows are charged a forfeiture fee. This is coming from the administration's philosophical functionality for this campus. Frills can be found in the art studio or the amazing Fashion Design workspaces.

The main Syracuse campus is separate from South campus, twenty minutes away and served by bus. It has a dining hall and a snack bar for the dormitory/apartment living. The university devotes good resources to safety and health, but they allow males and females to live together at South campus. The male-female ratio shows far fewer men here, like colleges and universities across the country. Syracuse in particular has a lot of realistic studies that young high school men can relate to. Guys, take a Syracuse campus tour, check it out.

Social Environment

Syracuse University has **13 schools and colleges**. Students identify with the **practical nature** of the curriculum. Most freshman students are admitted to the College of Arts and Sciences. The other Divisions and Schools can be quite competitive with very limited transfer options especially the Newhouse School of Public Communications. Each school and college has a connection to specific areas within the city's infrastructure. The university awarded its first winners of the Industry Seed Funding Competition in 2016 for small businesses in New York State with few strings attached.

There are many **different types** and groups of people at Syracuse. Close to one-half of the student population identifies as a minority. The university has **many layers of administrative programs and offices** in place that seek to support undergraduates adjusting to college life. The Syracuse website is designed for future students and current students. It is trendy and presents the option that students will live on campus. More detailed information is found in Word documents across the website.

There are living and learning communities within some of the dormitories which have peer-to-peer mentoring. Although students on this campus have historically been resolute, in Fall 2014, a large group of students along with faculty gathered at the Chapel to draw attention to issues facing diverse groups. They gave the Chancellor a list of 40 grievances.[71] Some professors held "teach-ins" on how this process relates to undergraduate education.[72] The university was awarded the 2013-2014 President's Higher Education Community Service Honor Roll with Distinction. The Chicago-based, non profit Interfaith Youth Core, partner of the Department of Education, along with other organizations awarded this honor.[73]

Compatibility with Personality Types and Preferences

Since Syracuse University is larger than most private universities and colleges, it has distinct social environments. Some schools appeal to the creative types who like their possibilities. However most of the schools and colleges tend toward objective practice (T) in preparation for graduation and employment. The administration's educational philosophy is to generate knowledge that meets the needs of the American workplace. Many of the degrees and courses are remarkably up-to-date and relevant as a result.

The students have not been expectant of wrap-around services. Most arrive on campus to secure their skill sets (S) and degree. The administration provides undergraduate services at the campus level. Campus-wide programs come from the different departments organized to support undergraduate residential life. A key feature of this is the strong emphasis on serving others (F), especially the citizens and businesses of greater Syracuse along with communities in New York State. The university administration encourages Syracuse undergraduates to become civically engaged (E).

Now read below about one of the majors that MBTI® research shows people of your type have selected since the mid-20th century. After, refer to Chapter Five for the 50 or so majors that can help you prepare for careers your type has selected. Most importantly, remember that this college description is a suggestion for exploration, not a commanding order. You can be successful in any major at any college.

PERSONALITY MATCH			
ISTJ	ISFJ	INFJ	INTJ
ISTP	ISFP	INFP	INTP
ESTP	ESFP	ENFP	ENTP
ESTJ	ESFJ	ENFJ	ENTJ

ISTP with an interest in design or art is going to smile when they see the Syracuse major in **Jewelry and Metalsmithing**. ISTPs will be in their element as they weld that last piece of silver in the senior portfolio for graduation. The major has a cap of five students per semester and requires an interview, but ISTP can get intense and creative with their goals. The department includes a full understanding of this craft including issues with current day metalsmithing.

ESTP is pretty realistic and the minor in **Forensic Science** will be about investigative facts. This study goes well with majors in chemistry, biology or psychology. With this minor, ESTP might go on to careers in medicine, science, engineering or the social sciences. The general background in this minor might also work with entry positions in regional police and criminal justice systems.

ESFJ fits well into the world of business when the career involves direct, daily interaction with customers. The major in **Real Estate** at Syracuse will likely support many of ESFJ's inclinations. Mixed use commercial/residential villages might appeal to this type. This Bachelor of Science degree focuses heavily on the management of commercial real estate finances. The core coursework is in marketing, accounting, finance and corporate mechanisms.

ESTJ likes to be organized and that works well for today's classrooms at all levels in the public schools. The degree Selected Studies in Education is for students who want a career in education but one that revolves around a specialty. The focus in Education, Technology and Media is solid choice for this type. ESTJ will pick up technical skills, but more important will study the effect that media has on our cultures in the American schools. It is designed for further graduate study.

ENTP could consider a minor in **Entrepreneurship and Emerging Enterprises**. New business ventures in the news get ENTP's attention. They are quick to spot a trend and would like studying start-ups or hybrid strategic partnerships. Through the Falcone Center undergrads take their start-up business plans, find the resources and take their product to the Syracuse campus and nearby regional markets. Guest lecturers bring another layer to this reality-based curriculum. ENTP, sometimes overly optimistic, might be surprised at the calculation that goes into successful start-ups.

ISFJ could look closely at the **Music Education** major. They will chose either brass, choral, woodwind, percussion or strings for the musical side of this study. The School of Education has the coursework for teaching competency and artistry for musicians in school settings. This type is usually thoughtful, cooperative, realistic and reliable. Wow, what a good high school teacher.

ISFP with a flair for dressing should look into the **Fashion Design** degree at Syracuse. It is unusual but so comprehensive. Undergrads start with basics in garment construction and fashion design concepts. Later courses are about fashion merchandising, CADS courses, patterns, textiles and more. This type will go for the handiwork of piecing together their own creations on paper through to production. Syracuse has an exceptionally rich curriculum in the hand-crafted arts.

ESFP will surely want to look at the **Retail Management** degree. This major offers subject studies that are not offered at most on college campuses. This degree is about retail store management from buying to customer relations and everything in between. There is a new concentration in Digital Retail Strategies offered in the School of Information Studies at Syracuse. Savvy ESFPs at ease with persuasion and fast-moving environments should look into this study.

INFP often pondering the meaning of their educational studies and personal growth is attracted to the helping professions. The **Social Work** has good bones for this type. INFPs are okay getting close to those in distress when they are providing guidance. This degree tends to be generalist in nature. Graduates have practical policy knowledge and the background in theory to recognize the relationship between the person and their immediate environment. It is this out-of-kilter relationship that social workers aim to improve.

ENFP with talent in design might explore the **Advertising** degree in the selective School of Communication. Beyond admission to the university, the Newhouse School requires a separate application but a portfolio is not required for this major. ENFP might join the student-run ad agency. Or they might decide to dual enroll for a double major in Information Studies, Management or Arts and Sciences. The facilities in the school are over-the-top with the latest digital equipment. The advertising major leans one of two ways, management or creative design.

ENTJ might go for the degree in **Marketing Management** at Syracuse. It uses project teams in many of the courses, like those found in large corporations. The major also looks at impact from competition, government regulation and the social issues that drive government mandates. A good example of this is front-load washing machines and top-load washing machines without agitators. Neither of these really do the best cleaning job, but corporations can only manufacture these two types now because they use less water for each load of clothes. However, they run much longer using much more electricity per load.

INFJ can juggle complicated ideas and connect them in a meaningful way. The degree in **Linguistics** at Syracuse pulls together knowledge from many areas in anthropology, geography, sociology, languages and psychology. This degree is excellent for graduate study in any of these fields. A minor in Classics would be complimentary since so much of our knowledge of the ancient world comes from the languages that were spoken. The degree could lead to study in law or with international NGOs.

ENFJ is imaginative and likes new challenges. The Syracuse major in **Science Education** doesn't lead to teacher certification but that is where the challenge comes in as well as the imagination. As community leaders question the quality of American education, some question the value of teacher certification too. Charter Schools, independent schools, online schools and faith-based schools are trying new concepts. At these schools, ENFJ may find pre-practicum and practicum experiences.

TUFTS UNIVERSITY

Office of Admissions
419 Boston Avenue
Medford, MA 02155
Website: www.tufts.edu
Admissions Telephone: 617-627-3170
Undergraduates: 5,177; 2,559 Men, 2,618 Women
Graduate Students: 5,730

Physical Environment

Tufts University is located on a slight rise in the Medford-Somerville area. The orange line subway station is a bus or 20-minute walk to campus. The **view of Boston** is rather peak-a-boo, depending on where you are on the campus. The residence halls are assigned by lottery each year with preference given to freshmen and sophomores. Upperclassmen are likely to live off campus. Additionally, there are special interest houses for students. The university maintains a large website presence for rentals in the area and many students live in surrounding neighborhoods walking or taking buses to the campus.

There are good eateries adjacent to campus for undergraduates, such as Buddy's Truck stop, a diner in a silver 1929 Worcester lunch-car. It points back to a historical period, just prior to the 20th century depression. The youngest of Millennials born in the late 1990s might visit places of the sweeping history of Boston over the centuries with so many structures of earlier times. This environment appeals to students who want **sophistication** and a top name university near Boston. The surrounding neighborhoods primarily consist of modest houses built in the mid 19th century to house the growing labor market for American industrialization. Nearby Airbnb, the website for finding local lodging, had good recommends for Buddy's. Both Airbnb and Buddy's are staples of the middle class families working independently to increase their income.

Social Environment

High achieving, intellectual students are attracted to Tufts' rigorous academics in the arts and sciences, engineering and pre-professional sciences. The university supports an even balance of men and women undergraduates on campus with about 40 percent identifying as minority. Developing and **stretching ideas** is a primary tool on this campus. Students who like **visual imagery** will enjoy Tufts' inclination to communicate by photographic and artistic design. It is formally part of the curriculum in partnership with the **School Museum of Fine Arts** in Boston and the campus Center for Scientific Visualization and the Department of Visual and Critical Studies.

Clubs and organizations are the biggest social outlet on this campus. There are a good number of dance performance clubs for sure. The university offers minimal support to fraternities and sororities although national trends show increasing membership. **Visualization** plays a role in a number of clubs like **JumboCast**. Run by the students, it webcasts all the athletic games on and off campus.

Political student organizations are also big and represent progressive perspectives quite well with less participation in clubs formed with conservative social concepts. **Advocacy** plays out on the campus and off campus. The University Chaplaincy is host to the interfaith student council which promotes and coordinates activism and service at local, regional and national levels. Two clubs, Friends of Israel and Students for Justice in Palestine, are among the several active, cause-related student groups at Tufts. In winter 2016, Tufts Armenian Club High hosted an action on campus calling attention to the 1915 Armenian Genocide.[74] The Tufts Labor Coalition, a student group, protested over janitorial cutbacks.[75] Undergraduates have **unique talents and hobbies** at Tufts and they apply those within the active clubs on this campus. Many undergraduates arrive on campus expecting to move on to graduate studies in medicine, allied health and veterinary science.

Compatibility with Personality Types and Preferences

Tufts University is taking scientific research into the emerging world (N) of visual imagery and visual utility. The lines are blurring between technology, art, science and visual applications on this university campus. To be sure, a lot of Tufts research remains oriented to the fundamental properties of basic molecular research. However, within their laboratories there seems to be an outward momentum (E) directed by the faculty and administration. The website and university publications readily present compelling messages about emerging technology and ideas (P) that can address current day problems in America.

Undergraduates travel off campus to observe and understand other ethnic groups. Internships and co-ops here are oriented to comprehend and document other cultures. Visual record keeping (S) is a favorite choice to capture and bring home the meaning of experiences abroad. Undergraduates of Tufts observe through media applications, confident in the knowledge of their discipline and ready to move forward into their professional careers with hyper-awareness of social and technological currents.

Now read below about one of the majors that MBTI® research shows people of your type have selected since the mid-20th century. After, refer to Chapter Five for the 50 or so majors that can help you prepare for careers your type has selected. Most importantly, remember that this college description is a suggestion for exploration, not a commanding order. You can be successful in any major at any college.

PERSONALITY MATCH

ISTJ	ISFJ	INFJ	INTJ
ISTP	ISFP	INFP	INTP
ESTP	ESFP	ENFP	ENTP
ESTJ	ESFJ	ENFJ	ENTJ

INTJ can be oriented to creative design. Tufts University offers a curriculum with the foundations of engineering and the function of human living spaces. The BS degree **Engineering in Architecture Studies** prepares graduates for advanced study in either architecture or design. Very thorough and often technically competent INTJ will go for state-of-the-art innovation. Metals, glass and polymers are all fun materials to use in construction but they require INTJ to spend a lot of time in the Mechanics of Soft Materials Laboratory.

ISTP could match up with the **Computer Engineering** degree while thinking of robots and control sticks. On this campus, ISTP will be nudged toward experimentation as well as ethical application. Undergraduates work in teams and also solo. ISTP is fine with either approach. This type wants to be efficient in their work and study. They avoid fussy stuff and will find the tools, logic and principles they need with the least effort. In this department, undergrads will learn the trade of software programming and engineering hardware systems. This combination focus is not often available and gives ISTP a chance to be creative in the labs at Tufts and also good job prospects for the future.

ISTJ will find the second major in **Biotechnology** good with a regular major in the social or physical sciences. The precise nature of biotechnology appeals to this type who can explore different career tracks through this study. It will provide the encouragement they need to keep exploring options until that right field jumps out at them. The department offers two courses that are basically introduction to research through field projects. ISTJ could look to medical practice, health administration or research and diagnostic skills in the pure sciences.

ESTP loves to find a solution that requires people and machines. They are pretty good at it too. Tufts University offers the very unusual **Human Factors** major. It is a very versatile degree, also called engineering psychology. Comfortable in their skins, they like to be in the center of the action. All of these skills will become major strengths as they design equipment, machines and systems for human use. Both client and ESTP will benefit from these projects that require safety, appearance and efficiency.

ENFP is enthusiastic and Tufts is a place of dreams that become active. The major in **Child Psychology** will be fascinating as it starts with the biological and social determinants of behavior. It is an exceptionally strong department with its research foundation, history of children's studies and many options for internships. ENFPs are long-range thinkers, good with abstract ideas and ready with a smile or a bit of humor. The degree leads into graduate studies and ENFP might take an international direction serving children in Eastern Europe refugee camps. With Russia's Putin and Islamic State, ISIS terrorism there are likely to be more unfortunate children caught up in misery.

ENTP is one who likes to predict future trends. The major at Tufts University in **Community Health** is just right for this. There will be field work along with the classes to understand the upheaval in American medicine since 2009. Large and complicated does not scare this type away. They will need to rely on their hunches and trust their intuition to find a balanced perspective in this interdisciplinary study, primarily presented with progressive social thought. In 2015, large numbers of the Millennial generation refused mandated insurance coverage despite fines by the government.

ESTJ likes to organize and analyze. The degree in **Biomedical Engineering** at Tufts has the tight structure that they look for in studies. Intense course work in math, sciences and engineering may have them wishing for side tracks in exploration and dreamy dialogue, but in the end that would not please them. How much more logical and objective does it get than designing devices for surgical insertion in the human body? Tufts University has a huge presence in human medicine through research and practice.

ENTJ has the stuff to take on the major in **Arabic** at Tufts University. They will take language courses in modern standard Arabic. The rest of the curriculum will be taught in English. Without coursework relevant to the political upheaval in the Middle East in the past ten years, it seems odd on this campus so attuned to news and social media. But confident ENTJ has the inclination to request independent studies and possibly to consider petitioning the university to add relevant courses in this area.

TULANE UNIVERSITY

Office of Admissions
6823 St. Charles Avenue
New Orleans, LA 70118
Website: www.tulane.edu
Admissions Telephone: 504-865-5731
Undergraduates: 8,353; 3,469 Men, 4,884 Women
Graduate Students: 5,178

Physical Environment

Few people can think of **New Orleans** and not conjure up images of the Super Bowl and French Quarter. Strong French influence shows up in architecture, cuisine, religion and ethnicity. Tulane and the city live together comfortably, the trolley travels straight into the heart of the city. Walk another three blocks and you are sitting at Café du Monde and looking at St Louis Cathedral, the oldest cathedral in North America and offering Catholic daily mass. The undergraduates come to love New Orleans and volunteer remarkable hours of service throughout the city.

Gibson Hall with its **Romanesque architecture** of stone over brick, built in the 1800s, mixes with modern and historic buildings on campus. Open Fall 2016, the Center for Catholic Life is modest but will offer reflection and a spiritual anchor when minor flooding from up country rains spreads across the city streets and sidewalks. Eco-friendly Lavin-Bernick Center is the hub of campus. **Environmental practices** are ever-present at Tulane. In Winter 2016 the Residence Halls competed in Tulane Unplugged for two weeks to see which one could reduce their electricity demand the most.

Tulane continually invests in **research**, especially at the graduate level. The research energy quickly seeps down to undergraduate courses, thus highlighting challenging concepts early on for students. Research spans across the many divisions in biology and especially concentrates on human medical advances.

Social Environment

Tulane University has a large variety of housing residences, each with a distinct atmosphere. They are designed for communication and student **leadership opportunities**. First and second-year students must live on campus. Undergrads refine leadership skills that tend to be service-oriented, not in the activist orientation. They generate community support and have been quite successful, many coming from the aftermath of hurricane Katrina. CACTUS is in its 44th year on campus and spearheads much of the student-led service success at Tulane. **Elected student leadership** within the collegiate community is very active on this campus.

An important statistic here is that about 80 percent of students come from outside the state of Louisiana. Many come from the Northeast, followed by the South Atlantic and the Midwest. They can be seen walking in flip-flops and reveling in the warm weather. Students come for the exceptional education, **campus cohesion** and direct **service in NOLA neighborhoods**. They are highly sociable and seek to build a wider, healthier community. Volunteering in **literacy work** is a popular choice.

With many service clubs to choose from and located in this international destination city, the undergraduates grow in professional experience. Tulane's message is clear: be a leader, **be engaged and be successful**. Those students with emotional power and resiliency do well here. It comes in most handy as students readily join the Mardi Gras celebrations and the vibrant, sophisticated city life.

Compatibility with Personality Types and Preferences

Tulane University is very much a reflection of its unique association with New Orleans, a city that blended cultural influences for centuries and sports a European style. As this fascinating history unfolded, Tulane's graduate schools developed similar to the formal European universities of past centuries. This philosophy grows out of research perspectives and translates downward to the undergraduate curriculum. Students at Tulane quickly get a wide exposure (N) to advanced concepts. They can observe how quickly those ideas travel into mainstream organizations. Administration emphasizes developing authentic leadership with service for NOLA neighborhoods and the local citizens approve.

Freshmen adopt the casual dress for the climate but they prepare for the formal worlds of business, government and the professions. For this reason, there is a precise order (T) to the coursework in the educational majors and minors. There also is a clear set of core courses designed to assure competencies (S) for all graduates of the university. These competencies in writing, foreign language, public service, mathematics and humanities drive home the expectation of accomplishment after graduation. There is continuous alliance between Tulane's curriculum and the demands of an advanced economy. Undergraduates are mindful of their future, outwardly (E) away from the campus experience but also in the city's neighborhoods. Faculty and administration are mindful of this juxtaposition (F). Successful Tulane students are typically characterized by their predisposition to thoughtful reflection and leadership.

Now read below about one of the majors that MBTI® research shows people of your type have selected since the mid-20th century. After, refer to Chapter Five for the 50 or so majors that can help you prepare for careers your type has selected. Most importantly, remember that this college description is a suggestion for exploration, not a commanding order. You can be successful in any major at any college.

PERSONALITY MATCH			
ISTJ	ISFJ	INFJ	INTJ
ISTP	ISFP	INFP	INTP
ESTP	ESFP	ENFP	ENTP
ESTJ	ESFJ	ENFJ	ENTJ

INFJ is enthusiastic about developing strategies. The very unique major in **Homeland Security** is in demand with the wave of Islamic State, ISIS terrorism in 2014-15. The course work is very pointed at emergency management and terrorism playing out within our national boundaries. Electives also point to the sources of international conflict with pertinent courses like The Arab-Israeli Conflict. The School of Continuing Studies offers this also as a minor. It focuses on leadership, hands-on training, critical thinking and decision making. INFJ has a pair of long-range glasses for disaster preplanning.

INTJ likes original, emerging activities. A professional career in architecture and design can easily work for this type if they have artistic talent. Tulane's minor in **Architectural Studies** and the major in **Engineering Physics** would give this quietly passionate type an impressive resume for entry into advanced architectural firms across our nation. After graduating from Architecture School, this type will advocate forcefully to test their material concepts in three dimensional design.

ISTP will enjoy the **Biomedical Engineering** degree at Tulane University because of the year-long research project. This type lights their own fire once they identify their mechanical passion somewhere within the research labs. Maybe it will be in the Material lab where research with polymer development from production to factory floor is emerging. The school also requires students to work on a team-designed project. This, too, fits in well with ISTP who enjoys working with others of the same interests and usually becomes the go-to person when the project hits a snag.

INTP might have to satisfy their curiosity about the **Bioinformatics** certificate at Tulane. They like to mix, match and invent computer programs. There really is no level of information management that is too complex for this type with powerful computing resources. This major is well-situated in Tulane's School of Public Health and undergraduates have access to a wealth of knowledge in the faculty at this prestigious, forward-thinking medical school. This is an emerging career field with the troubled roll out of the government's Affordable Health Care Act in 2014.

ESTP can find the finance world pretty attractive with elements of risk and investment. The major in **Finance** at Tulane University has a good curriculum that explores these two critical concepts. Elective courses that might attract ESTP would be Risk Management, Advanced Trading and Games and Decisions. During breaks they might just drop over for a coffee in the graduate business school to network and relax.

ENFP doesn't usually go into business careers but the major in **Management** might change their mind. In this Business School, undergrads study social issues along with business concerns as products and services move to market. ENFP will go for the generalist approach to become a well-rounded manager which is the goal of the department. Stepping out into the small corporations in a entry level position would work for perceptive, versatile ENFP.

ENTP goes for the pure physical sciences because of the possibilities in those fields. The minor in **Engineering Science** at Tulane will add a big element of interest for ENTP who might be majoring in communication or business. Technological experience or know how is such a large segment across many job markets who must use it to market or produce their services. Just think of Google, a pusher of information mostly, but it is all delivered through electronic media. This type doesn't want to be left out of the pivotal action and this minor will get them a seat at the table.

ESFJ will be delighted with the major **Psychology and Early Education** in the School of Science and Engineering at Tulane. Yes, you read that right. The psychology department is right where it needs to be with the physical sciences since emergent research in psychology is always focused on the brain and its chemical pathways. Sensitive, caring ESFJ will be more interested in the human development side, the historical foundation of the discipline. It will be a fabulous asset not only in elementary classrooms and preschool programs, but also for community organizations with outreach programs for struggling families.

ESTJ usually moves into positions of authority. They like realistic career paths that are directly supported by their academic degrees. The major titled **Legal Studies in Business** works pretty well for this purpose. It is a curriculum that offers specific background in areas like real estate and insurance. This type might also might look at the complex structure of business taxation. ESTJ could also use the major to enter law school. Regardless, this type will focus on the goals: theirs and the firm's.

ENTJ is quite comfortable in leadership positions. The degree in Management with a major in **Marketing** leads straight into the world of enterprise and competition. Coursework in this study emphasizes planning and management of products or services in retail markets. The elective courses are going to check the boxes for being relevant and fascinating, like the Personal Selling Lab. With their long-term vision, the first ENTJ position after graduation could be consulting to national or international companies.

UNION COLLEGE

Office of Admissions
Schenectady, NY 12308
Website: www.union.edu
Admissions Telephone: 518-388-6122
Undergraduates: 2,302; 1,276 Men, 1,026 Women

Physical Environment

Union College has a remarkable history with its founding shortly after the American Revolutionary War in 1795. This college has **alumni of national accomplishment**, like William H. Seward, Abraham Lincoln's Secretary of State, and U.S. President Chester A. Arthur. The beauty of the campus dates back to the late 1700s, when it was founded as a non-denominational college. The **Nott Memorial** is easily recognizable for its **16 sides of Russian-like architecture**. It serves as a visual anchor on this campus of other attractive buildings that match the innovation and delight of the Nott. Located in Schenectady, a 30-minute drive from the Albany airport, the city is not in the Snow Belt so it gets an average of **three good snow storms** each year.

The Peter Irving Center **interfaces teaching and research** with IBM's considerable donation of Intelligent Cluster Computing. This exceptional facility points to the administration's confidence in the undergraduate student body. Butterfield Hall includes a scanning electron microscope that faculty and students alike use for research. It is hard to overestimate the value of the **laboratory equipment** here since other small liberal arts colleges do not have this kind of equipment. It also is hard to get your head wrapped around the **interest and optimism** that generates on this exclusively undergraduate campus.

Social Environment

The social environment at Union College can be described in one word: **community**. Each student is assigned to a **"Minerva house"** which puts on social event after social event. The Minerva houses develop student initiative, collaboration and accomplishment. There are also Socials held by fraternity and sorority houses. The Henle Dance Pavilion is a beautiful setting for rehearsals and small performances. Reamer Center, home to many student organizations, is the campus hub with all the fast food stops. Students like their sports, the gymnasium, ball courts, hockey rink and pool. All in all, this campus is a bit isolated and students define and rely on **their own leadership** for social outlet.

Many sign up for **service learning** through the curriculum and often design their research for the benefit of others. The Office of Religious and Spiritual Life welcomed the Interfaith Youth Core Better Together program.[76] The Core, a Chicago-based nonprofit, is partnered with the Department of Education and questioned by some in theological circles.[77] Core training in 2015 included voicing religious or non-religious values, mobilizing student leaders and acting together according to common values.[78] Union undergraduates also have a local chapter of **Active Minds**. This national student club was started in recent years by the Millennial generation.

It is an outreach and encourages awareness of those with mental disabilities, pretty much ignored by news and social media.

Union is one of a select few liberal arts colleges whose **engineering** program has a foundation in the humanities. Their core curriculum includes history, science, math and study abroad to gain exposure to other cultures. About 75 percent of all students will travel and learn off campus. Students here want to connect with their professors who they value and look to for subject expertise. They expect to explore the **pre-professional fields**. They learn to present research findings formally in writing and much of it will be published as co-authors with their professors. Graduates move on to advanced studies in business, education, law or medical administration. These professional degrees are completed on campus with nearby universities. For those who move directly into the job market, their confidence and resumes stand out with **exceptional research background and determination**.

Compatibility with Personality Types and Preferences

Students and faculty at Union College reach out, intending to latch on to the future (N) of ideas and concepts. Together, they form a community that prefers to integrate current knowledge with every day common social and physical reality. As a result, personal connections are quite important at Union College. Friendships and mentoring are viewed as a primary foundation for learning (F). Analysis and discovery is the other side of this balanced coin. Undergraduates here carry the responsibility to be prepared for change in the coming decades. They want to remain open (P) and be able to identify and understand concepts in research literature. They want to bring that information to their own undergraduate study and apply it in their own research designs. The individual departments offer a wide selection of coursework for exploration. This breadth in the curriculum encourages students to sample across subjects well into the junior and senior years. Faculty interface social context with technical and scientific concepts. Student-centered research is designed to teach undergraduates how to interpret data and question the results. It features traditional mentoring, investigative methods and advising for oral and written communication.

Similarly, the residential life here is vibrant and thoughtfully planned (J). Education crosses the boundary into the residential life programs. International study is designed to understand foreign cultural perspectives as applied to the undergraduate's academic major. The international sites are selected for this purpose and not chosen for arts, culture or service. Integrated knowledge is uppermost at Union College and the administration's humane perspective is very much a part of this integration.

Now read below about one of the majors that MBTI® research shows people of your type have selected since the mid-20th century. After, refer to Chapter Five for the 50 or so majors that can help you prepare for careers your type has select-

PERSONALITY MATCH			
ISTJ	ISFJ	INFJ	INTJ
ISTP	ISFP	INFP	INTP
ESTP	ESFP	ENFP	ENTP
ESTJ	ESFJ	ENFJ	ENTJ

*ed. Most importantly, remember that this college description is a suggestion for explora-
tion, not a commanding order. You can be successful in any major at any college.*

INFP is one to support a cause or select a career field based on a social issue. The
degree at Union College in **Psychology** is nicely tailored for this passionate learner.
First years will survey this evolving field. Professors mentor students to think logically, evaluate research claims and use resources as a starting point for their own research. Juniors and seniors will complete a student practicum, independent project,
independent study, term study and thesis. INFP interfaces their written work with
their ideals.

INFJ is a thoughtful type and a darn good fit for Union College. A degree in
Philosophy focuses on mankind's expanding knowledge over time. This large effort
will refine INFJ's own ethical beliefs. The curriculum in philosophy is a sequence
that grows in complexity right along with the undergraduates. INFJs will consider the honors thesis in preparation for graduate study in law, health or the social
sciences.

INTJ is okay to declare a minor in an emerging field. They would get a first class
introduction to **Nanotechnology** at Union College. Students will acquire basic information about the properties of matter. With that foundation, they will explore the
limits and ability of a 'nano' and come to find its uses in tissue engineering, textiles,
energy, filtration, construction and more. This minor is for those heading off to engineering or graduate school in the sciences.

ISFP doesn't mind changing it up for a good reason. The degree in **Computer
Science** flexibly fits with majors in other departments across the college. Electives are
in bioinformatics, robotics, web programming and in game development so ISFP
will head off to other departments for integrating their research. It is all about applying the magic of Computer Science to conundrums in other fields. Social responsibility and the technical knowledge travel together at Union college and this is great
for values-driven ISFP.

ENFP has big horizon when it comes to interests, but there must be abstraction
and variety. The major in **Geology** can deliver both. At Union College, ENFP will
be very active in field studies which lead directly to independent research papers.
The department has a long, long list of advanced equipment to analyze the rocks at
molecular levels. This degree is all about going backwards in geologic history and
predicting how the rocks got from there to here. Abstract, big picture. ENFP is all
for that.

ENTP might be intrigued by the thought of a career in astronomy. If ENTP has
mathematical acumen and interest, the major in **Astronomy** at Union College is a
great choice. This ingenious type will show up as a first year with thoughts of the
important astrophysical research. Star formation, galaxy evolution and other subjects
might have jumped into ENTP's awareness in high school when New Horizon's
Pluto probe declared that it was not a planet. Union offers this major with active
advanced research, not to the mention black holes and gravitational waves of Winter
2016 discovery.

ESFJ goes for productive partnerships between business and government. This
traditional type is optimistic about conventional organizations in our communi-

ties. The curriculum in **Science, Medicine and Technology in Culture** is all about tension between society and progress. Subjects like the Scientific Revolution, the Philosophy of Science and Technology and Human Values justify ESFJ optimism in face of doubts about scientific progress. It will bring support to their underlying value of conventional society.

ESTJ has the tenacity to deal with all the drama surrounding energy conservation, especially since Pope Francis came forward with moral support to stop wasteful use of energy. But first this type will have to get all of their facts organized. Union College has just what ESTJ likes in a nice little study called **Energy Studies**. The course Heat, Light and Astronomy will point to the possibility of future energy production in space.

ENFJ is about helping others realize individual goals. The major in **Anthropology** at Union College takes a wide look at all the specializations in the field. Faculty mentoring will be very important in this very wide field. ENFJ will partner with their professor to find the topic that captures their attention. The department reviews the fields of anthropological medicine, environmental anthropology, economic anthropology, urban anthropology, anthropology and religion, psychological anthropology and several more. Wow. We said it was a wide field.

ENTJ will find the major in **Neuroscience** at Union College has three tracks in studying the human brain: bioscience, cognitive or computational. With a career choice in psychiatry, the cognitive track will work. The bioscience track works for a medical profession. If its computational neuroscience, careers in artificial intelligence are calling. Considering the Islamic State, ISIS terrorism of 2014-15, ENTJ might turn toward the power and accomplishment that comes with national defense positions.

THE UNIVERSITY OF CHICAGO

Office of Admission
5801 S. Ellis Avenue
Chicago, Illinois 60637
Website: www.uchicago.edu
Admissions Telephone: 773-702-8650
Undergraduates: 5,738; 2,938 Men, 2,755 Women
Graduate Students: 9,359

Physical Environment

The University of Chicago is located on the south side of the city in the **Hyde Park**, population 45,000. At the turn of the 19th century, the original campus was built of **neo-Gothic rectangular** structures along several city blocks which enclose the main quadrangle. In the 21st century a **minimalist architecture** has spread throughout. Boxed in by settled cityscape, U Chicago has razed dated historical structures. Buildings like the Research Institute are replaced with sharp, pointy edges and cantilevered wings that house the same departments but with a new name. The campus is laid out on the grid system with undergraduate housing on the north and south sides. Bicycles are recommended but when the Lake Michigan winds and winter blow in, they are impractical. Depending on what side of the campus rectangle you come in from you might see aging residential structures, historic edifices under the care of the local preservation society, parks or indigent neighborhoods.

Students use the **university bus** system to travel into the academic facilities which are essentially between North Hall and South Campus. Some dormitory halls are located off campus with a 15-minute walk to the academic center. With North Hall and other **dormitory quads** coming on line in 2016, the university is bringing undergraduates back on campus. The **Laboratory Schools** is an academic complex and residence for two thousand students with study spaces and dining spots within. It also is the center for early childhood education laboratories, performing and visual arts spaces, libraries and faculty offices. You might think of these as **mega dormitory quads** and they reduce the need for undergraduates to travel around the campus each day. The adjacent neighborhoods prompt awareness and safety conscious travel. Many of the 38 residential houses are located in 11 dormitories.

Social Environment

The college environment is a bastion of **controlled intellectual space**. Here there is everything for the **brilliant, reserved** student. Incoming undergraduates are intense about accumulating knowledge and proud to be on a campus of advanced International Research. One-third of the undergraduate study is reserved for The Core. These **required courses** center undergraduate dialogue on primary texts and principles. The Core is composed of elective studies but there are some courses required by the college and faculty reflecting their socially progressive views.

The **Center for Leadership and Involvement** is the gateway to activity on campus that is not academic. The college seems to provide resources to organizations that meet Center goals for undergraduate education. Social activities are guided in this manner. In 2016 a new club formed to advertise and get improved membership for the other 300 clubs on campus. The student government association, class of 2019, elected four women as their representatives. College media announced this single gender representation pointing out that men dominated these positions in the past. It was their response to those who jested the elections.[79]

In summer 2015, one student joined an outside group that barricaded themselves inside a campus building. They protested the university's decades long refusal to provide adult trauma treatment at the campus medical center, just blocks away from areas of violence.[80] Two days later, about 60 students and alumni barricaded a university building over projected budget cuts.[81] For some on campus, social concerns are high priority and they will find time to advocate. **Intellectual inquiry** is the goal of just about every undergraduate student.

Most students intend to move on to graduate study and research. They are not often distracted from their academic studies outside of typical social fun. After the day's heavy intellectual lifting, **intramural teams** and athletic fitness take over. Each residence hall has many teams for the ongoing competitions at multiple locations and with plenty of equipment. It is all accessible in the new mega dormitory quads. **Dance Marathon** raises funds for charity and has been a hit since it started in 2004. Undergraduates take **occasional breaks off campus** visiting artistic, blues and jazz clubs in distant downtown Chicago.

Compatibility with Personality Types and Preferences

University of Chicago is an analytical machine (T) with fuzzy edges. They honor tradition (J) and history in a number of ways which can serve to inform logic on this campus. At the same time, the graduate research relentlessly seeks new truths that seem to pop up with the passing of each decade. The list of scientific discoveries at U Chicago, such as carbon-14 dating, is remarkable.

The university's amazing intellectual resources and infrastructure are quite separate from the undergraduate experience. The websites for many disciplines are designed for graduate students and current research. Information about the undergraduate studies is usually found in the academic bulletin. The undergraduate education is formed and administered by the college, the college deans and their staff.

As undergraduate students arrive they are more than ready to explore the historical texts and speculate on what was meant by the author (N). This interesting way of looking into the past for knowledge is a hallmark of the university, as well as a contradiction. These students arrive as freshman with the belief that the next four years will intensely focus on the present to further discovery and develop their understanding of the world. Yet the college reserves the first two years for historical wisdom. Undergraduates will learn to look for novel ideas (P) in their last two years through all time and space mediums. Their very personalized body of knowledge of past and future forms the jumping off point to advanced research and intellectual work that will last throughout their careers. University of Chicago draws students who are conventional in some ways but always anxiously driven, and determined to impact the future. The university strongly supports **civic engagement** with many programs and centers. That philosophy is well-reflected across the campus environment.

Now read below about one of the majors that MBTI® research shows people of your type have selected since the mid-20th century. After, refer to Chapter Five for the 50 or so majors that can help you prepare for careers your type has selected. Most importantly, remember that this college description is a suggestion for exploration, not a commanding order. You can be successful in any major at any college.

PERSONALITY MATCH

ISTJ	ISFJ	INFJ	INTJ
ISTP	ISFP	INFP	INTP
ESTP	ESFP	ENFP	ENTP
ESTJ	ESFJ	ENFJ	ENTJ

INFJ who has a spiritual bent will very much be interested in the **Religious Studies** major in the Divinity School. It is designed to study and critique the purpose of religious practice. INFJ is attracted to philosophy and human values. The course topics of Buddhism, Christianity, Hinduism, Islam and Judaism methodically review their sources and problems. Focus is on religious claims, the community of believers and how they self-interpret their religion. INFJ will study one area in depth to produce the senior paper.

ENFP smiles broadly when they see that U Chicago has a course named **Big Problems**. It is not a major but offers a choice of subjects each year for seniors. The topics change but nicely include interests of the wide-ranging ENFP. As expected, Big Problems are unsolvable. The students will study the problem with optimism and explore skills intended to make a positive difference. ENFPs will have no trouble stretching their imaginations wide enough to comprehend topics in 2015-16 like Drinking Alcohol or Understanding Wisdom.

INFP takes real enjoyment in finding patterns in stuff that isn't related at all. That could be a major in **Geographical Studies**. The Committee on Geographical Studies, founded in 1934 as a graduate study of research, offers the major and is home to some of the most advanced study in the field. We have never seen courses in Advanced Geographical Information Systems or GIS. INFP will be able to peer at these satellite maps looking for patterns all day long.

ENTJ who likes numbers is going to really enjoy the **Applied Mathematics** major at U Chicago. This department organizes the undergraduate degree with the cumulative character of math and the emerging state of mathematics. Faculty actively promote the evolution of modern day math usage in disciplines across society. ENTJs with their visionary mind will use their secondary field in the physical sciences or computational neuroscience. ENTJ will expect to launch an academic career with mathematics on graduation.

INTJ will find lots of room to maneuver with the **Physics** major at U Chicago. The courses are broadly interdisciplinary. INTJs will first get grounded in the fundamental studies of matter, energy and force. This can be followed with further technical courses that move in the direction of medical, atmospheric or environmental sciences. INTJs love the process of discovery. This department will totally support their movement toward professional careers in research or corporate enterprises like Tesla.

ENTP will find the **Law, Letters and Society** major here taught by faculty from the law school. As ENTP moves through the sequence of coursework and research, they will gain clarity on how society is organized, shaped and controlled through the application of laws. This study showing the nature of power and its application will interest ENTP. The school presents legal studies as a system that developed from western legal thought. The course selection will feature Machiavelli, Marx and other thinkers of free will and relational thought.

INTP is good with research because it satisfies their curiosity. The major in **Jewish Studies** is an intense study of the Jewish nation through text, culture, language and history. Starting with archeological evidence around 1500 BC, INTP will learn of Abraham who formed the peoples and the nation that occupy the Israeli territory today. Yes, this will be enough to keep INTP in the library overnight, unaware that others have departed for a game or two of water hoops in North Hall pools.

ESTJ likes to do away with the illogical and inefficient. This is a great characteristic if you intend to major in **Economics**. Mathematics modeling and the modern economy are the focus. A good research topic would be the pharmaceutical industries' initial resistance to the Affordable Health Care Act. They changed their position after administration deal makers in 2009 agreed to put no price controls on drugs. It is ironic that U Chicago is in the vortex of progressive power politics reshaping much of the American landscape this past decade.

ISTJ is going to get the facts straight and there will be no missing links in that line. You can count on it. The major in **Geophysical Sciences** is a good bet for ISTJ who will use their tremendous powers of concentration. This type may struggle with the Bachelor of Arts degree, but the Bachelor of Science has the structure they like and leans toward an integrated use of math, physics, chemistry and biology. The study of earth, atmospheric and planetary sciences goes with either degree. After careful evaluation, ISTJ might focus on the origin and history of Earth. With that decision made, ISTJ's strengths come back into play big time.

ISFJ who is attracted to nursing, as they easily can be, might look into **Biological Sciences** through the college's Biological Sciences Collegiate Division. It will be an ideal preparation for the medical field or perhaps as professor of nursing. The division offers the Bachelor of Science which does not include electives outside of the general education requirements of the college itself. The Bachelor of Arts has more elective options outside of the major. About 90 percent of the students will be involved in undergraduate research activity.

ISTP goes for numbers and sometimes will apply them even to social conundrums in high school drama. The major in **Statistics** is a good choice for this type, yet ISTPs with their touch of humor will want more than numbers to keep them busy. In the Division of Physical Sciences, this department offers choice to combine the major with any other field in the natural or social sciences. This type is likely to move toward the physical sciences since they are often technically quite competent. Now let's see how you do that? Four girls want to go to prom with thee guys, now if you assign a number or value/data point to each of the seven names…got it?

UNIVERSITY OF MIAMI

Office of Admission
P.O. Box 248025
Coral Gables, FL 33124-4616
Website: www.miami.edu
Admissions Telephone: 305-284-4323
Undergraduates: 11,273; 5,497 Men, 5,776 Women
Graduate Students: 5,501

Physical Environment

University of Miami is only a few miles from downtown Miami and less than **20 minutes from South Beach**. This inviting, pleasant campus is surrounded by the residential neighborhoods of Coral Gables. Students get downtown quickly by hopping the metro at the stop adjacent to campus. The main campus circles around Lake Osceola at its center. The Shalala Student Center is perched on the edge of the lake is the place to meet and relax. On Earth Day in the Spring, the faculty and students form a hand held chain around the entire lake on campus. It is a collective **Hug for the Earth** and points to the sustainability studies at UM whose location is so very close to the endangered Everglades. Campus architecture is modern and functional at warding off the direct sun and its energy demand on air conditioning equipment.

With excellent fall and winter weather, students get around by bicycles, pedestrian sidewalks or the shuttle system which is a must since the campus is quite large. A new overhead pedestrian walkway, started in Spring 2016, will improve safe walking across US 1 and Mariposa Court. Safety is a big UM concern in the adjacent residential neighborhoods. The campus runs a free shuttle service on demand by students who call in. **Benches and outdoor chairs** are placed around the campus. Two main dining halls on opposite sides of the campus serve students in the traditional multistory dormitories for undergraduate residential life. Upper class students move off campus more often or rent an apartment with friends.

The graduate academic departments and research laboratories at University of Miami are imposing in size, presence and national importance within their disciplines. Undergraduate students who would like to perform research will apply through the centralized office and identify which professor-mentor they would like to work for.

Social Environment

Slightly less than half of the students on campus are from Florida with the other half coming from large Midwestern states, the eastern seaboard and California. Approximately 60 percent of the undergraduates identify as a minority. Students who attend U of Miami are academically **high achieving** and arrive with outgoing attitudes and extracurricular interests to match. First-year classes can be large, especially the **general education classes**. Upper-level classes have fewer students, some with as few as 20 students or less. Academic advising is handled differently within each of the schools. The Business School uses an **Advising Team** for students to schedule meetings with their assigned professors. In the College of Arts and Sciences, freshmen get a first year advisor in the department of their declared major or meet with general counselors. Undergraduates may declare majors within any of the nine academic schools at the university. There is a flexible policy for double majors and interdisciplinary majors.

University of Miami has a very active and well-resourced **Student Government**. It is patterned after the United States government with a Senate, Executive Office, Courts, etc. Much of the informal social environment is organized and channeled through this group of elected students. Campus-wide social activities are popular. The university is really supportive of the 33 Greek fraternities and sororities who generate more social options on campus. Volunteer Service is pretty well organized by the students. **PhilADthropy** is a good example where 13 teams of communication undergraduates develop free ad campaigns for hundreds of local nonprofits. The **Canes'** football team draws a huge crowd and they usually make it to a playoff bowl.

Resident faculty and professional staff are in each dormitory. Together with student representatives they plan academic and social activity. Juniors and seniors can apply for housing in the Villages which is apartment-style. First year students must live on campus together in designated dormitories. Residence Halls are coed and operate traditionally with men and women on alternate floors, singles and doubles with common restrooms. Visiting hours for guests and Quiet Hours lend cohesion and stability to the dynamic daily experience on campus. This arrangement acknowledges the hyper social experiences of young people in America today. University of Miami is mindful of these challenges and focuses on undergraduates' emotional health.

Compatibility with Personality Types and Preferences

University of Miami in Florida is a large presence in the collegiate liberal arts world. It is a big campus with big undergraduate student numbers similar to a regional state university. Undergraduate energy on this campus tends to move in two directions: one is negotiating the demanding, dynamic curriculum and the other is big Miami. Students who like this university come to terms with the city's social intensity in their own way. Some embrace it with vigor, others sample it as needed for a break from the demanding academics. Regardless of social inclinations, students here are on the ball, paying attention, pursuing a goal (S).

The educational curriculum has many majors not frequently found at liberal arts campuses. The faculty does not actively overlay political perspectives within the disciplines or their curriculum. The campus is geared for analytic learning with expectations for precise content (T) by both the professors and students in the classroom. Fuzziness is reserved for pillows in the dormitory. It is an ideal campus for the socially adept who can take advantage (E) of the exciting international culture, yet show up in class the next day prepared. It is also just right for quieter types who often keep their nose in the books, yet want to experiment with new social venues in college. They can drop into the city anonymously for an evening of observation with a friend or two. UM graduates are productive, astute citizens in the workforce which is a pretty darn good paraphrase of the UM mission statement.

Now read below about one of the majors that MBTI® research shows people of your type have selected since the mid-20th century. After, refer to Chapter Five for the 50 or so majors that can help you prepare for careers your type has selected. Most importantly, remember that this college description is a suggestion for exploration, not a commanding order. You can be successful in any major at any college.

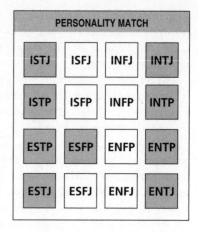

PERSONALITY MATCH

ISTJ	ISFJ	INFJ	INTJ
ISTP	ISFP	INFP	INTP
ESTP	ESFP	ENFP	ENTP
ESTJ	ESFJ	ENFJ	ENTJ

INTJ likes tough academic subjects. A good day for this type connects abstract information with reality and comes up with a new concept. UM offers a double major in **Marine Science** that is paired with one of the other physical sciences: geology, biology, chemistry, meteorology, physics or computer science. Visionary INTJs will have no trouble seeing the connections between these disciplines studying in this department at this university a few short miles from the Atlantic ocean. After graduation, advanced degrees for academic teaching/research posts or government and industry might call out to this type.

ISTP loves to discover the how and why of things. The **Audio Engineering** option is part of the BS degree in electrical engineering. The fun part for ISTP is that this option is integrated with the School of Music. ISTPs will secure the code or get a door key for access to the audio labs. This degree can open entry level positions in medical instrumentation, analog/digital manufacturing and, for sure, the music entertainment industry.

ISTJ is conscientious, thoughtful and competent. It is a habit and a goal. The **Health Science** degree offered in the School of Nursing gets graduates ready for admission to specialized health professional schools. During their studies, they will learn in the School's Center for Nursing and Health Studies located in downtown Coral Gables. This facility has classrooms, research and simulation with a three-bed suite for ISTJ to practice their interaction with patients. With all the background in health care at this personal level, ISTJ has what they want to make that next career decision.

INTP could like the major in **Ecosystem Science and Policy**. The curriculum is heavily focused on literature and recent research findings. Faculty are expecting undergraduates to learn about remediation also. The Everglades is a massive remediation study by itself and now going through restoration from well-intentioned, but damaging, projects in the mid-20th century. INTP is energized by problems of this complexity. INTPs often become absorbed in study and only occasionally want to head out for a social break.

ESTP can promote goals with spontaneous action in their lighthearted way. It could become a full-blown career after finishing the program in **Public Relations** in the School of Communication. ESTPs accurately read the tea leaves and will like developing a consistent, targeted message. The department requires a second program and ESTP might go for Media Management. It would be considered a minor.

ESFP might dust off their fifth grade recorder or hang onto that marching band horn to look closely at the unusual major, **Music Therapy**, offered at UM. This type, often attracted to the helping professions, might also have a bit of the performing artist within. They will like the pre-practicum to learn about assessment, goal setting, intervention and data collection. This major is accredited through therapeutic organizations. Health care centers across the nation require therapists to be accredited. ESFP will be good-to-go with this very professional degree from the School of Music. This therapeutic field is exploring treatments for difficult personality such as autism and Alzheimer's.

ENTP tends to be a risk-taker who might go into business. The UM major in **Entrepreneurship** together with the professional advisors at the business school is ideally located with nearby international, dynamic Miami. The school sponsors an annual business competition for undergraduates that awards thousands of dollars to the winners. Naturally assertive, ENTPs will be looking for partners to enter this contest. Although not known for their practicality, their creativity often sparkles.

ESTJ and authority go nicely together. It is a serious and honorable business for this type to make decisions and supervise with their skills and knowledge. The major in **Management** at UM develops those very skills. International Miami alerts traditional ESTJs to new possibilities in commerce. They will explore business practices and get one-on-one mentoring from professionals in the metropolitan area. After consideration, this type may opt for the minor in business and major in urban studies or government.

ENTJ likes to sign in on time. They develop an innovative, on-time leadership style. The UM School of Business and UM School of Nursing offer the major in **Health Sector Management and Policy**. ENTJs will understand that it points to executive positions in medicine, health insurance or health administration. The troubled overhaul of the American health industry from insurance to medicine is fertile ground for future ENTJ careers with this major.

UNIVERSITY OF PENNSYLVANIA

Office of Admissions
1 College Hall
Philadelphia, PA 19104-6376
Website: www.upenn.edu
Admissions Telephone: 215-898-7507
Undergraduates: 9,746: 4,897 Men, 4,849 Women
Graduate Students: 11,550

Physical Environment

U Penn is located in busy and bustling West Philadelphia, a few blocks from the Schuylkill River. Unlike several other Ivy and Ivy-like universities, U Penn has transformed a blighted, indigent neighborhood adjacent to campus with **extraordinary innovation and commitment**. After twenty years devoted to planning and ongoing construction, the campus offers a park-like setting. It is an interesting **mélange of historic buildings** in Federal, Colonial, Romanesque and Modern vertical style. The varied architecture represents several periods that sit together nicely. Modern additions like New College House have the typical glass, metal and angles, but there are also large expanses of wood, warming and familiar. College Hall was the first building in 1872 on U Penn's campus and the statue of Ben Franklin at the front entrance was there to witness it. He calls for a sense of pride in **American history** that many Millennials are unfamiliar with. Their public and independent high schools have dropped core courses in U.S. government and history.

Shoemaker Green is a reclaimed space that looks like an ordinary green lawn but actually recycles ground water and reduces heat intensity during the summer months. **Pennovation** Center is the new laboratory for commercialization of research and business incubation. Well, okay, we think that means starting up new businesses. The philosophical perspective at U Penn is good with for-profit industries. The **Neural and Behavioral Sciences** houses undergraduate studies in psychology and biology and facilitates emerging research and interface between these two disciplines. If you are going on a campus tour ask about the Sing Center for Nanotechnology and the Smilow Center for Translational Research too.

All first year and most sophomores live on campus in the College Houses, essentially **tall dormitory towers**. New College House opened 2016 is one of about **50 different housing options** on campus. However, most upper class students live off campus. The new Hub 3939, privately leased, is a mixed-use residential facility for undergraduate and graduate students quite near campus. The nearby Penn track is handy enough for most students to exercise on campus. The libraries are housed separately by subject and are clearly designated for either undergraduate or graduate use. U Penn is a very organized place indeed.

Social Environment

The very large majority of U Penn students are **valedictorians** of their high school graduation class. They were likely to be athletes and/or **student leaders** who started service projects in their hometown community. They tend to come from all over the U.S. and around the world. Just under 50 percent identify as a minority. They are **innovative, goal-driven and independent**. Once on campus, undergrads move through the first two semesters fulfilling core and general course requirements. Each of the Schools of Business, Nursing, Engineering and Arts and Sciences sets their own core distribution. However, there is flexibility and classes may cross over into any of the other undergraduate schools. With basic study completed, undergrads will move into majors and minors including undergraduate research.

University of Pennsylvania is over the top in their **encouragement** for undergraduates who want to tackle research in addition to their basic studies. The national laboratories and noted national faculty are not held out separately from the undergraduate academic departments. There are multiple advisements that initiate and help students find the right research for their study. Equally desirable, there seems to be no overriding university philosophical agenda narrowing options in which political direction to pursue research.

Many students will want to continue volunteering in service clubs and activities. The curriculum offers a significant number of **service learning** courses in West Philadelphia. Students will also find social outlets in the performing arts, athletics and residential programs. Harrison Saturday night is put on by the Harrison House. Since all of the Houses at U Penn are themed in some manner, Harrison is themed in Fun. So they weekly provide some kind of activity. This speaks to the confidence the administration places in students shaping undergraduate social experience since the dormitories are staffed by regular student Resident Assistants. Ben Franklin would approve that undergraduate students plan their own soirées and university budget is not diverted to a staff of professionals whose job is to plan social soirees for undergraduate students.

Compatibility with Personality Types and Preferences

University of Pennsylvania is unique among the most prestigious American universities in a number of categories. Probably the singular and most important factor is that of their founder, Ben Franklin. On this campus, the American Founding Fathers have a presence and appreciation. His lifetime achievements influenced a foundation of practicality and innovation that is holistically in place today. Three hundred years later, as one looks closely at the course of studies available to undergraduate students, you will see a curriculum of which he would likely approve. Penn is also unique for their extraordinary flexibility (P) between the four schools and the number of double majors they encourage. The research laboratories are definitely pushing the state-of-the-art as other institutions of similar size and resources. But U Penn is okay with the concept of business enterprise and some of their laboratories take on unique creative energy (N) in that direction.

Undergraduates at U Penn like the concept that you gather all the known information and then see how it can be applied. This type of knowledge can be advanced into the near future for the benefit of society as well as the bank account of the innovator. Academic philosophy demands students understand how things work and how they will be used. The favorite learning tool for this is logical analysis (T). Students drawn to U Penn are logical thinkers. The happy student knows that the universe is predictable (J) and will be evolving for the better as soon as they graduate and get out in the marketplace. And speaking of a predictable universe, how about that theory of relativity ultimately proven in Feb 2016 when gravitational waves hit our sensors from two black holes colliding eons ago. Woo hoo Albert Einstein. We're thinking Ben would approve of this too.

U Penn excels at real world applications of knowledge (S) too. The sciences are stellar and cross academic boundaries with an emphasis on integrated knowledge. The new Translational Research Center is more than over the top, gathering the biomedical research departments under one roof. The educational philosophy is also viewed in part as a "repository of knowledge." Between these two perspectives, the university continues to play a much-needed, pivotal role in the well-being of the nation.

Now read below about one of the majors that MBTI® research shows people of your type have selected since the mid-20th century. After, refer to Chapter Five for the 50 or so majors that can help you prepare for careers your type has selected. Most importantly, remember that this college description is a suggestion for exploration, not a commanding order. You can be successful in any major at any college.

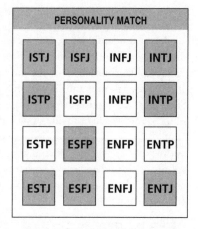

ISTJ at U Penn will want to look into the Huntsman Program to use their excellent memory for foreign language in an environment that demands accuracy and efficiency. A language like **Russian** combined with the **International Studies and Business** curriculum is a solid choice for the business world, a comfortable place for ISTJ. This type can cut through to the core with precision while conducting business in a second language with aggressive, savvy East European entrepreneurs. With Russia's Putin on the march with invasions in Ukraine and Syria, this expertise will be in demand. Western governments have failed at containing him, but he might be hemmed in by independent business corporations getting a double bang for their buck.

ISFJ has an appreciation for fine design. The concentration in **Real Estate** will fine tune that appreciation assessing large real estate developments. The Wharton School of Business and Management is an incubator for financiers and developers. The faculty is critically aware of the impact of government regulations and mandates during the past ten years coming from a host of offices and bureaucrats. Upon graduation, ISFJ could join a brokerage and pick up the experience needed to move into top firms. An alternative might be to join a regional, national or international architectural firm. This reflective type might also consider joining independent religious organizations that generate affordable housing in third world countries. Ben Franklin, an international at heart, would approve of that.

INTJ is quite the visionary with original ideas that rule. With a little artistic talent, U Penn's major in **Digital Media Design** could be a good one. Only a few types would go for a Bachelor of Science in Engineering focused on graphics. But INTJs have the determination to create new expression and ways of communication. This will work for all the international companies that are pushing their version of the iPhone. Now you see why INTJ is looking at this degree. They often hold themselves to a very high standard and that travels well in mega corporations like Google and Amazon. Yet maybe independent INTJ will develop virtual reality without a mega corporation. Media programming applies practical knowledge without the risk of physical failure. Ben Franklin has a smile on his face.

ISTP might want to take up a career in the military. The Navy Reserve Officer Corps fits in well on this campus that honors American presence in the world. This type is a natural troubleshooter when it comes to practical problems. The Economics degree with a concentration in **Actuarial Science** will open rewarding career tracks in weapons development. ISTP goes for machines and moving parts on which to drop their pragmatic numbers and details. In 2014, the administration reduced the DOD budget to pre-WWII levels. Patriotic defense workers hope to reduce government corruption and waste as huge dollar weaponry is contracted out. They can use the support of loyal actuaries like ISTP.

INTP likes to take on studies that others pass up. Neuroengineering and genetic engineering fit in that category. They possess an intense curiosity. The **Bioengineering** disciple in the School of Engineering is more than pretty special. Once again we have the Ben Franklin perspectives influencing the curriculum. After all, how much more practical does it get than working on the artificial heart that could become reality in the near future? There will be two options for INTP after finishing the sophomore year. They can take the BS engineering degree or the more flexible Bachelor of Applied Science which is about going on to medical school or medical research.

ESFP absolutely gets the real world of "what's happening now." There is no fuzzy-headed, wanderlust thread in their observation of the day. U Penn's Wharton School of Business concentration in **Insurance and Risk Management** will take advantage of this skill. This type thrives on interaction with others and a challenge. The detailed study of risk assessment tools will keep ESFP's attention. As a resourceful and realistic personality they want to offer the best products with a flair and a smile also typical of their type. They can recall and juggle large amounts of data. It works in this exacting science. This concentration prepares ESFP to tackle region wide assessments like that generated after the BP oil spill in the gulf. BTW, shrimp are going gang busters since that event.

ESFJ smoothly travels in the world of **Nursing**. The U Penn's Nursing School develops advanced research design that improves nursing practice. Priority one for this type is a healthy, well-functioning, caring environment. The degree in nursing is interdisciplinary and viewed through ethical, wellness and community perspectives. That is unusual in the nursing field. In fact, ESFJ can get a dual degree selecting a second major or minor in the School of Engineering, Business School or College of Arts and Sciences. It is not required though, and this type might want to devote all studies to nursing.

ESTJ is good at spotting inefficiency and impracticality. Yes there is a difference. Ask an ESTJ. They do well as civil servants in city, state or national government.

Fortunately, competent decision making tends to be ESTJ's work style. With the U Penn major in **Urban Studies** this type will gain knowledge and credibility to wield authority in some of the most demanding municipal environments. ESTJ might go to Detroit or Chicago for the required fieldwork in junior year working with a public or independent community group. This internship requires students to attend seminar at U Penn. But perhaps Face Time or Skype could fill this requirement for needed guidance and feedback if ESTJ is in the Midwest. U Penn itself has done an amazing job revitalizing the neighborhoods surrounding the campus. Over-the-top changes in the outdoor physical spaces on campus are pleasant and designed for sustainability.

ENTJ could look at U Penn's Wharton School and settle on **Health Care Management and Policy**. This field offers the complexity and big picture that ENTJs need for satisfaction. It also offers the potential for a spiraling climb to the top in an industry that seems to be very good at spiraling. This type has the acumen to develop successful plans in complex environments. The medical fields of today include artificial hearts, indigent services and technical diagnostics. Executives require sophisticated knowledge of litigation, courage and an absolute moral compass. With the government 2,000 pages of bureaucracies and rulings in Affordable Health Care, there is a very slippery slope to inefficiency and manipulation of the public. ENTJs, with a U Penn degree in this field, will get all the skills to stay upright.

UNIVERSITY OF REDLANDS

1200 East Colton Avenue
Redlands, CA 92373
Website: www.redlands.edu
Admissions Telephone: 800-455-5064
Undergraduates: 3,779; 1,624 Men, 2,155 Women
Graduate Students: 1,554

Physical Environment

Located in the **small town** of Redlands, inland about 60 miles east of the Pacific Ocean, University of Redlands was founded by the American Baptist Convention in 1909. The surrounding ecology gets students to focus on the delicate balance between nature and man. They can be in the semi-arid mountains within minutes for field studies or recreation. The administration understood then and now the **nature of space** and how it plays a critical factor in **shaping human activity**. The lovely cream stucco buildings and red tile roofs at this college speak to nature's beauty. The **Center for Spatial Studies** is a hub for GIS undergraduate research. It is novel and successful at teaching undergrads to look at their field of study through satellite imaging. It applies to all things on earth and is well connected to the older discipline of geography, before environmental studies came along. The Center also highlights **cooperation** and campus-wide planning across the academic departments. Redlands is remarkable for this and it shows up repeatedly, like the student majoring in English who created a multimedia map, using GIS, to present Holocaust survivors' travel and experience after WWII.

The university has always identified with the larger American scene opening its doors to those of all faiths. The spiritual communities are active on campus. U Redlands has also been consistently loyal to American principles and the **American experience** of three centuries. The curriculum is optimistic, exploratory and skill-building for resilience and **patriotic citizenship**. The terrorism spreading across the world in 2014-15 has not directly found its place in the curriculum as of yet. It is highly likely to. However, the students themselves have formed LiNK, Liberty for North Korea and their awareness of critical international issues, in addition to sustainability, is a tribute to the administration.

The **Hunsaker University Center** looks out at the science quad, library and sports complex. It acts as a hub for all the athletically-inclined on this campus. The 24-hour library study lounge with outdoor study nooks and outdoor water polo hint at the combination of fun/learning here. On the other side of the quad, the Johnston School for Integrative Studies is almost a second college within the Redlands campus.

Social Environment

Student life is blended with academic life. The aim of the faculty and administration is to develop students who will choose wisely in a complex world. All students will complete a service learning course or volunteer community project. There is a healthy **entrepreneurial focus** that seeps down from the business school. This approach to enterprise is found in courses across most academic majors. Faculty and administration encourage undergraduates to be successful individuals in enterprise as well as passionate in service. Students on this campus have not made demands or protested about more services for themselves. They are focused outward toward others who have serious needs at local, national and international levels. Most Redlands students care about **social order**, and finding new solutions to old problems. They arrived on campus as leaders of their high school. They are **smart, ready and excited** to start their freshman experience. Slightly more than half of the students identify as a minority.

The **student government** is very active with judicial and executive offices that put on campus arts and entertainment. The residence halls also plan for socials with students and professional staff working together. Each House develops its own **Community Standard**; again students working with staff to create the guidelines. There is a wide variety of housing including California Founders Hall with all-female and all-male communities. There is a lively **Greek community** with chapter houses for the local sororities and fraternities on campus.

The Johnston School students take classes in their own residence hall where they live and self-govern. Their educational experiences is all about creative writing. Once selected for this program, they design their "major" starting with their chosen faculty advisor. Their three-year academic schedule is exploratory and centered on the craft of writing. They will get written evaluations each semester, no grades. But they are not isolated. They take elective courses with grades just on the other side of the quad.

Compatibility with Personality Types and Preferences

University of Redlands does a great job blending order, structure (S), creativity and openness into a strong, consistent campus culture. The environment is comfortable, healthy and energetic. The administration and faculty devote most of their effort and resources toward the learning experience. Faculty are familiar with learning methods and theory for young adult learning. The social experience on this campus takes its direction (J) from the academic life. Students socialize "early and often." Their gatherings (F) are likely to have a couple of purposes, one being beneficial activity. This nicely reflects part of the college mission to develop "circular diversity."

There is just a hint of the Quaker morality on this campus. Productivity at all levels of administration has service for others as a focus. In decades past, the founders hoped to educate students who would come to appreciate other cultures by studying formal belief systems from around the world. The administration and faculty still hold this cross-cultural foundation as uppermost while guiding the student population through their educational studies. At the same time, American culture and heritage is valued and studied for its historical richness and underlying national strength.

PERSONALITY MATCH

ISTJ	ISFJ	INFJ	INTJ
ISTP	ISFP	INFP	INTP
ESTP	ESFP	ENFP	ENTP
ESTJ	ESFJ	ENFJ	ENTJ

Now read below about one of the majors that MBTI® research shows people of your type have selected since the mid-20th century. After, refer to Chapter Five for the 50 or so majors that can help you prepare for careers your type has selected. Most importantly, remember that this college description is a suggestion for exploration, not a commanding order. You can be successful in any major at any college.

ENTP should like the mix of finance and economics. This could lead to a career in investments and U of Redlands offers a BS degree with a major in **Financial Economics**. With first year calculus, ENTP is cleared to move on to upper level courses in Micro and Macroeconomics. The course in Corporate Finance opens the basic understanding of many for profit enterprises. This is critical since liberal arts colleges sometimes move away from enterprise in favor of nonprofit services. Yet many in the job market work at profit-driven businesses like Google, Ford and Disney World. With this preparation, ENTP will follow their keen intuition and entrepreneurial spirit when Redlands faculty tells them to trust their hunches.

ENFJ is a good fit on the Redlands campus. The major in **Government** focuses on the political scene in Washington D.C. The major highlights the impact on ordinary citizens by government bureaucracies and political influence. ENFJ is a heartfelt thinker and may find some of these government programs less helpful after a thorough study. Redlands has historically supported traditional, independent American industry. This type will look to faculty advising to navigate mixed messages from the national media.

ENFP might enjoy the unusual major in **Environmental Business** developed by faculty from both disciplines. Undergrads will explore how large established companies can improve their ecological practices while manufacturing goods or providing services. Think of it as "green business." The growing focus on sustainability is driving worldwide manufacturing concerns to retool or design green initially. ENFP will relate to constant change in this discipline and bring their enthusiasm to partnerships in business. Redlands has excellent training in GIS, a critical skill for this business degree.

INFP is another excellent fit at University of Redlands. In **Creative Writing**, the English department focuses on the process rather than a type of literature like poetry, short stories or theatrical plays. Vision-driven, INFPs march to their own tune during the collegiate years and creative writing can become an expression of their closely held values. The department regularly bumps up its Visiting Speakers Series with artists from out of town. INFP can incorporate their thoughts with noted writers.

INFJ, the deep thinker, may wonder why a minor in **Human Animal Studies**? The answer is careers in wildlife conservation, veterinary medicine, counseling therapy, zoos or wildlife rehabilitation centers. It is also a field that would take them out of their head, reserving some of that deep thinking for their major in the physical sciences. The program is unusual and this original thinker might pick up a second minor in creative writing.

ESFJ wants to get right in the middle of helping others improve. It could be help for a person or a small organization. The BA degree in **Communicative Disorders** prepares for career directions in preschool and elementary special services. The department also offers the Masters degree which is certification for directly providing therapy to individuals. However, independent community programs and nonprofits would hire ESFJ with just the bachelor degree to develop and run programs for at-risk youth in group settings.

ESFP would find the degree in **Business Administration** at U Redlands just the right mix between objective study and humane perspectives. This campus is remark-ably encouraging of experiential learning through the internship, study abroad and travel abroad options in May and the summer. The business curriculum presents the basic business skills in a thorough manner. ESFPs need and crave action so their typi-cal gift of gab with sound business practices might make for VP of Sales within five years at local, regional, national or international corporations. The department has a strong international orientation.

ISFP can definitely find a place at U Redlands and it might just be the **Biology** major. There is a solid pre-med advising program that covers all the bases. Tentative ISFP gets benefit from this one-on-one of advising. The course Observations in the ER will be an excellent learning experience for this type. They naturally take quick decisive action in crisis situations and might cement their choice of medical specialty in Emergency Room.

ISFJ can be generous, giving, helpful and thoughtful. It is great for careers in the health care. The major in **Biochemistry and Molecular Biology** is excellent as an introduction to this new field that mixes chemistry with biology. Professors across the nation refer to it as the intersection between chemistry and biology. This field has grown since the DNA mapping at the turn of the century. It would be ideal for ISFJ to consider a career in genetic counseling that would require advanced graduate study, but less than a medical degree.

UNIVERSITY OF RICHMOND

28 Westhampton Way
Richmond, VA 23173
Website: www.richmond.edu
Admissions Telephone: 804-289-8640
Undergraduates: 2,984; 1,445 Men, 1,539 Women
Graduate Students: 530

Physical Environment

The University of Richmond is nestled into forest and hills with Westhampton Lake at the center of the campus. The campus grounds reveal a **landscaped valley** reminiscent of a country club. The Tyler Haynes Commons is not only a student center, but also functions as a bridge over the ten-acre lake. Students take in the views of water and woods through floor-to-ceiling windows. It's no surprise why this campus is often cited as one of the most beautiful in the U.S.

U Richmond was founded as a Baptist seminary in the 1800s with Westhampton College for women added in 1914 on the opposite side of the lake. In the late 1980s, the university opened the **Jepson School for Leadership** which sought to define leadership through the lens of the humanities. Queally Hall, an important addition to the Robins School of Business, includes a finance trading room. Similarly, the Gottwald Science Center gathered the biology, chemistry and physics departments together offering a remarkable opportunity for research with advanced electronic instruments. There are many **athletic** fields and a sports complex supporting 17 NCAA Division I teams.

Social Environment

This university is flexible with dual degrees, double majors, concentrations and minors in the social sciences, humanities and pure sciences. The faculty were offering **interdisciplinary** learning decades before other colleges formed biology and chemistry into a new major called biochemistry. Undergraduate research here was a way to teach leadership several decades ago too. Again U Richmond was ahead of the learning curve.

Undergraduates recognize the structure and appreciate it, especially because it is structure with flexibility. The **Honor Code** is a defining experience for a U Richmond student. It is completely run by the students and they learn to organize and follow through using their own guidelines. The Honor Code has historical roots with stability. It is a formal document that has been modified over the years by Roberts Rules of Order. Again, here you see the **flexibility and structure existing together**.

Students live in single-gender housing. Each of the 15 halls are self-governing. The traditional dormitories give these youngest of the Millennial generation a breather from the highly sexualized media content that streams across their iPhones today.

Most incoming students plan to take freshmen studies without declaring a major. As freshmen, they will **explore abstraction** and theory in the First Year Seminars by critical reading, thinking and communication around one of the topics offered. In this way, the faculty and administration move students forward to declare a major, hopefully, at the start of the sophomore year. That is when many departments start their sequence of courses. For those still uncertain, there are minors and concentrations to expand the declared major.

It all adds up to a rather intensive collegiate experience intertwining ethics, reality and life for **expectant, optimistic undergrads** who see a lot of advantages in a community that is **cohesive and productive**. Advocacy clubs like Amnesty International are **focused outward** on behalf of others who have serious life issues. SSTOP is the student organization that raises awareness off and on campus about human trafficking. Very few student organizations call attention to this travesty right within America. The fourteen fraternities and sororities offer traditional leadership, service and social activities on campus. Eight Left Feet is a ballroom dancing club that requires no experience to join and our favorite.

Compatibility with Personality Types and Preferences

University of Richmond can be viewed as a study in contrast. Warm, southern grace coexists with a classical, time-honored format for education, yet the administration reacts quickly to the pulse of emerging trends in modern America. Richmond's overall academic philosophy leans toward acquiring evolving knowledge (N) even if it requires rewiring bureaucratic agendas. Yet there is equal value in their history and traditions established by rational thought on the university's founding (T). It is reflected in the two residential colleges—Richmond College for the men and Westhampton College for the women. And so it goes, back and forth, two distinct educational philosophies ruling, depending on the particular department, depending on the need, depending on the individual student declaring a major for undergraduate study.

Some majors are best described as transformative, bold and innovative. Others are conventional in their course curriculum. Here, journalists report the information, aggressively and boldly recording facts that do not look pleasant. Yet they also avoid forcing the reader to adopt a specific viewpoint. It's admirable and uncommon journalism. Above all, U Richmond is an intellectual environment that places the highest priority on acquiring knowledge with traditional respect for the historical institutional practices and codes.

Now read below about one of the majors that MBTI® research shows people of your type have selected since the mid-20th century. After, refer to Chapter Five for the 50 or so majors that can help you prepare for careers your type has selected. Most importantly, remember that this college description is a suggestion for exploration, not a commanding order. You can be successful in any major at any college.

PERSONALITY MATCH			
ISTJ	ISFJ	INFJ	INTJ
ISTP	ISFP	INFP	INTP
ESTP	ESFP	ENFP	ENTP
ESTJ	ESFJ	ENFJ	ENTJ

ISTJ who appreciates the tried-and-true could go for the **Accounting** major. The mind of a typical ISTJ is almost computer-like. Their ability to take in and use information will be perfect for this traditional discipline. ISTJs often are rather private individuals who appreciate the confidentiality required in the accounting world. This type sees the asterisks and actually reads the fine print at the bottom of the page. U Richmond undergraduate study in the business curriculum is equally precise. The department stresses the theory behind accounting and its many purposes.

ISFJ talented in the arts will do well in Richmond's strong **Studio Arts** department. Undergraduate students will be exposed to a broad spectrum of art techniques and mediums. At the conclusion of four years, ISFJs entering career tracks in the arts will have a strong collection of work for their portfolio. The art department faculty is culturally rich with one professor documenting the condition of the declining arts in Sarajevo after the 1992-95 Bosnian civil war in which 8,000 Muslim men were killed. ISFJ will find this sobering and supportive of revealing their own emotions in their artistic work.

INFJ can go for careers in business if people-oriented in actual practice on the job. The **Management** concentration in the Robins School of Business works for them. The curriculum allows INFJ to get the building blocks of entrepreneurship in place first. The department centers much around ethics in leadership and decision making. Combined with a major in Economics, INFJ could consult in human resources and help activate new business lines that require refocusing employee qualifications.

INTJ is an independent, quiet leader more often than not. Richmond has two rather nice options for this type who thinks big and original. The **Military Science and Leadership** program of studies has a long, successful history. It is part of Army ROTC which leads to a commission as a second lieutenant on gradation. INTJ could major in any degree offered at UR, with a full scholarship. The **International Studies Concentration in Africa** makes sense because the continent is pivotal with national instability and China's increasing investment in certain African nations. As a military intelligence expert or foreign service officer in the state department, INTJ will bring value in this field.

INTP gets the intellectual freedom they want with the **Economics** major in the School of Arts and Sciences. The curriculum focuses on economic theory, business economics, international economics, public policy and quantitative economics. This wide-ranging major suits independent, pattern-oriented INTP with options and wiggle room to exercise their global curiosity. For the occasional INTP who might want to open up their own business, the Business School offers the BSBA in economics also.

ENTP who looks closely at **Rhetoric and Communication Studies** could declare this major. The coursework should appeal to this critical thinker. Contemporary Oral Argumentation will help them soften their sometimes abrupt tones as they put a position out there. Add in the minor in **Leadership Studies** and you will have a very competent, powerful ENTP change agent. The major is rarely offered and comes from the traditional educational perspective of the university.

ENTJ will find the **Marketing** concentration very handy for their entrepreneurial dreams. The Business school offers this concentration with their **Accounting** major. With a minor in **leadership**, ENTJ would have a tidy resume for graduation. After several years with a national business consulting firm, this type might enter corporate business as an accountant with visions of CEO. The school focuses on preparation to land a lead assignment immediately after graduation.

ESTJ has what it takes to make an effective parole officer, and U Richmond has the **Criminal Justice** major. The degree surveys the effects of crime on society and reasons behind criminal behavior. The Virginia Victim Assistance Academy is an unusual resource not often available to students entering this career track. As an undergraduate degree, the major can lead to immediate employment or be a strong stepping stone to graduate study in criminal justice, public administration, social work, sociology or law. Ever mindful, practical ESTJ will narrow down the choice early in their studies at U Richmond.

UNIVERSITY OF SOUTHERN CALIFORNIA

University Park
Los Angeles, CA 90089
Website: www.usc.edu
Admissions Telephone: 213-740-2311
Undergraduates: 18,740; 9,285 Men, 9,455 Women
Graduate Students: 22,729

Physical Environment

The USC campus in **metropolitan Los Angeles** is surrounded by the glitz of nearby beaches, high-end shopping and legendary film-production houses so students get familiar with **public transportation choices**. It takes about one-and-a-half hours to travel by train, bus, taxi or rental car from the LAX airport to USC. It is a tight, **compact**, campus with yet another transportation maze. Good old-fashioned foot traffic or bicycles are the best choice but you will see the occasional car driving by looking for a parking space.

The residence halls on campus are divided into five communities, each with a different lifestyle. One has the lectures, arts, music and philanthropy. Another has world cultural programs. The North and South communities divide up the social calendar and host events for all undergraduates. The university has a **national reputation** in a lot of categories. It is a leader in digital records and digital representations of information, think Hollywood. But the one many know about is Trojans Football which makes USC an **athletic powerhouse**. The weather and emphasis on sports encourage lively activity on campus at all hours of the day and night.

The national research labs are designed for the USC **innovative, independent professors**. Knowledge is defined as translational in the 2011 USC Strategic Plan. That means USC faculty follow research design for the purpose of global citizenship. What might be the purpose of global citizenship knowledge? It might be the discovery and initiation of products and services for all humans on earth. Regardless, it is a lofty goal.

In 2016, there are **many multimillion dollar projects** across the campus in the schools of business, cinema, dance, sciences, journalism and more. To get into more detail about the massive research commitment, you can click on USC research and find centers categorized by subject area and alphabetized too. Without bothering to count it looks like there are close to 100 **mega research centers**.

Social Environment

The 18,000+ students on campus make up a **dynamic** student body with 60 percent identifying as a minority. This campus attracts those who get along well in a large community filled with very different talents and social styles. Students are vibrant and place equal value on **social learning** and academic learning. In the perfect location for interdisciplinary studies, USC is a powerhouse of ideas on the **Pacific Rim**. The pre-professional programs and business school pull in practical types who value traditional careers that are in demand. Here also, the **amazing research labs** give students awareness of emerging knowledge as assistants and contributors. **Internships** in metropolitan LA offer just about any experience you can dream up. There are the pure sciences, think Lockheed Martin, and the entertainment, think Disney and Los Angeles Rams, yes they're back. Business enterprise and political leadership will form around L.A.'s bid for the 2024 Olympics. Driven by an economy with few jobs for them, the human services for lower class, indigent and struggling middle class families occupy the opposite end of this spectrum.

In the evening, students are outside, talking, walking and playing pickup games. The dormitories are contemporary, functional in design. Housing is guaranteed to all freshmen and returning sophomores. Within the five residential communities, there are eight Residential Colleges. All of these are governed by the **Residential Student Government** which offers a whole lot of leadership positions and points back to the social learning that these undergraduates expect. The RSG essentially runs the social action on this campus. They plan celebrations for American traditions like Mardi Gras for all to attend. The dormitory also has professional staff and live-in faculty but they do not have the heavy hand of social control we have observed at a few other prestigious places.

USC is **exceptionally well-managed** with written charters published as PDF files on the USC website. There is little confusion about the purpose of the residential life in this high-density living community. Administration and faculty provide the structure and they expect the students to provide the leadership and energy to do the rest. The Middle East crisis in 2012 generated student protests for both Israeli and Palestinian positions. The administration, citing safety concerns, ushered the opposing sides away from the area with the use of the landscaping crew that came to redesign the square. In 2014 students questioned the bookstore policy on T-shirt procurement in third world countries. The administration published their procurement history of the T-shirts in a PDF file and posted it on the website.

Compatibility with Personality Types and Preferences

Wow is the word that comes to mind when thinking of USC. Also independence, dynamic and invention become part of a good description. Here, intellectual and physical energy combine and the product mirrors thriving, spontaneous Los Angeles (E). Educational philosophy focused on research at the university level drives and definitely rules this huge collegiate community in a studied way. There is a magnetic-like attraction to the unknown (N) that seeps out of the labs and travels into the undergraduate experience. There seems to be an institutional mandate to transform the boundaries of human knowledge.

The undergraduate students themselves are expected to actively push forward after graduation contributing as global citizens. They arrive as freshmen who are ready, smart, independent, expectant and optimistic. A review of the USC catalog reveals that critical thinking (T) and logical, disciplined approaches to learning are the favorite learning tools. Students are good with the incredible number of majors, minors and concentrations on this campus made available with their undergraduate degrees (S). They are resilient and able to access the many offices and professional mentors for guidance for their career direction after graduation.

Of equal importance, the undergraduate student body mirrors the administration's concern for others within the larger community. The Engemann Student Health Center is both caring and rational in its delivery of services to the young undergraduate students. This predisposition for noticing and caring about others seems to extend to visitors, employees, scientists, inventors and other individuals who find themselves on this campus for a few hours or a career (F).

Now read below about one of the majors that MBTI® research shows people of your type have selected since the mid-20th century. After, refer to Chapter Five for the 50 or so majors that can help you prepare for careers your type has selected. Most importantly, remember that this college description is a suggestion for exploration, not a commanding order. You can be successful in any major at any college.

PERSONALITY MATCH			
ISTJ	ISFJ	INFJ	INTJ
ISTP	ISFP	INFP	INTP
ESTP	ESFP	ENFP	ENTP
ESTJ	ESFJ	ENFJ	ENTJ

ESFJ will get the purpose of **Health Promotion and Disease Prevention Studies** from the words alone. This type is responsible and supports following the rules. The "shoulds" and "should nots" in human health care are covered in the course Theoretical Principles of Health Behavior. This type has a good amount of empathy for others in trouble. They find answers in courses like Social Exclusion, Social Power and Deviance. Their loyal nature is an anchor for patients and peers in large and small health organizations.

INFJ is quietly persistent and powerful with their gift of insight. The **Biophysics** undergraduate degree on this campus is going to use these INFJ talents. Introduction to Quantum Mechanics and Its Applications is a course that could launch INFJs into the world of graduate research. One of many research strands is that of Space Science where faculty is studying atomic processes and molecular gasses in the spectral region of extreme ultraviolet through infrared rays. So there, how about those rays.

INTJ who likes both creativity and computers will have to find those pathways that straight line data bits permit creativity to squeak through. The stable nature of physics won't be much more accommodating either. But in the USC undergraduate degree in **Physics/Computer Science** there might be enough wiggle room for INTJ's original ideas. Its solid coursework in math, computing and physics helps with the senior Final Project. Maybe this project will move along the lines of current USC high performance programming for massively parallel machines. We suspicion that physicists who detected gravitational waves from a black hole merger recorded in February 2016 were using a little of that massively parallel machine capability.

INFP can drop into the **Health and Humanity** undergraduate degree and search for life's meaning during four undergraduate years. They could clarify their possible contribution to the field by taking bioethics, aging, ethnicity, the mind and biology. The department requires two thematic modules and INFP might go for Health/Aging and Health/The Mind. The abstract nature of these two lets them focus on human potential and that is a very comfortable place to be for this type. The Armenian

Diaspora Community in Southern California, a short Maymester course, offered Spring 2016, sits well with this degree.

INTP is drawn to complicated patterns. Complex, large systems with incoming random data gives them a chance to unravel riddles. The unusual minor at USC in **Operations and Supply Chain Management** introduces numerical volume at imaginable levels. Think what could happen if even half of the 4,000 fuel pumps on all the 737 airliners started leaking in the same month. There could be fuel puddles at the waiting gates of the national and international airports. That is not the problem though. How do you get parts to all the mechanics to change it out on the flightline? By the way, don't disrupt the airline schedules. INTP can function and stand up to the intense pressure that always surrounds these decisions.

ENFP doesn't like to make a decision too soon. In the **Policy, Planning and Development** degree they can take elective coursework across health, sustainable planning, real estate development, law and social innovations. ENFP is in a perfect place at USC with this degree. Los Angeles has it all. The city is rich with human resources, physical infrastructure and intellectual potential. After graduation, this type might just work in each area through multiple career progressions. This will keep ENFP's need for variety and interest pretty well satisfied.

ENTP with a flair for business will want to take USC's cool minor, the **Pacific Rim**. It could pair up with a major in communication or business. Either way, it gives this type the elbow room they want in their studies. ENTP can see into the future spot-on if they have developed the intellectual discipline to filter their insight. USC will help them with the filter part. ENTP will reciprocate with original essays for courses like Global Strategy. But this type needs to learn how to write during the first two years of college or they will suffer grade-wise in their written work.

ENTJ who is not majoring in business but wants to pick up the basic tools should look at the minor in **Organizational Leadership and Management** at USC. Three classes in particular should call out to this type: Power, Politics and Influence, Designing and Leading Teams and The Art and Adventure of Leadership. This last course is probably their motto and they should wear it on a T-shirt.

ENFJ has a vibrant humor that audiences love. The undergraduate degree in **Communication** will let ENFJ fine tune their natural charisma. The sophomore course in Public Speaking is rock solid at USC. The art of presentation is part of the Los Angeles entertainment culture dating from the first talkies through to *Star Wars - The Force Awakens*. This type is likely to be a social science or humanities major, so the courses in this minor will be a nice addition and change from their usual focus in the helping professions.

ESFP is going to love the Bachelor of Science in **Arts, Technology and Business Innovation** at USC. It is a excellent example of the university's transformative and translational knowledge. Okay, forget those words. It means that the curriculum will come from the departments of business venture management, design, engineering and computer science. It is team taught and interdisciplinary. At this university, this personality type, this degree, this location points to career directions that are loaded with potential.

ESTP is going to thrive with the day-to-day action of a career in real estate. USC rolled out a new Bachelor of Science degree in **Real Estate**. This university has the resources to quickly reorient faculty and content that matches the needs of society. The city of Los Angeles is a natural laboratory for ESTP, an easy-going and natural networker. To get started they can drive around the metropolitan area to catalog different kinds of infrastructure. It will take a GPS, good driving skills and about 10 months to understand L.A. But ESTP can handle the drive with skill, acquire L.A. acumen and professionally move on to any other American metropolis.

ISTP can select a minor in **Construction Planning and Management** and be successful in technical business environments. The studies in this minor include management of resources and reading the political tea leaves in how resources get divided up. This type is best, without equal, in the application of technology in a production schedule. But this minor helps them with the planning and management that they don't come by naturally. With this in place, ISTPs can be exceptionally effective in an industrial setting.

UNIVERSITY OF TAMPA

401 West Kennedy Boulevard
Tampa, FL 33606-1490
Website: www.ut.edu
Admissions Telephone: 813-253-6211, 888-MINARET
Undergraduates: 6,823; 3,002 Men, 3,821 Women

Physical Environment

Imagine leaving the business district of Tampa, crossing the bridge of the **intercoastal waterway** and then coming upon a palace with wrap-around verandahs, honeycombed archways and minarets on the roof. You will be looking at Historic Plant Hall, UT's admissions and administration center. UT is oriented outward and internationally. There are many internships located overseas. There are actual class trips that travel overseas. There are new majors coming on line that reflect international concerns like the **cyber security major** in the Business school.

New dormitories, open in 2014 and 2015, are **minimalist** in design. They are spacious and just about what young professionals would rent in cosmopolitan communities. However, housing is tight on campus and is reserved for incoming students. Major construction, cranes and new facilities have defined campus for about ten years now. The Student Health Center is not easily matched by most colleges of similar size. The newest UT nursing laboratories include sophisticated simulation equipment. The academic buildings completed in 2010 dramatically expanded the life science curriculum. The athletic complex functions as a sports showcase for past and present UT athletes. It is also a medical clinic, training facility, conference and banquet space, not to mention indoor courts for student hoops. Even extension to the parking lot in 2015 hoisted the Entrepreneurship Center to the top floor with more classrooms and faculty offices tucked around the corner. UT also operates a **financial trading room** that gives business majors real experience. There really isn't much old here with the one exception of Historic Plant Hall.

Social Environment

University of Tampa is a good fit for those students who want to continue their solid high school academic and extracurricular experience. Students are mindful of social media and outgoing here. Ready for the next level of education, they are expectant and ready to **absorb instruction**. Students get in on the **latest trends** in arts and culture. They come from New England and the Midwest, about one half are from Florida and approximately 40 percent identify as minority. The Greek fraternities and sororities are popular on campus, providing outlets for service, leadership and socials. The students at UT are just a bit more on the city sophisticate side than the typical first year student in college. Many activities are held on campus since the surrounding neighborhood is mostly conference hotels. Division II UT teams compete very well and often place in their sport, like 2014 Division title holders in women's volleyball.

AT UT the faculty and administration carefully shape programs and policies. However, historically there has been no spiritual presence on campus. In 2010 the Sykes Chapel and Center for Faith and Values was dedicated. This transformation in spirituality came through the guidance of the Chicago-based, nonprofit Interfaith Youth Core, a partner of the Department of Education.[82] In 2009, UT's Resource Team cast a vision for the Chapel that incorporated existing university values and goals into new three learning domains. During the process, College deans were asked to nominate faculty who were opposed to the new Center and they were recruited to the Resource Team.[83] Two years later, Eboo Patel, founder and executive director of the Core, spoke in Sykes Chapel, acknowledging the university for acting as a pilot for the Chicago-based nonprofit.[84] Some in the theological community question this nonprofit.[85] Training undergraduates from across the nation in the Interfaith Youth Core program, Better Together, a recent blogger spoke of its emphasis to voice religious or non-religious values and engage others to act together according to their common values.[86] Mindful of its nonsectarian policy, UT supports Better Together's dialogue, education and advocacy.[87]

Undergraduate students at UT experience an **intensive, solid program in writing** that introduces the reasoning skills needed on this **reality-based**, hands-on campus. Faculty is devoted to **current content and trends** in their field. The students expect to step into professional settings after graduation. Faculty and administration philosophy present a curriculum with experiential learning and service learning for the purpose of personal development. Professors and undergraduates meet in **strong mentoring** sessions. Relationships are the primary vehicle for learning alongside the actual curriculum.

Compatibility with Personality Types and Preferences

At UT, there is a strong focus to move successfully and directly into the future workplace. It results in practical, cutting-edge knowledge (S). The faculty is devoted to providing high quality experiential learning. To this end, there is an attraction to technology and the faculty assertively introduces its use across the curriculum. Mindful of the global marketplace of ideas and employment, they bring outside experts early and often to the campus or forge international internship agreements with partners overseas. With a great number of cultural perspectives on this campus, there is easy awareness and sensitivity that translates into serving the community. It all serves to encourage orderly (J), methodical perspectives and pragmatic academic majors at UT. The international presence of the city draws from many differing backgrounds and they blend their outlooks and expectations giving a trendy, energized feel to this campus. They focus on getting prepared for the next step and the atmosphere on campus is professional in its own way.

PERSONALITY MATCH			
ISTJ	ISFJ	INFJ	INTJ
ISTP	ISFP	INFP	INTP
ESTP	ESFP	ENFP	ENTP
ESTJ	ESFJ	ENFJ	ENTJ

Now read below about one of the majors that MBTI® research shows people of your type have selected since the mid-20th century. After, refer to Chapter Five for the 50 or so majors that can help you prepare for careers your type has selected. Most importantly, remember that this college description is a suggestion for exploration, not a commanding order. You can be successful in any major at any college.

ISTJ will like the direct nature of instruction in the **Criminology** major, especially the Criminology Scholars' Program. This very exacting type prefers to cover all the bases. The annual Scholars Seminar presented by a local area expert in the field could find this type sitting in the front row, diligently taking notes. The department also offers a bachelor degree in **Forensic Science** which, as with most majors on this campus, has excellent job prospects on graduation. UT is ideal for the investigative sciences with its strong international presence and environment.

ESTP with an interest in athletics could excel in the field of **Sport Management**. Tampa's Sport Management curriculum provides undergraduate students with a good exposure to all of the academic disciplines that intersect the billion dollar sports industry—finance, economics, media, fund raising, event management, stadium management, legal issues and the list goes on. This popular major has 250 students and ESTP, good with large bustling settings, will start to build their personal network with these peers.

ESFP will like the variety and action in the **Marine Science Biology** major. ESFPs, often possessing a vibrant personality, would be ideal ambassadors in wildlife conservation. UT has a waterfront laboratory about 20 minutes from campus. Students stop in to gear up for field studies around the Florida keys. It is also a research lab for faculty and students alike.

ESTJ could be very comfortable with the major titled **Financial Enterprise Systems**. At UT, the focus is toward a comprehensive exploration of the markets and regulating institutions. UT faculty are educating undergraduates to take on functions in the 21st century. It is not surprising that this major features accounting principles and practices as well as finance. Since ESTJs are natural administrators, they will be more than capable of directing action in the fast-paced financial world.

ESFJ could go for the **Human Performance** degree. It is centered on individual physical fitness. This type's strong sense of responsibility and genuine caring for others fits in nicely with this degree. It is ideal for immediate, meaningful employment as wellness directors, private trainers and fitness technicians at exercise centers across the country. The degree can also be a solid stepping stone for graduate studies in allied health fields, also a favorite occupation for this type.

ENFJ often builds consensus with ease. They are attracted to potential and their strong people-centered values connect with the major in **Government and World Affairs**. International organizations might tap into ENFJ's strengths as a new manager of direct service programs in third world countries. Turning the Possible into the Probable is the motto on their T-shirt. But before any of this, ENFJ must select a concentration from American Government, Law and Government, World Affairs or General Government.

ISFJ often appreciative of the arts might look at the BA degree in Art with concentration in **Art Therapy**. This is an unusual degree but the faculty prepares graduates for entrance into a Master's degree program that will lead to national certification. ISFJ is a behind-the-scenes innovator who will work well with young clients in therapeutic settings. Some children with serious trauma will respond only to certain types of therapy, and art therapy is one of them.

VALPARAISO UNIVERSITY

Office of Admission
Valparaiso, IN 46383-6493
Website: www.valpo.edu
Admissions Telephone: 219-464-5011; 888-468-2576
Undergraduates: 3,260; 1,573 Men, 1,677 Women
Graduate Students: 1,256

Physical Environment

Valparaiso means "Vail of paradise." The university, located in the city of its name, population 33,000, is about 75 miles southeast of Chicago. The architecture on this campus reminds you of the elongated, horizontal lines of Frank Lloyd Wright. The campus buildings are **golden** in color, **striking, functional and flat** as they sit on the campus horizon. Surrounded by mid-20th century homes, each different than the other, and well-cared for yards, Valpo is in a comparatively safe residential neighborhood. Students can take a bus, train or limo from the Chicago or Midway airport. On campus, they use bicycles in good weather and take the campus bus in bad weather. Occasionally you will see zip cars on campus.

The **Chapel of the Resurrection**, of prairie-style architecture, is a clear **moral reference point** on this campus, where it marks the physical and emotional center of the college. The Fites Engineering Innovation Center is designed for undergraduates with laboratories and learning spaces. The **Harre Union** centralizes student services and is a fave campus meeting spot, if for no other reason than the campus dining options are here. The Union has performance spaces and many student offices and services. Christopher Center in the Library is the other place to catch a bite and crash in the **24-hour study lounge**. There are nine residence halls with traditional dormitory-style doubles, singles, suites and apartments. When the campus starts to close in, students head up to Chicago or travel to the near-by beaches of Lake Michigan in the early fall or late spring.

Social Environment

The **ethical underpinnings** on this **Lutheran** campus stand out as a big part of the undergraduate social and academic experience. Many students attend **candlelight evening** or morning prayer since about one-third are Lutheran and 20 percent are Catholic. The Global Leaders living and learning community brings awareness of international cultural values to the campus. The core curriculum explores multiple ethnic cultures within the United States. **Initiative and leadership** usually top off the day once academic study is done. The **elected student council** administers the Honor Code and Student Activities budget. Student athletes are in charge of the intramural and recreational teams. The **Crusaders** are really big at Valpo. About 20 percent of undergrads compete in Division I Athletics. Many of the students are **musically talented** and join campus ensembles, jazz, hip hop or groups to perform in the Harre Union.

Student organizations and events usually have some element of volunteering or service too. In 2015, the inaugural Dance Marathon raised $10,000 for charity.

Fraternities and sororities also take on large community service initiatives. Pretty much all of the professors tailor **service learning** for their undergraduates, occasionally overseas, but often for the benefit of local neighborhoods.

Two-thirds of the student body is from the Midwest states, those states of the Mississippi River basin and others from New York, California, Colorado and Texas. Students are attracted to the **pre-professional** programs in business, engineering and nursing. Many expect to secure a job on graduation and get involved with community leadership at some level. **Midwestern** values of efficiency and hard work are alive and well at Valparaiso University.

Compatibility with Personality Types and Preferences

Two abstract principles consistently hover over the Valparaiso University campus. Faith and learning move together within this realistic community and within each individual student. Learning takes off for first year students with expectations that undergraduates will ethically define their understanding of the world. Despite this very conceptual expectation, Valparaiso is quite grounded in the here and now. The administration philosophy strongly supports practical, realistic learning experience (S) through internships, projects and competitions. Technology is embraced and ever present on the campus along with faith. Student organizations and student behavior adopt a consistent emphasis on service and caring (F), yet the campus is full of activity and fun also. At Valpo, students are interacting with each other on a continual basis (E). The arts, athletics, service, learning, spiritual study and dorm confabs can all be silly or serious. In this lighthearted and honest environment, the administration expects both faith and learning will develop serving both the graduating students and the Valpo campus that they will shape in the passing four years.

Now read below about one of the majors that MBTI® research shows people of your type have selected since the mid-20th century. After, refer to Chapter Five for the 50 or so majors that can help you prepare for careers your type has selected. Most importantly, remember that this college description is a suggestion for exploration, not a commanding order. You can be successful in any major at any college.

PERSONALITY MATCH

ISTJ	ISFJ	INFJ	INTJ
ISTP	ISFP	INFP	INTP
ESTP	ESFP	ENFP	ENTP
ESTJ	ESFJ	ENFJ	ENTJ

ENTJ is busy preparing for leadership at reality-based Valparaiso. The major in **American Studies** centers on the philosophical underpinnings of American society. The ENTJ who wants to move into a career associated with government will have a very sound understanding of our nation. Course electives point to the balanced nature of the academic philosophies on this campus. Three courses deal directly with critical turning points in the nation: the Revolutionary Period, Civil War and Reconstruction and Depression and War 1929-1945. It seems so evident that this would be available to students at all liberal arts colleges electing to America Studies, but it is not the case. Many colleges shape this major through a particular filter of their choice—be it ecology, ethnicity, gender or economics. ENTJ will have a balanced view of the nation at Valpo, with its failures and successes.

ESTJ could use the knowledge gained in Valpo's **Actuarial Sciences** major with a career in corporate finance or insurance. This type is comfortable with facts and the expectation of decision. The world of high finance definitely fits this description. ESTJ is not fatigued with responsibility. In this major, they will learn to put a dollar figure on future risks. Now that could be a big responsibility if you are writing up a bond for an electron microscope at the Los Alamos National Laboratories.

ESTP is a natural for Valpo's **Sports Management** major. This major requires a minor in **Fundamentals of Business** or **Business Administration**. Some students will go for a double degree or a double minor. Valpo is okay with each of these. The courses Psychology of Sport and Sport and Society help ESTP understand their role in management as a promoter or as the public contact for parents enrolling junior for little league baseball. After graduation ESTP will look to youth sports, corporate positions, college athletics, amateur sports or professional sports. In each setting, business savvy will keep ESTP on the management team. The major is offered by the Department of Kinesiology and really adds quality elective courses.

ESFP takes kindly to helping others through informal chit chat. The concentration in **Criminology** is a good choice for this type sympathetic to young children and adolescents. The course in Urban Sociology sends on-the-go ESFP to nearby Chicago. Here they will find internships with community organizations. Chicago's Southside neighborhood has suffered from decades of distrust and hopelessness. ESFP with foundations of the Lutheran faith will bring a Christian perspective and could coordinate with faith-based communities in the neighborhood on service research.

ISFP has a technical side to their personality and Valpo has the right degree and approach for this type who would like a career in **Civil Engineering**. ISFPs enjoy being out of doors. The practical courses in geotechnical, structural transportation, water resources engineering and environment protection appeal to this type. ISFPs prefer to leave abstraction stuck between the pages of books located on library shelves. The senior project will put this Type, often a bit too humble about their skills, together with peers to design, build, test and evaluate a project, all within a realistic budget.

ENFJ doesn't usually go for economics, but might look twice at the Valpo major **International Economics and Cultural Affairs**. The department approaches the economics through a people perspective. Students will also take advanced foreign language courses from a region that they choose in Europe, East Asia or Latin America. The department focuses on redistribution of resources designed for certain social outcomes. ENFJ will learn to evaluate success and failure of these social programs through theological, moral reasoning. They will survey the realistic limits of the courts, government, business and nongovernmental organizations.

ISTJ will like the field of accounting because it is so very fact-based. This type is a mastermind with data and will not shrink from the idea of the certified public accountant exam after graduation. Their own thoroughness and follow through pretty much points to a "pass." ISTJ can choose from two options at Valpo. The Bachelor or Business with a major in **Accounting** plus the second major qualifies to sit for the CEP exam. For impatient ISTJs, although there are not very many, this is more focused and completed in four years. A second choice that qualifies for the CEP exam is to take the BBA with the major in accounting followed by a Masters in Accounting, also at Valpo. Either way, they will learn in a realistic internship. Okay, maybe this is too much information. Think of it as a 4 year or 5 year path to the CEP exam.

ISFJ supervises with the people as number one priority. Add in their wry sense of humor, and they have a great start for the **Management** major in Valpo's College of Business. After all who wouldn't want a boss like this? The department has a business core on the principles and tools of enterprise. Later courses then follow with a focus on ethics, communication and problem solving. The business background will move ISFJ toward staff positions. They might advise employees on the nature of their performance or be advising higher execs on sustainability issues in manufacturing. Either way, ISFJ will be people-focused.

ESFJ is often gifted with the art of conversation. They are good listeners too, paying attention, organizing and storing up the information. The major at Valparaiso in **Marketing** at the College of Business will use all of this when students research and develop promotion strategies for nearby businesses. Valpo has that layer of ethics and loyalty that traditional ESFJ will like. With social media streaming across iPhones continuously, more corporations are looking to new practices like eco-friendly manufacture and promotion that sits within Christian morality. Caring ESFJs will find this is just the right approach to marketing.

VANDERBILT UNIVERSITY

2201 West End Avenue
Nashville, TN 37325
Website: www.vanderbilt.edu
Admissions Telephone: 800-288-0432
Undergraduates: 6,851; 3,426 Men, 3,425 Women
Graduate Students: 5,835

Physical Environment

Vanderbilt University, just a mile from Music City in downtown Nashville, was founded by **Commodore Cornelius Vanderbilt**. Today, we all just call it "Vandy." The Commodore wanted this college to be an intellectual center for the region and the nation, with powerful connections to industry. Ironically, there has never been a College of Business at Vanderbilt. The university moved toward enterprise formally with the 2016 opening of the Innovation Center. It is the place for all faculty and students with an idea that could play out in private commerce. The Center has primary focus in two Vandy areas of expertise, **education and health care**. Vanderbilt **research** is always pushing the state-of-the-art in human health, presently working on the artificial kidney.

Historically, the university has supported American perspectives of world leadership and continues to do so at regional levels. In response to the Islamic State, ISIS terrorism of 2014-15, the School of Engineering joined private industry to develop cyber-security training for information systems. It will be for IT managers at federal, state and local levels of law enforcement. Historic American global influence is found in the **Vanderbilt Television News Archive** with abstracts of all network newscasts since 1968. The Blair School of Music echoes the overall Vanderbilt heritage, providing an education that has traditional heritage while honoring artistic innovation. Nashville's booming music industry also calls out the rich musical heritage of the surrounding Appalachian Hills.

The campus sits in the middle of the **arboretum** of huge magnolias and oaks, tying together a varied architecture, from Victorian, mid-20th century to current day modern. The **sprawling landscape** finds multi-story student housing across the campus. The Sarratt Student Center is the social hub for campus with student services, outdoor seating and plenty of snack shops. The Recreation Center at other side of campus is huge and offers programs across all ages, intramurals, classes and athletics. First year housing is close by and with many snack shops in the dorms and with this gym, first years have to be happy. On the north boundary of campus, students navigate a busy four-lane road. They are warmly welcomed in the many eateries, pubs and coffee shops with summer ice-creams by curb-side. This is where students can find a bit of the Americana without the carefully planned collegiate environment.

Social Environment

Vandy undergraduates often come from well-funded public or independent schools. Their resumes show high school extracurriculars and participation in community arts, service and athletics. One-third of the students are from the southern states, one-third from the Midwest and the remaining from the east and west coasts. Forty percent identify as a minority. Undergraduates are tuned into the social problems streaming across their iPads and the national news media. They find Vanderbilt faculty have both conservative and progressive social perspectives. In January 2015 students protested against a senior professor lecturing on the Charlie Hebdo attacks. Citing freedom of speech, in November 15 the administration resisted escalating demands by students to condemn her.[88]

Intramurals, club sports and cheering for the 'Dores are popular on campus along with social activities provided by the university. Yet, the mild winter weather, handsome campus, canopies of shade in the Arboretum and Nashville's social vibrancy are memorable. The order of business when class lets out in the extended spring and fall afternoons finds the 'Dores relaxing in the day and each other's company on this **social campus** of southern historical friendliness.

All freshmen live in the Ingram Commons within one of 10 houses. For all others, the university supports learning-living communities often based on academic interests and sponsored by academic departments. All sophomores, juniors and seniors must petition to live off campus. Presently there is a lottery for the few permitted off campus spaces. Fourth Fridays are student talent shows in the Sarratt Lounge budgeted by the Residential Life program. **Greek fraternities and sororities** offer independent leadership experience, service and socials for all to attend.

Bright, **high-performing and expectant**, undergraduates step up to the **academic demands**. Many intend to go on to graduate studies. Research is the historical backbone of Vanderbilt and administration philosophy orients undergraduate research primarily through the summer research program. Faculty actively bring their current research findings forward to the undergraduate students through the curriculum and upper level student independent studies.

Compatibility with Personality Types and Preferences

Vanderbilt students acquire state-of-the-art knowledge in their chosen discipline during their four years on campus. The educational philosophy is intensely focused on this drive for excellence. Acquiring and refining knowledge (T) is priority number one. The basic foundation courses in each discipline are very strong (S). Students log conventional time with their iPads reading in the humanities, arts and social sciences. In the physical sciences they take pencils to paper pads learning formulaic reasoning or activate their calculators. After the extensive core of liberal arts courses and department required courses (J), independent studies follow in the senior year. The curriculum is loaded with observation and skill-building in the social sciences. In the pure sciences, the undergraduate research is competitive. A few students with graduate school in mind are brought into the labs to assist professors in their research. The student body is quite energized (E) and well-organized. They actively define their own social experience with the participation of the residential life programmatic structures. They are civically-minded young adults who were active in high school service and will remain so throughout life.

Now read below about one of the majors that MBTI® research shows people of your type have selected since the mid-20th century. After, refer to Chapter Five for the 50 or so majors that can help you prepare for careers your type has selected. Most importantly, remember that this college description is a suggestion for exploration, not a commanding order. You can be successful in any major at any college.

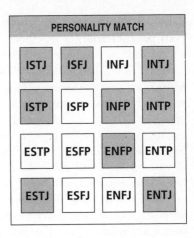

PERSONALITY MATCH

ISTJ	ISFJ	INFJ	INTJ
ISTP	ISFP	INFP	INTP
ESTP	ESFP	ENFP	ENTP
ESTJ	ESFJ	ENFJ	ENTJ

ISTJ is a natural administrator who wants to be totally prepared for leadership if a position should come their way. Vanderbilt has the best major for getting ISTJ ready. The major in **Human and Organizational Development** starts with effective management skills in analysis, technology communication and organizational development. The Education Policy Track goes on to prepare ISTJ for positions in consulting, research, charter schools and metropolitan school districts. But first ISTJ will become familiar with educational policy through the social, political and economic filters common in America today.

ISTP could find the **Biomedical Engineering** degree at Vandy fascinating. The course in Foundations of Medical Imaging is a study of technical absorption, reflection and scattering of energy. It is basic knowledge if you are going on to take the later electives in biophotonics, tissue engineering or imaging. The precise technical methods in this degree appeal to unemotional ISTP. It has the reality factor that is necessary for them to stay interested. Vandy's exceptional engineering college developed this degree in the mid-1960s and it has been state-of-the-art ever since.

ESTJ can pick up management credentials at Vandy through the minor in **Scientific Computing**. It combines with the **Biomedical Engineering** degree and prepares this type to follow their inclination to take charge while clearing up shades-of-gray imaging results. Given this, ESTJ might take undergraduate research for credit during the senior year and apply some of their new computational skills from this minor. ESTJ could get real project management experience with big data problems that show up in advanced bioengineering study. Or they might just head for medical school.

ISFJ is a gentle soul and will be most welcome in the **Child Studies** major. At Vandy, students study childhood up to adult years. Key studies in this major are in developmental psychology, language and learning. ISFJ will be fascinated with human development. It speaks to their very rich personal perspectives. The degree is intended for advanced study in psychology, education, child advocacy and pediatric nursing. Through their understanding and preference for realistic approaches this type becomes excellent at management positions in the field.

INFP might like to use their long-range vision throughout a career. The major in **Early Childhood Education** focuses on thinking and reasoning in toddlers and early childhood. It will require that ability to look at developing sensory awareness of the toddler brain. They will bring this information into educational practice. As a double major with **Communication of Science and Technology**, INFP will pick up skills in the natural sciences, engineering and statistics. On graduation they could move into publishing, education or policy careers. Politically-motivated trends in public school education sometimes run counter to child development and INFP is curious enough to catch it.

ENFP of childhood music lessons or high school band could go for the **Musicology and Ethnomusicology** major in the Blair School of Music. It is an intense study of all music varieties and style from choir chants to Broadway musicals to, of course, the blues. With New Orleans about six hours by car, an internship is in the making. Music in the French Quarter, played on the streets by the local musicians, is brilliant and replicates the level of excellence in the Blair School of Music. They will also study the cultural influence of music during all historical periods and spiritual music as an expression of belief.

INTJ will find the **Mathematics** department at Vandy offers a great jumping off point for a lifetime career in cyber security. Across the globe American influence is not welcome now. Our defense forces are at levels below that of WWII, so America and the Department of Defense are vulnerable targets. INTJ will show a level of intensity in their expression as they walk into their class Error-Correcting Codes and Cryptography. Formerly a sophomore level course, it is now a class for juniors because of the advances in computing that have been fuelled by mathematical algorithms.

INTP has the triple "i"—intense, internal, intuition. That will help with the degree in **Chemistry** at demanding Vandy. The physical facilities and labs are outstanding. The department requires analytic thinking and all kinds of conceptual schemes can be dreamed up for their senior independent work. Professors interface their advanced, national research findings with coursework in the classes. INTP will graduate with state of the art knowledge in this field. But first they must be mindful of Vandy's objective style. Creativity is fine here, but accidents that could have been prevented and being late are not so well-tolerated.

ENTJ will jump right into Game Theory with Economic Applications. This course has the entrepreneurial bent and is sufficiently complex to keep ENTJ's busy mind engaged. This course is an elective in the joint major **Economics and History**. It is a new degree and pretty intriguing to this type. They will get the full economic tool box of analytics and theory. They will focus equally on the history and origins of modern society through production of capital and the redistribution required for an economy and a nation to remain viable.

WABASH COLLEGE

P.O. Box 352
Crawfordsville, IN 47933
Website: www.wabash.edu
Admissions Telephone: 765-361-6225
Undergraduates: 926 Men

Physical Environment

Wabash College is 45 miles northwest of Indianapolis and is proudly referred to as **My 'Bash** by current undergraduates and alumni alike. The college is remarkable for several reasons including its place as an all men's institution and their exceptionally active, loyal alumni. The **Center of Inquiry in the Liberal Arts** conducts assessments across the nation's small liberal arts campuses. It offers workshops and conferences on the collective nature of each undergraduate student population that arrives annually on campuses across the nation. It is an invaluable service for all higher education and is the gift of the remarkable Little Giants of Wabash College.

The **Athletic Center** is nothing short of spectacular with its **Olympic-size pool**, lots of exercise equipment and weight rooms. It is a magnet for athletic students who go on to many Little Giant's Division III titles in multiple sports. The **Fine Arts Center** is also a big draw for artistically-inclined guys who want to do big art in the outdoor classroom space. The Salter Concert Hall is here as well with individual practice rooms for aspiring musicians. The New House dormitory, open 2016, joins nine fraternity houses and college-owned apartments. The Wabash **Center for Teaching Religion and Theology**, funded by the Lilly Endowment, is active with grants and resources for all American colleges with Religious Studies in their curriculum. It is another gift to the American community of small liberal arts colleges.

Social Environment

Tradition rules at Wabash College. The Tuttle **Chapel** is hoppin' on Thursdays with loud, guy-type clowning around with song and satire. Chapel services and gatherings are the spiritual anchor for the campus. Throughout the academic year, different groups compete to see who can belt out the **Old Wabash refrain** the loudest on the front porch. That kind of enthusiasm is captured by professors who dialogue with students in **pointed discussions** that become **ongoing debates**. Especially in the first year there is a lot of talk on **character development**, such as what it means to be a **Wabash Man** and **The Gentlemen's Rule** which calls for students to act with responsibility, be accountable at all times. The **role of men** in the larger American society is a serious topic given the diminished numbers of men in higher education as well as all the professions. Every first year takes the Spring course, Enduring Questions. It points to the abstract, **reflective** nature of the Wabash community.

Athletics and **friendly competition** are a daily habit. Forty percent of students who come here play one or two varsity sports. Wabash college football, wrestling, baseball and basketball teams are hotbeds for men intent on toning up their muscles and physical agility. Three-quarters of all students play in intramurals. **Fraternities, student clubs** and **residence halls** all generate intramural teams for weekly competitions against each other. Service for others is ongoing and starts the second day on campus for freshmen who head out in the afternoon to volunteer in Crawfordsville.

Wabash College appeals to a wide range of personalities. About 70 percent are from Indiana, 25 percent identify as a minority and they come from 33 states. High school athletes appreciate Wabash. Socially outgoing guys come to Wabash. Leaders in high school clubs appreciate Wabash. Eagle scouts go for Wabash. Quiet guys in the physics lab think Wabash is a great place. Guys who expect to be better students in college than high school come here too. Casual conversation on this campus ranges from sports to women to careers. You can't underestimate the cultural guidance of the **alumni** on this campus. They frequently guest lecture, they sponsor internships in their businesses, they support the off campus internships with scholarship funds that help the guys travel out of country. Most of all, they model successful, ethical graduates of Wabash. Homecoming, The **Big Bash 2016**, is the largest event on campus annually and speaks to the remarkable memories of men graduating this college.

Compatibility with Personality Types and Preferences

Wabash College has done a great job of incorporating learning styles with moral behavior into a strong mix that serves a variety of undergraduate men. The administration of this guys-only college really understands the perspectives of their entering freshmen. New students quickly hear about humane concepts (F), awareness and analytic thinking. As undergraduates progress toward graduation, they learn through trial and error (T) how one is expected to honor the Wabash community and prepare for citizenship in (E) the larger society. Faculty in all departments use experiential (S) learning. Undergraduate students travel frequently to locations within the U.S. and overseas through their courses. Professors make great use of immersion learning on short four-to-five day trips to connect students to the world beyond campus. The faculty use of abstract conceptual learning (N) is featured in Wabash's classics curriculum. The curriculum works equally well for two opposite learners: the hands-on, give-me-the-facts student and the abstract, discussion-based learner. Students who are attracted to Wabash are confident that this single-gender environment will give them the best of both worlds—the caring world that builds community and the traditional guy world that loves athleticism and power.

Now read below about one of the majors that MBTI® research shows people of your type have selected since the mid-20th century. After, refer to Chapter Five for the 50 or so majors that can help you prepare for careers your type has selected. Most importantly, remember that this college description is a suggestion for exploration, not a commanding order. You can be successful in any major at any college.

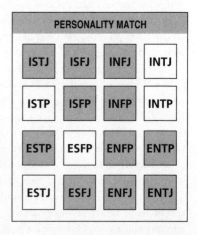

PERSONALITY MATCH

ISTJ	ISFJ	INFJ	INTJ
ISTP	ISFP	INFP	INTP
ESTP	ESFP	ENFP	ENTP
ESTJ	ESFJ	ENFJ	ENTJ

INFP pretty much has to have their personal values lined up with daily living. The major in **Philosophy** lets this type fine tune their inner values as they study across the centuries of thought. Study of the classic Western texts by reading, writing and discussion in class covers a wide range of topics with unfamiliar perspectives. The Pre-Law advising on campus supports the philosophy major for a legal career in advocacy. Undergraduates have a creative Philosophy Club that gives campus-wide talks on subjects that the guys relate to like drones in the sky.

INFJ is a creative type that goes for change to make life better for others. The **German** major or minor with pre-professional advising in **Health and Allied Sciences** lets this type focus on international careers. The 2014-15 mass immigrations from Islamic State, ISIS terrorism in the Middle East place value on current European cultural awareness. INFJ just might work with an international organization that is delivering health services in these camps. Perhaps after that experience, INFJ returns stateside for a medical specialty degree.

ISTJ is going to love studying **History** at Wabash College because it requires five areas of competence and this type likes accuracy above all else. The History major and **Pre-Law** advising sets a clear career path for this realistic type. Historians and lawyers use analytical skills, interpretation and oral/written expression required in this major at Wabash. The practice of law is always about changing or keeping a current practice or decision, so grounding in the past is critical for a good oral argument.

ISFJ with their usual good sense of color and space might go for the major in **Studio Art** or **Art History**. ISFJs without the talent can elect the Art History major with its strong coursework in the classics. Both majors explore visual expression of abstract ideas. Not to worry about how to translate these studies into a career because Wabash has a pre-professional concentration in **Business**. On this small campus, faculty in both departments can advise ISFJs on developing an affordable line of three dimensional art pieces for big box stores like Walmart or Lowes garden shops.

ISFP likes to work with their hands and enjoy the outdoors. The major in **Classics** at Wabash College focuses on Greek and Roman ancient literature, history, art and archeology. With this major, ISFPs might want to check out the **Education Studies** minor too. Wabash offers a secondary teaching license in the state of Indiana if ISFP applies by spring of junior year. Ten weeks in the public high schools has that hands-on learning they like. They can specialize in artifact collection and study, bringing this interesting art into high school lesson plans of independent, parochial and charter schools.

ESTP likes to take calculated risks for the most part. When the intramural competitions are done for the evening, ESTP tackles math formulas for their **Physics** major. This field is full of hands-on work in the labs once the first year basics are finished. Undergrads assist professors with their faculty research. ESTP might go for the astrophysics research here at Wabash. Perhaps they will even study Spacetime, predicted by Einstein at the turn of the 20th century and proven in February 2016 when two black holes were observed in massive collision. It's all about gravitational wave theory.

ENFP can be a very compassionate soul and the study of **Religion** just might appeal. The department has a remarkable position in national higher education religious study, not to mention the Wabash national reputation. Enthusiasm for the classics on campus easily supplements ancient religious texts. Professors actively mentor students in this major that can lead to further theological studies and the worlds of medicine, law and business. During the last weeks before they graduate, the men of this major give chapel speeches that serve as a reflective pause in the closing days and weeks on campus.

ENTP will be front and center when the conversation turns to speculation. The classic major in **Rhetoric** with a concentration in **International Studies** is great for this type. ENTP is curious and will try to figure out how and why individuals accept and filter the conflicting stories they hear. All in all, they will deconstruct positions put forth in the public square. As a speaker ENTP has to overcome starting too late with too few details followed by rambling thoughts. If they get this down, they can become powerful personalities of creative, long-range thinking. Off campus study and summer internship in Europe or Latin America will open doors for several possible careers.

ESFJ will like studying **Biology** at Wabash College. The science building has all the bells and whistles to support a hands-on, research-driven curriculum. ESFJs go for harmony and experiential learning. The field studies, internships and lab experiments bring this degree into the real, practical world. Off campus study is usually funded through one of the six programs that Wabash College operates for undergraduates. Students get travel and living expenses to locations outside of the country and nationally. These internships are called Immersion Studies and they often mean students live and work with local citizens in their field.

ENFJ will like the independence that comes with a career in **Psychology** and the opportunities to help others one-on-one. Emerging research in this field is the focus of the department. Students will learn the critical nature of the scientific method and be able to apply it when they research journals and papers. There is much to be reviewed in new concepts about behavior and the brain. Upper class work focuses on students generating their own concepts and formulating the scientific methods to answer it. Professors prefer that undergraduate research is service-oriented. It all works for ENFJ.

ENTJ will find the minor in **Business** to their liking along with their entrepreneurial interests. The 21st century business environment requires leadership and long-range planning. For the largest of our corporations like Ford and General Electric that means international long range business plans. The **Political Science** major is a solid choice for an ENTJ looking for those executive management positions in their later career. The Wabash Student Council is self-governing and ENTJ might run for a leadership position on it. It is practically an internship, as the guys operate with an annual budget of $400,000 for the campus activities and outreach.

WAKE FOREST UNIVERSITY

1834 Wake Forest Road
Winston-Salem, NC 27109
Website: www.wfu.edu
Admissions Telephone: 336-758-5201
Undergraduates: 4,867; 2,336 Men, 2,531 Women
Graduate Students: 2,921

Physical Environment

Wake Forest University is about a 90-minute drive north of the Charlotte International Airport. In the low Appalachian Hill country, it was founded by Baptists in the early nineteenth century. The campus has many two, three and four-story red brick buildings mostly in the Federal style. This plain, familiar architecture points to the nature of the university which offers academic study reflective of current day American culture. The Wait Chapel, the largest indoor seating space on the campus, serves as an auditorium. **The Barn**, of classic A-frame structure and metal roof, is unique and perfect for its location reserved for student-hosted parties and events.

There are many new buildings at WFU and older facilities have been renovated, so stepping on campus is like coming across a well-designed, contemporary, open space mall. The **Benson Student Center** is one of several hubs on campus with all the student organizations and services. Other dining spaces, looking very much like neighborhood restaurants, serve as gathering spots across the campus. Another new dormitory will open in Fall 2017. These latest dorms have software to monitor utilities usage by the students. The university has an **extensive intranet** that serves as the communication center and authoritative information center across all academic and social segments of the campus It is like a massive old fashioned bulletin board, the go-to-place.

Social Environment

Wake Forest University appeals to students who want academic study and regular social activities minus passionate agendas. Over-the-top enthusiasm is reserved for Wake Forest football and basketball, always in the playoff bowls and title championships. In high school, WFU students were **reliable, enthusiastic** and outgoing in student government, in high school clubs and events like homecoming. They find they can do the same on this campus. Students bring **spirit to athletic games** and love their mascot the Demon Deacon, distinctive in his 1890s black garb, yellow tie and tall stove pipe hat. There is a **club sport** for most extracurricular interests from bass fishing to karate and all in between. **Intramurals** are similarly expansive with inner tube water polo, all the in-betweens and table tennis.

Wake Forest University's strong social and athletic traditions (J) on campus help undergraduate's transition from high school to a successful collegiate experience. In fact, the campus honors many of the vibrant, fun collegiate stuff of the old classic movies. WFU social events are plentiful. Students join **chartered social organizations**/clubs which are approved after review by several committees and receive financial support and resources from the university. **Greek life** provides a level of leadership and opportunity that is independent of some of the residential life oversight.

Fraternity and sorority chapter members live together on floors in the larger residence halls. There are also many smaller residences all formed around common interests. Undergraduate students are employed as Resident Advisors in the dormitories and are members of the various committees that plan and approve campus-wide social events. Seniors can live off campus with permission and under circumstances called out in the university's Social Regulations and Policies.

Most students hope to address problems in American society and some join student organizations for this purpose. They look to explore action through their own initiative within the structure of campus organizations. They develop leadership skills through partnership with established local and national service and political organizations. A good example of this is the Wake Forest chapter of the Roosevelt Society which models itself after a think tank and addresses ecological issues. WFU undergraduates, **questioning, occasionally unsure**, hear familiar American cross currents and look for resolution within historic, time-honored collegiate practice.

Compatibility with Personality Types and Preferences

Undergraduates here really come to cement a career that is realistic and in demand. They attend classes with purpose and manage their time well. They approve of the stable, fun social activities available to them. The campus is organized traditionally by levels of administrative leadership that grant approval for extracurriculars that meet collegiate social goals. The WFU curriculum quickly embraces current day movements in American society. The faculty have primary responsibility for content and educational practice within their department's curriculum. Depending on the department, undergraduates will find conservative social constructs or progressive social perspectives, like the Department of Psychology on gender stereotypes.[89] Students submit applications for undergraduate research positions to join faculty in their research. Students have other opportunities like Spring 2016 - Election Travel where the group travels nationally and students are randomly assigned to volunteer or work in paid positions on primary campaigns of presidential candidates.

Through study, discussion and logical analysis (T) students secure skills and knowledge at WFU. Freshman will have classes that introduce critical reading, thinking and writing. It pushes students to develop personal values and explore ethical positions. After the first year, undergraduates sign up for and essentially secure advising in the academic departments. Faculty encourage students to prepare for difficult issues that will be raised in courses during senior year. Pass/ Fail grading is an option for upper class students. Undergraduate students typically apply and compete for research internships. The national research is usually directed toward current day social issues, emerging sciences and designed for publication. The administration philosophy leans heavily toward student accountability in educational choices.

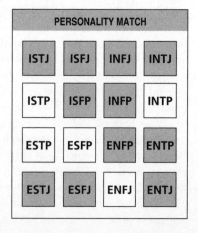

PERSONALITY MATCH

ISTJ	ISFJ	INFJ	INTJ
ISTP	ISFP	INFP	INTP
ESTP	ESFP	ENFP	ENTP
ESTJ	ESFJ	ENFJ	ENTJ

Now read below about one of the majors that MBTI® research shows people of your type have selected since the mid-20th century. After, refer to Chapter Five for the 50 or so majors that can help you prepare for careers your type has selected. Most importantly, remember that this college description is a suggestion for exploration, not a commanding order. You can be successful in any major at any college.

ENTJ will feel comfortable with the wide range of financial courses in the **Economics** major. The Economics of Entrepreneurship course compares economic theory with the actions of successful entrepreneurs, past and present. This type will be at ease in the uncertain world of economics. ENTJ is likely to move into a professional environment such as law, business, medicine or government as an expert advisor.

ISTJ will really appreciate the extensive course selection in the **Biology** Department. ISTJs are attracted to comprehensive, demanding classification systems in the huge world of insects and the department has the curriculum for this focus. The undergraduate research is solid and ISTJ must identify the professor who is researching in this area and set up an appointment to apply as an assistant. The rest is lab work. The career field is in need of Millennials to come on board since many Baby Boomer entomologists are retiring.

ESFJ places physical fitness high on their priority list. The degree in **Health and Exercise Science** is all about fitness. The course in Physiology of Exercise totally covers human health in muscle tone and the cardiovascular, pulmonary and endocrine systems. ESFJ is people-centered and is comfortable with jobs at the community and local level, so positions in fitness centers are good. Other options with this degree include professional schools in the health sciences.

ISFJ should look at the courses in the **Anthropology** department at Wake Forest. This major can be excellent or watered down by the department focusing on a current issue or social perspective. WFU has the excellent version. ISFJ is patient with the details and empathetic. Undergrads in the major can volunteer or get work study at the WFU Museum for Anthropology. The course Feminist Anthropology is nicely balanced with the course Masculinities Across Culture. This is one of the rare American Liberal Arts Colleges that actually offers course work on the male gender.

ISFP is likely to be comfortable with the mission of Nature Conservancy. The interdisciplinary minor in **Environmental Studies** gives a wide look at how government policy changes land use. The damage caused in the Everglades by the 1930s government projects and the Department of Energy 2015 damage to Colorado's watershed will encourage trusting ISFP to carefully research programs offered by nonprofit organizations and government bureaus.

ESTJ will be drawn to the business school major in **Finance**. The requirement in strategic management focuses on startups and those in early production or those expanding overseas. Since these courses really study the nature of competition in fast moving markets, ESTJ will get a good sense of when to make the tough calls. The department encourages undergrads to team with MBA students in presentations for start-up business ventures.

ENFP often can be found in sales. The concentration in **Marketing** at WFU is a good choice. The School of Business has a strong MBA program with active connections to start-up grants. Undergraduate students can apply to work in teams with the MBA folks who are designing sales campaigns themselves. This type is fairly persuasive and will enjoy the action in marketing which is always changing and heads off boredom.

ENTP is often drawn to concepts in **Political Science**. The subject is likely to be fascinating for ENTPs. WFU has a solid department that offers an objective curriculum. Recent undergraduate papers looked at complex subjects reported simplistically by the media. The curriculum is without social bias of conservative or progressive views. ENTPs, curious, independent and analytical, will get the freedom to interpret and encouragement to explore. Regional upheaval and explosive social movement generated by the American withdrawal of forces and historical commitments in the Middle East are ideal for this type drawn to complexities.

INFP could like the looks of the very credible **German Business** emphasis in the Department of German and Russian Languages. They must take the language requirement through the second year. After that they will focus on cultural understanding and take a sequence in basic skills for German business study abroad. On graduation they will be eligible to take the Goethe Institute certification in business proficiency in German.

INFJ values independence and harmony. Within the Department of **Religion**, INFJs will find a solid foundation of survey courses in the major world religions. WFU has a field school in Tell Keisan, Israel. Undergrads will spend four weeks in excavation and one week of political, religious study in Jerusalem. The department offers a rich study in Christian texts and history. Here INFJ will get an exceptionally clear inquiry into the religious faiths.

INTJ speculates a whole lot and it can lead to an idea for action. This consistent thinker often excels in research. The major in **Chemistry** at Wake Forest is ideally oriented toward research. INTJ has independence and objectivity to select a line of departmental research and apply with the professor for an assistant position. Put this together with a follow on career path that includes research and development in the pharmaceutical industry and this major becomes an INTJ action plan.

WASHINGTON AND LEE UNIVERSITY

116 North Main Street
Lexington, VA 24450-0303
Website: www.wlu.edu
Admissions Telephone: 540-463-8710
Undergraduates: 1,890; 952 Men, 938 Women
Graduate Students: 374

Physical Environment

Washington and Lee University is located in the **quaint and historical** town of Lexington, population 7,000. Surrounded by farm land, horse pastures and the Appalachian Mountains, the university appeals to students who are comfortable with traditional venues. Campus architecture is all the more remarkable because George Washington bequeathed his 20,000 shares of James River canal stock for seed money. Confederate General Robert E. Lee is buried with his horse within sight of the historical center. Mindful of history, the entering class walks through traditional southern wrought iron gates flanked by federal style, red brick, academic buildings. Each of these have their front porticos decorated with massive **white columns**.

The Colonnade, on the National Historic Register, is in the traditional center of campus and highlighted by an expansive green lawn. In the 20th century, the campus grew toward the ridge and now reflects the futuristic side of Washington and Lee with up-to-date everything. The university is now in a long term construction project started with The **Village Square** of upper division housing and natatorium, open 2016. The New Neighborhood when it is completed will look more like an open air mall with smaller shops and residences. Accomplished high school athletes are attracted to the university because of the excellent sports facilities. Students socialize in the Elrod commons, the library, the ivy-covered classroom buildings and Greek houses. The profound sense of American tradition and community is apparent to all who walk the campus.

Social Environment

W&L students are eager to learn the concepts, knowledge and expectations that give them a head start in **pivotal career fields**. They are **high-achieving**, expressive, ambitious and hard-working. Some will come from socially and historically influential families. Undergraduates expect to be challenged by a **rigorous academic** curriculum and faculty at W&L is more than happy to oblige. The educational experience is **intense and individualized**. It starts prior to arrival on campus in the fall. First years are advised about time management and introductory studies that require **discernment**. Faculty engage students with **dialogue and conversational hypotheses**. It is a favorite teaching practice and students acquire this conversational engagement by the end of the first semester. The administration developed the unique four-week **Spring Immersion Term** in addition to the two regular semesters. Faculty wanted to push fun into the intense learning syllabus to finish off the academic year. It is a key feature of the education and each student takes one course for credit. Rather like a capstone in some ways, they are elective in nature and become W&L memories of happy note. Successful students take advantage of the academic peer tutoring and several other supports on campus. Some students will settle into academic mentoring with their professors that goes beyond the course curriculum. The speaking tradition and Honor System point to individual and community accountability. Service learning is typically focused on issues of poverty and sustainability that are well interfaced throughout the curriculum. The administration has greatly expanded the resources and curriculum in reference to **poverty within the American community**.

The student body here forms close ties. The First Year Experience settles all freshmen into small sections of about ten individuals within the residence halls. They each have an upper division student to help them adjust to college life. Only seniors are permitted to live off campus. All student residence halls are governed by trained student residential staff. The university does not place professionals within the dormitories to program or administer social policy. It is very consistent with the administration philosophy of independence with accountability. The **Greek system** is exceptionally strong on this campus, the great majority join and live in the chapter houses on campus. Student organizations tend to move toward lighthearted entertainment as an alternative to the intense dialogs that float across campus all day. The club sports, intramurals, fitness and outing club also provide counterpoints to the intellectual life. As graduates, they will have academic **poise and acumen** to interface with the distinguished W&L alumni network often leading to further opportunity.

Compatibility with Personality Types and Preferences

Clarity of thinking, originality (N), analysis, precision and attention to current societal trends do a good job of characterizing the Washington and Lee academic environment. Logic and the art of concentrated thinking (T) are in demand on this campus. Incoming undergraduate students are encouraged to adopt the W&L value of honoring intellectual inquiry. Seminars, courses and clubs all offer guideposts in respect to current day practices and issues. The Mock Convention is an intense two-year effort by the student body to predict the presidential candidate of the sitting national minority political party. On this campus, the undergraduate student interfaces knowledge with persuasive communication so as to take a credible place in the public square. Successful students here are keen and assertive. The Johnson Symposia and Shepherd Program offer leadership opportunity and service initiative at the regional and national levels.

W&L offers many sophomore-level courses with advanced content and broad expanse across the disciplines. Many of these are open to undergraduates, others are open after consent by the professor. At W&L undergraduates are grounded in the leading-edge present and mindful of our American past. But where is the American Studies major?

Now read below about one of the majors that MBTI® research shows people of your type have

PERSONALITY MATCH			
ISTJ	ISFJ	INFJ	INTJ
ISTP	ISFP	INFP	INTP
ESTP	ESFP	ENFP	ENTP
ESTJ	ESFJ	ENFJ	ENTJ

selected since the mid-20th century. After, refer to Chapter Five for the 50 or so majors that can help you prepare for careers your type has selected. Most importantly, remember that this college description is a suggestion for exploration, not a commanding order. You can be successful in any major at any college.

ENTJ is an exceptionally fine fit for Washington and Lee. Direct, decisive and conceptual, they will be drawn to the Williams School. Among the exciting entrepreneurial projects within the school is the **W&L Student Consulting**. This group of business students advises client nonprofit companies on a variety of strategies. One of our favorites was the work they did with the John Adams National Historical Park, This type will also want to sign up for the Williams School of Business course in Entrepreneurship and enter a competition judged by W&L alumni with their own excellent business credentials.

ENFJ would likely approve the program in Teacher Education at W&L. The program and licensure is offered together with the local public state university. Both the minor in Education and the other in **Education Policy** require field work and practicum in the schools. ENFJ, sometimes idealistic, might go for the policy track to look at the Common Core. This controversial program was not adopted by several states, including Virginia. ENFJ will have independent opportunities to explore the reported failing grades of the 2014 Common Core assessments nationwide.

ENFP is okay with difficulty as long as they can be enthusiastic in clearing it up. ENFPs usually excel in any major that captures their imagination. The program in **Neuroscience** requires solid coursework in several different sciences and this is a nice overview of possibilities for joining faculty in their ongoing research. The department is now centering on how the brain takes in sensory information like sight, sound, smell and touch. This BS degree opens doors in many directions of advanced study.

INFJ could bring metaphor to some of the nuts and bolts logic that travels on this campus. Should they disagree with a particular statement, which they are likely to do, it may be done with a touch of grace. The **Medieval and Renaissance Studies** program is ideal for INFJ's exceptional insight. The European populations of the 1300s to the 1600s has an amazing storehouse of internet journals, societies and academies. There will be a deep enough well of mystery and metaphor to keep INFJ happy on this campus of nuts and bolts.

INTJ takes nothing for granted. If this type needs to rearrange the principles of **Physics** and the basics of nature, so be it. W&L faculty would likely permit and enjoy the ensuing mayhem—for a short time. Reality can bring INTJ back to earth in the Concrete lab where structural behavior is studied in faculty research for cementitious materials. Yes, that is spelled correctly. Go figure or take a tour of the W&L School of Engineering and Physics. Follow this with a tour of Christchurch, New Zealand. Thanks W&L.

ENTP can be comfortably assertive at W&L. With strong ideas and big personas in abundance at W&L, quick-thinking ENTPs will receive the intellectual stimulation they crave. The **Mock Trial** might provide ENTPs the jury box and audience to which they will put forth their courtroom litigation strategies. Direction for this program comes from the Department of Politics and ENTP should look into this major because it evenly balances exploration of citizenship, theory and global politics. It is a complex, abstract study. ENTP is all for it.

INTP is intellectually curious and contemplative. Their powerful minds may be underestimated when they are typically quiet in the classroom. However, faculty at W&L will spot intellectual potential and draw out this type. INTP and the major or minor in **Philosophy** makes sense. The department's Root Lecture Series brings faculty of psychology, religion and philosophy on a rotating basis. This outside perspective gives INTP extra filters to run abstract concepts by. That is okay because INTP is detached and will remain objective, though intensely curious.

ISTJ comfortably takes in large volumes of facts, checks them for accuracy and then stores them away. ISTJs won't be overwhelmed with the intensity of ideas here; rather, they will endure and conquer. The **Pre-Law program** is an additional sequence of elective courses of current political issues likely to find their way into the courts. All taught by the philosophy department faculty, they are well-balanced and absent political agendas of correctness.

ISTP often goes for a technical and statistical field of interest. The W&L **Environmental Studies** major is interdisciplinary and ISTP can select elective courses that move in the direction of documenting and assessing field studies of current issues. It requires direct observation and their environmental capstone project could be about any of several problems in the watershed near this university. For the occasional ISTP interested in policy, this major can be focused in those directions too. Regardless, they will be studying remediation successes and failures. Think of the Department of Energy's contamination of Colorado water sheds in 2015. Answers are illusive, yet political motives inundate this field.

WASHINGTON UNIVERSITY IN ST. LOUIS

One Brookings Drive
St. Louis, MO 63130-4899
Website: www.wustl.edu
Admissions Telephone: 800-638-0700, 314-935-6000
Undergraduates: 7,336; 3,596 Men, 3,740 Women
Graduate Students: 6,696

Physical Environment

Washington University is located in St. Louis about five miles from the Mighty Mississippi River and Famous Arch. A visit the admissions office here will take you into iconic Brookings Hall, the most photographed at Wash U. A bit like a European castle, with gates open, it influences other structures on campus to follow in the same Gothic design. Much of the campus is built into the side of natural sloping ground and architects have taken advantage with delightful facilities like the new Olin Business complex. The atrium allows light to stream down below into the basement of the amphitheater. There is seemingly endless construction of new facilities that support the professional schools at Wash U. They are too numerous to write about. Other recent expansions to the undergraduate academic facilities focused on expanding the Faculty's **advanced national research**. The transformation of the Danforth Campus continues with more construction starting in 2017. The Board of Trustees would have it no other way, both professional schools and university academics are priority number one.

The library is often packed with students who are studying or hanging out between classes. Another favorite place on campus is the Holmes Lounge because of its comfy leather chairs and its **gorgeous ceiling**, heavily inlaid with carvings. The **Danforth University Center** also has an interesting ceiling with colored panels. Make sure you notice ceilings across this campus. Delmar Loop expanded the perimeter of the undergraduate campus. **The Lofts** remind you of downtown urban renewal efforts—safe, clean and inviting. Built with sustainability as a starting point, The Lofts point to a considerable commitment of budget and call attention to sustainability which is also a number one priority.

Weather is really unpredictable here because of Missouri's geographic location on the continent. Cold Canadian air pushes down to meet Gulf warm air streaming eastward. When classes start at 8 a.m., freshmen arrive in shorts and T-shirts. When class is over at 8:50 a.m., upper division students pull their wraps out of backpacks, head out for a warm study space, and smile at the falling snow. It's all part of **dynamic Wash U**. The best transportation around this large campus is by bike. Architects made it a high priority with new landscapes between the buildings. The League of American Bicyclists recognized Wash U as **very bike-friendly**.

Social Environment

When first-year students arrive at Washington University's Danforth campus, they come with **stellar high school accomplishments**. The majority will come from the eastern half of the United States. They may ponder the optional Wash U pass/fail grade options but each department sets its own guidelines. There is some academic competition on campus since the university attracts many pre-professional students. Wash U's own prestigious schools of law, medicine and business call out to those interested in advanced study. Students arrive on campus expecting to find new pursuits and there are tons of new pursuits. **National initiatives and national research labs** offer ongoing points of entry for undergraduates who wish to apply for a position in established studies. There is also an extensive **Office of Undergraduate Research** that mentors students with selecting and presenting research findings of interest to them.

Other than their resumes, Wash U undergraduates are ready to leave their high school social experience behind. They are okay with structure brought into the Wash U social environment. The administration philosophy obliges with the **Undergraduate Council**, a group of students, faculty and administrators. The council conducts continuous assessment and makes regular adjustments based on its findings. The social web on campus is constantly monitored and tweaked to meet residential life programmatic goals. The **Interfaith Campus Ministries Association** is a comparatively new office funded by one of many alumni endowments. It meets monthly and refers undergraduates off campus for pastoral counseling. All local religious faiths are encouraged to communicate through the office and offer outreach to undergraduate students. The Graham Chapel is used for concerts, plays and lectures.

There is a nice and easy flow of interaction between students. One-quarter join **Greek life** and become really involved in it. Chapter houses are located North Side of the Danforth Campus. After the first year on campus, undergrads can choose from a large variety of housing options. Many will choose The 40 and both this area and the North Side are basically self-contained with all the amenities of metropolitan lifestyles. **Strong friendships** form during this first year that remain in place through graduation on this campus. Student organizations form mostly around intellectual, cultural and political orientations. Most students on campus are not inclined to be activists for a cause. However, Spring 2014 students staged a 17-day sit-in where hundreds joined a campaign to remove a member of the Board of Trustees over his CEO position in coal industry. Seven students were arrested as they tried to enter the Board of Trustees meeting, demanding to talk with the member.[90] For those, undergraduates ready to leave the campus bubble, a quick trip out to Forest Park, cite of the 1904 World's Fair, is delightful with its museums, zoo, planetarium and many athletic fields.

Compatibility with Personality Types and Preferences

Washington University consistently ensures its academic environment supports discovering and disseminating knowledge. The university is really exceptional at both activities and commended especially for their efforts to bring knowledge into the public square of usefulness. A great deal of ecological research is developed with local habitats like the box turtle project that Wash U, St. Louis Zoo and Forest Park work together. The Ozark Mountains are at the center of many research designs for sustainability of the ecology. Many of the major academic divisions look to support public communities struggling with social and infrastructure problems. You might think of it as Service Research. Thank you Wash U.

Like-minded students at Wash U seek to be part of this vibrant energy. It reflects their wish to grow in understanding of themselves (I), become active and expert at giving back. Faculty and administration support a stable community with a strong undercurrent that highlights the responsibilities inherent in teaching and learning—the two-way street. Teacher and student collaboration is common on campus.

Exceptionally bright students who are predisposed to analysis and objective thinking (T) excel here. Academic activity is ever present in the classes, in the extracurricular clubs and the social gathering of friends. Faculty soften the academic edges with individual encouragement, collaborative and team learning. Mentoring students is a high priority for faculty. The student-professor relationship often moves into the research labs and grows within the academic structure (J) of research. Graduates are focused on achievement and move easily onto prestigious advanced studies as well as influential positions in business. Wash U has a predisposition to send out graduates who are highly skilled in developmental research.

Now read below about one of the majors that MBTI® research shows people of your type have selected since the mid-20th century. After, refer to Chapter Five for the 50 or so majors that can help you prepare for careers your type has selected. Most importantly, remember that this college description is a suggestion for exploration, not a commanding order. You can be successful in any major at any college.

PERSONALITY MATCH			
ISTJ	ISFJ	INFJ	INTJ
ISTP	ISFP	INFP	INTP
ESTP	ESFP	ENFP	ENTP
ESTJ	ESFJ	ENFJ	ENTJ

INFP will find the major in **Urban Studies** at Washington University absolutely in synch with their desire to work for a greater cause. This major offers a broad curriculum cataloging ills and issues within American urban settings. The department is clear in their prediction for a future of densely populated cities with considerable power to shape lives within and across national and international boundaries. Juniors are encouraged to apply for the senior honors program. INFP is likely to do this and naturally develop a well-supported thesis proposal. Wash U social life is sufficiently intellectual for this type, too.

INFJ is drawn to creating new ideas. The minor in **Bioinformatics** is an unusual course of study offered jointly by the engineering school and the biology department. It is an emerging field and will give this type opportunity to push the boundaries. This minor combines nicely with a degree in computer science, biology or engineering. Creative INFJ will likely choose a major honoring their inclination to help others. Majors in computer engineering or biology with this minor could lead into advanced degrees and implanted electronic devices that monitor diabetic levels in the blood stream.

INTJ is attracted to complex, tough problems. The major in **Operations and Supply Chain Management** offers a peek at the complexity of moving parts around the globe to support manufacturing and service operations. Graduates of this major also get involved with raw materials, parts, storage, pricing and repair of products. Business competition is intense under free trade and globalization trends. Competitive environments get INTJ enthusiastically in the game. They might be quiet but they usually are part of the solution. Their self-contained nature reserves energy for their internal thinking.

ISTP likes investigation and the major in **Archeology** requires a good bit of speculating. Students in this major explore the nature of artifacts and collection through field studies. This type also likes to be outdoors because of the freedom and activity that comes with leaving the desk and iPad behind. At Wash U, they can expand their preparation for this career by selecting a study abroad experience that takes them into active archeological digs. The emphasis on academics over social learning on campus appeals to this type. www.shovelbums.org has a whole list of current field studies.

ISTJ relates well to the goals of the **Health Care Management** major. Graduates are expected to think precisely and develop useful frameworks that address problems. Both easy for ISTJ, they prefer to gather all the facts and review them objectively then reach a decision. The financial mechanisms in the troubled national health care roll out of 2014 are under constant scrutiny. The ISTJ in this major will have to put on their investigative answer to find financially sound mechanisms in the 2,000 pages of this legislative act. This type has a quiet humor and will find themselves in demand as a study buddy

ISFJ will not be surprised by the comprehensive studies in the **Fashion Design** major at Wash U. The graduates of this Bachelor of Fine Arts Degree bring a strong set of skills to fashion creation for mass production and high fashion apparel. ISFJ might join an established sports line of clothing for Millennials after graduation. This career honors the type's own value for a pleasing, comforting human environment. Their typical attention to detail is perfect. They can handle the repetitive routine in the seasonal deliveries for yet another ski season.

ENTP ever ingenious and looking to come up with original ideas. Look into the Earth and Planetary Sciences degree at Wash U. This type is constantly available for intellectual discussion that fits so well on this campus. The department offers four majors and the **Environmental Earth Sciences** looks darn good. This appeals to ENTP who likes variety with its large list of interesting electives to choose from. The intensity of dialogue on campus will delight this type who is always ready to debate— on either or both sides of an issue.

ENTJ attracted to the idea of business will find the major in **Economics** at Wash U quite interesting. The department loads the curriculum with mathematical models applied to inflation and government decision making. This university is very much focused on the social issues and the Center for Dynamic Economics is proof positive. ENTJs have an objective mindset which they can put to use while moving through the curriculum in this major. It will be this type who suspicions misinformation reported by the national media. A second major in the School of Business would be ideal for faculty mentoring to sort out and identify the truths underlying economic decisions. A minor in political science wouldn't hurt either.

INTP has the curiosity and time to speculate about the unusual elements to be found in **Geobiology**. This discipline is primarily an advanced graduate level of study. However, INTP can take advantage of the open doors on this campus and speak directly to faculty conducting research. The unknowns within the planet's historical record will definitely catch INTP's attention and rev up ponderings of sorts. INTPs will approach those unknowns as if they were puzzles to be solved and time is no obstacle, there will be decades to find the answers.

WESLEYAN UNIVERSITY

237 High Street
Middletown, CT 06459
Website: www.wesleyan.edu
Admissions Telephone: 860-685-3000
Undergraduates: 2,928; 1,397 Men, 1,531 Women
Graduate Students: 296

Physical Environment

Named in honor of John Wesley, the founder of the Methodist Church, Wesleyan University sits mid-way between Hartford and New Haven, on old Route 66, in quaint Middletown. The striking element on the campus is the lovely **Andrus Quad** that functions as an athletic stadium and a favorite meeting place for students who want to play a casual game of Frisbee on a sunny day. On game day, portable stadium seats are brought out, placed on the gentle slopes defining the quad, and undergraduates cheer on the Cards' of Division III baseball, football and track. The rest of the year, the Andrus is a soft depression of green lawn and quite welcoming. Otherwise, the campus is distinguished by weathered red brick facilities of early 19th century, 1960s and recent buildings of utilitarian style. A busy road separates campus from the adjacent neighborhoods also of 19th century architecture.

The quirky **Usdan Center** is central to the campus energy and the meeting place for all who spend their days in this expectant environment. The traditional residence halls on campus are supplemented by 150 small homes outside of the campus perimeter, but still owned by the university and considered college housing. Other options are themed residences on and off campus. The university is remarkable for their careful use of resources. In fact, their portable planetarium anchors the astrophysics studies on campus and actually travels off campus for outreach to local school groups.

Social Environment

Incoming Weslies quickly form small groups of like-minded friends during the first year. These interests become solidified as an identity for the group and they look to find their next residence in one of the hundreds of small homes through the annual general room selection process. As these groups often remain together moving from one house to another over three years, they generate a unique collegiate social environment with individualized interests translating into passions and advocacy. The administration philosophy supports this with the Office of Community Service providing resources to groups who are advocating for a cause. There is a requirement for action advocacy in some of the themed housing.

In Winter 2014, the university president joined 1,000 students marching across campus into Middletown protesting discrimination of blacks in the criminal justice system.[91] In Fall 2015 an op-ed in the campus newspaper sparked turmoil on campus when an editor criticized Black Lives Matter.[92] Subsequently, the campus newspaper had its budget cut in half, along with other actions that pressured the student newspaper into publishing an apology.[93] There were other students and alumni who believed the newspaper caved into the pressure.[94] The administration responded by stating there is no right not to be offended.[95] Weslies have historically been inclined to action and protest. In 2010, the campus offered undergraduate training by Department of Education partner, Interfaith Youth Core of Chicago, with the Better Together program. Students talked about using religion as a tool for cooperation and mobilizing students from all faith backgrounds.[96]

Greatly involved in the life of the mind, most students bring expectations of change for American society. Academic study throughout the curriculum is **discussion-prone**. Within Wesleyan's Open Curriculum, undergraduate advising is by faculty in the declared major and focused on meeting requirements for graduation. There is a large component of **service learning** on campus with many student organizations centered around outreach to the nearby community. In the classroom there is no excessive competition for grades. Weslies are inclined to ask how their senior undergraduate research experience will radiate outward off of the campus and into the larger world.

The administration and faculty on campus is oriented to the progressive social perspective. There are very few courses within the overall curriculum that reflect across the centuries of the American experience. Coursework focusing on our nation is primarily about the 20th century minority ethnic experiences and pop culture. There seems to be no evidence of the large, unwelcome European immigration in the early 1900s. In this environment, undergraduates **develop** finely-tuned opinions.

Compatibility with Personality Types and Preferences

The Wesleyan campus is for people-centered (F), creative (N) students who come to search for truths. They arrive on campus with a questioning predisposition and will find plenty of company. Though they are likely to experience questions about their idealistic positions, it is the predominant nature of the campus. The administration's philosophy consistently supports activist practice and policy. However, a less vocal community of undergraduate students and alumni are more mindful of practical considerations than practiced across the campus. Their voices can be heard in student organizations like the Patricelli Center for Social Entrepreneurship.

Students are encouraged to develop their own core beliefs about the world around them, albeit there is little support for conservative conceptual understanding. Armed with information, introspective Weslies mull over these social values with their academic studies providing a counterpoint. The undergraduate curriculum explores human endeavor in the pure sciences, efficient use of national resources and progressive social constructs in society.

Now read below about one of the majors that MBTI® research shows people of your type have selected since the mid-20th century. After, refer to Chapter Five for the 50 or so majors that can help you prepare for careers your type has selected. Most importantly, remember that this college description is a suggestion for exploration, not a commanding order. You can be successful in any major at any college.

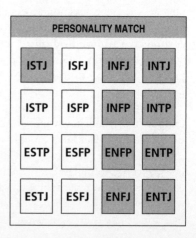

PERSONALITY MATCH

ISTJ	ISFJ	INFJ	INTJ
ISTP	ISFP	INFP	INTP
ESTP	ESFP	ENFP	ENTP
ESTJ	ESFJ	ENFJ	ENTJ

INFJ is often well-prepared in the labs and will be rewarded for remaining glued to the microscopes in the **Molecular Biophysics** certificate at Wesleyan. It will require additional course work beyond their major but may advance INFJ in admission to other programs or employment. The field is advancing by genetic leaps and bounds due to the recent advances in gene mapping. INFJ will like weekly reviews of research at the Molecular Biophysics Journal Club. Deep conversation is a preferred learning method for this type. Computer Science is growing presence in this discipline.

INTJ applies analytical power to find new information. The major in **Astronomy** at Wesleyan is very good at developing passion in this precise, yet remote science. That combination of adjectives is just fine with this type who is attracted to the improbable. Here INTJ will be able to take courses and conduct research in the professional observatory on campus. Possibly they will co-author papers with their professors utilizing the portable planetarium. How cool is that?

ENTP will learn needed presentation tools in the certificate program for **Informatics and Modeling**. This type often has original, creative concepts but also struggles with getting them into the conversation in a productive way. This sequence of courses introduces the use of computational science to set a framework for analysis. There are two approaches within the program and ENTP will do well to discuss the best approach with their major advisor on campus.

ISTJ at Wesleyan is likely to appreciate the **German Studies** minor because it surveys the political culture of the recent past and present day politics. This type likes to collect information in factual form and then rearrange it to fit into larger concepts. Wesleyan is an ideal campus for this and ISTJ will enjoy getting lessons in the abstractions from fellow high flyers on this campus prone to conceptualization. With European instability on the rise because of Islamic State, ISIS terrorism, cultural awareness of this key western European nation is needed by many enterprises and organizations.

INFP interested in writing will carefully bring analysis to the certificate in **Jewish and Israel Studies** at Wesleyan University. Over a three-year period, courses are offered covering the biblical Israel, Diaspora, Spanish Expulsion, Jews in Eastern Europe, the Hebrew Bible and the various forms of Judaism. It is a great companion study to any degree, especially the physical sciences, since it involves no labs. The studies in this major could correlate with the Christian Genocides in 2014-2015 by Islamic State, ISIS terrorists in the Middle East and Africa.

ENFP will find the **Art History** major at Wesleyan ideal because the faculty teaches art through cultural history. Rather than overly focusing on the visual art techniques and style, ENFP will take advantage of their strong insight while finding the human story in paintings. The curriculum requires a regional focus, either Asian, European, American or African. Much course work is interdisciplinary and is outside the traditional concept of art history.

ENFJ will appreciate the nature of team work used in **Archaeology**. The major requires ENFJ to design their own curriculum which is interdisciplinary at Wesleyan. The combination of mentored encouragement and enthusiasm is a favored learning experience for this type. It is offered as a minor or major which can be nicely paired with studies in the physical sciences that are often required to interpret the archeological dig sites. American study seems to be underrepresented in course offerings, similar to the curriculum in the art history department.

INTP will like the pure pursuit of science in the **Molecular Biology and Biochemistry** major. This type could easily be attracted to the transmission of genetic information. Undergraduate research in the junior and senior year with faculty is very accessible. INTP will sign up for a half or full credit with the professor of their choice in the research that interests them. They can repeat the course again with a different professor or the same one. Faculty mentoring in this difficult science is good at Wesleyan. This major moves across chemistry, computer science, biology and occasionally psychology, so double mentoring with two professors in different departments is a good option.

ENTJ is a strategic planner and might enjoy pulling together a linked major in the College of **Integrative Sciences**. ENTJ will get the whole tamale in this degree. It is primarily a physical science degree of their choice which becomes their declared major. But then they link to another department and perform intensive research between the two disciplines. They will do a summer undergraduate research, two to four seminars of research for credit, advanced research seminar or senior thesis tutorial, a senior capstone colloquium and present all of this to peers in the program. BTW they will always be in the Journal Club. We told you it was the whole tamale, and it won't be too much for this type.

WILLIAMS COLLEGE

Office of Admission
800 Main Street
Williamstown, MA 01267
Website: www.williams.edu
Admissions Telephone: 413-597-2211
Undergraduates: 2,045; 1,007 Men, 1,038 Women

Physical Environment

Nestled at the base of the Berkshire mountains in the north-west corner of Massachusetts, Williams College tends to feel remote. On quiet fall days, one can imagine the clip-clopping of 19th century horses and buggies. Now the area and campus appeals to hikers and snowboarders. **Kellogg House**, over 200 years old, has a documented history of continuous use. After recent renovation it became a Living Building, self-sufficient with its own water, energy, materials, agriculture and health performance characteristics. The historical youngster at Williams College is **The Log** donated by the class of 1941. After a sustainable renovation, it reopened in 2016 to hoorahs by all past graduating classes.

Williams College, an intellectual academic powerhouse through the centuries, has deep historical bones. When artifacts are discovered or brought out of storage, they are **valued, conserved and repurposed**. The administration, alumni, students and locals are regularly reminded of **Williams' history** going back to Colonial times. The Sawyer Library and the **Williams College of Art** have holdings spanning that 300-year history. The Prendergast Digitization recently cataloged thousands of visual images. This collection by the artistic Prendergast brothers joined Williams' already notable holdings of original paintings and artifacts. Undergraduate students are actively recruited to volunteer at the museum as guides or assist the professional staff.

The extensive Science Complex pulls in many pre-med, pre-vet and science-loving students and houses nine departments of the physical sciences. The **Paresky Student Center** of soaring, arching glass windows is the major hub for socializing and dining. The undergraduates remain long after finishing their meal, next to their forgotten dishes piled up on tables. In fact, Williams College has updated or constructed much across the campus over the past decade. The town itself, a short way down Mohawk Trail, may offer the best chance now to hear those horses and carriages. Students and faculty might take their zip cars into the small establishments that also cater to visiting parents and Williams' employees.

Social Environment

Many **bright students** are drawn to Williams College's prominent reputation in New England. They also come for the **progressive social views** held by many in this collegiate community. About half of the students identify as a minority. The academic environment is continuously **expectant** and intellectual boundaries are pretty permeable. Many courses are cross listed and taught as interdisciplinary. It prods **discussion and connection** that always reaches for a new understanding or clarity. Peer learning is a feature of the campus with students often giving informative presentations to each other outside of the classroom. About one-half of the undergraduates sign up for **Tutorials**—two students meeting weekly with their professor who critique each other's work over the semester.

Williams undergraduates are **introspective and very aware**. As first years, some will identify with an organization or club and thereafter each conversation, each club meeting is exploratory and raises awareness or sympathy for that identity. In this way, many students develop an expectation for action. The social atmosphere on campus is one of ever-present **collective values**, held by differing groups with a variety of views. In October 2015 a student club uninvited a speaker whose views were seen as conservative.[97] Several students supported a prominent alumni protesting over the campus endowment in oil stocks.[98] Both the university president and president of a student club cancelled speakers as opinions flew both ways, for and against the speakers.[99] It is ironic that these introspective students at Williams college, searching for meaning and affirmation, look outside of themselves for that answer. There is almost a reflective melancholy on campus.

The administration's philosophy strongly supports aggregate learning and this comes into the curriculum through service learning, experiential learning by teams of students and the peer learning. Most students live on campus for this reason, although a few seniors are permitted off campus each year. The residence halls are formed into four **Neighborhoods** and they are responsible for much of the light-hearted entertainment on campus. The Neighborhoods are **self-governed** by a student Leadership Team. They cooperate with each other sharing budget, resources and responsibility for planning campus-wide events. On a fall days, the student body comes out wearing purple to cheer on the Division III football games. They know the winter will close in and hours of conversation will be logged inside over hot chocolate.

Compatibility with Personality Types and Preferences

Education at Williams College is a process (P) rather than a goal. The process exists in an educational community of discussion, collaboration and earnest exploration (N). Students bring a lot of energy (E) and intensity to their undergraduate major studies and extracurricular activity. A good hour from Albany, NY, the Williams campus is a buffer from the contemporary American scene. That sets up idealistic expectations for the social and academic experience. Professors expect students will be giving back to the community through service and experiential learning. Students expect to bring personal commitment and action to their individual viewpoints.

The more reserved undergraduates excel with the one-on-one faculty-student relationship (I). Many also come for the close (F), directed study with their professors and department advisor. Faculty across the physical sciences are engaged with peers at other research universities across the country. Speakers in the Biology Colloquium offer undergraduates awareness of emerging research in national laboratories at other colleges and universities. Williams' own advanced research is actively interfaced with leading national institutions. The college is distinguished by this unique combination of conversational dialogue, social purpose and history.

Now read below about one of the majors that MBTI® research shows people of your type have selected since the mid-20th century. After, refer to Chapter Five for the 50 or so majors that can help you prepare for careers your type has selected. Most importantly, remember that this college description is a suggestion for exploration, not a commanding order. You can be successful in any major at any college.

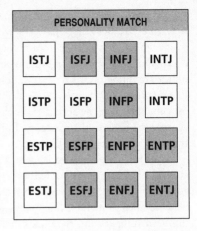

ENFP would do well to take advantage of the in depth offerings of the **History** department. The faculty is abundantly informed of historic American tradition and foundation across three centuries. ENFPs love to be inspired and creative. How about combining this major with a publishing house specializing in texts for America's school children? Perhaps the creative ENFP will convince local school boards to reintroduce American government and history in their core subjects for graduation. The course American Immigration History includes the early 1900s European influx that is not often included in studies of our nation at American liberal art colleges and universities.

ENTP would do well to pursue the **Leadership Studies** concentration at Williams College. The faculty offers a collection of courses that explore the power relationships between leaders and followers. Since ENTPs are drawn to the worlds of power, they can find themselves in positions of authority. At the same time, these creative thinkers can become tongue-tied when trying to express their vision. The course in Art of Presidential Leadership exposes ENTPs to strategies and they will likely select a few for their own tool box. Local initiatives in service leadership are an established part of the concentration for undergraduates and others in the Williams community.

ESFJ frequently moves into the world of health care. At Williams College, the **Biology** department includes balanced molecular, cellular, organismal and ecological study. It is perfect for advanced degrees in the life sciences or those wishing to go into education or education policy. The close advising on this campus is ideal for ESFJ who wants harmony and the time to carefully move in directions that value others and society. The Williams Tutorial is also likely to really appeal to this type who thinks best when they are talking out their thoughts.

ENFJ can delight in the new challenge of the **Classics** major at Wesleyan and the **Critical Languages** program. Williams has no formal language requirement and undergraduates study the Graeco-Roman world through literature, history, art and the social sciences. At the same time, there is a nice program for forgotten languages like Hebrew. It is a self-study with tutorial supervision by qualified native speakers. ENFJ studying Hebrew will have a distinct advantage in reading translations of the classics. Essentially they might, with help, explore original text in Hebrew and bring greater depth to a tutorial with another classmate.

ISFJ often is a stickler for technical accuracy. The intriguing concentration in **Maritime Studies** combines easily with **Biology**, a good choice for ISFJ, or another science major. This concentration looks at maritime naval power, ocean studies and oceanic history. Viewed as interdisciplinary by Williams, a good study would focus on the troubling claims of the Chinese of ownership of the Senkaku/Diaoyu Islands in September 2012. It would be a realistic peek at the international world of power influenced by oceanic access. ISFJ who is cool with reality can see that international aggression falls into that category. Plus, ISFJ would like to leave abstraction between the pages of books in the library.

ENTJ has the characteristics and style of legal courtroom witnesses and consultants. The degree in **Geosciences** at Williams compliments sustainability and is a good choice for this type who expects to be recognized as an expert in their career field. Faculty provides a fine overview of the massive forces that shape our planet, think earthquakes and river basins like the Mighty Mississippi. The department really hones in on the oceans' circulation which speaks directly to climate influence and change.

INFJ likes to study complex problems in a relaxed way that is free of due dates. The degree in **Political Economy** at Williams looks at the connection between public policy and available economic resources. Curriculum examines political goals resulting from the administration's progressive social views of fairness, 2006 through 2017. To sort out answers, INFJs could take advantage of the Tutorial that pairs a professor with another student in debate. This type possesses a dose of stubborn once in a while and may opt for a different interpretation than in the curriculum. A second senior capstone could address the European restructuring of economic policy to handle the massive immigration waves resulting from Islamic State, ISIS terrorism in 2014-15. The European Union, in 2015, formally declared Genocides of the Christian, Yazidis and other ethnic religious minorities by the Islamic State, ISIS.

INFP will possibly be drawn to the **Theatre** major at Williams College. This department views dramatic performance as an interpretive tool and undergrads study western and non-western theater. INFPs love to tell their story and present their original thoughts through written work. They are rarely "talking heads." With their creative spirit in overdrive, a career in drama and therapy could emerge. Williams College students in theater typically double major so theater/psychology makes sense.

ESFP has the enthusiasm and spontaneity to spin a degree in **Classics** into designer floral landscapes and interior decor in cities like New York City, London or Los Angeles. ESFPs will stretch their imagination and refer to classical concepts of design for interior and exterior botanical landscapes. Ancient Roman architecture blended indoor and outdoor living spaces together and would be great inspiration. Williams' course in Field Botany would be critical for this direction, along with perhaps a minor in Biology.

YALE UNIVERSITY

38 Hillhouse Avenue
New Haven, CT 06520
Website: www.yale.edu
Admissions Telephone: 203-432-9316
Undergraduates: 5,477; 2,793 Men, 2,684 Women
Graduate Students: 6,859

Physical Environment

Yale is the **second-oldest private institution** of higher education in the nation and has been at its present location in downtown New Haven since 1716. Many of the buildings reveal their age, all the more so since they are located directly adjacent to city sidewalks and streets. Yale and New Haven have evolved together over the centuries and appear much like other midsize cities of retail stores with older neighborhoods and some evidence of decay. City streets and campus tend to blur together and Yale students remain aware of their surroundings. It is, however, striking to see Yale's ultra-modern glass-and-metal buildings of 21st century architecture in the mix with their somewhat tired-looking neighbors. Construction cranes and closed off streets make it a bit confusing to figure where the center of campus might be.

However, the rest of Yale University is extraordinary and superlative to say the least. To comprehend the Yale **national research laboratories** is to imagine one of the disciplines, let's say biology, and realize that Yale Biology is akin to all of the hospital research institutions in, lets say, the city of Boston. It is an allegory but likely to be a true allegory. A noticeable amount of research and faculty at Yale move in socially progressive directions, highly supportive of feminist views. Sometimes in contradiction to those perspectives, other research or individual faculty will suggest alternative views. In winter 2016, a Yale Sociologist publishing research summarized, "It's time to stop ignoring the role men play in reproductive outcomes."[100]

The Yale **literary archives** might best be understood if one thought of the literary holdings at the British Museum. Do undergraduates have access to these? Yes, they do. Nevertheless, it is hard to believe that an undergraduate student will leaf through the pages of the **Tyndale Bible, 1534**, acquired by Yale in 2014. Three centuries of collecting has positioned the Yale historical archives to be topped only by the collections of advanced nation states while equal to or beyond their peer institutions.

Dormitories at Yale are always referred to as Residential Colleges, but more specifically by their individual names. They actually reduce the need to be out and about on the campus after traditional class hours. Each of these buildings has many features like a small theater, courtyards, spaces for dance, exercise, art, music and of course dining. Two more Residential Colleges are under construction and scheduled to open August 2017. They will provide for slightly larger incoming classes, if finished on time, for 2017 and beyond.

Social Environment

Undergraduate students reside at one of the **12 residential colleges**, located in the most central and well-traveled areas of the campus. Students live spaciously within these recently renovated facilities that appear and function like fine hotel/ conference centers. Each become **cohesive communities** of approximately 200-300 students. Complete with their own budget, faculty families and a professional live-in staff, students are encouraged to think of the college as their family. Each house has its own Master who takes all meals with the students in the dining hall. As an older "family member," they actively mentor the residents with academic advising too. They also schedule student **social and academic gatherings** at weekly afternoon English teas. Most teas feature a well-known speaker, celebrity or authority and are designed for smaller groups of 10-40 students with similar interests. These twelve Colleges function as ideal communities where students come to always expect a positive social and intellectual experience.

Yalies are socially **sophisticated** for the most part. Slightly more than half identify as a minority and there is widespread **talent** and intellect among the **bright, driven, expectant** student population. Much of Yale residential life revolves around performing arts, club/intramural athletics and their 500 student organizations. The Alliance for Dance at Yale has 17 different types of dance groups and serves to advocate for dancers on campus, with an outreach to high schools in the Hartford area. Yale clubs often serve two purposes, one for extracurricular entertainment and the other to advocate for its purpose.

The university leadership aggressively establishes outreach to the local, national and international community through undergraduate academic studies designed to interface as service projects. **Dwight Hall**, a nonprofit organization independent of Yale, registers required Senior Projects and Senior Capstones, student-led groups and individual and group projects. Funding and administrative support is included and approximately 3,500 students use the system for their own coursework requirements. Much of the work falls under the umbrella of socially progressive design for public citizens and children. The Dwight Hall mission is to nurture undergraduate students as leaders of social change.

Yale students are **very aware**. Period. Of many things--politics, black holes, art, algorithms, history, cancer, wealth, Moxie Marlinspike, Syria, ibuprofen, zinnias, the Mississippi River. Individual student perspectives become part of the aggregate knowledge on campus. The overall Yale social and academic environment lives within the framework of **relativistic values**. Contradictions can and do exist. In Fall 2015 an email sent out by Yale committees and offices identified inappropriate Halloween costumes. A Residential College professor replied by email, stating there should be room for provocative costumes, alluding to free speech. That pushback email was received by the students as violating basic respect for minority culture and livelihood.[101] Student campus-wide protests followed charging Yale administration with racial insensitivity. The dean of the college recast the discussion with perspective that the exchanges were uncivil but did not violate free expression. The Residential College Master, married to the professor who sent the push back email, resigned.[102] The President formed a task force to consider projects and policies related to diversity and inclusion, along with a $50 million dollar initiative to increase faculty diversity over a five-year period. Yalies are all, equally, caught up in a search for truth.[103]

Compatibility with Personality Types and Preferences

Yale University leadership places premier priority upon the undergraduate student body. This is unlike other peer institutions of similar reputation whose primary purpose seems to move toward advancing knowledge through research in national laboratories. Rather, Yale intends to impact the national scene through the caliber and abilities of its graduates. As such, all resources at all levels are tailored for the student academic and social experience. In fact, the social experience is considered to be the most distinctive feature of undergraduate life. Residential life, think of that as the social experience, is tailored for the whole student body and tightly structured through a variety of offices and mechanisms.

All Yalies have unique talents, but they all share an expectation of impacting society on graduation. Each residential college student population is selected to be very much alike in talent and ability. It is also important to understand that Yale is admitting students of near professional-level talent. That means there will be visual artists of Advanced Placement caliber, possibly with their own exhibitions, in each of the Residential Colleges. The 12, soon to be 14, pretty much differ in their architecture only.

Yale faculty expects and intentionally benefits from collaboration between students and with students. The resultant reciprocal learning brings knowledge of current trends within society to the campus. The academic environment includes educational practice for all 16 personality types. Each student is assured that the materials and educational resources are in place to develop their undergraduate field of study.

The collections of specimens and artifacts in the archival vaults have to be a delight for the student who prefers to see, touch, listen and smell (S) while learning. Students must use their imagination (N) to propose and identify the classes and learning experiences that will push them forward in their major. As a result, there is considerable informal interfacing with the exceptional faculty within the residences and within the academic departments.

The curriculum has flexibility (P) through the special divisional major and electives which allow study outside of the programs offered without limitations or constraints once approved. The science laboratories are equipped beyond wild wishes to support undergraduate proposals with a disciplined approach (J) in research design. Strands of study and knowledge that might be offered as seminars (T) or independent study at smaller liberal arts colleges become full-fledged courses or department programs at Yale. The student who arrives really missing (F) hometown friends and family will find solace in the 12 residential colleges where friendships will quickly develop under the tutelage of the Chief in charge.

The less outgoing students (I) will find it possible to select programs and studies with small numbers of like-minded peers. Faculty within the major will mentor academically, offering the student that one-on-one, preferred single point focus. In this way and other educational practices, Yalies look inward. Yet the student who derives energy from others (E) will find that Yale educational philosophies absolutely demand interaction and collaboration. This is all the more necessary as some level of course work is completed in the community. The curriculum well honoring all learning styles is viewed as the best way to advance the aggregate knowledge of the whole student body. Indeed, there is not a personality type that is not very well-supported at Yale.

Now read below about one of the majors that MBTI® research shows people of your type have selected since the mid-20th century. After, refer to Chapter Five for the 50 or so majors that can help you prepare for careers your type has selected. Most importantly, remember that this college description is a suggestion for exploration, not a commanding order. You can be successful in any major at any college.

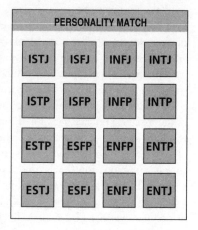

INFP can be driven by their personal beliefs. Often this is a private journey that leads INFPs down some pretty creative paths. During their upperclass years, this type will want to move ahead in spite of any scheduling or limiting obstacles. They can be relentless in pursuing knowledge for a vision of an improved world. The **Yale Summer Session** gives them a little lagniappe, Louisiana talk for an extra slice of bread, to squeeze in a needed course prior to graduation. Their ease with writing can be put to good use in these more concentrated summer classes. INFPs can be creative at the art of overachieving. The courses offered are for one credit each.

INFJ occasionally enters the dynamic world of national or international corporations. At Yale, INFJs can combine knowledge of their undergraduate major with a Bachelor of Arts in **Engineering Sciences**. It offers three educational tracks for the non-science major who wishes to move into the world of business. INFJs will have their big-picture-glasses on during all the course work and can quickly spot an opportunity to bring advanced engineering applications into the practical world. This program is perfect for INFJs who can major in any social science of their choice.

INTJ will probably ponder the **Special Divisional Major** at some point through the first year at Yale. INTJs are bent on translating their visions into reality. They are pretty original and their novel ideas can be difficult to understand. It is possible that even Yale may not have the direction of academic study they require. In this case, INTJs can present their request to the appropriate faculty committee and hopefully be given the go-ahead. This type has the persistence and personal strength to follow the process through to the decision. Should it not come out in their favor, the vision will still live on, perhaps now altered to assure success next time.

INTP will constantly be delighted and absorbed with the major in **Physics and Philosophy**. How much more complicated could it get? For this type, that is just what they need to keep their intense search for clarity in check or at least occupied. INTPs see the world through patterns and expect those patterns to be useful at some level, even if it is an abstract level. The required course in logic will help with this. There will be seven physics courses, six philosophy courses and the Senior Requirement which has choice between physics research or philosophical paper.

ISTP is going to be a first class participant in the **Bulldog Bots**, the robotics undergraduate student club at Yale. This club plays around with machines that are directed and powered by computers and people on the ground. ISTPs will only play with machines if they do something practical or interesting. They will see that the Bots at least do the interesting part. ISTP may also want to look closely at the **Environmental Engineering** degree which requires monitoring of air and water. Of course, mechanical devices stuck in odd locations on Earth must be controlled by folks who like Bots, no we mean, robotics.

ISTJ is swell at picking up huge amounts of specific data and storing it for immediate or future use. Once gathered, this type enjoys analysis and formulation for categories and concepts. ISTJs are a natural for **Archeological Studies** at Yale. Their senior research project, required for this major, will be a comprehensive study through logical analysis of their individual observations of an archeological find. ISTJs will devote months to this work and must be careful not to get caught up in perfectionism.

ISFJ with an artistic talent has the dedication to develop a portfolio of studio art work during five terms of Yale's introductory art courses. They must develop a portfolio that will be submitted for admission to the major in sophomore year. This gentle realistic type might concentrate in photography to capture their deep appreciation of family and personal meaning. The **Art** major explores all modern day and traditional studio arts. ISFJs will bring their excellent visual memories to the forefront in any medium they choose. Their typical sensitivity for others will find a home within this community of fellow students and faculty. The department utilizes international professionals in addition to Yale faculty.

ISFP prefers to actively and directly work with information. The major in **Near Eastern Languages and Civilizations** has archeology mixed into the major and immersion learning. A chance to visit ancient civilization sites brings a great deal of meaning and understanding for ISFP away from the traditional academic classes. It is very relaxing for this type. The required literacy in the languages with visual meaning in ancient hieroglyphics also makes the study a tad easier for ISFPs. The senior essay will require translation of ancient texts from one of the civilizations. Perhaps Yale's Egyptology Center could pass ISFP's safety concerns for a study abroad.

ESTP is quick to get the picture and it could actually be a 3D visual picture. The major in **Computing and the Arts** at Yale is interdisciplinary as well as pretty darned unusual. Think about live entertainment like rock concerts, Disney on tour or live theatrical performances. All of these are making big time use of large screen visuals sometimes simply using air as the background screen. At Yale, ESTP will learn about the current computing tools for professional artists. The last minute glitches in the show, with thousands waiting in the audience, are a specialty of magic work that most ESTPs have up their sleeve.

ESFP should find the major in **Sociology** quite appealing because this type is focused on current realities. This Yale curriculum is proof positive that a balanced study of social ills can be presented with conservative social perspectives in comparison to social progressive perspectives. In fact, of all the majors, in all the descriptions of interdisciplinary study we have yet to see anything as comprehensive and empirical as this phrase in their introduction to Social Policy Analysis: "The capabilities and limitations of four fundamental tools of policy: markets, networks, bureaucracies and legislation." The department courses also include the exploration of employment and family-based policy strategies for alleviating poverty; challenges to the view religion is an archaic force destined to dwindle away; social movement theory used to analyze the emergence and evolution of Islamic movements from the early twentieth century to the present; and ways in which political operatives and journalists attempt to structure and restructure such relationships to their benefit.

ENFP often go into teaching. Here at Yale, the major in **Cognitive Science** would be ideal for a career in education policy or follow on Masters Degree in Education. The major is organized as an interdisciplinary study with courses in psychology, linguistics, philosophy, computer science, economics and neuroscience. Yes, that is definitely interdisciplinary. It is also ideal for a career in public or independent schools across America. A broad intellectual background will help when underperformance in American schools is regularly questioned.

ENTP is fascinated by the world and quite capable of finding multiple shades of meaning through their expansive insight. The three language courses in **Polish** hold advantage for this creative type. But it might be their interest in the Political Science major that leads them toward Eastern European languages and culture. ENTPs only have to think about Russian Invasions in 2015 to see the utility of speaking a little Polish on the international stage. However, Yale offers multiple lessons in humility. ENTP must concentrate on a good number of solid details in their Senior Essay if it draws comparison between the Ukrainian invasion and potential for Russian encroachment on Poland.

ESFJ is forever curious about others. This type is more than capable of collecting and cataloging information for future benefit on behalf of people and their organizations. The course in **Study of the City** at Yale has advantages for this type. American cities are attempting to serve all populations and they have multiple programming needs. This course offers a look at those in need. This course would be a dynamite elective for the excellent Sociology major at Yale.

ESTJ often zeroes in on challenges that exist in the real world rather than an Ivory Tower. They will be right at home here at Yale. The dynamic, hard-to-predict field of economics can be paired with a second discipline. At Yale, the major is called **Economics/Mathematics** and it offers formulaic solutions for the somewhat chaotic environments ESTJ likes to organize. This curriculum studies economics as a national "food source" and correlates it with the decline of national wealth. This type will especially enjoy the department's Seminars that emphasize student interaction and reading professional articles.

ENFJ will find the **History** department at Yale with nationally recognized faculty and remarkable national archives at their ready for research. This degree can be shaped toward many careers and this type might like studies in Public Policy. The undergraduate students learn to speak to broad audiences and to craft historical subjects into stories of interest. Wow. That just about describes one of the premiere talents of this type. After graduation, this gifted public speaker could bring their new found understanding to international NGOs struggling to provide third world services. Areas like those on the border of Islamic State ISIS activity, are susceptible and manipulated by their historical and ethnic rivalries. Competent ENFJ will be at the ready with historical practice in their area of study.

ENTJ has the competitive drive to hang in there for the valuable fifth year of the **Public Health** degree at Yale. This type will be happy with the combination BA-BS and the Masters level degree awarded on completion. ENTJ may seize the opportunity to analyze the troubled roll out of the national health plan in 2014. They have the strategic thinking to do this and the leadership skills to get it into the public square.

CHAPTER 7

THE TABLES OF COLLEGES RECOMMENDED FOR PERSONALITY TYPES

This is a comprehensive listing of the colleges and majors assessed in this book that are compatible with your Personality Type. It is important to understand that this list is not exclusive and students can be successful at any college. Our basic premise is that the colleges within these tables represent collegiate environments that are excellent fits for the indicated Personality Type and characteristic learning style.

The reader is reminded within each of the 82 college descriptions that the Personality Type information provided is supplemental and it is best used in conjunction with other factors such as size, distance from home, social environment, admission and financial considerations, etc.

Sixteen Personality Types and Colleges

ISTJ
American University
Amherst College
Beloit College
Boston College
Boston University
Brandeis University
Butler University
California Institute of Technology
Claremont Colleges–Pomona
Claremont Colleges–Scripps
College of Charleston
College of Wooster
Columbia University

Connecticut College
Dartmouth College
Davidson College
Denison University
Duke University
Emory University
Florida Southern College
Furman University
George Washington University
Georgetown University
Georgia Institute of Technology
Hamilton College
Harvard University
Johns Hopkins University
Kalamazoo College
Kenyon College
Lynchburg College
Marquette University
Massachusetts Institute of Technology
Middlebury College
Northeastern University
Northwestern University
Notre Dame University
Oberlin College
Princeton University
Roanoke College
Rollins College
Saint Louis University
Stanford University
Tufts University
University of Chicago
University of Miami
University of Pennsylvania
University of Richmond
University of Tampa
Valparaiso University
Vanderbilt University
Wabash College
Wake Forest
Washington and Lee University
Washington University
Wesleyan University
Yale University

ISFJ

Amherst College
Bates College
Beloit College
Boston College
Brandeis University
Butler University
Case Western Reserve University
Claremont Colleges–Pitzer College
Claremont Colleges–Scripps
Colby College

Colgate University
College of Wooster
Columbia University
Connecticut College
Davidson College
Denison University
Elon University
Emory University
Florida Southern College
Furman University
Georgetown University
Georgia Institute of Technology
Guilford College
Harvard University
Haverford College
Johns Hopkins University
Kalamazoo College
Kenyon College
Lynchburg College
Marquette University
Muhlenberg College
Northeastern University
Notre Dame University
Occidental College
Pepperdine University
Princeton University
Redlands University
Roanoke College
Rollins College
Saint Louis University
Salve Regina University
Stanford University
Swarthmore College
Syracuse University
Tufts University
University of Chicago
University of Pennsylvania
University of Richmond
University of Tampa
Valparaiso University
Vanderbilt University
Wabash College
Wake Forest
Washington University
Williams College
Yale University

INFJ

Agnes Scott College
Amherst College
Bates College
Beloit College
Bowdoin College
Brown University
Carleton College

Case Western Reserve University
Claremont Colleges–Claremont McKenna
Claremont Colleges–Harvey Mudd
Claremont Colleges–Pitzer College
Claremont Colleges–Pomona
Colgate University
College of Charleston
College of Wooster
Columbia University
Connecticut College
Davidson College
Denison University
Duke University
Emory University
Florida Southern College
Furman University
Georgetown University
Guilford College
Hamilton College
Hampshire College
Harvard University
Haverford College
Hendrix College
Kalamazoo College
Lawrence University
Massachusetts Institute of Technology
Middlebury College
New York University
Oberlin College
Occidental College
Princeton University
Redlands University
Salve Regina University
Sarah Lawrence College
Stanford University
Swarthmore College
Syracuse University
Tulane University
Union College
University of Chicago
University of Richmond
University of Southern California
Wabash College
Wake Forest
Washington and Lee University
Washington University
Wesleyan University
Williams College
Yale University

INTJ

Agnes Scott College
American University
Amherst College
Bates College

Bowdoin College
Brown University
California Institute of Technology
Carleton College
Case Western Reserve University
Claremont Colleges–Claremont McKenna
Claremont Colleges–Harvey Mudd
Claremont Colleges–Pomona
Claremont Colleges–Scripps
Columbia University
Connecticut College
Dartmouth College
Duke University
Emory University
George Washington University
Georgetown University
Hamilton College
Hampshire College
Harvard University
Hendrix College
Johns Hopkins University
Lawrence University
Massachusetts Institute of Technology
Middlebury College
New York University
Northwestern University
Oberlin College
Occidental College
Princeton University
Sarah Lawrence College
Stanford University
Swarthmore College
Tufts University
Tulane University
Union College
University of Chicago
University of Miami
University of Pennsylvania
University of Richmond
University of Southern California
Vanderbilt University
Washington and Lee University
Washington University
Wesleyan University
Yale University

ISTP

American University
Amherst College
Boston College
Boston University
Bowdoin College
Brandeis University
California Institute of Technology
Carleton College

Case Western Reserve University
Claremont Colleges–Harvey Mudd
Claremont Colleges–Pomona
Claremont Colleges–Scripps
Columbia University
Connecticut College
Dartmouth College
Davidson College
Emory University
George Washington University
Georgia Institute of Technology
Hamilton College
Harvard University
Johns Hopkins University
Kenyon College
Marquette University
Massachusetts Institute of Technology
New York University
Northeastern University
Princeton University
Saint Louis University
Salve Regina University
Stanford University
Syracuse University
Tufts University
Tulane University
University of Chicago
University of Miami
University of Pennsylvania
University of Southern California
Vanderbilt University
Washington and Lee University
Washington University
Yale University

ISFP

Bates College
Beloit College
Boston University
Bowdoin College
Brandeis University
Brown University
Butler University
Case Western Reserve University
Claremont Colleges–Pitzer College
Colby College
College of Charleston
College of Wooster
Davidson College
Denison University
Elon University
Florida Southern College
Furman University
Guilford College
Hampshire College

Harvard University
Haverford College
Hendrix College
Kalamazoo College
Kenyon College
Lynchburg College
New York University
Northeastern University
Pepperdine University
Princeton University
Redlands University
Roanoke College
Rollins College
Saint Louis University
Salve Regina University
Sarah Lawrence College
Swarthmore College
Syracuse University
Union College
University of Southern California
Valparaiso University
Wabash College
Wake Forest
Yale University

INTP

Agnes Scott College
American University
Amherst College
Bates College
Bowdoin College
Brown University
California Institute of Technology
Carleton College
Case Western Reserve University
Claremont Colleges–Harvey Mudd
Claremont Colleges–Pitzer College
Claremont Colleges–Pomona
College of Wooster
Columbia University
Connecticut College
Dartmouth College
Davidson College
Duke University
Emory University
Georgetown University
Hamilton College
Hampshire College
Harvard University
Haverford College
Hendrix College
Lawrence University
Massachusetts Institute of Technology
Middlebury College
Northwestern University

Oberlin College
Occidental College
Princeton University
Stanford University
Swarthmore College
Tufts University
Tulane University
University of Chicago
University of Miami
University of Pennsylvania
University of Richmond
University of Southern California
Vanderbilt University
Washington and Lee University
Washington University
Wesleyan University
Yale University

INFP

Agnes Scott College
Bates College
Beloit College
Bowdoin College
Brandeis University
Brown University
Carleton College
Case Western Reserve University
Claremont Colleges–Harvey Mudd
Claremont Colleges–Pitzer College
Claremont Colleges–Pomona
Colgate University
College of Wooster
Columbia University
Davidson College
Denison University
Duke University
Elon University
Florida Southern College
Guilford College
Hampshire College
Harvard University
Haverford College
Hendrix College
Lawrence University
Massachusetts Institute of Technology
Oberlin College
Occidental College
Pepperdine University
Princeton University
Redlands University
Saint Louis University
Sarah Lawrence College
Swarthmore College
Syracuse University
Union College

University of Chicago
University of Southern California
Vanderbilt University
Wabash College
Wake Forest
Washington University
Wesleyan University
Williams College
Yale University

ESTP

American University
Boston College
Boston University
Butler University
California Institute of Technology
Case Western Reserve University
Claremont Colleges–Claremont McKenna
Colby College
College of Charleston
Columbia University
Dartmouth College
Denison University
Elon University
Florida Southern College
Furman University
George Washington University
Georgetown University
Georgia Institute of Technology
Hamilton College
Harvard University
Johns Hopkins University
Kenyon College
Lynchburg College
Marquette University
Massachusetts Institute of Technology
Muhlenberg College
New York University
Notre Dame University
Northeastern University
Princeton University
Roanoke College
Rollins College
Saint Louis University
Salve Regina University
Stanford University
Syracuse University
Tufts University
Tulane University
University of Miami
University of Southern California
University of Tampa
Valparaiso University
Wabash College
Yale University

ESFP

Agnes Scott College
American University
Boston College
Boston University
Brandeis University
Brown University
Butler University
Case Western Reserve University
Claremont Colleges–Harvey Mudd
Claremont Colleges–Pitzer College
Colby College
Colgate University
College of Charleston
College of Wooster
Denison University
Elon University
Florida Southern College
Furman University
George Washington University
Georgetown University
Georgia Institute of Technology
Guilford College
Hampshire College
Harvard University
Kenyon College
Lynchburg College
Marquette University
Massachusetts Institute of Technology
Muhlenberg College
New York University
Northeastern University
Northwestern University
Redlands University
Rollins College
Saint Louis University
Salve Regina University
Syracuse University
University of Miami
University of Pennsylvania
University of Southern California
University of Tampa
Valparaiso University
Williams College
Yale University

ENFP

Agnes Scott College
Bates College
Beloit College
Boston College
Boston University
Bowdoin College
Brown University
California Institute of Technology

Carleton College
Case Western Reserve University
Claremont Colleges–Harvey Mudd
Claremont Colleges–Pitzer College
Claremont Colleges–Pomona
Colgate University
College of Wooster
Columbia University
Dartmouth College
Denison University
Elon University
Florida Southern College
Furman University
George Washington University
Georgetown University
Guilford College
Hampshire College
Harvard University
Haverford College
Hendrix College
Johns Hopkins University
Lawrence University
Massachusetts Institute of Technology
Muhlenberg College
New York University
Northwestern University
Occidental College
Princeton University
Redlands University
Salve Regina University
Sarah Lawrence College
Stanford University
Swarthmore College
Syracuse University
Tufts University
Tulane University
Union College
University of Chicago
University of Southern California
Vanderbilt University
Wabash College
Wake Forest
Washington and Lee University
Wesleyan University
Williams College
Yale University

ENTP

Agnes Scott College
American University
Amherst College
Bates College
Boston College
Bowdoin College
Brown University

California Institute of Technology
Carleton College
Case Western Reserve University
Claremont Colleges–Claremont McKenna
Claremont Colleges–Pomona
Colgate University
College of Charleston
College of Wooster
Columbia University
Connecticut College
Dartmouth College
Duke University
George Washington University
Georgetown University
Georgia Institute of Technology
Guilford College
Hamilton College
Hampshire College
Harvard University
Haverford College
Hendrix College
Johns Hopkins University
Lawrence University
Massachusetts Institute of Technology
Middlebury College
New York University
Northwestern University
Notre Dame University
Oberlin College
Occidental College
Princeton University
Redlands University
Sarah Lawrence College
Stanford University
Swarthmore College
Syracuse University
Tufts University
Tulane University
Union College
University of Chicago
University of Miami
University of Richmond
University of Southern California
Wabash College
Wake Forest
Washington and Lee University
Washington University
Wesleyan University
Williams College
Yale University

ESFJ
Agnes Scott College
American University
Bates College

Beloit College
Boston College
Brandeis University
Brown University
Butler University
Claremont Colleges–Claremont McKenna
Claremont Colleges–Pitzer College
Claremont Colleges–Pomona
Claremont Colleges–Scripps
Colgate University
College of Wooster
Columbia University
Davidson College
Denison University
Elon University
Florida Southern College
Furman University
Georgetown University
Guilford College
Harvard University
Haverford College
Kalamazoo College
Lawrence University
Lynchburg College
Marquette University
Muhlenberg College
New York University
Northeastern University
Notre Dame University
Occidental College
Pepperdine University
Princeton University
Redlands University
Roanoke College
Saint Louis University
Salve Regina University
Sarah Lawrence College
Swarthmore College
Syracuse University
Tulane University
Union College
University of Pennsylvania
University of Southern California
University of Tampa
Wabash College
Wake Forest
Williams College
Yale University

ESTJ
American University
Amherst College
Boston College
Boston University
Brandeis University

Butler University
California Institute of Technology
Claremont Colleges–Claremont McKenna
Claremont Colleges–Pomona
Claremont Colleges–Scripps
Colby College
College of Charleston
Dartmouth College
Davidson College
Duke University
Elon University
Emory University
Florida Southern College
Furman University
George Washington University
Georgetown University
Georgia Institute of Technology
Hamilton College
Harvard University
Johns Hopkins University
Kalamazoo College
Kenyon College
Lynchburg College
Marquette University
Massachusetts Institute of Technology
Muhlenberg College
New York University
Northeastern University
Northwestern University
Notre Dame University
Pepperdine University
Princeton University
Roanoke College
Rollins College
Saint Louis University
Syracuse University
Stanford University
Tufts University
Tulane University
Union College
University of Chicago
University of Miami
University of Pennsylvania
University of Richmond
University of Tampa
Valparaiso University
Vanderbilt University
Wake Forest
Yale University

ENFJ

Agnes Scott College
Amherst College
Bates College
Beloit College

Bowdoin College
Brandeis University
Brown University
Butler University
Case Western Reserve University
Claremont Colleges–Claremont McKenna
Claremont Colleges–Harvey Mudd
Claremont Colleges–Pitzer College
Claremont Colleges–Scripps
Colby College
Colgate University
College of Wooster
Columbia University
Connecticut College
Dartmouth College
Davidson College
Denison University
Duke University
Elon University
Emory University
Florida Southern College
Furman University
Georgetown University
Georgia Institute of Technology
Guilford College
Hampshire College
Harvard University
Haverford College
Hendrix College
Kalamazoo College
Lawrence University
Lynchburg College
Marquette University
Middlebury College
Muhlenberg College
New York University
Northeastern University
Notre Dame University
Occidental College
Pepperdine University
Princeton University
Redlands University
Roanoke College
Saint Louis University
Salve Regina University
Sarah Lawrence College
Stanford University
Swarthmore College
Syracuse University
Tufts University
Union College
University of Southern California
University of Tampa
Valparaiso University
Wabash College

Washington and Lee University
Wesleyan University
Williams College
Yale University

ENTJ

American University
Beloit College
Boston College
Boston University
Bowdoin College
Brandeis University
Butler University
California Institute of Technology
Carleton College
Claremont Colleges–Claremont McKenna
Claremont Colleges–Pomona
Claremont Colleges–Scripps
Colgate University
College of Charleston
Columbia University
Connecticut College
Dartmouth College
Duke University
Elon University
Emory University
George Washington University
Georgetown University
Georgia Institute of Technology
Hamilton College
Harvard University
Johns Hopkins University
Kalamazoo College
Lawrence University
Lynchburg College
Marquette University
Massachusetts Institute of Technology
Middlebury College
Muhlenberg College
New York University
Northeastern University
Northwestern University
Notre Dame University
Oberlin College
Occidental College
Pepperdine University
Princeton University
Roanoke College
Rollins College
Saint Louis University
Stanford University
Syracuse University
Tulane University
Union College
University of Chicago

University of Miami
University of Pennsylvania
University of Richmond
University of Southern California
Vanderbilt University
Wabash College
Wake Forest
Washington and Lee University
Washington University
Wesleyan University
Williams College
Yale University

NOTES

1. Byron Tau and Peter Nicholas, "Time Gap Found in Clinton Emails," *Wall Street Journal*, 1 Oct. 2015: Section, Politics.

2. Marc Daalder, "Amherst College Students Are Occupying Their Library Right Now Over Racial Justice Demands," *In These Times*, 14 Nov. 2015, 14 Mar. 2016 <http://inthese-times.com/article/18603/amherst-college-students-are-occupying-their-library...>.

3. "President Martin's Statement on Campus Protests," *Amherst College*, 15 Nov. 2015, 14 Mar. 2016 <http://www.amherst.edu/amherst-story/president/statements/node/620480>.

4. Cindy Wooden, "In Africa, Pope Highlights Peace and Unity," *One Voice*, 4 Dec. 2015, 1+.

5. John Branch and Orient Staff, "Students and administration clash, causing tension at Bates," *The Bowdoin Orient*, 27 Mar. 2015, 14 Mar. 2016 <http://bowdoinorient.com/article/10104>.

6. Clayton Spencer, "President Clayton Spencer's letter about recent campus events," *Bates*, 9 Mar. 2015, 14 Mar. 2016 <http://www.bates.edu/president/2015/03/09/letter-campus-events/>.

7. Rebecca Goldfine, "Teach-in Offers Day Devoted to Climate Change, Racism, Social Justice," *Bowdoin*, 2 Oct. 2015, 14 Mar. 2016 <http://community.bowdoin.edu/news/2015/10/teach-in-offers-educational-day-devoted-to-climate...>.

8. Sohrab Ahmari, "How to Fight the Campus Speech Police: Get a Good Lawyer," *Wall Street Journal*, 3 Jan. 2015: Section, Opinion.

9. Associated Press in Providence, " NYPD commissioner Ray Kelly shouted down at Brown University Lecture," *the guardian*, 30 Oct.2013, 15 Mar. 2016 <http://www.theguard-ian.com/world/2013/oct/30/nypd-commissioner...>.

10. Tara Culp-Ressler, "Red Tape Won''t Cover Up Rape': The Silent Protests That Are Sweeping College Graduations," *Thinkprogress*, 18 Jun.2014, 4 Mar. 2016 <http://www.thinkprogress.org/health/2014/06/18/3450390/red-tape-rape-college-protest/>.

11. Douglas Belkin, "For College Students, History's a Mystery," *Wall Street Journal*, 15 Oct.2014: A6.

12. Peter Fricke, "Pomona president: racism protests come from inability to fight Trump," *CampusReform*, 5 Jan. 2016, 4 Mar. 2016 <http://www.campusreform.org/?ID=7129>.

13. Hannah Oh, "CMC Students Feel Marginalized, Demand Resources and Resignations," *The Claremont Independent*, 12 Nov. 2015, 4 Mar. 2016 <http://claremontindependent.com/cmc-students-feel-marginalized-...>.

14. Korn, M., & Belkin, D., "Backlash Develops Over Student Protests," *The Wall Street Journal*, 20 Nov. 2015, 11 Mar. 2016 <http//:www.wsj.com/articles/backlash-devel-ops-over-student-protests-1448063437?cb=logged0.9506288125862927&cb=logged0.677682278844695>.

15. Watanabe, T., & Rivera, C., "Amid racial bias protests, Claremont McKenna dean re-signs," *Los Angeles Times*, 13 Nov. 2015, 4 Mar. 2016 <http://www.latimes.com/local/lanow/la-me-In-claremont-marches-20151112-story.html>.

16. Joseph Dickson, "Addressing Campus Climate Diversity Issues-Living Document," *Pitzer College*, 14 Dec. 2015, 4 Mar. 2016 <http://www.pitweb.pitzer.edu/president/diversity/...>.

17. "Rally at Colby Against Racist Yik Yak Comments," *Inside Higher Ed*, 17 Apr. 2015, 5 Mar. 2016 <http://www.insidehighered.com/quicktakes/2015/04/17rally-colby-against-racist...>.

18. Jaleesa Jones, "Colgate University students ask#CanYouHearUsNow," *College*, 24 Sep.2014, 5 Mar. 2016 <http://www.college.usatoday.com/2014/09/24/colgate-university-students-ask-canyouhearusnow/>.

19. "University Messages Progress Report," *Colgate For All*, 29 Jun. 2015, 5 Mar. 2016 <http://www.colgate.edu/campus-life/diversity-and-inclusion/colgate/colgate-for-all>.

20. Emily Bazelon, "Have We Learned Anything From the Columbia Rape Case," *The New York Times Magazine*, 29 May. 2015, 15 Mar. 2016 <http://www.nytimes.com /2015/05/29/magazine/have-we-learned-anything...>.

21. NBC Connecticut, "Connecticut College Closed Monday to Address Recent Hate Messages," *American Renaissance*, 30 Mar. 2015, 15 Mar. 2016 <http://www.amren. com/news/2015/03/connecticut-college-closed-monday-to-address...>.

22. Victor Skinner, "VIDEO: 'Black Lives Matter' protesters rage against students in Dartmouth library," EAGnews.org, 16 Nov. 2015, 15 Mar. 2016 <http://www.eagnews. org/dartmouth-black-lives-matter-protesters-confront-students-in-school-library/>.

23. Alexandra Samuels, "Blackout demonstration at Dartmouth results in controversy, confusion," *College*, 17 Nov. 2015, 6 Mar. 2016 <http://www.college.usatoday. com/2015/11/17/blackout-demonstration-at-dartmouth-results-in-controversy/>.

24. Brian Chen, "Protesters Deny Physical Harassment, Gain Vice Provost Ameer's Endorsement," *The Dartmouth Review*, 17 Nov. 2015, 15 Mar. 2016 <http://www.dart review.com/protesters-deny-physical-harassment-gain-vice-provest-ameers-endorse-ment/>.

25. Mark Washburn, "Davidson students protest police shootings; disrupt holiday festival," *The Charlotte Observer*, 6 Dec.2014, 6 Mar. 2016 <http://www.charlotteobserver.com/ news/local/article9242129.html >.

26. Jon Guze, "Student Protest at Duke," *The Locker Room*, 22 Nov. 2015, 18 Jan. 2016 <http://lockerroom.johnlocke.org/2015/11/22/student-protest-at-duke/>.

27. Valerie Bauerlein, "In Campus Rape Cases, Some Men See Injustice," *Wall Street Journal*, 11-12 Apr. 2015: A1+.

28. Associated Press, "Duke Cancels Plan for Muslim Prayer Call," *Wall Street Journal*, 16 Jan. 2015: Section, U.S.

29. Blake Dickinson, "Duke to Establish Islamic Studies Center, Create $1.5 Million Endowed Professorship," *Duke Today*, 9 Nov.2005, 8 Mar. 2016 <http://today.duke. edu/2005/11/islamstudies.html>.

30. "Numen Lumen Pavilion dedicated," *Elon University*, n.d., 15 Mar. 2016 <http://www. elon.edu/e-net/Article/68964>.

31. "Mapping Interfaith Cooperation to Your Campus Mission and Values," *IFYC Interfaith Youth Core*, n.d.: Page 3+, 7 Mar. 2016 <http://www.ifyc.org/sites/default/files/u4/ Mapping.pdf>.

32. Ben Brazil, "What is Interfaith Dialogue for?," *Youth Theological Initiative*, 14 May.2013, 8 Mar. 2016 <http://yti.emory.edu/what-is-interfaith-dialogue-for/>.

33. Scott Greer, "University's board votes to keep its Chick-fil-A despite student protests," *Campus Reform*, 29 Apr.2013, 7 Mar. 2016 <http://www.campusreform.org/?ID=4727>.

34. Michael Bodley, "Luminaries stages silent Ferguson protest for racial equality," *The Pendulum*, 1 Dec.2014, 7 Mar. 2016 <http://www.elonpendulum.com/article/2014/12/ elons-luminaries-stages-stream-silent-ferguson-demonstrators-protest-racial-inequality/>.

35. Guha, A., & Mehrotra, K., "Students Protest Racism on Clifton Road, List Demands for Administration," *The Emory Wheel*, 11 Nov. 2015, 7 Mar. 2016 <http;//emorywheel. com/students-protest-racism-on-clifton-road-list-demands-for-adminstration?>.

36. "Message to the Emory community," *Emory News Center*, 12 Nov. 2015, 7 Mar. 2016 <http://news.emory.edu/stories/2015/11/upress_message_to_emory_community/index. html>.

37. "Emory Leadership Response to Student Concerns," *Emory News Center*, 2 Dec. 2015, 7 Mar. 2016 <http://news.emory.edu/stories/2015/12/upress_response_to_student_con-cerns/index.html >.

38. "The Fourth Annual President's Interfaith and Community Service Campus Challenge Gathering," *ACPA College Student Educators International*, n.d., 15 Mar. 2016 <http:// www.myacpa.org/events/fourth-annual-President's-interfaith-and-community-service-campus-challenge-gathering>.

39. "Georgetown Hosts Interfaith Youth Core Interfaith Leadership Institute," *Berkley Center*, n.d., 8 Mar. 2016 <http://berkleycenter.georgetown.edu/events/georgetown-hosts-interfaith-youth-core-interfaith-leadership-institute>.

40. Brazil, "What Is Interfaith Dialogue For?," 14 May.2013.

41. "Ongoing Projects, Initiatives, & Programs," *Georgia Division of Tech Student Life*, n.d., 8 Mar. 2016 <http://www.engage.gatech.edu/content/ongoing-projects-initiatives-programs>.

42. Brazil, "What Is Interfaith Dialogue For?," 14 May.2013.

43. Douglas Belkin, "Asian-Americans Allege Harvard Admissions Bias," *Wall Street Journal*, 15 May. 2015: Section: U.S., Education.

44. "Report of the College Working Group on Diversity and Inclusion," *Harvard University*, Nov. 2015, 8 Mar. 2016 <http://diversity.college.harvard.edu/files/collegediversity/files/diversity_and_inclusion_working_group_final_report_2.pdf>.

45. Nathan Koppel, "Haverford Speaker Criticizes Students," *Wall Street Journal*, 19 May.2014, Section: Politics.

46. Saralyn Lyons, "Johns Hopkins students, administrators gather for 'an honest conversation' about race, racism on campus," *Hub**, 1 Dec. 2015, 10 Mar. 2016 <http://hub.jhu.edu/2015/12/01/black-student-forum-johns-hopkins>.

47. Ken Anselment, "Framework for a more inclusive Lawrence," *admissions@lawrence*, 11 Jan. 2016, 10 Mar. 2016 <http://blogs.lawrence.edu/admissions/2016/01/framework-for-a-more-inclusive-lawrence.html>.

48. Mullins, B., Belkin, D., & Fuller, A., "Colleges Show Their Lobbying Might," *Wall Street Journal*, 9 Nov. 2015:A1+.

49. Joseph Brusky, "Four Marquette University Students Arrested While Demanding School Make Changes," *OccupyRiverwest*, 28 Apr. 2015, 10 Mar. 2016 <http://occupyriverwest.com/us/marquette-students-rise>.

50. Brian Fraga, "Was Marquette Professor Disciplined For Upholding Church Teachings?," *National Catholic Register*, 25 Jan. 2015:11.

51. William Navarre, "MIT students protest Ferguson grand jury decision on campus," *The Tech online*, 5 Dec.2014, 10 Mar. 2016 <http://tech.mit.edu/V134/N59/blacklivesmatter.html>.

52. Zach Despart, "9/11 flag vandalism shocks Middlebury College," *Addison County Independent*, 16 Sep.2013, 11 Mar. 2016 <http://www.addisonindepenent.com/201309911-flag-vandalism-shocks-middlebury-college>.

53. Hilary Lane, "Students join nationwide protests against the killing of two black men," 69NewsWFMZ-TV, 5 Dec. 2015, 4 Mar. 2016, <http://www.wfmz.com/news/news-regional-lehighvalley/Local/muhlenberg-college-students-stage-a-sitin-over-the-garner-and-brown-cases/30084546>.

54. Lauren Caruba, "In Focus: Students demand Native American studies, recognition of Evans' role in Sand Creek Massacre," *The Daily Northwestern*, 1 Mar.2013, 15 Mar. 2016 <http://dailynorthwestern.com/2013/03/01/top-stories-in-focus-students-demand-native-american-studies-recognition-of-evens-role-in-sand-creek-massacre>.

55. "John Evans Study Committee," *Office of the Provost*, May.2014, 15 Mar. 2016 <http://www.northwestern.edu/provost/committees/equity-and-inclusion/study-committee-report.pdf>.

56. Ben Strauss, "N.L.R.B. Rejects Northwestern Football Players' Union Bid," *The New York Times*, 17 Aug. 2015, 15 Mar. 2016 <http://www.nytimes.com/2015/08/18/sports/ncaafootball/nlrb-says-northwestern-football-players-cannot-unionize.html?_r=0>.

57. Tim Moran, "Black Lives Matter Group Makes Demands at Northwestern," *Evanston Patch*, 2 Dec. 2015, 15 Mar. 2016 <http://patch.com/illinois/evanston/black-lives-matter-group-makes-demands-northwestern-o>.

58. "Lecture: Interfaith Leadership in the 21st Century," *Campus Ministry*, n.d., 11 Mar. 2016 <http://campusministry.nd.edu/about/events/2015/01/15/31785-lecture-interfaith-leaderhip-in-the-21st-century/>.

59. Marvin Krislov, "Response to Student Demands," *OberlinOnCampus*, 20 Jan. 2016, 11 Mar. 2016 <http://oncampus.oberlin.edu/source/articles/2016/01/20/reponse-student-demands>.

60. Ed Stetzer, "InterVarsity 'Derecognized' at California State University's 23 Campuses: Some Analysis and Reflections," *The Exchange A Blog*, 6 Sep.2014, 11 Mar. 2016 <http://www.christianitytoday.com/edstetzer/2014/september/intervarsity-now-derecognized-in-california-state-universit.html >.

61. Madison Galdi, "Occidental College president 'happy to resign' over student demands," *CampusReform*, 17 Nov. 2015, 15 Mar. 2016 <http:www.campusreform.org/?ID=7005>.

62. Jim Tranquada, "Oxy Student Protest Updates," *OXY*, 23 Nov. 2015, 11 Mar. 2016, <http://www.oxy.edu/news/oxy-student-protest-updates>.

63. Mary Hui, "Administration Reaches Agreement With Student Demonstrators," *Princeton Alumni Weekly*, 20 Nov. 2015, 12 Mar. 2016 <blogs.princeton.edu/paw/2015/11/adminstration-reaches-agreement-with-student-demonstrators/>.

64. "Princeton Faculty Letter in Support of Student Protests," *A 21st Century Archive of African American Studies*, 20 Nov. 2015, 12 Mar. 2016 <aas.princeton.edu/2015/11/20/support-letter/>.

65. Korn & Belkin, "Backlash Develops Over Student Protests," < http://www.wsj.com/articles/backlash-develops-over-student-protests-1448063437?cb=logged0.9506288125862927&cb=logged0.677682278844695>.

66. James Anderson, "St Louis University Occupation Ends, But Movement for Justice in Ferguson Continues," *In These Times*, 25 Oct.2014. 12 Mar. 2016 <http://inthesitimes.com/article/17287/st_louis_university_occupation_ends_but_movement_for_justice_in_ferguson_c...>.

67. Bhattacharjee, R., & Shore, D., "Students Protest Stanford's Decision to Not Expel Student in Sex Assault Case," *NBC Bay Area*, 12 Jun.2014, 12 Mar. 2016 <http;//nbcbayarea.com/news/local/Students-Protest-Stanford's-Decision-to-Not-Expel-Student-in-Sex-Asault-Case-262972151.html>.

68. Elena Kadvany, "Stanford University processes fail victims of sexual assault, students say," *Palo Alto online*, 22 Jan. 2016, 12 Mar. 2016 <http;//www.paloaltoonline.com/news/2016/01/22/stanford-university-processes-fail-victims-of-sexual-assault-students-say>.

69. Suzanne Goldenberg, "Students occupy Swarthmore College in fossil fuel divestment protest," *theguardian*, 19 Mar. 2015, 12 Mar. 2016 <http://theguardian.com/environment/2015/mar/19/students-occupy-swarthmore-college-in-fossil-fuel-divestment-protest>.

70. "How does the Board come to decisions when discussing complex issues such as divestment?," *Swarthmore College Bulletin*, Summer 2015, 12 Mar. 2016 <http://bulletin.swarthmore.edu/summer-2015-issue-iv-vol-cxii/steadily-engaged>.

71. Paige Carlotti, "Syracuse sit-in protest enters 8th day," *USA Today College*, 11 Nov.2014: Page 1, 12 Mar. 2016 <http://college.usatoday.com/2014/11/11/syracuse-sit-in-protest-enters-8th-day/>.

72. Carlotti Page 5.

73. Kathleen Haley, "Syracuse Recognized on President's Higher Education Community Service Honor Roll," *Syracuse University News*, 27 Jan. 2015, 12 Mar. 2016 <http://news.syr.edu/syracuse-recognized-on-president's-higher-education-community-service-honor-roll-81141/>.

74. Arin Kerstein, "Tufts Armenian Club participates in national protest against denial of Armenian Genocide," *The Tufts Daily*, 5 Feb. 2016, 13 Mar. 2016 <http://tuftsdaily.com/news/2016/02/05/tufts-armenian-club-participates-national-protest-denial-armenian-genocide/>.

75. Nicole Fleming & Jennifer Smith, "Tufts students to begin hunger strike over job cuts," *Metro*, 3 May. 2015, 3 Mar. 2016, < https://www.bostonglobe.com/metro/2015/05/03/tufts-students-begin-hunger-strike-support-university-janitors-targeted-for-layoffs/O30YeVmPxq6cJz8PPOmkVL/story.html.>

76. "Religious and Spiritual Life," *Union College*, n.d., 13 Mar. 2016 <http://www.union.edu/campus/diversity/religious/>.

77. Brazil, "What Is Interfaith Dialogue For?," 14 May.2013.

78. Leah Nussbaum, "IFYC Summer Experience," *Syracuse University* Hendricks Chapel, 8 Jun. 2015, 12 Mar. 2016 <http://hendricks.syr.edu/spotlights/Leah Nussbaum.html>.

79. Sarah Zimmerman, "Reppin' the South Side," *The College*, n.d., 13 Mar. 2016 <http://college.uchicago.edu/uniquely-chicago/story/reppin-south-side>.

80. Samuel Esposito, "Trauma center protestors arrested at University of Chicago," *Chicago Sun Times*, 4 Jun. 2015, 13 Mar. 2016 <http://chicago.suntimes.com/new/trauma-center-protesters-arrested-at-university-of-chicago/>.

81. Miriam Shestack, "Students Protest University of Chicago Budget Cut, Say Admin Is Acting Like a Corporation," *In these Times*, 6 June. 2015, 13 Mar. 2016 <http://inthese-times.com/article/18021/students-protest-university-of-chicago-budget-cuts-say-admin-is-acting-like...>.

82. "Sykes Chapel and Center for Faith and Values," *The University of Tampa*, n.d., 13 Mar. 2016 <http://www.ut.edu/sykeschapel/?trumbaEmbed=view3Devent%26eventid%3D91944273>.

83. "Mapping your Campus Mission.," Page 1+.

84. "UT Helps Pilot Interfaith Movement," *The University of Tampa*, 16 Mar.2011, 13 Mar. 2016 <http://www.ut.edu/UT-Helps-Pilot-Interfaith-Movement.aspx>.

85. Brazil, "What Is Interfaith Dialogue For?," 14 May.2013.

86. Nussbaum, "IFYC Summer Experience."

87. "Better Together," *Spiritual Life*, n.d., 13 Mar. 2016 <http://www.ut.edu/spiritual/>.

88. Adam Tamburin, "Vanderbilt chief responds to call to suspend Carol Swain," *The Tennessean*, 11 Nov. 2015, 13 Mar. 2016 <http://www.tennessean.com/story/news/education/2015/11/11/vanderbilt-chancellor-responds-call-suspend-swain/75607986/>.

89. Alex Cohen, "#WhereisRey? The psychology behind gendered toys," *Take Two*, 11 Jan. 2016, 14 Mar. 2016 <http://www.scpr.org/programs/take-two/2016/01/11/45869/whereisrey-the-psychology-behind-gendered-toys/>.

90. Jeff Biggers, "Breaking: 7 Washington University Students Arrested Protesting Peabody Coal," *Ecowatch*, 2 May.2014, 18 Feb. 2016 <http://ecowatch.com/2014/05/02/students-arrested-peabody-coal/>.

91. Olivia Drake, "Students Lead Black Lives Matter March through Campus, Middletown," *Wesleyan University*, 9 Dec.2014, 19 Feb. 2016 <http://newsletter.blogs.wesleyan.edu/2014/12/09/blacklivesmatter/>.

92. Jonathan Turley, "Wesleyan Student Writes Column Criticizing 'Black Lives Matter' Movement And Critics Respond By Demanding The Defunding Of The Newspaper And The Editors Apologize," *Jonathan Turley*, 25 Sep. 2015, 14 Mar. 2016 <http://jonathanturley.org/2015/09/25/wesleyan-student-writes-column-criticizing-black-lives-matter-movement-and-critics-respond-by-demanding-the-defunding-of-the-newspaper-and-the-editors-apologize/>.

93. Kaitlyn Schallhorn, "College Newspaper Loses Thousands in Funding After Publishing Negative Black Lives Matter Op-Ed, " *The Blaze*, 20 Oct. 2015, 14 Mar. 2016 <http://www.theblaze.com/stories/2015/10/20/college-newspaper-loses-thousands-in-funding-after-publishing-negative-black-lives-matter-editorial/>.

94. Valerie Richardson, "Campus paper budget yanked in dust-up over 'Black Lives Matter' op-ed," *The Washington Times*, 20 Oct. 2015, 19 Feb. 2016 <http://washingtontimes.com/news/2015/oct/20/wesleyan-students-slash-campus-newspaper-budget-af/?page=all>.

95. Michael Roth, "Black Lives Matter and So Does Free Speech," *Wesleyan University*, 19 Sep. 2015, 14 Mar. 2016 <http://roth.blogs.wesleyan.edu/2015/09/19/black-lives-matter-and-so-does-free-speech/>.

96. Marina Melendez, " 'Better Together' Kick-Off!! November 22, 5-7pm DFC," *Wesleyan University*, 22 Nov.2010, 14 Mar. 2016 <http://classof2014.blogs.wesleyan.edu/2010/11/22/better-together-kick-off-november-22-5-7pm-dfc/>.

97. Josh Logue, "Williams College students invited a prominent critic of feminism to speak. Then the backlash started." *Slate*, 22 Oct. 2015, 21 Feb. 2016 < http://www.slate.com/articles/life/inside_higher_ed/2015/10/williams_college_uninvites_suzanne_venker_after_student_backlash.html >.

98. Jim Levulis, "Williams Alum Returns Honorary Degree In Protest Of College's Climate Plan," WAMC Northeast public radio, 23 Oct. 2015, 21 Feb. 2016 <http://wamc.org/post/williams-alum-returns-honorary-degree-protest-colleges-climate-plan#stream/0>.

99. Susan Svrluga, "Williams College cancels a speaker who was invited to bring in provocative opinions," *The Washington Post*, 20 Feb. 2016, 1 Apr. 2016 <https://www.washingtonpost.com/news/grade-point/wp/2016/02/20/wi...>.

100. Bess Connolly Martell, "Yale sociologist to the CDC: Don't leave men out of the reproductive equation," *Yale News*, 15 Feb. 2016, 1 Apr. 2016 <http://news.yale.edu/2016/02/15/yale-sociologist-cdc-don-t-leave-men-out-reproductive-equation>.

101. Justin Worland, "Why a Free Speech Fight is Causing Protests at Yale," *Time*, 10 Nov. 2015, 24 Feb. 2016 <http://time.com/4106265/yale-students-protest/>.

102. Tessa Berenson & Haley Sweetland Edwards, "Exclusive: Yale's Dean Defends 'Safe Spaces' Amid Campus Protests," *Time*, 9 Dec. 2015, 24 Feb. 2016 <http://time.com/4141125/yale-protests-free-speech/>.

103. Sarah Brown, "After Criticism, Yale Sets Aside $50 Million over 5 Years for Faculty Diversity," *American Renaissance*, 3 Nov. 2015, 15 Mar. 2016 <http://www.amren.com/news/2015/11/after-criticism-yale-sets-aside-50-million-over-5-year...>.

ABOUT THE AUTHORS

ROSALIND P. MARIE AND C. CLAIRE LAW advocate that students learn to recognize the nature of social and cultural trends emerging on college campuses today. These trends can shape your college experience. Refer to FindThePerfectCollegeForYou.com for an explanation of how to utilize this type of information in your college search.

MARIE has pursued a lifelong interest in education as a school psychologist and independent educational advisor. She currently advises 20-somethings who are transferring from community college or returning to college with new career goals. Her background includes counseling, testing and parent support at public and independent schools in Idaho and Alabama. In 1995, Marie opened an independent consulting service advising parents and students seeking admission to boarding school, college or therapeutic programs. She has served on regional and national boards in the fields of education. Marie holds a Master's degree in Psychology, Counseling and Guidance and an Educational Specialist Degree in School Psychology. Retired from the United States Air Force Reserves in 2000, she divides her time between Huntsville, Alabama and Eagle River, Michigan with husband John and too many pets.

LAW founded "Educational Avenues" in 1999 (www.eduave.com) and guides parents and students through the college admission and financial aid process. In addition to counseling hundreds of American students and international families, she teaches prospective independent educational consultants at UC-Irvine Extension. She began working in college admissions in the late 1970s at Carleton University in Canada, the Art Institute in Atlanta and Bryant University in Rhode Island, where she served as the Director of International Admission. She then worked for AMS-Education Loan Trust, a Sallie Mae lender under the FFEL Program. Law has a Master's degree in Human Development and enjoys helping students discover their natural gifts and identify colleges where they can be successful. She resides on Daniel Island, South Carolina.